902858834 5

Please return/renew this item by the last date shown.
Items may also be renewed by the internet*

https://library.eastriding.gov.uk

* Please note a PIN will be required to access this service
- this can be obtained from your library

D1341821

BEFORE
BLETCHLEY
PARK

PAUL GANNON

BEFORE BLETCHLEY PARK

THE CODEBREAKERS OF THE FIRST WORLD WAR

The History Press

First published 2020

The History Press
97 St George's Place, Cheltenham,
Gloucestershire, GL50 3QB
www.thehistorypress.co.uk

British Library Cataloguing in Publication Data.
A catalogue record for this book is available from the British Library.

ISBN 978 0 7509 9246 6

Typesetting and origination by The History Press
Printed and bound in Great Britain by TJ Books Limited

Contents

Introduction

On 17 January 1917, Nigel de Grey, a young Naval Intelligence officer, hurried to the office of his wartime superior, Captain William Hall, Director of Naval Intelligence. Once inside, de Grey impatiently spluttered out his question, 'Do you want to bring America into the war, sir?' The short, dapper captain, known to his subordinates as 'Blinker' Hall because of his rapidly blinking eyes, was immediately alert. 'Yes, why?' he inquired. De Grey brandished a piece of paper, exclaiming, 'I've got a telegram here that will bring them in if you give it to them!'

The war was at a critical stage. A dreadful, bloody stalemate on land and sea was consuming lives at an awful rate. The military offered no obvious way of breaking the deadlock. The United States' entry to the war, however, could shift the balance and bring the dreadful slaughter to an end. But neither the US Government nor its people wanted to join the Europeans' imperial war. If de Grey was not exaggerating the import of the telegram, then whatever he had discovered could be decisive.

De Grey was one of the handful of people who worked in Room 40 of the Admiralty in Central London. Their task was to break German naval and diplomatic codes and ciphers. This particular telegram, sent from Berlin, via Washington, to the German representative in Mexico, was intercepted in London on its journey. De Grey, and a colleague, Dilly Knox, had made out only some passages of the message. But what they had revealed was enough to send de Grey dashing off to Hall's office. The German Foreign Secretary, Arthur Zimmermann, proposed in the telegram that Germany and Mexico join forces in waging war – 'conduct war jointly; make peace jointly' – against the United States. When the telegram's contents were fully decoded and revealed to the US public, it helped propel the United States into the war, ensuring Germany's defeat.

This intercepted message is Room 40's most renowned achievement. Yet, the Zimmermann telegram was just one of many thousands of wireless and telegraph cable messages systematically intercepted throughout the war and decoded by Room 40, and by its War Office equivalent, MI1(b).

The existence of these codebreaking activities was kept secret during the war, though soon afterwards some details were exposed. But it was only in the early 1980s that a semi-official account of Room 40 was written by Patrick Beesly, a Naval Intelligence officer at Bletchley Park in the Second World War. He had access to some of the Room 40 archives and his book became the standard work. Many previously secret documents have since been opened at the National Archives in Kew, including several on the Zimmermann telegram and on the secretive MI1(b), enabling us to update the story of First World War codebreaking.

★★★

History, it is frequently asserted, is written by the victors. And this case certainly seems to fit that idea. Assuming that we do not dwell too long on what 'victory' actually means, Britain was among the states that determined the shape of the settlement imposed at Versailles in 1919. British codebreakers in the First World War peeped into the secret military, naval and diplomatic messages of Germany and its allies, and also into the diplomatic messages of neutrals, including the United States, Spain, the Netherlands and Greece.

British codebreaking was part of the overall effort that achieved victory. And, by helping to bring the United States into the war, codebreaking was critical in determining who would be the winners and the losers. So the story would seem, at first glance, to be a classic case of history written by the victors; but it is not such a simple matter.

This book tells the story of the First World War using those intercepted messages. In that sense, it is history intercepted, decoded and translated by the victorious side – but as written by the vanquished. The intercepts allow us to hear the voices of German military and naval commanders (seldom, though, of the lower ranks) and also of diplomats, politicians and spies. There are orders couched in military jargon, often about apparent trivia such as switching on harbour lights, but also debates between diplomats, civil servants and politicians about operations and strategy and even the allocation of blame when things went wrong. When combined, the intercepts reveal how the German military and government understood and organised their war.

The geographical spread and range of topics covered in those messages is astounding. They reveal how Room 40 and MI1(b) gave British military leaders an oversight of their enemies' activities on a global scale: on every continent and in every ocean; in the air war; the espionage and sabotage war; and the propaganda and diplomatic war. The story, however, has been cast into the shadows by the better-known efforts at Bletchley Park during the Second World War.

This is also a story about people. The cast of characters who peopled Room 40 and MI(1)b is as replete with brilliant academics and unworldly eccentrics as the more renowned codebreakers of Bletchley Park. And a few accounts from the individuals who toiled night and day between 1914 and 1918 have survived, allowing us to get a feel for what it would have been like inside Room 40 or MI1(b) and to glimpse behind the mask of command and the veil of secrecy.

★★★

This book was originally published in shorter form as *Inside Room 40*, but since publication of that title new documents and other material have become available, revealing the story in greater depth, so this edition is substantially larger. Some further accounts of First World War code-breaking and other material relating to the story can be downloaded from www.paulgannonbooks.co.uk.

Acknowledgements

I am very grateful to George Lasry and colleagues for sharing material on their deciphering of the Goeben and Breslau messages.

My thanks go to Dr Tim Matschak who advised me on some obscure German terms, and to David Williams and Reg Atherton for useful discussions on cryptographic issues. Also thanks for help with access to files go to the staff at the National Archives, Kew; Churchill Archives Centre, Churchill College, Cambridge; British Library Reading Room, London; Post Office Archives, London; and the Imperial War Museum, London. Also thanks to Mark Beynon of The History Press who commissioned this book and to Alex Waite for working on the preparation of the book in the midst of the COVID-19 pandemic.

Prologue

Few in Britain or elsewhere in Europe really expected war in 1914, even if war appeared a desirable approach to some, even if it had been much discussed in the press, and even if repeated crises between European powers had come close to war over the past ten years but not to actual war. Indeed, even after Archduke Franz Ferdinand, Crown Prince of the Austro-Hungarian Hapsburg Empire, was assassinated in Sarajevo on 28 June, few imagined that war was on its way – let alone a war that would be without previous parallel in number of deaths, injury, agony, starvation, disease and economic dislocation.[1]

David Lloyd George, the British Chancellor of the Exchequer, wrote in January 1914:

> Our relations with Germany are infinitely more friendly than they have been for years … [Britain and Germany] seem to have realised what ought to have been fairly obvious long ago … that there is everything to gain and nothing to lose by reverting to the old policy of friendliness which had been maintained until recent years between Germany and this country.[2]

Lloyd George was an enthusiastic reformer and moderniser. He had introduced the first serious provisions for a welfare state in Britain – pensions, unemployment benefits and health insurance. He had other great projects at the centre of his attention in mid-1914 – reform of the House of Lords, Home Rule for Ireland and votes for women. He was just one of many European politicians who were taken by surprise at the intrusion of war into domestic politics. He wrote in his *War Memoirs*:

I cannot recall any discussion on the subject in the Cabinet until the evening before the final declaration of war by Germany. We were much more concerned with the threat of imminent civil war in the North of Ireland. The situation there absorbed our thoughts.[3]

After a cabinet meeting on 24 July, Foreign Secretary Sir Edward Grey asked ministers to remain in their seats for a briefing on the 'situation' in Europe. It was very grave, he told them, but hopeful.

As it was July, the diplomatic holiday season was under way and many diplomats and politicians were away when the crisis struck. The German Kaiser Wilhelm II sailed off on his annual cruise in the seas off Norway. The French Chief of Staff, Ferdinand Foch, 'did not hesitate to go to his estate in Brittany ... Sir Edward Grey saw no reason to delay a planned fishing trip [and] several military and political leaders were in fact vacationing in soon-to-be enemy countries'.[4]

As the crisis intensified towards the end of the month, 'the weight of [telegraphic] traffic between governments swamped the relatively primitive international communications system, so that vital cables became subject to chronic delay', waiting to be decoded.[5] To circumvent the delays, in the days when the German Foreign Office feared Britain would join the war if Germany attacked Belgium, the German Foreign Secretary sent a telegram to his ambassador in London saying, 'As long as England remains neutral our fleet will not attack the northern coast of France and we will not violate the territorial integrity and independence of Belgium.' It was sent in plain language, 'evidently in the hope of its being intercepted. And, in fact it was the censor, and not Lichnowsky [the ambassador], who communicated it to the Foreign Office.'[6]

Any lingering prospects of defusing the increasingly tense situation evaporated in the summer heat. Instead, the great powers were drawn into widening the conflict, constrained by commitments made in their alliances, and propelled into war by their own precipitate demands, transmitted around Europe by telegraph to empty foreign offices. When a satisfactory reply to an ultimatum was not received in the short time allowed, war was declared.

Austria-Hungary declared war on Serbia on 28 July. As it had already withdrawn its ambassador, it had to notify Serbia by telegraph – the first time war had been declared by telegram.[7] Russia and Germany, supporting respectively Serbia and Austria, declared war on each other within days. Russia's involvement threatened to drag in its entente allies, France and Britain. But 'even then,' said Lloyd George, 'I met no responsible Minister who was not convinced that, in one way or another, the calamity of a great European war would somehow be averted.'

However, Germany's plans for war with Russia involved knocking out France, by attacking through Belgium, before the sluggish but numerous Russian Army could mobilise. Once Russia mobilised, Germany was able to claim it was responding to Russian aggression and attack both Russia and France.

Britain sent an ultimatum to Germany on 4 August, demanding a declaration of respect for Belgium's neutrality by midnight European time (11 p.m. British time). Lloyd George described it as:

> ... a day full of rumours and reports, throbbing with anxiety. Hour after hour passed, and no sign came from Germany. There were only disturbing rumours of further German movements towards the Belgian line. Then evening came. Still no answer.

The prime minister, Foreign Secretary and Home Secretary were 'all looking very grave'. Shortly after 9 p.m. a telegraph message, from the German Foreign Office to the German Ambassador in London, was intercepted at the Central Telegraph Office. It was translated and sent to the anxious huddle of senior ministers. It read, 'English Ambassador has just demanded his passport shortly after seven o'clock declaring war'.[8]

This was the first news received from Germany in response to the British ultimatum. No word had reached London from the British Ambassador in Berlin (the Germans having held up his telegram reporting on his meeting with the German Foreign Secretary). 'We were at a loss to know what it meant,' said Lloyd George.

Ministers debated whether they should use the intelligence gained from the intercepted message to begin British Army mobilisation without waiting until the deadline. They also wondered whether to start naval operations scheduled for the commencement of hostilities, such as cutting German international submarine telegraph cables to isolate it from the outside world. The ministers debated:

> Should this intercept be treated as the commencement of hostilities ... should we unleash the savage dogs of war at once or wait ... and give peace the benefit of even such a doubt as existed for at least another two hours?[9]

In the end they decided to wait until Big Ben had chimed in the eleventh hour of that disastrous day.

***

Ten years earlier, in 1904, British warships and overseas cable stations had been instructed by the Admiralty to intercept foreign military and government messages and to forward copies to London.[10] The earliest surviving copies in the National Archives of those intercepted messages date from March 1914. Even these were not decoded until November 1914, after copies of German naval code books had come into British possession. But we can benefit from hindsight and read the messages to see how Germany prepared for war and then signalled its start to distant German naval and merchant ships and to its far-flung colonies.

The first recorded intercepts were taken by wireless operators on Royal Navy ships – such as *Glasgow*, on patrol in the south Atlantic. Other surviving intercepts were telegraph messages sent over British-operated international submarine cables. The Eastern Telegraph Company made copies of telegrams passing through the hands of its operators in places such as Rio de Janeiro and Cape Town.[11] The volume of intercepts increased as war drew closer.

Some of the decoded messages reveal Germany preparing to distribute cipher keys and code books ready for use in the event of war. For example, on 20 March 1914, a message sent in the name of the Kaiser to the German Legation in Montevideo contained instructions about which ciphers were to be issued to which secret agents in Buenos Aires and Rio de Janeiro. On 5 May, the *Admiralstab* (Admiralty Staff) sent out details of new ciphers to the German cruiser *Königsberg* at Dar es Salaam in German East Africa (present-day Tanzania).

Other messages, for example one on 18 March, were about potential suppliers of coal and places where discreet re-coaling of German warships could take place if war did break out. A cable message on 9 April, from Berlin to a German gunboat in Manila, instructed the captain to record details of ships seen surveying the waters near both German and British territories in the Far East. These were all matters that could properly be seen as the daily tasks of a navy in times of peace. This included being prepared for war to break out at any time and so these messages are not evidence of an intention to go to war, any more than British interest in intercepting and recording incomprehensible encoded messages should be taken as anything more than diligent preparation.

After the assassination of Franz Ferdinand, the tone of the messages changed. The telegrams now conveyed a tension that was absent from the earlier signals. As the political crisis deepened, both the German and the British navies were put 'on alert' in July. This was something that could be done without provoking war in the way that mobilisation of land armies would inevitably mean war was about to break out.[12]

On 7 July, Berlin sent a telegram to the gunboat *Eber*, which was undergoing boiler repairs at Cape Town (in the British territory of South Africa), warning that the 'political situation at home [is] not free from difficulty. Development is to be expected in eight to ten days. When is your boiler cleaning finished?' Later that day, the *Admiralstab* advised the captain to 'conclude no written agreements of any description with [the] Consul General. Destroy any that exist.'

In mid-July the German cruiser *Scharnhorst*, at Yap in the German Marshall Islands, was informed that an 'Austro-Hungarian note has been presented to Serbia on 23 July. Political development cannot be foreseen. Await further developments at Penope Island [in New Guinea].' On 26 July, the warship *Königsberg* was told:

> Diplomatic relations have been broken off between Austria-Hungary and Serbia. Tension between Dual Alliance [Germany & Austria-Hungary] and Triple Alliance [Russia, France & Britain] possible. It is presumed that England will maintain an expectant attitude.

Most of the above messages were cable traffic intercepted by the Eastern Telegraph Company. But, on 26 July, a message was intercepted at an Admiralty wireless station at Dover. It informed the Commander of the German High Seas Fleet, 'We have received news that Russia has broken off manoeuvres and sent the troops back to their depots [indicating intended mobilisation]'. The message also urged the naval commander to 'hasten the return of Wilhelm'.

Even though the political situation in Europe had been getting steadily worse through July, Kaiser Wilhelm had gone off on his summer cruise in his imperial yacht *Hohenzollern*, to the Norwegian fjords (where his captive guests were subject to his excruciatingly adolescent practical jokes). Cancelling his trip might have given the impression that Germany was eager to exploit the crisis following the assassination of Franz Ferdinand. Going through with the voyage would signal that everything was normal. But once war loomed it was vital to ensure the Kaiser's speedy return.

On 29 July, the *Eber* in Cape Town was told to 'leave on some plausible pretext and go to Lüderitz Bay' in German South-West Africa (Namibia today). The captain dragged his vessel out of the harbour 'in a hurry, half [her] boiler tubes not working and in a heavy sea'. The next day a message from the German Navy's main wireless station, at Norddeich in northern Germany, informed the captain of the cruiser *Strassburg*, 'War has broken out between Austro-Hungary [*sic*] and Serbia … in the present state of affairs the English Channel is still passable'.

The same day, warning messages were sent out from the German wireless station at Nauen, near Berlin. This was the world's most powerful wireless transmitter, capable of transmitting as far as North America, southern Africa and East Asia. The messages issued orders to bring into play the preparations for coal supplies and secret re-coaling places. And a plain-language message was sent to all German merchant ships, 'Threatened with danger of war. Enter no English, French or Russian harbours.' The merchant captains were also told to keep an eye on the movement of foreign warships and to report them to the *Admiralstab*.

The next day, all merchants were ordered to run for the nearest neutral port to avoid being captured by British or French warships. Cruisers stationed at German colonies in Africa and Asia were told to start attacking enemy warships and any merchant ships flying enemy flags. Berlin instructed the cruiser *Dresden*, 'Do not come home but carry on cruiser warfare. We will send coal.'

German agents in South America, Spain, Portugal and other places were told to start clandestine operations. Details of the payments of thousands of marks to agents were transmitted from Berlin to distant posts. In return, Berlin received intelligence reports, some of them no doubt of value, but many made up of wild rumours, such as the message notifying that 'a secret confidential agent reports that on Thursday 15,000 Englishmen arrive in Alexandria from Malta'.

On 2 August, German colonies were told to keep Berlin informed about what was happening far from the homeland:

Send regularly by wireless short messages on the political situation. The big wireless station here [at Nauen] is open for reception continuously by night and day … also [encipher] wireless [messages] in case the political situation becomes more acute. Put the catchword Delta before the call sign.[13]

The same day, a message to many recipients, transmitted by cable and wireless, said, 'Hostilities have commenced against Russia. War with France certain: hostilities will probably begin on 3 August. Great Britain very probably hostile. Italy neutral. Acknowledge.' On 4 August, a cable message to German cruisers read, 'Declaration of war between Germany and Great Britain is to be expected hourly.'

★★★

The world war had begun. The outbreak of the armed conflict was marked by a bombardment of wireless and cable messages from Nauen and Norddeich. To help boost morale at the start of the struggle, a message on 5 August to all warships from the *Admiralstab* cancelled all outstanding punishments for breaches of discipline. More importantly, arrangements were made for cruisers to meet up with supply ships (with essential fuel and food) at quiet points on the coasts of South America and Africa and at remote islands in the Pacific Ocean.

Two German warships, the *Goeben* and *Breslau* in the Mediterranean, were instructed on 4 August to head as quickly as possible to Constantinople (Istanbul). The flight of the two ships from the clutches of the Royal Navy was an important early propaganda victory for the Germans (see Chapter 7). Berlin was delighted to hear of even a minor success and wanted more details. On 11 August, Berlin sent a congratulatory message: 'His Majesty the Kaiser directs the captain to send in a report of your escape.'

Propaganda was to become a key part of the First World War, both on the home fronts and in neutral countries. On 12 August, the powerful German wireless station at Nauen sent out a joyous message: 'Our army has won a decisive victory at Mülhausen, Alsace, against the French Army Corps. Spread the word.' Details of other victorious clashes of arms were similarly reported, for example on 20 August, celebrating 'incomparable bravery' by German forces storming and conquering a strong point on the Western Front.

The log of intercepts is silent between 23 August and 9 September – except for a single message intercepted in Shanghai on 6 September. This reported that the Japanese were expected to arrive off the coast of Tsingtao, Germany's colonial territory on the coast of mainland China, which had been acquired in 1898 to great national pride. The apparent German wireless silence – or perhaps it was difficulties in intercepting signals at the British listening stations – ended on 9 September, with a wireless message from Nauen to Windhoek, in German South-West Africa (Namibia), giving details of British blockading lines off the African coast. On 22 September, Nauen told Windhoek, 'All lines of communication have been compromised except perhaps no. 163.' This referred to the disruption, by the British Navy, of the coal and supplies bases set up before the war for German cruisers. From now on, such messages become quite common.

Around this time, the British, by much immensely good luck, came into possession of the main German naval code books. And, following French success in September in breaking German Army cipher keys in north-western France, the British also worked out how to break the naval cipher keys. A message dated 21 October, sent from Nauen to the German ship *Roon*, was intercepted in Melbourne. It was sent in a non-secret code, but with a secret cipher (which it appears the Australian Navy had broken). It reported:

> My activity has been rendered difficult because the collier [ship] has been detained by the government. Nevertheless 1500 tons of coal are stored for use in case of necessity at Tjilatjap [Java] on board steamer Sydney …

This could stand as an example of many such messages reporting on the German struggle to create – and the British to crush – German cruiser warfare on the high seas. But what makes it interesting for our story is the combination of the use of a public code book and a secret cipher. A handwritten note in the log of messages records that 'it was from this message that "Key B" was discovered, by guessing the [code] group for *Roon*'.

On 13, 22, 25 and 27 November, messages sent to German cruisers and colonies warned that one of the three main German naval code books and its cipher key had been 'compromised' by British naval forces. Along with the ability to decode German naval and military messages on the Western Front, the war was to enter a new phase of a prolonged bloody stalemate. As we will see in the chapters that follow, codebreaking was, eventually, to help break the stalemate.

1

Munitions of War

In 1913 the British Government's Committee of Imperial Defence drew up a list of items that a naval blockade would aim to prevent reaching enemy countries in a future European war. The list included supplies with obvious military significance: ammunition, projectiles, explosives, nitric acid and so forth. There were also some more obscure items on the list – including a sort of rubber known as gutta-percha.[1]

The Assistant Surgeon to the Presidency in Singapore, Dr William Montgomerie, reported on gutta-percha to the London Society of Arts in 1843. He had ventured into:

> [A] place much infested by tigers, to which it is necessary to proceed on foot, so it would be a venture of some risk to proceed to this spot; but I have offered a reward for specimens of the flowers and fruit of the tree.[2]

Sourced from the *Palaquium gutta* tree, which grew almost exclusively in the forests in Malaya and Singapore (both then British colonies), gutta-percha had a key difference from rubber. Though solid at normal temperatures, when heated it became soft and could be moulded into virtually any shape. When it cooled down it hardened but retained the moulded shape. Native Malayans used it for various purposes such as knife handles and walking sticks.[3] In Europe it found uses as consumer products such as ear trumpets, corks for soda-water bottles, and golf balls. It had plenty of industrial uses too: belts for machinery, industrial tubing, suction pipes and acid-tank linings.

This handy but niche material became truly important, however, as an insulator for undersea electric telegraph cables.[4] Demand for gutta-percha grew rapidly in both Britain and Germany. However, in Germany the Siemens company hit problems in sourcing the supplies it needed. As recorded by a German historian of telegraphy, 'It was necessary to acquire it from the British Gutta-Percha Company that had the supply of raw gutta-percha entirely in its hands'.[5]

Like rubber, gutta-percha was extracted from the bark of trees, but unlike rubber it did not flow easily. To achieve maximum output the trees were cut down and several large cuts made into the bark. Each felled tree only produced about 5kg of raw gutta-percha – yet the telegraph industry demanded tens of thousands of tons.[6] Within a few years, thousands of trees had been chopped down and supply was threatened as an ecological disaster loomed.

Gutta-percha was a classic example of a raw product extracted from the colonies and shipped back to the homeland where it was processed by an increasingly sophisticated industry. In enabling the global telegraph network, the seemingly low-tech produce of trees from distant jungles was at the heart of high tech of the time. The global telegraph network lay at the heart of the most advanced form of financial capitalism and trade, aided the exploitation, control and administration of Britain's colonies and dominions, and boosted the organisation and effectiveness of Britain's military forces. Thus it was that, as war in Europe loomed, gutta-percha was declared to be a contraband product.

★★★

Soon after the invention in the 1840s of the electric telegraph, Western European countries had busily constructed dense domestic telegraph networks. The next step was to link those domestic networks across national boundaries. Technically, this was a straightforward task on the Continent (assuming political barriers did not stand in the way), but crossing the seas was another matter. For Britain, one of the leaders in developing telegraph technology, however, it was a vital necessity, both economically and politically.

Imports of food and cotton were vital and of growing importance as the nineteenth century progressed.[7] Indeed, imports greatly exceeded the value of exports of manufactured goods from Britain, so the difference had to be made up as 'invisibles', such as shipping (where Britain was the world's 'common carrier') as well as finance/insurance and the provision of capital (where the British again dominated).

From the middle of the nineteenth century, the British economy became increasingly dependent on services.[8] Control of the international telegraph network enabled further development of global trade and services

It was not just the control of the gutta-percha supply that turned Britain, and London in particular, into the centre of the burgeoning global telegraph industry. Experience with the manufacturing process, not just of the cable itself, but also the sensitive transmitting and receiving equipment, was also centred in and around London. The cable-laying (and vital cable-repair) ships were nearly all British. The companies that operated the cables, too, were mainly British, most notably the Eastern Telegraph Company (with a dozen or more variously named subsidiaries). And the very size and spread of the British Empire gave the impetus to build an ever more extensive international network.

The first submarine cable link was laid across the Channel between Britain and France in 1849 but worked for just a short time. A second attempt in 1851 proved more effective. The Channel cable enabled Paris Bourse closing prices to be known in London's Stock Exchange 'within business hours'.

By 1854 there were some twenty cables linking Britain to Ireland and the Continent.[9] The first attempt to lay a cable across the Atlantic in 1857 was a failure, but another attempt in 1858 was initially successful. However, after a couple of months, a fault developed in the insulation some 300 miles west of Ireland. Before it failed, one message sent by the British Government to Canada cancelled an order for transporting two army regiments across the Atlantic, saving the Treasury the sizeable sum of £50,000 in transportation costs.[10]

Although submarine cables were useful for the government, the funding of the transatlantic and many subsequent cable projects was the work of the City of London. Knowledge of the prices in US markets for grain and other supplies was eagerly sought. Once a cable joining Britain and North America was laid successfully, international cable communications rapidly became essential to modern economies. As one US observer noted, 'Wealthier Russian peasants quickly became attuned to the need to price the wheat they grew for export so as not to be undercut by imports from America.' On the quayside in Nikolayev, a Ukrainian port on the Black Sea:

Peasants on arrival at the market with their grain were asking, 'What is the price in America according to the latest telegram?' And, what is still more surprising, they knew how to convert cents per bushel into kopecks per pood.[11]

Initially, the cables shadowed the main trading routes. These first international cable-laying projects were financed by private concerns (kick-started by compensation paid to British telegraph companies on the nationalisation of domestic telegraph companies). As the turn of the century approached, the profitable cable routes were, by and large, completed, and it required government involvement to initiate new routes that would serve imperial needs more than commercial ones – such as the enormously expensive transpacific cables. By this time, the British Government, the colonial authorities, the self-governing dominions and the British military and navy were conscious that they possessed a communications infrastructure for the Empire. Other countries built local links that connected regional clusters of their own colonies, but, except across the Atlantic, they had to link in to the global British network for long-distance spans to their own colonies.

The British Government increasingly understood the importance of the global network, but also feared its vulnerability. Thus, they sought to ensure alternative links, following different routes, in case one cable suffered technical problems – or was cut by an enemy power. It became a key objective that the British network consisted entirely of British-controlled links that touched land only within the Empire. The global web of cables was dubbed the 'All Red Network' after the colour used on maps to show territories belonging to the Empire.

★★★

At first Britain's dominant role in the global cable network was seen as just another example of a comparative advantage that one economy had in a specific economic sphere. But, towards the end of the nineteenth century, this laissez-faire attitude came under pressure. Growing economic protectionism, even as more and more countries came to rely on international trade to supply their population with food, became a cause of conflict and mistrust between nations.

Germany, only united in the aftermath of Prussia's crushing victory over France in 1870–71, was a latecomer to Great Power status. However, its economic might grew rapidly and by the end of the nineteenth century was outstripping the British economy. 'The pace of German industrial growth and innovation was frantic.'[12] But its political and imperial status did not match that of Britain, France or Russia.

Continental industries gained from the advantage of adopting the latest methods, while British industries lagged behind, concentrating on traditional industries and technologies.[13] Growth of industrial production in Britain slowed. By 1913, Germany sold more manufactured goods in Europe than did Britain. However, there were balancing factors. Essentially, Britain, Germany and other leading powers grew economically interdependent.

Germany became one of Britain's best customers, as well as its most important supplier.[14] And Britain continued expanding its service sector to make up for its relative decline as the 'workshop of the world'. London was the financial capital of the world:

> The world's bank, the world's clearing house, the world's greatest stock exchange, the only free market for gold, the chief source of money and credit to facilitate international exchange, and hub of the global communications network.[15]

Although Britain began to fall behind in the technologies that characterised the 'Second Industrial Revolution', especially the electrical and chemical industries, there was an important exception to that generalisation: in the telecommunications and cable sector Britain held its own.

However, perceptions mattered and German advances in the sector grabbed the limelight. As the historian Richard Evans put it, 'The widespread belief in Britain that Germany was forging ahead economically before 1914 fuelled anxieties about the rise of an economic rival that translated all too easily into political and military forms.'[16] This feeling of growing vulnerability was therefore a factor in the growth of Anglo-German antagonism.

★★★

The term 'imperialism' entered the English language in the 1870s:

> The cult of empire began in Britain in 1877 with the proclamation of Queen Victoria as Empress of India ... by the 1890s imperial propaganda could be found everywhere, on railway bookstalls, in political meetings, in novels, magazines and history books. ... Already by about 1880, however, nationalist and political politicians in many European countries were beginning to dream of the conquest of other parts of the world.[17]

Between 1874 and 1914, European nations grasped more than 8.6 million square miles as colonies. Although keen to avoid clashes with other imperial powers, the German Chancellor, Otto von Bismarck, allowed Germany to acquire German South-West Africa, Togoland, Cameroon and German East Africa, as European powers rushed to acquire any unclaimed territory in the 'Scramble for Africa'. By the end of 1884 Germany's African empire encompassed almost 1 million square miles, making it the fourth-largest colonial power on the continent.

A similar frantic search for island territories in the Pacific began after Bismarck approved the annexation of the Bismarck Archipelago, New Pomerania, the northern Solomon Islands, the Marshall Islands and Nauru. The multilateral rush to grab the last of the available territories was effectively over by the mid-1890s, but not before it had added to the brew of mutual distrust between the European Great Powers.

This was the situation facing Wilhelm II, the young and impetuous monarch who became the Kaiser in 1888. By 1890, he had forced the resignation of Bismarck, who had acted as a restraint on Wilhelm's ambitions. These stretched to wanting a navy to match Germany's emerging imperial role, and this added a new and critical factor to Anglo-German antagonism:

> [Wilhelm] became convinced that Germany was engaged in a life or death struggle for the remaining unclaimed pieces of the globe, and those nations which did not get their share would enter the twentieth century under a crippling handicap. ... [he] became fixated on the idea that Germany needed a strong navy for the high seas, with big battleships. In a crisis between France and the Ottoman Empire over Crete in 1897, the British side with their naval power were able to end the dispute while Germany sat on the sidelines.[18]

In 1898 Wilhelm launched a programme to build a navy to rival that of Britain, challenging the British insistence that it must have a navy at least as big as the combined naval power of its two largest rivals. The year before, Wilhelm II had appointed Rear Admiral Alfred von Tirpitz as State Secretary of the Navy.

A driven, charismatic figure, Tirpitz guided and dominated the navy programme. He aimed to build a fleet at least two-thirds of the size of the British Royal Navy and capable of winning a naval battle in the North Sea. The Royal Navy, with its global interests, he thought, could not concentrate its entire fleet in the seas around Britain, thus leaving it vulnerable to a German attack in its home waters.[19]

Wilhelm envisioned a navy that would allow Germany to enforce its will on a global scale, as was currently possible for the Royal Navy (although, by this time, the British, realising they could not compete with the United States and Japan, had agreed naval spheres of influence with both these rising powers).

Wilhelm's plan would have required the building of fast cruisers – something that did not appeal to Tirpitz, who wanted large battleships. He won his struggle with Wilhelm, insisting, 'Our fleet must accordingly be so equipped as to be able to perform at its best between Heligoland and the Thames.' It needed to be big enough to force concessions from Britain: 'rapprochement through deterrence' at least.[20]

However, little thought had been given to how Britain would react. It was this long-term plan to develop a navy capable of challenging Britain's Royal Navy that was the key factor behind the growth of Anglo-German antagonism.[21] In 1902, the emperor told the British premier, Arthur Balfour, that the youthful German Empire:

… needed institutions in which it could see the unified idea of Empire clearly embodied. … His Majesty went on to repudiate the foolish notion that we were building a fleet in order to attack others. He had no interest at all in gaining or losing a few palm trees in the tropics. Such questions of colonial borders could always be settled easily, with a little goodwill.[22]

Not surprisingly, the British were unimpressed by such professions of innocence, fully aware that the purpose of having a navy was to exercise power. At a meeting in Germany in August 1908, the British Undersecretary of State, Sir Charles Hardinge, expressed the 'grave apprehension' of the British to Wilhelm about the German programme of naval construction.

Wilhelm told him, 'We needed our navy to protect the rapid growth of our trade.'

To which Hardinge responded, 'But it always stays at Kiel or Wilhelmshaven or on the North Sea.'

Wilhelm snapped back, 'As we have no colonies and no coaling stations, that is our base. We have no Gibraltar or Malta!'

Hardinge replied, 'Your trade cannot be protected from your base.'[23]

The British response was to out-build the Germans in numbers of vessels and to build bigger, more powerfully armed ships. As Sir Edward Grey, the British Foreign Secretary, put it in December 1906:

The economic rivalry (and all that) do not give much offence to our people, and they admire her steady industry and genius for organisation. But they do resent mischief making. They suspect the Emperor of aggressive plans for *Weltpolitik* [world politics], and they see Germany is forcing the pace in armaments in order to dominate Europe and is thereby laying a horrible burden of wasteful expenditure on all the other powers.[24]

★★★

In 1896, Kaiser Wilhelm sent a congratulatory telegram to President Kruger of the Boer Transvaal on defeating a raid, led by Leander Starr Jameson on the Transvaal state. Although denied by the British Government, Wilhelm and his advisers believed that Britain was indeed behind the raid and lauded Kruger's success in 'defending the independence of his country against external attack'. He considered sending troops to aid Kruger but stepped back from such a dangerous provocation of Britain.[25]

The British controlled cable communications to southern Africa, but the Kaiser's telegram was allowed to go via a British cable. However, it was leaked to the London press, who published it even before it had reached Pretoria.[26] Though some modern writers argue that the telegram was not provocative but mild in tone, at the time it caused great annoyance in Britain,[27] and it marked the deepening of tension over Germany's imperial ambitions and Britain's control of cable networks.

Another incident occurred over Germany's plans to install its own transatlantic cable. The main line of communication between Germany and the Americas was via a cable from the Frisian Islands to Valentia in Ireland, where traffic was transferred to an Anglo-American cable to North America. German companies complained that the route was congested and that their messages received a low priority. So Germany wanted its own cable from Cornwall to the Azores and on to New York.

The British turned down the German application to land a cable in Cornwall. 'The British government evidently hoped, by its action, to prevent the emergence of a rival cable node between the Eastern and Western Hemispheres, one through which information would flow outside the control of Britain.'[28] But this did not work out as the British expected. Instead, Germany laid a cable direct to the Azores, thus bypassing Britain and ruling out any British control over messages – or the opportunity to read them.

More conflict over cables arose during the Boer War of 1899–1902. As war between British South Africa and the Boer republics loomed, the

British authorities introduced censorship of communications on the two cable routes between Europe and southern Africa. Cable messages passing through London for South Africa were scrutinised to see if any were from Boer friends and supporters in Europe. All telegrams in code or cipher were forbidden except those from governments to their representatives in southern Africa. In March 1900, the two Boer republics asked Germany to seek mediation with Britain on their behalf. The Kaiser, however, would only do so if both sides wanted its involvement and if the request came from a third party. The German Chancellor drafted a telegram, explaining this, to be sent to the Boers. Wilhelm, aware of British eavesdropping, insisted the cable be sent in plain language so that 'London knows about it and must hear of our answer at once'.[29]

This habit of interfering with German messages led the German Government to plan its own independent submarine telegraph cable network. As one German wrote:

It was England itself which, in the nineties, sounded a fanfare before an unsuspecting world and repeatedly used its almost total power over cables for national-political purposes in a manner that was extraordinarily painful for the other European peoples.[30]

During 1899, negotiations between Germany, Britain and the United States led to the German acquisition of the West Samoan islands. Bernhard von Bülow, Germany's Foreign Secretary from 1897, wrote to Wilhelm:

Those islands, where Germans have worked for so long and so diligently, and which serve as a base for our trade in the Pacific Ocean with Polynesia, Australia and Western America, have great commercial value. Greater still is their maritime significance for our inter-oceanic shipping, in view of the future Panama Canal and the projected world cable link. But the place which the islands occupy in the nation's heart is of even higher value.[31]

Bülow's words reveal the fuzzy nature of Wilhelm's imperial objectives. It is unclear if it were trade, inter-oceanic shipping, national sentiment, or pride in having one's own cable links that was most important, or whether they were all seen as equally necessary reasons for possessing colonies and cables.

Two further German transatlantic cables were laid in 1900 and 1902–03 to support the growing trade between Germany and the United States and

South America. However, when Germany tried to extend its cable links through Turkey, the Near East and on to the West Pacific, British fears were again aroused.[32] Wilhelm aimed to match and displace Britain's pre-eminent global empire, starting with plans to build a railway between Berlin and Baghdad, with a telegraph line built alongside the railway:[33]

> In this case, at least, the driving force behind the German Reich's imperialistic urge for expansion was not the financiers, as is often claimed, but the dreams of world power cherished by the monarch and his diplomats. The railway, together with the [planned German] battle fleet, became the quintessential expression of Wilhelmine aspirations for world power.[34]

The British Government blocked finance from the City of London for the railway to prevent perceived German challenges to its power in India. The Foreign Secretary, Lord Lansdowne, observed, 'Until now England had sole control of the shortest route to India. With the construction of the Baghdad railway this would no longer be the case.'

Germany could come a step closer to providing the shortest telegraph link to the India Ocean. Not only that, but Russia also had interests in the area and was pushed closer by German ambitions towards Britain, its traditional rival in the area.[35] The Kaiser and his senior politicians, in their plans for a bigger empire, were treading on the toes of other powers.

Then, in 1913, Britain put pressure on the Turkish and Portuguese authorities to deny permission for a German cable between their territories. Sir Edward Grey's view was that 'Germany has no great commercial need for a cable such as that described and he is accordingly led to the conclusion that the object of their request is political'.[36] Germany was denied its own cables in the Indian Ocean thanks to British determination to clamp down on competition to its dominant position.

Thus were Wilhelm's ambitions thwarted. Germany was left with building a small number of cables linking Pacific islands and its base in Tsingtao, China, partly in conjunction with the Dutch and – to avoid the necessity of using British cables back to Europe – using a US cable across the Pacific, continental America and the Atlantic. This was a costly option, but at least the Dutch acquired two routes from the Netherlands to their Asian colonies that did not touch on British territory.[37]

Another unlikely cable alliance was created between Germany and France. Despite the persistent enmity between them, they agreed to combine their independent cables to form a common link to South America – France having suffered repeated incidents in the last decade of the nineteenth century of Britain delaying its telegrams for diplomatic and colonial advantage. Britain's cable policies alienated friend and foe alike. However, around this time a new technology was emerging that threatened British communications hegemony.

2

Breakout

In 1911, Italian forces invaded the Ottoman provinces of Cyrenaica and Tripolitania (present-day Libya) in a grab for colonial territory. The invasion led one of the most celebrated inventors of the era, Guglielmo Marconi, inventor of wireless telegraphy, to travel immediately from London to Italy to help his native country. Naturally, the Italian navy used Marconi's equipment. On the other hand, the Ottoman forces were, conveniently for the patriotic Marconi, users of a rival wireless system supplied by the German company, Telefunken.

The bombardment of the Libyan coast by Italian warships destroyed the Ottoman's coastal Telefunken stations. A few months earlier, the Marconi Company had tendered for the contract to supply wireless systems to the Ottomans. Although the Marconi system allegedly received better scores for signal strength and reliability, the German system was chosen – due, it was said, to diplomatic pressure from the Germans on the Turkish Ministry of War.[1]

Marconi was gleeful as he watched the action:

I visited yesterday the remains of the Telefunken station at Derna which was destroyed by this ship. It was supplied with four large towers about two hundred feet high and a building placed between the towers which contained the engine and instruments ... a few days later ... the [Italian] admiral called ... by wireless and informed the operators, in French that if they wished to save their skins they had better get out of the way as the station would be shelled in ten minutes. They were seen to close up [the station] without a fight ... The most impressive sight I have seen during the war was the bombardment by our and other ships of a Turkish position during the night. I never saw anything more like what could be described as hell on earth.[2]

To many modern historians the Italian attack on Libya was one of the opening moves leading to the First World War. The Ottoman Empire was the 'sick man of Europe' and Italy's assault sparked off a rush for its territories, leading to the two Balkan Wars of 1912 and 1913 and then to the crisis that followed the assassination of Franz Ferdinand in Bosnia in 1914.

The Italian military had expected an easy takeover of the two provinces, but met unexpectedly fierce resistance and were soon confined to a coastal strip. Although, for the Libyans and the Italian troops, the war and associated atrocities dragged on until 1912:

For Marconi, the war was short and exhilarating. He was to do patriotic duty, reposition himself with respect to his German rivals ... The success of the Italian wireless campaign convinced both Britain and Germany to invest heavily in developing the new technologies. ... As wars go, the Italo-Turkish War was a minor conflict. It seemed to be an easy victory for Italy, ... But the war was financially ruinous for Italy, bringing disillusionment with [Italian prime minister, Giovanni] Giolitti that would create the instability of the next few years and foster the radicalization of Italian politics and the rise of Mussolini.[3]

★★★

The traditional story is that when Marconi first developed a wireless system, he and his ambitious mother approached the Italian authorities who expressed no interest in the young Italian's invention. Marconi then exploited his British mother's nationality and connections by taking his wireless to Britain, where he found more willing minds. This story has been repeated in the many biographies of Marconi, but according to the most recent academic biography published in 2016, by Canadian professor Marc Raboy:

[There is] no documentary evidence that the Marconis actually contacted the Italian government before Annie [his mother] and Guiglielmo left for England in February 1896, although they certainly considered doing so. Research suggests that Marconi himself made the claim only once, in a

1923 letter to Mussolini that was certainly politically motivated. The story became part of the mythology of fascism, used by both Marconi and Mussolini's regime as evidence of the incompetence and lack of patriotism of Italy's liberal governments of the 1890s and 1900s.[4]

In the 1920s and 1930s, Marconi became a strong supporter of the Italian Fascist government, becoming an *ex officio* member of the Grand Council of Fascism. In 1926, he proudly proclaimed, 'I always claim for myself the honour of having been the first fascist in radio telegraphy.'[5]

As Raboy recounts:

Archival documents reveal that there are two versions to most of the stories about Marconi's early life: a heroic version, in which an unusually gifted genius overcomes incredible odds to prevail; and a more prosaic version in which, by a combination of intelligence, determination, attention to wise counsel, class privilege, and plain good fortune, he achieves success. Marconi himself became a master at fostering ambiguity between these two versions of his biography; it was an ambiguity that served his interests.[6]

London was the obvious place for Marconi to promote his invention. He spoke English without a trace of a foreign accent, sounding to his British listeners just like any other educated Englishman. He received a mixed response in London. He was coolly received by the General Post Office (GPO), which was conducting its own experiments with wireless communication, but he got a more enthusiastic reception from the Royal Navy and the marine insurance market, Lloyd's. Both appreciated the potential of ship-to-shore communications for safety at sea. The navy also saw possibilities for advancing centralised control of warship movements and operations.

In September 1896, the Royal Navy and the GPO observed tests of Marconi equipment. According to an official report:

I witnessed near Salisbury, in damp weather, signals transmitted to a distance of one and one-third miles through the air without wires … This was done in both fine and very rainy weather … These experiments have been continued in the presence of … [officials] between stations hidden from each other by rising ground, but the extreme distance to which all-round signals can be sent … such as would be useful to a fleet, have not yet been ascertained.[7]

Very rapidly the distance increased to scores and then hundreds of miles.

The Admiralty not only allowed Marconi to test his sets at sea in their warships, it also worked with his company to develop reliable working systems that could transmit over many miles under all sea conditions.[8] The Royal Navy also spotted security issues. Vice Admiral Sir Henry Lawson, commanding the Channel Fleet, observed in August 1900, following trials, 'As any possible enemy can decypher spelt messages it is very desirable to code signals when ... within wireless distance of an enemy.' It was, he said, advisable to use the 'Cruiser Code' as much as possible to make the messages secret.[9]

Wireless was taken up much more eagerly in the Royal Navy than in Wilhelm II's Imperial Navy:

> Admiral Tirpitz, the German navy minister, appreciated the value of wireless but thought that new equipment should only be adopted when it had been fully proven. When he did succumb to pressure to deploy German wireless sets, they performed badly, so Tirpitz's opinion against early adoption was reinforced. Thus, in 1914 the German navy was faced with the urgent challenge of implementing wireless technology into its ships.[10]

On the surface, it might seem as if the wireless transmitter was the key invention. But really it was the receiver that was at the core of Marconi's success – the ability to distinguish 'signal' from 'noise'. Marconi was driven by the urge to receive messages over longer and longer distances. In 1901, Marconi first achieved transatlantic signalling from Caernarfon, in North Wales, to North America (though it took until 1907 to develop a reasonably acceptable commercial service). Marconi's emphasis on sensitive receivers gave the Royal Navy a significant advantage in the interception stakes when the war started.

★★★

One day in 1903, two men called William both happened to visit Rome at the same time. One was Kaiser Wilhelm II, head of the German Empire. The other was Guglielmo Marconi, the returning hero; the Italian boy who had gone to London to turn his invention into a commercial proposition. Now he was visiting the eternal city to be made a citizen of Rome.

The 'other Guglielmo', as the Italian press humiliatingly dubbed the Kaiser, was there to visit the Pope. The German Kaiser's parade to the Vatican caused chaos in Rome, and Marconi was late arriving at the ceremony with the mayor where he was due to receive his fellow countrymen's token of admiration. All the same, the public adoration for Marconi rather pushed the touchy Kaiser's reception into the shade.

Wilhelm did not like Guglielmo. His drawing away of public attention did not help relations between the two men when they met later that day as dinner guests of King Victor Emmanuel. There were also more weighty reasons for the discord. Marconi reported:

> The Kaiser's conversation with me and his general attitude were strangely characteristic of the role of omniscience which he had already assumed at the time. After having congratulated me on my work and my wireless he proceeded to tell me that he considered that I was wrong in 'attempting to obstruct wireless communications from German ships'. I told William of Hohenzollern that although I thanked him for his advice I felt confident both on technical and other grounds that the course of development for wireless telegraphy which I was following was the right one … At dinner whenever the King of Italy tried to direct the conversation towards wireless telegraphy and its achievements the Kaiser just as resolutely headed it off towards other subjects.[11]

The Kaiser's tetchy mood derived in part from an incident in 1902 involving his brother, Prince Heinrich, who had voyaged to the United States on the German liner *Kronprinz Wilhelm*. Throughout the trip, Heinrich (who was to become commander of the German Imperial Navy's Baltic fleet during the First World War) was impressed at being able to send and receive messages via the Marconi wireless set that had been installed on the ship. However, the return journey was on a different German ship, *Deutschland*, which was kitted out with a German wireless set. The messages transmitted from this ship were not received – or more likely, were ignored – at Marconi Company wireless stations. The German ship was thus unable to send or receive any messages until it neared the German coast and came into range of German land wireless stations.

Marconi claimed that the problem was a technical one, even blaming the German ship's wireless set for being out of order. But this was no doubt a lie. The reality was that there were commercial motives for the Marconi Company's policy of only communicating with its own wireless sets. Wilhelm was livid. Many other Germans – and indeed many Americans – shared his anger at Marconi's business practices, which were aimed at strengthening his company's dominant position in the wireless market.

Germany, however, soon provided Marconi with his most significant commercial and technological competition. This was of little surprise, given the strength and vitality of the German electrical industry. Professor Adolf Slaby was one of the pioneers of German wireless technology. He had attended an early wireless test by Marconi with the British GPO in May 1897 – the first experiment sending wireless signals across a wide body of water, the Bristol Channel. Slaby had heard about Marconi's experiments and asked to be permitted to attend. Marconi was against having the German professor observe his work, but the GPO overruled him. On returning to Germany, Slaby applied what he had seen to his own substandard system and claimed it as his own work:

> Slaby seemed to be acting as an agent for Siemens as well as the German navy with the blessing and urging of the Kaiser; also he had his own scientific and financial interests to promote. Exactly what he was doing was never fully clear.[12]

Another German professor, Ferdinand Braun, was also working on his version of wireless equipment, and in July 1899 was reported to be ready to demonstrate it to Lloyd's. There were claims it could transmit and receive over greater distances than those achieved by Marconi. But an intelligence despatch by a British naval attaché in Germany suggested:

> [The] report is too vague and devoid of technical details to enable any opinion as to the value of Professor Braun's system to be formed … [the experiments at Cuxhaven] have been of quite a private character and no report of the results of his experiments has, so far at least, been made by Professor Braun.[13]

Braun soon started working in collaboration with the Siemens firm that had been experimenting near Kiel (the base of the German Imperial Navy). Siemens had also been conducting experiments at Berlin with the Prussian Government, and according to British diplomatic despatches, 'using some entirely new method', said to be very successful, 'that is to say, far superior to those obtained hitherto according to Marconi's system'. But another naval attaché reported from Germany, 'As regards Marconi's system it is not considered Germany is at present in advance of us'.[14]

Marconi, recognising the importance of the German market, applied in 1896 for a patent in Germany for his system, but its award was delayed until 1900, giving the German companies time to develop their own technologies without infringing on Marconi patents. Slaby had written to Marconi in January 1899 declining an attempt by Marconi to collaborate. 'As far as I know it is excluded that foreigners will be admitted to the [German] experiments. The only way for you to get into business with our navy is with a German firm.'[15]

In 1903, under pressure from the Kaiser, Siemens and AEG merged their wireless operations in a joint venture under the name Telefunken, forming a German competitor to challenge Britain's Marconi Company.

Although the Kaiser was deeply conservative in his beliefs about the desirability of untrammelled monarchical governance and, in his social views:

> ... when it came to educational policy and the promotion of technological innovation, however, Wilhelm II showed himself to be incredibly progressive ... In his peculiar way he combined the court culture of absolutism and a class warfare approach towards millions of his subjects, on the one hand, with genuine enthusiasm for the modern world of technological progress on the other.[16]

Thus, the international struggle for a share of the worldwide market for wireless sets was often bitter. Between 1909 and 1914, Marconi's share of overall international sales market inevitably fell, from 67 per cent to 39 per cent, as more manufacturers joined the market (although it still sold many more wireless sets in 1914 than in 1909 as the overall market grew rapidly). Telefunken's share jumped from 10 per cent to 33 per cent.[17]

Table 2.1 – **Wireless sets in use from Marconi and Telefunken, 1909–10**

Year	Marconi		Telefunken		Other		Total
	No.	**%**	**No.**	**%**	**No.**	**%**	
08/1909	161	67	24	10	55	23	240
10/1910	203	63	53	16	66	20	320
07/1912	900	37	798	33	752	32	2450
01/1913	1047	37	871	31	879	31	2797
01/1914	1521	39	1281	33	1100	28	3902

Source: Michael Friedewald, *Telefunken und der deutsche Schiffsfunk 1903–14*[18]

Marconi's attempt to monopolise the wireless industry failed, and he had to accept that Germany had succeeded in building its own potent position in the sector:

In Marconi's business plan ... was the key part of an even grander ambition. As far as the company was concerned, its goal was to create a global communications network. The biggest obstacle was what Marconi called the 'Telefunken wall' of high-level German political support for the rival firm. ... Even some British ministers were considering giving Telefunken contracts if they quoted lower prices than Marconi, it was said.[19]

By 1908, despite the politics of the matter, Marconi began thinking about striking an arrangement with Telefunken to co-operate, and the two companies signed a deal in January 1911 to form a jointly owned subsidiary.

Marconi was a determined businessman. The health of his company was what mattered to him. He wanted to erect a global chain of wireless stations. If they could be set up on British territory, that was fine, but if not, he would erect them on another country's land. 'Marconi's cosmopolitan, internationalist vision [was that] wireless should serve the whole world, not a particular national interest. (The only time he diverged from that position was where Italy was concerned.)'[20]

While, in Britain, plans to build an Imperial Wireless Chain faltered due to government concerns about cost (and an 'insider trading' scandal involving, among others, Lloyd George), Germany began building a wireless network linking its far-flung colonies and attempting to evade the stranglehold of the British dominance of global cable communications.[21] By mid-1914, both countries had provided their home navies, armies and governments with enough radio systems to equip them with an essential weapon for conducting the world war that broke out in the summer.

★★★

At the end of July 1914, a delegation of engineers from Marconi Company visited the world's most powerful wireless station at Nauen, near Berlin. Work had just been completed on upgrading the wireless station so that it could transmit signals as far as 5,000km. The station at Nauen sat at the heart of a developing global network of wireless stations along with two other long-range wireless stations that were operational in Germany, Eilvese and Norddeich. A station in Tsingtao, China, could reach as far as Yap in the Caroline Islands, where another German station linked to the Central Pacific island of Nauru in the Marshall Islands. Nauru's wireless station, in turn, linked to the distant mid-oceanic island of Apia in German Western Samoa. Several of the wireless stations (including Rabaul in German New Guinea, and at Yap) were still under construction as war approached.[22]

Germany's African colonies were equipped with a series of smaller wireless stations, but all were in touch with a powerful station at Kamina, in Togo, which had a range of 3,000km, enabling it to communicate with Nauen. Kamina was the hub for the African colonies, keeping them in touch with the homeland. A station at Windhoek in German South-West Africa, in mid-1914 was being developed with a fairly powerful wireless system which could theoretically transmit almost as far as Nauen (when it was working, and atmospheric conditions were favourable). Two further powerful German stations were situated in the United States, at Sayville, working with Nauen, and at Tuckerton, working with Eilvese in Germany. A third long-distance transmitter on German soil, at Norddeich, handled communications to and from around 1,500 ships of the German Imperial Navy and merchant vessels at sea in the Eastern North Atlantic, the Norwegian Sea, the Baltic Sea, the North Sea, the Channel and as far south as the Cape Verde Islands.[23]

Back in Berlin in July 1914, the Marconi visitors were, according to an official Marconi Company history, 'afforded the usual friendly courtesy and generous hospitality by their German hosts. Their programme included visits to various factories and research establishments associated with the Telefunken Company.' The 'grand finale' of the trip was:

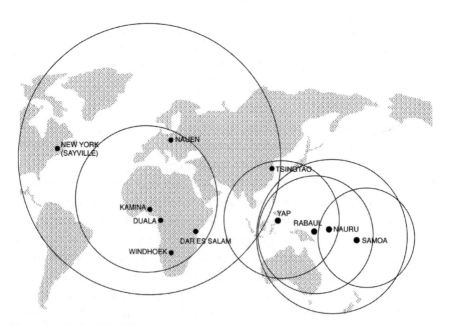

Map 2.1 – Major Wireless Stations in the German Empire, August 1914

… an inspection of the high-power station at Nauen, at which 200 kW high-frequency alternators and massive new antennas had recently been installed. The complete equipment was shown to the British party which shortly afterward left to take the night boat home.[24]

Immediately the party of Marconi Company engineers departed the station on 29 July, the Nauen station was closed for normal service and handed over to military authorities who had been waiting in the wings. Other parts of Europe were effectively already at war and Nauen was needed to play its role in co-ordinating the communications of the German military and naval operations, diplomatic and espionage activities, and for communications in organising the trade in war supplies.

★★★

Historian Annika Mombauer, in her survey of the debates between historians on the causes of the First World War, writes that all of the accounts she discusses:

… might be regarded as highly contentious by some historians. There is no interpretation, no 'factual' account of the events that led to war that could not be criticised or rejected by historians who favour a different explanation of the origins of the war.[25]

It may have involved, directly and indirectly, many millions of people, but the First World War was begun by a very small number of people from the ruling elites. It is estimated that the Kaiser consulted just seven people over Germany's decision to go to war. Following the assassination in Sarajevo of Crown Prince Franz Ferdinand in recently annexed Bosnia, the Habsburg elite blamed Serbia. They were determined to go to war against Serbia. According to one historian of the Central Powers:

Now was the time to strike to prove the Empire's vitality and to smash its enemies before they coalesced into an invincible coalition. In July 1914 Habsburg leaders were desperate men. They were ruthless because they felt they had nothing to lose.[26]

Austria-Hungary's only real ally was Germany. Many, but not all, historians are also convinced that Germany was set on a war to vanquish its foes. The

German elite around Wilhelm II feared the *Kaiserreich* was being encircled by Russia to the east and France and Britain to the west. So, to avoid being isolated and left alone to face the entente powers, Germany clung tightly to Austria-Hungary. This, in turn, meant German backing – in the form of the notorious 'blank cheque' of support for whatever action Austria-Hungary decided upon – for the Habsburg aims for a quick and decisive victory over Serbia. 'Vienna wanted war, and the German leadership understood as much. They could have restrained the Austrians, and chose not to do so. But certainly they did not frogmarch a reluctant Habsburg Empire to war.'[27]

German diplomats urged Austria-Hungary to act quickly. Yet they delayed delivering their ultimatum to the Serbs for two main reasons: first, much of the army was on leave helping out with the harvest; and second, it was an attempt to throw the French off the scent. The French President Poincaré was due to visit Russia, and the Austro-Hungarians wanted to prevent the two allies consulting on a response to any ultimatum. So, the delivery of demands to Serbia was held back until the French delegation, departing St Petersburg on 23 July, was at sea returning to France.

However, this trickery was put at risk when the Russians intercepted cables sent from Vienna to the Austro-Hungarian ambassador in St Petersburg, enquiring about the date on which the French were due to sail home. The Russians had already derived from a diplomatic source in Vienna roughly what the Austro-Hungarian Foreign Secretary intended to do. The intercepted telegrams were decoded, and the Austro-Hungarian ruse revealed.[28] The Russians and French strengthened their alliance during the French visit, giving French backing to a strong Russian response to the Austro-Hungarian actions, and setting the scene for war.

Russia saw Serbia as an ally and also feared that if it did not act in response to the Habsburg aggression, it would lose access to the Dardanelles and its only all-year-round sea outlet for its critical money-earning wheat exports. Russia's involvement brought Germany into a stand-off with the Romanov Empire in the east. It also meant an immediate German attack on France through Belgium, which, in turn, meant that Britain, an ally of both Russia and France, would probably be dragged in as the British elite feared that Germany could become the dominant power on the Continent and thus be in a position to threaten the Empire by menacing the Royal Navy from Channel ports. Also, British leaders reasoned that if the country stood aloof from the war, it would suffer whoever was victorious.[29] Thus did a desire for a quick regional conflict in the Balkans initiate what turned into a prolonged world war.

3

The Longest Link

William Le Queux's novel, *The Invasion of 1910: With a Full Account of the Siege of London*, describing a fictional invasion of southern England by the German Army, sold over 1 million copies. Published in 1906, just as the Anglo-German naval antagonism was reaching fever pitch, it was one of a popular genre of invasion scare stories – such as the much more readable *Riddle of the Sands* by Erskine Childers, which recounts an unravelling of a German plot to launch an invading army from the tidal inlets around the islands nestling in the German Bight. By contrast, Le Queux's book reads more like a gazetteer of southern England, interspersed with plodding descriptions of army shoot-outs. But at least Le Queux had studied his subject closely and worked out a militarily practicable route for the advance towards London for the German forces from their landing place on the eastern coast.

However, when his book was taken up by the *Daily Mail* for serialisation, the author had to adjust the path to be taken by the German Army to pass through towns that had higher sales of the newspaper than his original route. The *Daily Mail's* time-honoured formula of creating fear and indignation demanded such changes. *Daily Mail* readers were more likely to be moved to fear by a foreign army romping through their own home town, rather than someone else's. They also needed to be raised to indignation by holding a suitable scapegoat responsible for the failure to prevent the brutal 'pike-helmeted gentlemen' ravishing *Daily Mail* territory. A fictional news correspondent reported on a failed British action to hold up the German advance at Purleigh, near Chelmsford:

From General down to the youngest Volunteer drummer boy, our brave soldiers did all, and more, than could humanly be expected of them, and on none of them can be laid the blame of our ill-success ... 'Who then was responsible?' it may well be asked. The answer is simple. The British public, which, in its apathetic attitude towards military efficiency, aided and abetted by the soothing theories of the extremists of the [pro-navy] 'Blue Water' school, had as usual, neglected to provide an army fitted to cope in numbers and efficiency with those of our Continental neighbours.

The first action of the fictional Teutonic invaders on landing was to cut the telephone and telegraph cables so that news of the invasion could not get through to London, hindering the British Army's response. Cross-Channel communications were also interrupted. However:

[It later] became apparent that the telegraph cables between the East coast and Holland and Germany ... had never been cut at all. They had simply been held by the enemy's advance troops until the landing had been effected. And now [the fictional German army commander] von Kronhelm had actually established direct communication between Beccles and Emden, and on to Berlin. ... At Emden, with its direct cable to the theatre of war in England, was concentrated the brain of the whole movement.

***

When the real war started, Germany invaded Belgium rather than Britain, but it did indeed set out to sever British communication links, especially its telegraph cables to allies and neutrals alike. The first to be cut were the easiest for Germany to gain access to – landlines from Russia to India via Turkey. Then, in September 1914, the Germans cut the British-owned cables in the Baltic Sea, which connected France and Britain to Russia. After that, they severed Black Sea cables in November 1914 (when Turkey joined the war on the side of the Central Powers).[1] Later, between May 1915 and April 1917, Germany made various attempts to cut all the cables leaving Britain, including cables to Iceland, Norway, Sweden, Denmark and the Netherlands.[2]

The Imperial Navy even developed grapplers and cutters that could be used on mine-laying submarines to sever undersea cables, but they were difficult to use and liable to failure. The transatlantic cables were left untouched – probably because they hoped to arrange with some neutral countries to send German diplomatic messages.

Further away, at the start of the war the German forces in German South-West Africa occupied a cable station belonging to the British-owned telegraph company, holding the staff as prisoners for nearly a year until they were liberated by troops from South Africa. However, British cable companies stopped communicating with the station, bypassing it, so that the German action had no effect on British communications.[3]

Two attempts were also made to cut British cables in the Pacific and Indian Oceans – both these actions were spin-offs from Graf von Spee's squadron of commerce raiders plying the waters of the Pacific and Indian Oceans looking for Allied merchant ships to capture and sink. Spee despatched one of his cruisers, the *Nürnberg* (subsequently joined by a support ship, *Leipzig*), to attack the remote mid-Pacific Fanning Island, a transit station in the British transpacific cable from Canada to Australia and New Zealand.

The link from Canada to Fanning Island was 5,600km, then the longest single submarine cable span in the world. The Pacific cable, funded by governments in the Dominions as well as the British Government because of its lack of commercial viability, was justified, according to the Colonial Secretary, Joseph Chamberlain, on the basis that 'the risk of war incident to the present route [to Australasia and the Far East] would be avoided by a cable in the opposite direction'. British planners also hoped that the island's inaccessibility was 'its chief protection against attack by a European enemy'.[4]

In early September, the island authorities were warned that a German ship might visit, so a lookout was posted to keep watch from atop a flagpole. When, on 7 September, he saw two approaching ships he shouted the alert, but as the ships were flying French flags, the islanders were relaxed about the landing parties who set out in small boats rowing towards the island (there being no jetty). Then, just before the landing party reached the shore, an officer jumped out of one of the rowing boats, pulled out a pistol and waved it around. Out at sea the warships drew in the French flags and raised the flag of the German Imperial Navy.

The cable station crew offered no resistance and the German landing party proceeded to damage the equipment in the cable station and to dredge up the cables close to shore and hack through them. The landing party then returned to their ships and sailed off. However, they had rather botched their work by failing to drag the severed end of the Fanning–Fuji cable out to deep water and failing to destroy key equipment. Within a few hours, the cable staff had dragged up the cable ends and temporarily spliced them to create a connection good enough to transmit news of what had happened to Fiji. The navy, although unable to spare any warships to escort it, sent a repair-cable ship to Fanning, and by mid-October the cable was fully restored.[5]

Another warship, *Emden*, split from Spee's squadron to roam the Indian Ocean and South China Sea seeking British merchant ships. The cruiser, along with one collier ship, proceeded over the next two months to capture or sink nearly two dozen merchant ships. In mid-November, the captain, Karl von Müller, after a daring bombardment of Penang, became even more ambitious.

The Cocos Islands group (also known as the Keeling Islands) and, in particular, Direction Island, was an important node in the British telegraph network. Three cables ran from Direction Island, one to Mauritius, another to Perth in Australia and a third to Batavia. The island also housed a British wireless station.

On approaching the islands, a landing party, commanded by First Lieutenant Hellmuth von Mücke, was sent ashore, with orders:

> ... to destroy the wireless telegraph and cable station on Direction Island, ... and to bring back with me, in so far as possible, all signal books, secret code books, and the like. ... We could discern the roofs of the European houses and the tower of the wireless station. This was our objective point, and I gave orders to steer directly for it.[6]

The crew considered destroying a schooner they passed on the way in, but that action was postponed, 'as I wished first of all to find out how affairs on shore would develop':

> With our machine guns and fire-arms ready for action, we landed at a little dock on the beach, without meeting with resistance of any kind, and, falling into step, we promptly proceeded to the wireless station. ... We quickly found the telegraph building and the wireless station, took possession of both of them, and so prevented any attempt to send signals ... We now set to work to tear down the wireless tower. ... The stays that supported the tower were demolished first, and then the tower itself was brought down and chopped into kindling wood. In the telegraph rooms the Morse machines were still ticking busily. What the messages were we could not decipher, for they were all in secret code.
>
> To locate and cut the submarine cables was the most difficult part of our task. A chart, showing the directions in which the cables extended, was not to be found in the station, but close to the shore we discovered a number

of signboards bearing the inscription, 'Cables.' ... Back and forth the steam launch carried us over the cables that were plainly to be seen in the clear water as we tried to grasp them with a couple of drags and heavy dredging hooks, which we drew along the bottom. ... With great difficulty at length we succeeded in getting the cable into the boat. ... we set to work upon the stout cables with crowbars, axes, chisels and other implements. After long and weary labour, we succeeded in cutting through two of them, and we then dragged the ends out to sea, and dropped them there. The third cable was not to be found in spite of our diligent search for it.

According to one British report, the Germans had actually spent much effort in hauling up and cutting one spare cable that went nowhere.[7]

But then events took an unexpected course. A member of the German landing party recorded:

Suddenly at 9 o'clock the *Emden* signalled with her search lights in the Morse code telling us to hurry up. We loaded the cutters hurriedly ... only to see the *Emden* putting out to sea. At first this maneouvre was quite incomprehensible; but she next fired a broadside and then shells began to drop all round her.[8]

In fact, the British staff on the island had seen the *Emden* approaching and sent a wireless distress message. It was picked up by a nearby Australian cruiser, *Sydney*, on convoy duty. Mücke later wrote, 'There was no longer any room for doubt; we knew that a battle was on in earnest.'[9]

The landing party prepared to defend the island, over which a German flag was now raised. The Australian warship being bigger and better armed than the German cruiser, there was little doubt about the outcome. The battle moved further away from the island as the *Emden* was repeatedly hit by shells.

As mentioned above, on the way in to the island the German landing party had passed a schooner that they had decided they would blow up on completion of their destruction of the cable and wireless equipment. But now Mücke decided that the schooner, the *Ayesha*, might offer an alternative to a one-sided battle with an enemy warship: 'I decided to leave the island on the little boat.' This led to a long odyssey as the German crew steered the schooner northwards in the hope of finding a way to friendly territory. They left Direction Island that same day and sailed to Yemen (part of the Ottoman Empire, an ally of Germany). From there they travelled overland to

Constantinople, arriving in June 1915, where they reported to Vice Admiral Wilhelm Souchon, commander of the German battlecruiser *Goeben*.

As at Fanning Island, it did not take long for the cables to be reconnected, restoring communications on the global British communications network. Despite German efforts, British control of the seas meant that the damage done to its cables and wireless stations was little more than a nuisance. Although the German Navy intermittently deployed submarines to attempt to cut British cables, the capacity of the global network was limited more by overload, as cable traffic grew rapidly during the war, than from enemy action.[10]

4

Urgent Imperial Service

The British policy of severing German cables and destroying German wireless stations evolved out of fear that the far-flung British communications infrastructure would be hard to defend and appeared to invite attack. The Committee of Imperial Defence concluded that 'great efforts will be made at the outbreak of war to isolate as much as possible the different parts of the Empire, and especially the United Kingdom'.[1] To counter this, the drive to create the 'All Red' network became a key policy – to such an extent that historian Paul Kennedy described it as a 'fetish'.[2] An Inter-Departmental Committee on Cable Communications, reporting in 1902, said, 'We regard it as desirable that every important colony or naval base should possess one cable to this country which touches only on British territory or on the territory of some friendly neutral.'[3] In this way, an extensive network offered the realistic prospect of building a secure global communications network.[4]

By 1908, the strategists were thinking about offensive operations, not just defensive ones. Disabling enemy networks:

> ... would no doubt be followed by reprisals. But even if the United Kingdom abstained from cable cutting, it would probably have no effect in influencing Germany ... seeing that there are places which it would be desirable for naval and military reasons to cut off from telegraphic communication in a war with Germany, or with Germany and her allies, the Sub-Committee are of the opinion that the right to cut cables, whether connecting neutral points or not, should be exercised whenever the exigencies of war demand it.[5]

Careful consideration had to be given to the potential for upsetting important neutrals, primarily the United States. Lesser nations mattered less:

> Discrimination must be exercised before any particular cable is cut, and care taken to minimise the inconvenience to neutrals, whose resentment if aroused might lead to hostility which would be inconvenient for us.

The policy was neatly summed up, 'Generally speaking, if France and Russia were in alliance with this country, it would be possible to isolate Germany from practically the whole world, outside Europe.'[6]

★★★

On the night of 4–5 August 1914, the Admiralty sent a prearranged telegram to the GPO requesting that 'cable cutting arrangements mentioned therein be immediately carried out'. At 1.52 a.m. the cable ship *Alert* sailed from Dover Harbour to the west of the Varne Lightship. Reaching this point at 3.15 a.m., the ship's crew dragged a grappling hook along the sea floor searching for German submarine telegraph cables. The first cable was found half a mile north of its charted position and raised at 3.35 a.m. It was cut by 3.55 a.m.

The crew then repeated the operation searching for four other cables. On finding each cable, it was raised to the ship and hacked apart with axes. Despite bad weather and 'torrents of rain' from around 6 a.m., by 10 a.m. the crew had cut the five cables from the German island of Borkum, of which two ran to the Azores (with onward connections to New York) and one each from Tenerife (with connections to South America and West Africa), Vigo and Brest. Then, three cables from Borkum and another German island, Nordeney, linking to Lowestoft, Bacton and Mundesley on the English coast were also hacked apart.[7]

The GPO reported, 'The effect of the expedition was to interrupt entirely all communication between Germany and all oversea countries (except Norway and Sweden) by direct cable.' A letter sent from the Cable Depot in Dover to the GPO headquarters recorded, 'Our little arrangement came off quite satisfactorily and as it was desired moreover.'[8] The GPO reported, 'Subsequent steps were taken to utilise the Channel sections' of the cut cables, for example, providing additional cable capacity between Britain and France. One part of a cable was also used to lay a new link between Britain and Russia.[9]

To tighten the communications noose even further, at the end of August a British ship cut the German cable linking Chefoo (Yantai), Tsingtao and Shanghai. Russia was a bit slower off the mark in cutting German access to cables to the Far East, but within a few days, 'all cable communication between the Central Powers and the outside world came to an end'.[10]

★★★

On 12 August 1914, Regimental Sergeant Major Alhaji Grunshi of the British West African Frontier Force[11] was the first British Empire soldier to fire a shot in the war. He was part of a force sent to destroy the high-powered German wireless station in the German colony of Togo, West Africa. Lomé, the coastal capital, fell on 12 August with hardly any resistance. But the real objective of the Empire troops was not the capital. Rather it was a village, Kamina, some 150km inland and the location of Germany's most powerful African wireless station.

The wireless set at Kamina could communicate with Nauen near Berlin and served as a relay point for the other German colonies in Africa: Cameroon, German South-West Africa and German East Africa. If Kamina could be taken out, all the German colonies on the African continent would effectively lose their connection to the homeland and Wilhelm II's dream of possessing a global wireless communications network would be shattered.[12]

On 5 August 1914, the Offensive Sub-Committee of the Committee of Imperial Defence 'strongly' recommended that British forces in the Gold Coast 'should be used for offensive purposes against Togoland with a view to destroying the wireless stations in that colony'.[13] About 2,600 Empire troops formed the attacking force, of which only about sixty were whites.[14] The German deputy governor, Major von Doering, 'signalled to Berlin that he planned to abandon the defenceless Lomé … and to fall back inland on Kamina'. The message was sent by wireless in plain language and intercepted by the British (probably as was intended).[15]

After Lomé fell, the Germans made a brief attempt at resisting the British advance along the Chra River on 22 August and did reasonably well. But, rather than continue to defend their temporary position they withdrew towards Kamina, some 33km further inland. It was reached by the British Empire troops on 25 August.[16]

The wireless station operatives did not mix much with either natives or other German settlers, whether colonial civil servants, merchants or

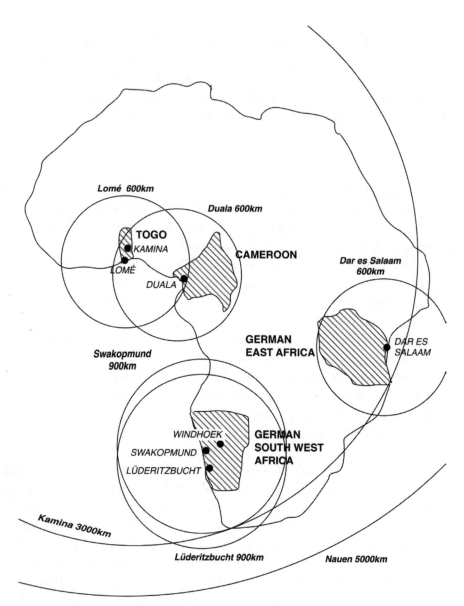

Map 4.1 – Major wireless stations in Germany's African colonies, August 1914

missionaries. The wireless station did not come under control of the local colonial authority and formed an isolated 'enclave'.[17] According to a German report, Kamina was a 'rather well fortified place' with good, deep trenches, but it lay in a depression surrounded by hills, so was vulnerable to artillery.[18] When news of the outbreak of war arrived in Kamina the wireless station staff were apprehensive. 'There was great concern for the safety of the station [as] … the station's large size made it difficult to defend from a military attack.'[19] The powerful transmitter needed a large antenna held aloft by twelve towers. Demolishing any one of them would suffice to stop the station from working.

Work on the station had only recently been completed, but with the approach of war it immediately became busy. Between 1 August and 22 August the station handled 229 messages in each direction between Berlin, other German colonies and German ships:[20]

From the notification of mobilization onwards Kamina was in service day and night. The wireless traffic piled up by the hour. The messages were for Windhoek, Duala, Dar es Salaam, and ships far and wide, which answered in similar quantity … The crew got stuck into their work … The initial wireless reports about the progress of the German army in Belgium were encouraging and strengthened our courage and raised our hopes, even if we had only a short time left in Kamina. But we did not worry as the war seemed unlikely to last much longer.

We received orders to ensure that the station should be demolished rather than fall into enemy hands in working order. It meant that work that had begun with such hope would end up as a mass of debris. … Enthusiastic participation of black staff in the destruction work could not be guaranteed so only whites would be used. … The ring of our enemies came ever closer.[21]

During the night the order came to destroy the station:

In the incredibly short time of five hours, the laborious work of several years was in ruins. The turbines and electric machines were destroyed as well as the cabling. The oil from the transformers flooded the transmitter room floor. … The toughest task was the destruction of the twelve towers. … A message had already been sent to Duala and Windhoek that 'If you hear nothing more from us, Kamina, the crew and the German colony of Togo is no longer in German hands'.[22]

Historian David Olusoga visited Kamina in 2014 and described the scene:

Surrounded by fields of crops and the mud and straw huts of the local Togolese farmers stand the ruins of a nerve-centre of European colonialism. Half-consumed by the vegetation lie huge rusted pieces of machinery. They are the heavy steel mounts on which enormous antennae once stood, along with giant water tanks which once cooled electric engines, and the remains of circular electric generators, brown with rust, some of them up-ended. Nearby are the concrete foundations of what once was a command centre, filled with weeds, overgrown with vines. The outlines of other buildings, perhaps outhouses or barracks, can still be traced in the red African soil. These physical manifestations are all that remains of a once vital hub for Germany's colonial communications: its radio station in Kamina – the *Funkstation Kamina*. [23]

> A telegram received on the 26 August [1914] … informed the S[ecretary] of S[tate] for the Colonies that … the wireless station as Kamina had been destroyed by the enemy, and that the enemy had sent a flag of truce on the afternoon of the 25 August offering, if given all the honours of war, to capitulate and stipulating for specific terms. [24]

The officer in charge replied that the enemy were not in a position to ask for terms and must surrender unconditionally, which they did and 'at 8.0 a.m. on the morning of the 27 August the British and French forces would enter Kamina'. [25]

The next target was Cameroon, with its wireless station at the coastal town of Duala. It was expected to be a tougher task than Togo. The British were intercepting messages sent to Duala and other German wireless stations in Africa from Nauen informing them of German victories in Europe, including the occupation of Brussels and the sinking of Allied submarines. [26] In Duala, the German authorities were informed by wireless from a German Hamburg–Amerika Line ship that British cruisers, including *Cumberland*, were close by and within range of Duala's Telefunken station. 'Feverish activity now began,' a German officer wrote after his capture. 'The first thing thought of was to block the entrance' to the river. This was achieved by sinking two large steamers, seven less sizeable ships and eighteen smaller ones still. [27]

The British spent several days seeking a route up the various channels of the Lungasi River using small boats, avoiding the sunken ships, mines and 'infernal machines' released to damage the approaching boats. [28] The infernal machines were in fact torpedoes which German forces attempted to launch from close up on two successive nights, though without success. On the second attempt a German officer, Willy Ebeling, was taken prisoner to his great annoyance:

Had I then suspected that I was surrounded by black spies, I should have chosen quite a different route for the second attack and should never have been taken prisoner by the English, but should now, with my comrades, be fighting in the Cameroon Highlands against the advance of the foe. Our betrayers had given the English accurate information as to where we could be caught. ... The hours and days which followed were full of ignominy for me. The blacks on board the *Cumberland*, our betrayers, received me with jeers, among them being King Dell himself – a German subject.[29]

Exploration of the river channels eventually enabled British troops to get close to the town. Although these operations were not directly successful, they made the German military authority worry about being attacked from the rear and were instrumental in bringing about surrender:

At 9.30 a.m. several loud explosions were heard and the tall wireless mast was seen to fall, and it was intimated by means of a white flag being hoisted over Government House and on the principal flagstaff, that the authorities were willing to surrender the town and neighbouring districts unconditionally.[30]

Confined on board a British ship, Ebeling wrote about how on Sunday, 27 September he heard:

... the news of the surrender of Duala. I could have wept ... There must have been terrible confusion. As our commandant saw on the approach of the enormous enemy forces that it was useless to attempt a serious defence of Duala, he, with his corps of officers and his black troops, withdrew to fortified places in the interior.[31]

Ebeling may have taken some pleasure later in the fact that it took many more months for the German forces to be forced to vacate Cameroon fully (eventually taking refuge in a Spanish enclave in 1916).

Next on the list of colonies to be dealt with was German South-West Africa (Namibia today), the most important and the most notorious of the German colonies in Africa. It was important because – unlike Togo, Cameroon or German East Africa – it was seen as suitable for settlement by Germans, with the potential to become a German equivalent of Britain's South Africa or Australasia. Clashes with the local inhabitants, who objected to the annexation of their lands for transformation into German farms, led to notoriety as the colony became the scene of an attempted genocide – the 'Kaiser's Holocaust' in the title of one book about the terrible events of the first decade of the twentieth century.[32]

In January 1904, rifle fire broke out between the native Herero and the German *Schutztruppen* (militarised police force). Without waiting to ascertain just what had happened, a young Lieutenant Zürm hurriedly sent a telegram to the Colonial Department in Berlin claiming that an uprising was under way. In a classic example of how the telegraph could result in the colonial tail wagging the homeland dog, the Colonial Office and the Kaiser back in Germany were alarmed and demanded a military response. The first commander sent out to crush the revolt (Hermann Göring's father) failed and was replaced by General Adrian Dietrich von Trotha who had gained a reputation for brutality in China during the Boxer Rebellion. The Kaiser called on him to 'end the war by fair or foul means'.[33]

Initially, the means chosen was to push the Herero inhabitants into the desert to starve to death. When this aroused complaints in the German press and the Reichstag, Trotha was told to seek other methods and he set up concentration camps, one of which became a death camp for the Herero and Nama. Tens of thousands died and survivors were reduced to 'virtual slaves'. Of about 50,000 Herero at the beginning of the uprising, only 15,000 were left alive at its end. By 1913 there were 1,331 German farms with 15,000 settlers in place of the previous inhabitants.[34]

It was into this tragic land that the First World War intruded in 1914 and 1915. The immediate attractions for the Committee of Imperial Defence were two medium-range coastal wireless stations, Swakopmund and Lüderitzbucht, and a higher-power station at the capital Windhoek in the interior. Theoretically, the wireless set at Windhoek was capable of transmitting as far as Nauen in Germany, but in mid-1914 it was only just in service and when working its practical range was limited by atmospheric conditions so it had trouble transmitting back to Berlin.[35] The British naval codebreaking unit Room 40 was aware of this problem, as a memo from its head, Alfred Ewing, in mid-October 1914 confirmed.[36]

On 6 August, the Colonial Office in London asked the government of the Union of South Africa in Pretoria to consider capturing the wireless stations:

> If your Ministers at the same time desire and feel themselves able to seize such parts of German South-West Africa as will give them command of Swakopmund, Lüderitzbucht and the wireless stations there or in the interior, we should feel that this was a great and urgent imperial service.[37]

The premier, Louis Botha, a Boer, saw advantages for the young South African nation. 'Nobody with any knowledge of naval strategy could believe that German South-West Africa, with its ports and powerful wireless station, could possibly be left undisturbed on the flank of an important sea route' and, therefore, if South African troops did not do it, it could well end up with Australian or Indian troops being used instead.[38] The South African Government also saw the war as an opportunity to take control of the German colony for itself.

First, however, a revolt against doing the British bidding had to be suppressed. Many Boers, including some government ministers, still smarted from the recent Boer War with Britain and saw that country as their real enemy. Germany was seen as a friend by the 'bitter enders' who saw in the war an opportunity to seek freedom from British influence, not for collaboration. The Boer revolt was ended by mid-January 1915, just as a message, intercepted by Room 40, showed that Berlin, following the destruction of the wireless at Kamina, was desperate to hear news from Windhoek. The message read:

> Nauen to Governor Windhoek: ... 1) Request news on the situation, especially in Angola; 2) How is the Boer Rebellion progressing? 3) Do you require landing of provisions and munitions and do you consider it possible? 4) Have the English occupied Swakopmund? 5) Have you destroyed the Swakopmund railway line? The situation in Europe is favourable to Germany. Signed Admiralty Staff.[39]

By then the attack on German South-West Africa was already well under way from the sea. The wireless station at Swakopmund was destroyed on 14 September 1914 and four days later troops landed at Lüderitzbucht. By spring 1915 the South Africans were attacking the interior of German South-West Africa from four directions. Hopes that the high-power station at Windhoek would provide a means of communicating with Berlin proved to be wishful thinking. A message intercepted by Room 40 in January 1915 revealed Windhoek lamenting, 'All we hear [from Nauen] is mangled groups every 8 or 14 days. Send via New York so we can understand better.'[40]

By May 1915, the South African troops had captured Windhoek, where the existing wireless station had been permanently put out of use by German authorities:

> After a second night spent by the roadside, Botha's party [heading to the capital to accept the surrender] saw rising out of the bush the wireless masts of Windhoek whose capture had been the primary purpose of the campaign

– at least as far as the British government was concerned. … Following the formal surrender, some of the South Africans went immediately to inspect the great wireless station … With its 360-foot masts, each resting on a huge glass insulator.[41]

Botha learned from intercepted German wireless messages that the German Governor intended to retreat northwards, perhaps into Portuguese Angola. So the Boer premier demanded unconditional surrender, which was achieved in July 1915. In Germany, the surrender was received with shock and disbelief. After the fall of Windhoek, there had been little news about the campaign and most Germans were unaware of the progress of the South Africa forces. One German commentary observed that it was 'the first British victory in the war and had been won by a Boer general'.[42]

The final German colony in Africa was German East Africa. The destruction of the German wireless station at Dar es Salaam was achieved rapidly, by bombardment from a Royal Navy warship off the coast, but a German warship, *Königsberg*, after sinking one merchant ship, took refuge in the forested Rufiji delta, south of Dar es Salaam, until the ship was finally attacked and scuttled in mid-1915. The crew removed the ship's guns and wireless and joined the forces led by Lieutenant Colonel Paul von Lettow-Verbeck in a prolonged resistance to the British in German East Africa.

The challenge to the British Empire troops was sustained, but it was never a strategic threat. All the same, its persistence caused some 10,000 casualties and created untold misery for the inhabitants in the areas affected by the fighting. The German forces also maintained an ability to communicate by wireless with Berlin.

The struggle in and around East Africa lasted to three days beyond the 1918 Armistice in Europe and (as intended) caused the diversion of forces that could otherwise have been deployed on more decisive fronts.[43]

★★★

The attack on Germany's more distant colonies in the Pacific had to be fitted into the need for the Royal Navy to deal with some other pressing tasks: the defence and transport of Empire troop convoys from South Asia and Australasia to the Middle East and Europe and dealing with German ships that threatened to disrupt Allied trade routes in the same waters.

The first target was the wireless station on the island of Yap in the Carolines. It was home to an important station with a range of 1,900km, linking to

Tsingtao (Germany's Chinese colony and its only overseas naval base), Rabaul (in the Solomon islands in German New Guinea), Nauru (in the Marshall Islands) and Apia (in German Western Samoa). The wireless station at Yap was destroyed by shellfire from the warship *Hampshire*, on 10 August 1914.[44] In September, the island, which was also a junction point for three German–Dutch submarine cables, was occupied by Japanese forces, who were formally British allies.

Shortly after Yap, the next target was the wireless station, still under construction, at Rabaul. In late July, a message told the staff to get the station in operation by October. 'This message amazed us, but we knew nothing of the storm clouds gathering on the European horizon,' recalled one wireless engineer. Suddenly, on 5 August, they heard a transmission announcing war with Serbia, Russia, France and England. 'It was assumed that the British would soon be coming, but no one knew when. We sat on the far side of the globe and could expect little protection.'[45]

Emergency work saw the wireless ready within three days to transmit to another Pacific wireless station, Nauru. On 12 August, observers in Rabaul spotted six warships gathering off the coast with the powerful Australian cruiser *Australia* as flagship. A landing party was sent ashore but was unable to find the wireless station and retreated. A month later:

At daybreak on 10 September the Australian warship again lay in the harbour. This time it was better prepared and equipped with 3,000 troops. Our fate was sealed. Yap, Samoa and Nauru were all silent and did not answer our calls any more. The island's small defensive squad fired on the enemy troops who were advancing towards the wireless station, killing or wounding some of the Australian attackers ... At 4 p.m. the commander of the defending troops announced he could only hold out for another hour. Station Rabaul transmitted its final call for help.[46]

Shortly after that, the mast crashed to the ground.

The day after the second attack on Rabaul, the Australians attacked Nauru in the Marshall Islands. A landing party was unopposed and found the wireless station had already been destroyed. It was brought back into operation by the Allies in January 1915.[47]

The operation to take control of the German wireless station at Apia in Samoa was being put together even before the war had started. On 2 August the Admiralty was advised that an 'expedition from New Zealand would serve a useful purpose if sent to capture Samoa, where Germany has a harbour and a wireless station'. The Naval Intelligence Division reported that the island was home to a fairly powerful Telefunken set with a range of up to 3,700km. It was located 8 miles inland and was served by a mast 120m high. The objective was to 'prevent [the island] being used as a base of operations by the armed German ships against our trade or as a [wireless telegraphy] centre of communications in the Pacific'.[48] The expedition was told to capture the wireless station undamaged so it could then be used to contact other British wireless stations – and also to 'intercept and report signals from unknown sources'.

When the staff at the wireless station learned that Britain had joined the war against Germany they were dismayed: 'We knew that this meant a death sentence for our colony.'[49] The German authorities hoped for a visit from one or other of Graf Spee's cruisers, but this was unlikely as the island offered no coal, no protected harbour and no forts:

> The wireless station was kept busy with ... the dispatch of warning messages to German ships, also with attempting to jam British and French ship- and land-station transmission. ... After the bombardment of the Telefunken station on Yap on 10 August 1914, we were cut off from all links to the homeland. ... we did not need to wait for long for the enemy to appear. On the morning of 29 August 1914 a lookout reported the approach of a fleet of eight warships. Could it be the fleet of Graf von Spee? It soon became apparent it was in fact a British dreadnought. ... The harbour of Apia smelt and steamed from all the grey colossuses.

Again, the German authorities ordered the wireless station staff to destroy the equipment:

> The procedure had already been prepared in planning for a military attack and arrangements had been made to put the equipment out of use to such an extent it would take some months to restore it to working order. However, the transmitter mast was not destroyed. One reason for this is that the mast was a symbol of German power and its destruction would not augur well for the prestige of Germany. And the Germans on the island reckoned on a short war.[50]

A telegram from the Governor of New Zealand to the Secretary of State for the Colonies in London, received at 3.18 p.m. on 2 September, reported, 'Expedition under my command with the assistance of the allied fleet occupied the town of Apia August 31.'[51]

While all this was going on, Graf von Spee's Pacific squadron was creating a headache for the Admiralty. At the start of the war it was based in Tsingtao on the Chinese coast. Fearing they could be stranded in the port, Spee took most of his ships to sea. In November 1914, the Japanese, with a token British contribution, blockaded and then invaded Tsingtao and the surrounding area, moved inland to lay siege to the base, captured it and prevented any further use of the high-power German wireless set there which had a range of 2,000km.[52] Thus, the last German wireless station in the Pacific region was closed down.

★★★

The Royal Navy, with the help of the Australians, New Zealanders and Japanese, could muster a much more substantial naval force than Spee, but had to deploy the ships spread around the vast spaces of the Indian Ocean, the China Seas and the Pacific Ocean. Tracking down Spee's ships was immensely difficult. Spee benefitted from faulty British intelligence (which suggested that he was in the South China Seas) and over-centralised command from the Admiralty in London (enabled precisely by the global reach of Britain's telegraph and wireless networks). But Spee also had problems of his own, in particular, replenishing his dwindling supplies of coal and ammunition.

Early in September, Graf von Spee's remaining ships gathered at Christmas Island – where they heard about the Allied occupation of Samoa. He took his flagship and two other ships to Samoa, hoping the Allied warship would have gone elsewhere, but leaving behind supply ships which he could sink. When he reached Samoa, he found no supply ships, so he sailed off. His visit was a mistake as well as a waste of time as he had given away his position, having been observed from the island and his presence reported to the Admiralty by wireless.[53]

The sighting of Spee at Samoa, combined with a message intercepted in Fiji or Samoa (sources differ) in early October, fixed his rough position and revealed his plans. Once decoded, the message revealed how Spee intended to head to the South American coast, rather than sailing west to the Indian Ocean (as the Admiralty in London was convinced he had intended).[54] The intercepted message led to the Admiralty sending a squadron under British commander, Admiral Cradock, who, despite being outgunned, attacked Spee's squadron near Coronel off the west coast of Chile, leading to a painful defeat for the Royal Navy on 1 November. Cradock feared that if he did not attack despite the overwhelmingly negative odds, his reputation would be damaged as had happened to a British commander who had let two German warships escape to the safety of the Black Sea at the start of the war.

Spee, aware that he would sooner or later be trapped, lost belief in his squadron's ability to survive and headed to the South Atlantic intending to make a dash through the British blockade back to Germany. On 19 November, Berlin advised the German Consul in Valparaiso to send wireless messages to Spee's squadron about coaling for the long return journey. The consul was told not to expect any wireless messages in reply as Spee needed to keep his whereabouts secret from British warships.

Eventually, Spee's ships were enticed (possibly by false leads planted by the newly appointed British Naval Intelligence chief, Captain 'Blinker' Hall) to attack the Falkland Islands in the South Atlantic. Spee received a report from a German agent in Punta Arenas that there were no British warships at the Falklands, but this was misleading as a powerful British squadron was steaming at speed directly for the islands, arriving just before Spee. He was attracted by the idea of destroying the British wireless station. Spee took the bait and, on 8 December, his ships were destroyed by the British squadron.[55]

Interception of wireless signals played a role in the battles of Coronel and the Falklands. The Royal Navy ship *Glasgow* was present at both battles and used wireless 'direction-finding' techniques to locate the enemy. On 13, 22 and 25 November messages sent to German cruisers and colonies warned that the German merchant code book (the HVB) and its key had been 'compromised' through capture by British naval forces. According to one historian:

> In the last resort, however, [German] cruiser warfare failed because the Germans could not conceal the movements of their ships. A steady stream of clues as to their whereabouts were picked up, often with great rapidity, sometimes in real time, and circulated with efficiency by the British between the Admiralty, local commands and pursuing naval units on the worldwide wireless and cable network.[56]

The Royal Australian Navy had its own codebreaker, naval officer Frederick Wheatley. He received intercepted wireless messages to and from German ships and gained access to cable messages to and from Spee's ships sent via Montevideo. Wheatley cracked a new cipher used with the HVB merchant shipping code book.

Wheatley's success in early November may have contributed to the eventual destruction of Spee's squadron at the Falkland Islands. It is also possible that Wheatley's achievement underlaid Room 40's own success at breaking German cipher keys which came around the same time.

A footnote in a file in the National Archives shows that a copy of another naval code book, the SKM (Signal Book of the Imperial Navy), was sent out to the south Atlantic for the *Glasgow* because its wireless telegraphy officer, Lieutenant Stuart, had intercepted and logged many signals. The file recorded:

> It is greatly to his credit that so careful a watch was kept though he cannot have guessed the remarkable results to be obtained … after the success of [Room 40] in the late months of 1914, a copy of a captured German signal book was sent to the South America Station and Stuart made such excellent use of it and the material he had so carefully collected that he was able ultimately to decipher a signal made by *Dresden* on [8 March 1915] giving the destination as Juan Fernandez where she was found and destroyed by *Glasgow* and other ships. This is one of the very few instances of the deciphering of an enemy signal that led to immediate and definite results.[57]

In August 1914, Germany still had two long-range wireless stations in the United States, Sayville (Long Island) and Tuckerton (New Jersey). However, in September, the US Navy took over control of the Tuckerton station. The Germans were allowed to continue to transmit messages between the United States and Germany. But, messages had to be sent in plain language as no coded or enciphered messages were allowed. This was problematic for Germany, though less so for military than for diplomatic and propaganda reasons. The German Ambassador in Washington, Graf von Bernstorff, later noted:

> As is known, American public opinion at that time had been given a one-sided view of the causes and course of the war, for England, who, immediately after the declaration of war, had cut our transatlantic cable, held the whole of the transatlantic news apparatus in her hands.[58]

He could have added that the British also exerted a global stranglehold on Germany's communications.

Historian Paul Kennedy summed up British preparations for the communications war:

> In retrospect, one cannot help but be impressed by the efficiency of the strategic advisory bodies, and particularly the Colonial Defence

Committee, in this matter of submarine telegraph communications. While vast shake-ups were needed in almost all branches of the navy and the army between 1870 and 1914 to bring them into line with the realities of modern warfare, those concerned with the cables policy appear to have been extremely professional and competent. Naturally, they possessed many advantages such as a great navy, an abundance of overseas posses-sions, and immense financial and technical resources within the nation itself; but credit for the skilful utilisation of all these factors cannot be denied. In their permanent striving for an effective cable communications system, in their rooting out all the weak links in the chain, and in their detailed defensive and offensive preparations, those strategists had not only helped to strengthen the military bonds of empire in peace time but also prepared that body better to meet the hazards and shocks which a world-wide war could present to it.[59]

5

Birth of a Legend

After the war started, German wireless messages were plucked from the airwaves, entirely on their own initiative, by amateur wireless enthusiasts who were acting illegally. Copies of the intercepted messages were sent to the Admiralty in London. But, because no one at that arthritic institution had given any thought to intercepting enemy messages, there was no plan to deal with the messages sent in by the amateur sleuths. So, they piled up on the desk of the Director of the Naval Intelligence Division, Henry Oliver.

The semi-official history of Room 40 says:

Oliver realised their potential value but had no staff who were not already fully occupied and certainly none with the slightest idea of how to set about the problem of code-breaking. One day in the first half of August, Oliver was walking across Green Park to the United Services Club in Pall Mall for lunch in the company of his friend the Director of Naval Education, Sir Alfred Ewing. 'It struck me,' Oliver recounted, 'that he was the very man I wanted.' He knew that Ewing had some interest in ciphers, because the latter had recently talked to him about 'a rather futile ciphering mechanism' which he had devised, and they had gone on to discuss 'novel methods of constructing ciphers.' Oliver told Ewing that development naval education would receive little priority until the war was won and offered him the task of setting up a code-breaking organization. Ewing promptly accepted.[1]

This is the official story of the birth of British codebreaking in the First World War – a truly British tale of lucky amateurishness that just about helps the country pull through in its hour of crisis.

The story grows in the retelling. One retired British admiral wrote:

> [Oliver] had these messages on his desk and was trying to make up his mind what to do with them when he chanced to meet [Ewing … who] had made a lifelong study of cryptology as a hobby and [who] asked to be allowed to study the messages.[2]

A member of the Naval Intelligence Division, Hugh Cleland Hoy, in a book about Room 40, has it that:

> Oliver, fired by his coincidence of need for a cryptographic expert and the hobby of [Ewing], decided to test his skill in all seriousness. He therefore handed him a few messages in code that had been intercepted from Germany. Great possibilities hung on the result and [Ewing] was equal to the task, for a few hours later the messages lay, properly deciphered, on [Oliver's] desk. [Oliver] looked at them and turned to Ewing, 'Can you undertake the formation of a department to carry on this work?' he asked. Ewing nodded.[3]

The point that gets exaggerated is the chance nature of the whole affair. Oliver's meeting with Ewing was just lucky coincidence and conveys an impression of slothful civil servants taking long leisurely lunches and strolls in the summer sunshine through Green Park. Even as the country went to war, decisions about who to appoint to vital posts depended on whom one happened to be lunching with. As one historian puts it, 'In the inimitable manner of which the British are so proud, it was amateurs who came to the rescue of a torpid officialdom.'[4] Some quite eminent historians have praised the amateurism of the British Intelligence effort, seeing it as a good thing. Professor Christopher Andrew wrote:

> The mobilization of British intelligence for the two World Wars provides at least a partial vindication for the now unfashionable virtues of British amateurism. To a remarkable degree the British intelligence system during the First World War was the result of brilliant last-minute improvisation by enthusiastic volunteers. That the volunteers failed to achieve … was due chiefly to the short-sightedness of the professionals.[5]

★★★

However, the standard account is in good part a cover story. It emerged in piecemeal fashion to provide a plausible narrative to accompany details of codebreaking activities that leaked into the public realm after the war. For each leak, there had to be an official story to play it down, emphasising the amateurism and luck. The cover stories were then repeated, and added to, becoming a comforting legend. Writers add or alter details to show a little originality in their account and avoid copying previous accounts too closely, so the legend accumulates dubious details.

All the same, the cover story is not pure invention, even if some aspects are highly misleading. And its debunking can be taken too far. One Italian historian, Alberto Santoni, has suggested that the British cover story was invented to give the impression that the British success at codebreaking during the First World War was pure luck, unlikely to be repeated in a later conflict. His view, and that of some others, is that British interception and codebreaking operations were systematic. They were undertaken from as early as March 1914, if not much earlier, possibly as early as 1904. The cover story was thus a key part of a cunningly effective British plan to trick its enemies into underestimating its codebreaking capabilities – so that Germany viewed scornfully the skill of British wireless interception engineers and cryptographers in the Second World War.[6]

But this takes matters too far and is too dependent on hindsight – and specifically on knowledge of the British success at codebreaking in the Second World War (and an apparent misreading of one particular file of intercepts in the British National Archives).[7] What actually happened is certainly nowhere near as amateurish and dependent on luck as the legend would have it, nor as calculating as the hard revisionist approach would imply. It is possible now to reconstruct a more nuanced account of the founding of Room 40 and its almost forgotten military counterpart, MI1(b), by bringing together a variety of documentary sources now available at the National Archives at Kew, near London, the Churchill Archives Centre at Cambridge, and the Post Office Archive in central London.

★★★

At the start of the First World War, France, Austria-Hungary and Russia all had diplomatic codebreaking operations, commonly known as 'Black Chambers', but Britain did not have a centralised cryptographic organisation. Its efforts were more diverse, set up and run by individual departments in Whitehall and by colonial or military authorities for specific imperial territories or wars. According to a historian of British intelligence, John Ferris:

By July 1914 British statesmen had some experience with and many expectations about the elements of signals intelligence. Rather than being a radical break with the past, the establishment of code-breaking bureaus in 1914 was the logical culmination of a long-standing trend. Few practices save cannibalism were beyond the pale for British statesmen, subject to the principle that they not be caught publicly in the act. ... Victorian and Edwardian governments collected intelligence as a matter of course, not through permanent and specialized organizations but, rather, a personalized system. Collection agencies were jury-rigged to meet specific problems and disbanded once these were resolved.[8]

The interception of Russian telegrams passing through India and Persia was formalised in 1858. The 'Great Game' was played out in the Middle East and Asia between Britain and Russia during the latter half of the nineteenth century, with the British fearful of Russia's designs on India, the 'jewel in the imperial crown'.

The British worried that local rulers might show favour towards Russia. In 1879, enciphered letters between the late Amir of Afghanistan and the Maharajah of Kashmir fell into British hands. The then Viceroy, Lord Lytton, wrote, 'Part of it is in a cipher of which the key is yet to find' – implying someone was looking for it.[9]

In 1904, Major George R.M. Church and Captain G.S. Palmer were sent to Simla to start systematic efforts to intercept Russian messages and break their codes and ciphers. Church had been a telegraph censor in Aden in 1900, so had some experience of eavesdropping and maybe of codebreaking too. One Indian Office civil servant argued, 'The tapping of messages is a recognised practice of continental governments, and I don't see why we should not follow it.'

There was some token resistance to the idea of intercepting the Russian telegrams. The Acting Viceroy, Lord Ampthill, was worried that 'the regular interception of correspondence telegraphic and otherwise is contrary to all English practice'. All the same, he acceded to it.[10]

In 1912, the Viceroy of India informed the India Secretary in London:

In the Army Department [in Simla] they have succeeded in discovering the Russian, Persian and Chinese Cyphers, and they are now able to decypher any telegram despatched from, or arriving in, India, or passing along Indian telegraph lines. Thus I was able to give you the other day the contents of a telegram from the Russian Consul at Bushire to the Russian Minister in Tehran, and we are able to control all the telegrams sent by the Persian Consul General to his own Government. We have quite a large file of Chinese telegrams that have been decyphered and that are quite interesting.

The telegrams detailed the Chinese negotiating position at the Simla conference and intrigues with Tibetan leaders:

This, the best secret intelligence which Britain had on any diplomatic matter between 1898 and 1914, shaped British policy throughout the Simla Conference. It did not lead to a concrete success for imperial foreign policy. However, it let Britain come far closer to the settlement which it desired than the India Office had believed the empire's 'exceedingly weak' position would allow.[11]

The British Army had its own separate intelligence operations. There are documentary records of the British Army gaining access to Russian and Turkish codes and ciphers in the 1870s and 1880s. For example, in 1875 the British military attaché in St Petersburg came into possession of some Russian messages and the key to the cipher used to hide the contents.

During the Egyptian campaign of 1882, the tapping of cables revealed that the Egyptian Army was doing its own bit of eavesdropping, so British Army Intelligence staff sent a few false orders over the telegraph cables hoping to mislead their opponents.[12]

[Following]… the occupation of Egypt … the intelligence branch of the expeditionary force was duly dismantled. Less than two years later, however, the British had once more hastily to piece together intelligence bodies for each of the several forces sent against the Mahdi in the Sudan … With the return of the troops from the Sudan to Egypt in 1885, a new permanent intelligence branch was founded in the [now British-controlled] Egyptian army under the command of British Officers.[13]

At the turn of the century, both sides in the Boer War tapped telegraph cables to listen in on the other. Boer eavesdropping was confined to southern Africa, but Britain could listen in elsewhere too. The 'Cable Censorship' intercepted cables in Cape Town, Durban and Aden, examining their contents.[14] In 1901, during secret negotiations, the British allowed Louis Botha, the Boer commander, to communicate in code with the Boers' president, Paul Kruger, in exile in Europe – with the messages going via British-controlled cables. The

British Army took copies of the messages and decoded them. The British claimed that the messages revealed nothing that they did not already know.

From about this time, the British Committee of Imperial Defence started to think systematically about what to do about submarine telegraph cable networks in time of war. And 1904 seems to be a key date – it was the year that the interception unit was set up at Simla and British warships were first ordered to intercept foreign naval wireless messages.

It was also the year that a 'Special Duties Section' was set up in the War Office, 'charged with the "study of ciphers, composition and issue of new ciphers, ... organisation of censor department for war, submarine cables ... Government telegraphic code"'. The first head of the section:

> ... was firmly convinced that the staff of his section 'must be experts at cipher, and must have a good knowledge ... of the cable systems of the world' and cryptography, 'a matter hitherto neglected,' needed to be 'taken up at once'.[15]

When Lieutenant Colonel James Edmonds took charge in 1906, 'to insure capable cryptanalysis would be available in wartime, [he] assembled a list of "experts in deciphering",' and arranged for training of suitable junior officers in order to build up 'a reserve of officers for intelligence duties in wartime'.[16] However, work on deciphering was restricted in the years before 1914, from the available evidence, to just one officer who also ran the library of intelligence information.

The Admiralty set up an Intelligence Department in the late 1880s. From 1904, serious efforts were made to 'lay the groundwork ... for transforming the Admiralty into a naval command centre through heavy investments in new intelligence and communications networks'.[17] Military and naval attachés at overseas embassies contributed intelligence, especially from Germany.[18] Again, at least one officer was engaged in examining intercepted encoded and enciphered messages – when war broke out, he became Room 40's star codebreaker.

★★★

By July 1914 many Indian and diplomatic authorities, including [Sir Edward] Grey [the then Foreign Secretary] and two successive permanent under-secretaries, Charles Hardinge and Arthur Nicolson, and at least three officers in the Boer war who achieved high command during the Great War, Henderson, Kitchener and Milne, had some practical experience with the use of signals intelligence. The same may be true of the two British commanders in chief on the western front, for both John French and Douglas Haig commanded columns in 1902 which had received copies of the captured Boer codebook. Moreover, Haig was the head of the Indian general staff and his intelligence chief during 1914–17, John Charteris, was a member of the Indian intelligence branch when the Indian code-breaking bureau was at work ... Before August 1914 the British Authorities had already decided to form cryptanalytical organisations during any war ... The army and probably the navy had incorporated limited preparations for signals intelligence into their planning for major wars. The intelligence authorities of Britain's fighting services planned to establish cryptanalytic bureaus in time of war and had at least an elementary idea of what this would entail.[19]

As we saw in the prologue, German wireless messages were intercepted, copied and kept by wireless operators at the Admiralty in London at the beginning of May 1914 and by wireless operators on at least one Royal Navy warship at least as early as March 1914. During July, as the international situation grew more fraught, the number of intercepted wireless messages increased. They are recorded as having been intercepted by the Admiralty at London or Dover, Port Patrick (Ireland) as well as Royal Navy ships and wireless stations in places such as Cape Town and Kingston (Ontario).

Wireless intercepts taken by the Marconi Company started to be recorded from the end of July. A message was intercepted at a new Admiralty 'policing' station at Stockton on 1 August. By 3 August, the number of stations taking messages increased and one entry reads, 'Taken at Admiralty, Chelmsford, Towyn, Stockton, etc.'[20]

★★★

The standard account, as we have seen, is that on the day war was declared or some time in early August (the accounts vary), Henry Oliver, Director of Intelligence Division, is supposed to have had that lunch with the Director of Naval Education, Alfred Ewing. They were old pals and it was just coincidence that Oliver and Ewing had, on a previous occasion, chatted about Ewing's amateur interest in the art of cryptography. So, Oliver, according to one account, scooped up the German messages piling up on his desk, stuffed them in his pocket and then set out to walk to the United Services Club for lunch.

The idea of two senior naval officers, in the first days of the war, strolling to lunch, no doubt in a fine August sun, is not quite in the same league as the story of an insistently insouciant Francis Drake in 1588 finishing off a leisurely game of bowls before slipping away to meet the Spanish Armada that had been reported approaching the Channel. But it is just as much a legend.

The start of the war meant an immense amount of work for Oliver. As head of Naval Intelligence, he had to ensure a flow of reliable information for a variety of naval operations ranged across the globe. Several such operations had been planned for the first days of any war, such as cutting German undersea telegraph cables; invading German colonies in Africa and Asia to destroy their wireless stations; clearing the home seas and distant oceans of German warships; organising intelligence for mine-laying and home port protection; and arranging the convoy of troop ships across the Channel and from the distant colonies and dominions of India, Canada, Australia and New Zealand. All these needed good intelligence on the whereabouts of German warships and forces.

And Oliver was no slouch. Indeed, he had a reputation as an extremely hard worker. Later in the war, after his promotion in November 1914 to Chief of Naval Staff, he hardly ever left his office, having a camp bed there, on which he napped for short periods. He also added to his own workload by refusing to delegate, and drafted naval orders personally.

One military historian has described the scene in the 'war room' at the Admiralty in London at the start of the war. It was, he says, 'wild, thousands of telegrams littered about and no one keeping a proper record of them'.[21] Thus, there is no reason to assume that the workaholic Oliver, on the extremely busy first day of the war (or thereabouts) would have found time for a leisurely lunch with a friend. He may well, of course, have arranged to meet Ewing, but it would certainly have been a working lunch, not an opportunity to catch up with an old chum.

Nor was it likely to have been a chance encounter. Oliver clearly wanted Ewing to undertake something to do with the war because one of Oliver's tasks was to set up the pre-planned Admiralty codebreaking unit. He had already identified Ewing as the man for the job. Oliver later recalled, 'Before 1914 the [naval] intelligence department had been trying without success to decode wireless cyphers. I wanted to put a big man on it.'[22]

Ewing was a big man figuratively speaking only. His son later wrote:

In private Ewing often expressed the regret that he was not taller, and remarked that a tall man can be impressive even when whispering brainless balderdash, whereas a short man like himself, in order to get the same result, must stand on tiptoe and shout solid sense.

If this is true, then Ewing must have learned very early in life how to raise himself up on his toes and bawl loudly, for he was marked out as a special student by his lecturers from his first days studying engineering at Edinburgh University. He was a 'very serious student' and his professor recommended he be employed, initially unpaid, at a telegraph cable manufacturing plant in east London (the centre of the world's cable manufacturing industry), assisting with electrical testing of cables.

His diligence brought payment, and, despite his tender years, he was sent to South America to help with cable repairs. Ewing first came into contact with codes at this time. He suggested to a colleague that they should encode their telegrams to each other when working in foreign countries to ensure commercial secrecy. He also learned to appreciate the importance of changing the code frequently to maintain confidentiality.[23]

In 1878, aged only 23, he was appointed a professor of mechanical engineering at Tokyo University and given the task of setting up an engineering studies department. While there, fascinated by the frequent tectonic activity, he invented the basic design for the 'seismograph' to measure earthquake intensity. He also worked on magnetism, coining the term 'hysteresis'. He was then offered the newly established chair of engineering at Dundee University. It was a step up, but not enough to occupy his burning ambition. His son said, 'Putting it bluntly, it is perhaps not unfair to say that all the time he was in Dundee he was working hard to get out of it.'

His shameless self-promotion bore fruit at the end of 1890 when he was appointed professor of mechanical engineering at Trinity College, Cambridge. Here, he worked as hard as ever, successfully establishing engineering as a subject fit to be studied in Cambridge. But even this was not enough for him:

> His energy, his capacity and appetite for work became almost insatiable; no grist was too small for his mill. Nor was he afraid to let other men see that he meant to succeed, and meant to get all the work he could, and the reward of that work.[24]

As well as his academic duties, he acted as an engineering consultant for big industrial projects, author of encyclopaedia articles and an expert witness in court cases – which he found 'pleasantly remunerative as well as excellent sport'.[25]

In 1902, Ewing was invited to become Director of Naval Education. The navy's leadership, in part at least, realised that the technical challenges of modern warships demanded an overhaul of the education and training of officers and ratings. New methods of selection were needed. New schools and training establishments were to be set up and a new curriculum devised. Marine engineering was to become a key skill as the modern warship was a mass of complex, interacting machines. But:

> Some of the old school did not relish the idea of an engineer rising to be an Admiral. Others considered that the [existing system of] competitive examinations should not be abolished ... other diehards thought that the change was an indictment against all previous Boards of Admiralty.[26]

One traditionalist protested:

> Under the new scheme of Naval Education a civilian settles the curriculum and issues reports upon the results, without showing how the results are obtained. ... What is required at this critical moment is the abolition of the office of the Director of Education and the reconstitution of the Committee of Education of the Admiralty, composed of naval officers.[27]

Nevertheless, Ewing's tough character ensured that 'the initial plan was adhered to'.

He rose to the top with the aid of considerable self-confidence and pretty sharp elbows. His achievements at Tokyo, Dundee, Cambridge and the Admiralty showed that he was entirely capable of beating many a taller chap when it came to doing a good job. His ability to build an organisation from new, to pick the right people and to get the job done, meant that, however squat his physique, he was indeed a big man, eminently suitable for a big job.

Ewing's interest in ciphers was also somewhat more professional than suggested by the references to his personal hobbyist's attraction to the arcane subject of cryptography. His early work with telegraph cables first brought the use of codes to his attention. Later, while at the Admiralty, Ewing sat on a pre-war Admiralty committee on codes and ciphers, including studying the potential use of machines to encipher and decipher messages (although one of Ewing's detractors within Room 40, William F. Clarke, later wrote that his experience on the committee 'taught him little or nothing').[28] Probably the 'futile' cipher machine was connected with this work. Far from being the fortuitously found amateur, Ewing had a suitable professional background.

★★★

Within a day or two, a handful of the navy's modern languages teachers found themselves being asked to volunteer for 'special duties' and to report to the office of the Director of Naval Education at the Admiralty. The first of these were Alastair Denniston, W.H. 'Bill' Anstie, and two naval instructors about whom only their surnames are known: Curtis and Parish.

Denniston was to be a key member of Ewing's staff, becoming his deputy. In 1914, he was a 33-year-old German-language teacher at Osborne, the Royal Naval College, with no knowledge of codes or ciphers. However, he was an excellent linguist, having studied at the Sorbonne and Bonn Universities. He had also written a German grammar book that was widely used in British schools. He was good at sports, winning, in 1908, a bronze medal at the London Olympics as a member of the Scottish hockey team.

He was to find a permanent new career for himself in cryptography. After the war, he became head of Room 40's successor, the Government Code and Cipher School, GC&CS. Despite some concern in the 1930s about his appointing friends and relatives to important secret posts, he retained that position until 1941. Denniston was also a short man and it is claimed that he was called the 'Little Man' by colleagues.[29]

Bill Anstie taught at the Royal Naval College in Dartmouth. He was to play a key role in breaking various German cipher keys and 'reconstructing' code books. William F. Clarke later described Anstie as 'a charming fellow who once shocked Sir Alfred Ewing by pinning up the notice of a sweep in Room 40 with the first prize a copy of the German code book'. Denniston commented that he was 'very sound', which may not seem overly fulsome praise, but for the terse and critical Denniston it was his highest compliment.[30] Yet, for the first week or so they floundered, overwhelmed by the seemingly unsurmountable task of making sense out of long lists of meaningless letters or numbers. Their first job was to learn the basics of the codes and ciphers.[31]

Within a week of getting started, Ewing was visited by Colonel George Macdonogh from the War Office, where a similar organisation had been set up under an officer with 'experience of deciphering in the Boer War', Brigadier General Francis Anderson, who had been called up from retirement.[32] Before the war, like the Admiralty, the War Office had only a single officer in its Intelligence Department looking at intercepted messages. The job had been given to the librarian of the General Staff Intelligence Department.

In December 1914, when the German military ciphers had been cracked, the cryptographers decided to look back at old intercepted messages that had been stored by the librarian. They discovered 'some perfect specimens of CHI and ZIF [ciphers] intercepted on 13 and 14 November 1913'.[33]

Unlike the Admiralty, the intelligence operations of the British Army were not controlled centrally. When the British Expeditionary Force (BEF) General Headquarters (GHQ) was set up in northern France it had its own intelligence units.[34] But coded intercepts were sent to the central unit in London. Its contribution was generally 'at the strategic level, providing training, a central repository of information and longer-term back-up to field units'.[35] It was initially called MO5(e) but its name went through various changes over the course of the war. To avoid confusion, I will stick throughout with its best-known name, MI1(b).

Anderson was a mathematician and in 1887 he had published 'Remarks on a Method of Deciphering Cryptograms'. Three years later, he became the British Army's cryptographer during the Boer War. In 1912, he established 'very close relations' with the French Cryptographic Bureau, one of the most advanced in Europe.

When the wartime unit was set up, Anderson was assisted by Major George Church from the codebreaking unit at Simla. Several others also joined the team. Four of them, Lieutenant G. Burnett, Captain Shirley Goodwin, Mr H.C. Steel and H.E.C. Tyndale, joined at the beginning of August, but left in mid-September and nothing is known about the reasons why they were recruited nor why they left.[36]

J. St Vincent Pletts, an employee of the Marconi Company, who joined the team on the 11 August, was one of the first of a handful of civilian recruits to MI1(b). He was followed by Oliver Strachey (brother of the controversial author, Lytton Strachey) who joined on 26 September 1914. He was transferred from the Indian Civil Service. His background may have been reliably high class, but he and his spouse were none too careful about keeping his appointment secret. His wife wrote to her mother that Strachey had been assigned 'to decipher codes and piece together scraps of wireless messages picked up from the enemy'.[37]

Strachey was to prove to be an extremely good cryptographer and stayed in the post-war codebreaking unit that had been set up under Denniston in 1918–19. He was joined in MI1(b) by another civilian, C. Bryans, on 4 October, and two army officers, 2nd Lieutenant G.C. Crocker and Lieutenant A.J. Quarry. They were based in Room 219 of the War Office on Whitehall.

Messages were at first intercepted at a powerful receiving station that was erected at South Lawn, Leafield, in Oxfordshire. Initially, the messages had to travel to London via Oxford and through several sets of hands before reaching the cryptographers, causing delay and introducing errors. Eventually, a telegraph line was installed which ran directly to the War Office.

The two units were told to work as one at this early stage of getting to grips with German Army codes and ciphers on the Western Front, and Room 40's naval work was relegated to second place. As Denniston later commented, 'Sir Alfred agreed to send a representative to work with General Anderson and then what might be called the prenatal life of the cryptographic section began.'[38]

Denniston and Anstie crossed Whitehall to the War Office, while Parish, Curtis and a new recruit, Lord Herschell, manned a 'watch' from Ewing's tiny office in the Admiralty. Herschell's father had been Lord Chancellor under Gladstone. The young aristocrat himself was a lord in waiting to Edward VII and then to George V and was a personal friend of the Spanish king. More pertinently, he was also a good linguist. However, he was not a natural cryptographer. Within a couple of months he was taken off cryptographic work to translate captured German documents. When the new director of the Naval Intelligence Division, Captain William 'Blinker' Hall (who replaced Oliver in November 1914), was appointed, Herschell became one of his personal assistants or 'fixers'. William F. Clarke dismissively described him as 'only a sort of honorary member'.[39]

Squeezed into Ewing's office or at the War Office, 'the first six weeks were entirely devoted to research, no real results being produced,' recalled Denniston. A German code book that had been bought by British Naval Intelligence before the war turned out to be a forgery. When work on army codes allowed, the volunteer schoolmasters spent their time looking for clues in the apparently random collection of letters or numbers in messages sent out from German transmitters at Nauen and Norddeich.[40]

Ewing searched out details of codes at the GPO and the Reading Room of the British Museum, trying to get to grips with the structure and working of different code books. William F. Clarke's accounts of Ewing leafing like a complete novice through 'old' code books are part of the legend. Code books were common features of commercial and administrative life at the time and anyone in professional life would have been familiar with them at work and possibly at home, too. Indeed, people even took them on holiday as there were special code books for tourists so they could send cheap telegrams back home. And, of course, Ewing was already quite familiar with codes from his work as a youth for a cable company. Ewing was deepening his acquaintance with codes, not initiating it. According to Denniston:

> Code books of German commercial firms were collected and the investigations proceeded, without however any discovery other than that Germany was communicating with her colonial governors and others … No one knew anything about wireless telegraphy procedure.

★★★

The urgent military need in August 1914 was to halt the headlong German assault, via Belgium, into northern France. The French commander-in-chief, Joffre, planned for major French offensives to take place on the French–German border, between Verdun and Switzerland. It took some time for him to accept intelligence reports showing that, in fact, the German plans involved a massive swing through Belgium:

> Unfortunately the German strategy had little in common with what the French had imagined it to be … the jaws of the immense [German] pincers were wide open, while the French, all unconscious, sat in the middle … entirely blind to the fearful gathering in the north.[41]

It was only in mid-August that Joffre began to shift forces to face this onslaught, although it was too late to avoid a forced, if organised, retreat.[42] The BEF was quickly put together and transported to France by the third week of August. It took its place on the threatened Allied left wing in time to join in the retreat.

The French had originally set up their own intelligence operation, the army's Deuxième Bureau, in the early 1870s, and had a long-standing involvement in interception and codebreaking (the French also had a codebreaking unit in the Foreign Office that was devoted to diplomatic interception). With no means initially of reading the content of the enciphered German messages, the Deuxième Bureau concentrated on the careful logging and analysis of the material they intercepted – where they were sent from, to whom, at what time and how often could be inferred from these logs when hundreds of messages were collated. Now known as 'traffic analysis', this allowed the French, somewhat belatedly, to start drawing up a more accurate picture of the structure of the German Army as it smashed its way through Belgium and into France.

Wireless technology was fairly new and rather clumsy to use in 1914. Wireless sets were large, heavy and unwieldy. They also needed their own generators to provide power and a tall mast to hold up an aerial. Several horses and wagons were needed to carry a single wireless unit. While size and power needs did not matter when it came to ships, on land they were serious drawbacks. Wireless was transportable, but not portable. So, early in the war, wireless sets were only issued to the headquarters of the commanders of the individual corps and armies, and also to cavalry formations, who had horses and wagons for transport and also traditionally had the task of undertaking reconnaissance for intelligence.[43]

MI1(b) realised that they had been mixing up army and naval messages. Also, they were confusing 'call signs' (used by wireless operators to identify themselves or their units) with code words within the body of messages. So, at this stage, it all meant next to nothing to the budding codebreakers. 'In those days,' said Denniston, 'the very amateur and inexperienced staff were greatly elated if they could obtain some sense from the [plain-language] intercepts.'[44]

Given that the 'plain language' was German military 'telegraphese', with a proliferation of abbreviations and jargon, we should not be too dismissive of this initial achievement. MI1(b)'s first record of an intercepted message was quite early on, possibly on 9 August. A logbook records that the message 'seems' to bear this date, but this is not certain. Unfortunately, there seems to be no record of the intercept or what happened to it.

The first challenge facing the operation was to get good-quality intercepts. As one cryptographer noted:

At this time and for weeks following, the reception of the intercepted messages seemed to present great difficulty to the operators of our stations – accuracy was very rare and in some cases the errors were very gross.[45]

Things improved, however, and in early September the cipher officer at BEF GHQ, Captain Henderson, reported that the operators were now able to distinguish between French and German wireless signals. A few days later, he suggested that many more messages could be picked up if a dedicated wireless interception station was set up.[46] According to Denniston, 'It was the time of the German advance into France and their movements could be dimly observed from the study of the *en clair* [plain-language]' messages.[47]

However dim things may have seemed to the British at that stage, thankfully, the French were far in advance when it came to interception and decryption.

At the outbreak of the First World War, the main French interception station was based at the Eiffel Tower. Staff there started to pick up German Army wireless messages on 4 August. From 11 August, the Germans were sending messages from Luxembourg, Belgium, Wölvre and Lorraine. Intercepting these transmissions enabled the French to start working out the identity of German Army units and likely routes of attack.[48]

In total, seven German armies attacked France, with the main strike force advancing through Belgium intending to envelop French forces from the German right wing and advance on Paris (a modified version of the so-called Schlieffen Plan). The key roles were played by the German 1st Army under von Kluck, on the outer right wing, and the 2nd Army under von Bülow on his left.

Kluck's army was identified early on as he signed some wireless messages to his commanders in his own name and some messages were sent in plain language. Indeed, in the rapid advance, the German wireless operators began to ditch the encumbrance of enciphering their messages and sent them in plain language, especially the 1st Army cavalry unit under General von der Marwitz.

Records suggest that the French broke the German cipher using two messages of the same length, a technique known as 'anagramming' (see Chapter 7) on 9 August. On 21 August, the French Army decryption unit made the first major cipher break and several messages were read. One message gave details of a planned attack on the BEF, who were informed on 23 August, a day before the attack.[49]

These messages gave the French and the British hints as to the operational plans of the Germans. But what did it matter? In a day or two, they fully expected to destroy the Allied armies, who were rapidly withdrawing back towards Paris. The war in the west would soon be over.

Indeed, right up until the first couple of days of September the German plan for a knockout blow looked likely to succeed. However, the German armies began to outrun their logistics and serious errors were made over the focus of the attack, worsened by a virtual collapse of communication between the supreme command of the German forces (OHL) and Kluck and Bülow – not helped by the distance between OHL and Kluck's headquarters being at the limit of their wireless range, nor by Kluck's tendency to ignore orders. Jealousy and pride also meant that Kluck and Bülow were not communicating with each other.

On 19 August, an intercepted message revealed the German logistical problems to the French. The situation worsened when Kluck's 1st Army started to advance faster than Bülow's forces. At the same time, the commander at OHL, von Moltke, decided to switch the target from the west of Paris, aiming instead for the destruction of the French Army north and east of the capital. An intercepted message of 28 August from Moltke read, 'His Majesty [the Kaiser] orders the German Army to march forward in the direction of Paris.' On 2 September, Moltke informed his commanders:

> The intention of the Supreme Command [OHL] is to throw back the French in a south-easterly direction, cutting them off from Paris. 1st Army will follow the 2nd [Army] echeloned back and additionally will ensure flank cover for the armies.[50]

But, although Kluck was ordered to fall back slightly to protect Bülow's advance, he declined to do as ordered, hoping to win the glory of leading the smashing the French Army. In doing so, Kluck exposed his own right flank.

Crucially, the French intercepted the messages conveying these orders and air reconnaissance confirmed Kluck's continued forward movement. A French counter-attack was made possible by the intercepted messages informing Joffre of the German Army's changed route of attack.

The cool-headed Joffre switched troops from the German–French border north of Paris to attack Kluck's exposed flank on 6 September. This forced Kluck to withdraw troops from his left to prevent the possibility of being enveloped. This, in turn, led to a gap opening up between the German 1st and 2nd Armies. The existence of the gap was identified by the French, in part from more intercepted messages and in part from aerial reconnaissance. French and British troops then attacked into the widening gap, forcing both Kluck and Bülow to retreat to north of the Marne. Intercepted messages on 10 September showed the Germans were widely retreating to stave off a more serious defeat.

So, during the first two weeks of September, the German plan to knock out France was destroyed at the Battle of the Marne. The Allied success was due in part to the 1,300 German messages intercepted by the French – some in plain language, some half in plain and half-enciphered, and some fully enciphered but which still revealed location, unit and direction of movement.[51] Initially, it was plain-language intercepts (and the increasingly effective use of 'direction-finding' wireless operations – see below) that informed Joffre's unflustered command decisions. He acknowledged that 'German wireless stations were one of our most precious sources of information'.[52]

Ironically, this happened only a few weeks after the Russians had committed the same error of using plain-language messages, leading to a spectacular German victory at the Battle of Tannenberg.[53] According to British Intelligence historian John Ferris:

> [The] victory on the Marne was no miracle. … *en clair* transmissions (combined with the solutions of encoded German traffic) warned the British Expeditionary Force of the precise time, location and strength of six full scale attacks on its front … Without this material, the British Expeditionary Force might well have lost the race to the sea, or even have been destroyed.[54]

The 'race to the sea' followed the Battle of the Marne as both sides tried to outflank each other to the north-west until they arrived at the coast and the static trench lines were dug in.

On 27 September, documents were captured that contained about fifty messages, allowing two full keys to be worked out and many more messages to be decrypted. The first major cryptanalytic breakthrough came on 1 October after the careful logging of all the intercepted German messages.[55] The German Army cipher system was called ÜBCHI by the Allies. It 'transposed', i.e. jumbled up but did not change the plain text (see Chapter 7). When used properly, messages were actually transposed twice, making it fairly hard to crack the cipher system.

Initially, only parts of the key could be worked out, but on 1 October an entire key was reconstructed. As the Germans used a single key which was changed fortnightly (the official instructions only vaguely advised that 'the key should be changed from time to time') once the key was discovered all messages sent with that key could be decrypted.[56] The example key given in the German instructions was the bellicose-sounding phrase, '*kampf und sieg*' (battle and victory).

The head of the French cryptographic bureau, Colonel François Cartier, at the end of the year, looking back on these hectic first days wrote, 'I need not tell you of the overwork I have had to sustain since the end of July. I have managed to cope with it, though I was often afraid I should succumb.'[57]

The news of the cipher breach spread quickly through the French Army and even outside the military. A senior French officer hurriedly issued orders to keep quiet about it, but information had already seeped out. On 4 November, *L'Homme Enchaîné* reported:

> We learn – from a reliable source – that Allied units intercepted a telegram addressed personally by the Kaiser to one of his generals (believed to be the Duke of Württemberg) of the absolute necessity of taking Ypres before 1 November.

Such a message did indeed exist, although it was sent on behalf of the Kaiser and not by him personally. A 'press indiscretion' also occurred in Britain on 3 November when the *Daily Mail* reported:

> Two German messages were tapped. The first ran 'Take Ypres by November 1st.' The second 'more men now and we have them.' The latter placed the British Army on guard.

As a result, procedures were tightened up in MI1(b) on the basis that 'the fewer people who see these messages in view of recent press indiscretion the better'.

However, the Germans appeared not to have heard the news and made no attempt to change the key they were using until late October. This time, it took the French just four days to break the key. When the key was changed again in November, it took three days, and the next change after that was cracked in just one day.[58]

At the end of October, a flurry of decrypts revealed that the Kaiser was planning a visit near the front at Thielt in Belgium on 1 November. The French planned to use the information to greet him with some bombing raids. Fortunately for Wilhelm, the orders from the French Army staff mixed up German and French time (which were one hour different) and the raids, which also involved the British, missed their target. Again the story leaked out.[59] *The Times* of London reported the attempt to kill Wilhelm. It was repeated by *Le Matin* on 7 and 8 November, but without mentioning a source.

This time, the German intelligence section did not fail to notice the news and concluded that the cipher system had been broken. A new cipher system, which was supposedly unbreakable, was introduced on 17 November. From that date, until the French broke the new system (known as ABC to the French and British) on 5 January 1915, no more German messages could be decrypted.

Between 5 October and 16 November the Allies had intercepted and decrypted nearly 600 German messages on the old ÜBCHI system, leading to the sending out of 169 intelligence telegrams to French, British and Belgian army units. As it happened, the end of the 'race to the sea' and digging of the trench lines meant that German use of wireless communications was vastly reduced. Thus, the temporary loss of this vital source of intelligence due to the careless security breach was not as serious as it might have been.

★★★

The British codebreakers did not take long to catch up with the skill being acquired by the French, who shared in full the details of their successes. It was on 2 October that the French delivered information about the captured cipher instruction documents to the British Army codebreakers and informed them that they had broken the ÜBCHI key system. The translated German cipher instruction document made its way to MI1(b) in London and was referred to as 'Exhibit II'.

Two days later, further intelligence reached London 'from Captain Henderson and his analysis of the system [based] on the surmise that Exhibit II is correct'. On 3 October, MI1(b) received some momentous news from GHQ in northern France: a cipher key of some twenty characters had been worked out by the British cryptographers at GHQ. The cipher used a 'double transposition' technique as described in 'Exhibit II'.[60] The British military cryptographers used the recovered keyword, '*zumstur-mwehrrechts*' ('to the attack force right'), to crack German messages dating back to 22 September.

Breaking the ÜBCHI system using a technique known as anagramming required a specific set of circumstances. Messages could only be deciphered if two or more messages of the same length, without errors and enciphered with the same key, were intercepted. 'These circumstances have but rarely been met with,' noted one cryptographer.[61] However, there is a record on 5 November:

Mr Strachey was successful in anagramming two messages of equal length and was thus able to get the key in use. The following telegram was sent to GHQ in France. 'It will be noted that the following is the solution of the German key now used 9, 1, 12, 8, 3, 13, 2, 10, 5, 6, 11, 4, 15, 14, 7. Two words in key ... *Mark Brandenburg* (solved 4.XI.14)'.

The string of numbers above is used in the transpositions (see Chapter 7). When the key was changed it took only two days to break it, 'Mr Strachey again successful with a double anagram regains the key'. The new key consisted of four words and was a bit more imaginative than the military and national slogans used thus far, '*Reise um die Welt*' ('travel round the world'). The head of Military Intelligence, General Macdonogh, wrote to the cryptographic bureau to say:

I believe that the last two solutions of 'special information' were worked out by the officers of your section. Perhaps you would let them know how useful we found them, especially the second one which arrived several hours before we received it from the French, thus enabling us to obtain valuable information much more quickly than would otherwise have been the case and hope they may be equally prompt in discovering [the new key].[62]

By 4 December MI1(b) was fine tuning its operation. A report noted that 'the complete operation of intercepting, deciphering, enciphering [and] sending out to GHQ and deciphering there has been carried out in some cases in well under two hours'.[63] 'No time was lost in getting down to decipher,' said Denniston. 'Watchkeeping' in the War Office was reorganised and more people were needed.[64]

The two British cryptographic teams organised their work in a systematic fashion. One of the civilians in MI1(b), C. Bryans, set about compiling a dictionary of German words found in deciphered messages. Such dictionaries were to play a vital role when it came to working out the content of new German code books. Another civilian, J. St Vincent Pletts, contributed some ground-breaking technical expertise by inventing a machine 'to lessen the labour in finding a key'. Unfortunately, we have no more information on this key-finding machine.

As mentioned above, not all communications intelligence was based on interception and decryption. Traffic analysis played an important role. It was based partly on the use of wireless sets that were specially designed to measure the compass bearing of enemy wireless transmissions without intercepting the messages being sent (although traffic analysis also exploited information derived from intercepted messages without decrypting them). If two, or better still three, direction-finding wireless sets, based in different locations, could each measure a bearing, these bearing lines could be drawn on a map. Where they intersected would reveal the physical location of the enemy transmitter (with the degree of accuracy depending very much on the distance of the enemy transmitter and the angle between the direction-finding stations).

Shortly before the outbreak of the war, a Marconi Company wireless engineer, H.J. Round, developed a wireless set that could be used to measure bearings. When the war started the War Office asked for Round to be seconded to the BEF where he initially installed two direction-finding stations in co-operation with the French Army. When these sets had proved their worth, a wider network was installed covering the whole of the Western Front.

Early in 1915, the Admiralty asked for Round to set up a similar network in Britain to track submarines, surface vessels and Zeppelins.[65] Naval direction-finding stations were set up at Lerwick, Aberdeen, York,

Flamborough Head, Lowestoft and Birchington. Later in the war, five stations were set up in Ireland to track German submarines patrolling the Atlantic approaches.[66]

Round made many advances in wireless technology right through to the Second World War, accumulating through his career some 117 patents in his name. One of his inventions during the First World War made it possible to fix the varying location of German spotter aircraft (which were used to direct artillery fire). In one week, as many as eleven German spotter planes were shot down as a result. He was said to be a 'bluff, sturdy, forthright extrovert, fond of the company of his fellows provided they were not fools'.[67]

On the other side of the front, the German Army paid little attention to interception and decryption in the first year of the war. It was only in mid-1915 that a centralised army codebreaking unit was set up in Germany (at Neumünster), but by that time the use of wireless on both sides of the static trench lines had been reduced substantially. And it was only after two years of war that the German Army had codebreakers based on the Western Front itself (at Spa in Belgium).[68] However, immediately after the 'race to the sea', a German Army cavalry unit intercepted some British naval wireless traffic after the drop-off in wireless traffic on the army front line.[69]

The British interception and codebreaking efforts were to pay dividends in the future. In the autumn of 1914, from the surviving fragments of information about the early days of British cryptography in the First World War, we can see that the combined unit had acquired important German documents and learned how to break German Army cipher methods. Within three months, a solid foundation had been put together for the next four years of war.

6

Code Capture

Even in autumn 1914 the war was a global one as Europe's empires clashed. The capture of some German documents, including important code books, took place during autumn 1914 in three quite coincidental events in various parts of the world. The locations were the chill waters of the eastern Baltic, the choppy waves of the North Sea and the balmy seas off the coast of Australia. However, it took some time for the material to make its way to London and Ewing's team. Despite the delays, the effects were to prove far-reaching.

In the Baltic, the Russians captured from a German warship two or three copies of the main naval 'signal' book, used to encode many of its wireless messages (we will look at the nature of the codes and ciphers in Chapter 7). Known as the '*Signalbuch der Kaiserlichen Marine*' (SKM), it was a major trophy for the Russians because all the copies should have been destroyed by the German crew of the *Magdeburg*.

On 23 August the *Magdeburg* was one of five ships sent to attack Russian shipping and harbours in the Gulf of Finland. The German ships became separated in thick fog and at half-past midnight on 25 August the *Magdeburg* ran aground on a sand bank.[1] She was unable to free herself, nor did an attempt by one of the other ships to tow her have any success. Later that morning, the captain, fearing Russian ships could not be far off, ordered the destruction of the ship's documents, including copies of the SKM. Explosive charges were placed so that the ship could be blown up before the Russians arrived. However, some of the charges went off prematurely and the crew started to abandon ship before the destruction of the papers had been completed.

At that point, several Russian ships appeared and started shelling. A Russian boarding party clambered onto the partially damaged German ship and, in the captain's cabin, recovered his copy of the SKM code book. One or two further copies (the sources differ on this point) were recovered from the sea.

The Russians decided that they would keep the waterlogged copies and give the dry copy to the British. It was handed over to the First Lord of the Admiralty, Winston Churchill, on 13 October. Churchill described the incident in his account of the war, published under the title of *The World Crisis*:

> At the beginning of September, 1914, the German light cruiser *Magdeburg* was wrecked in the Baltic. The body of a drowned German under-officer was picked up by the Russians a few hours later, and clasped in his bosom by arms rigid in death, were the cypher and signal books of the German Navy and the minutely squared maps of the North Sea and Heligoland Bight. … The Russians felt that as the leading naval Power, the British Admiralty ought to have these books and charts … [Later in October] I received from the hands of our loyal allies these sea-stained priceless documents. We set on foot at once an organization for the study of German wireless and for the translating of the messages when taken in. At the head of the organization was placed Sir Alfred Ewing.[2]

Over the years, this account has been repeated many times – despite the fact that the copy of the code book in the National Archives at Kew has clearly never been immersed for some hours in seawater.

The improbability of the code book-clasping corpse has even been cited by conspiracy theorists as 'evidence' that the entire story of the capture of the code book is a fake. But Russian sources suggest that one copy was indeed found in the arms of a drowned German sailor. No doubt Churchill was told of this and could not resist adding the extra drama to his story. The reader will no doubt spot some errors in Churchill's account – including the misleading placing of the appointment of Ewing and the setting up of his organisation as happening *after* receipt of the code book in late October. But the most conspicuous feature of the story is its colour – the dead sailor gallantly clasping the secret code book.

Around the other side of the world another German code book had already been captured. This time it was a merchant code book (the *Handelschiffsverkehrsbuch*, or HVB). It was captured from a German ship, the *Hobart*, on 11 August in an Australian port by a boarding party from the Royal Australian Navy. They wore civilian clothes and claimed that they were customs officials to trick the captain – who did not know that war had broken out – into granting them access to the ship. When their ruse was uncovered, the captain attempted to remove secret papers from behind a panel in his cabin. He was arrested and the hidden papers seized. On 9 September the code book was sent by boat to Britain, also arriving at the Admiralty at the end of October.

A third code book, the *Verkehrsbuch* (VB, or 'Traffic Book'), was recovered, allegedly, from the North Sea during November. A small skirmish took place between five British ships and a much inferior German squadron of four smaller vessels, all of which were quickly sunk. One of the masters of the stricken German ships put all his ship's confidential documents into a lead-lined chest and ditched it over the side. The chest was 'miraculously' trawled up from its resting place on 30 November by a British trawler. Among the prizes was a copy of the VB.

By early December this code book too had found its way to Ewing's team. The term used to describe this find – miraculous – is not my choice, but that of the codebreakers themselves, who referred to the story of the code book's recovery as the 'miraculous draft of the fishes'. This may, of course, be another cover story.

In an early draft of a chapter on codebreaking in a secret internal history of the naval war, written by Room 40 staff at the end of the war, this event is not described. However, there is a reference to the recovery of important documents with far-reaching consequences in Persia during the autumn of 1914. The author of that document wrote, 'The [VB] book was actually taken from a consulate in Persia at an early period in the war.'[3] However, this story does not seem to appear in the final version of the document, whereas the 'miraculous draft of the fishes' does find its way in.

The SKM, HVB and VB were not the only code books in use by the German Navy, military and government at the time. There were several diplomatic codes and ciphers as well as army and naval ones. Several such codes and ciphers will figure later in the story. It is possible that the author of this post-war document has confused the acquisition of the VB with some other code book. Certainly, some important secret documents, including two different diplomatic code books, were captured in Persia fairly early in the war, so possibly he has confused the two events.

Whatever the truth about the acquisition of the VB code book, by the start of winter 1914 Ewing's team had in their hands three vital documents. The bulk of the daily messages sent out by the German Imperial Navy were coded with the SKM and other important naval messages made use of the VB. The HVB was the least important of the three, but it was still useful.

It is important to point out that the coded messages were also routinely enciphered (see the next chapter). Having the code books was not enough to read intercepted messages. It was also necessary to be able to break the cipher system.

Before the three code books were captured, most of Ewing's staff were working on military messages for the War Office. In November, Assistant Paymaster Erhard Rotter was transferred to Ewing's team from the Naval Intelligence Department where he was the main German-language expert. Rotter was the officer who had looked at intercepted messages before the war earlier at the Admiralty, as mentioned by the then Director of Intelligence, Henry Oliver. Some writers have suggested that Rotter had been active in cryptography for some years.

Rotter took up occupation in an office next to Ewing and set to work on trying to relate the intercepted messages to entries in the SKM code book. According to a later account written by William F. Clarke, Ewing did not understand the nature of the problem and insisted that Rotter should take the intercepted messages and for each group of characters in each message, write down the SKM entry. As most of the messages were actually coded and then enciphered as well, this process produced a mass of nonsense.

Clarke claimed that Ewing insisted that Rotter carry on with the task regardless of the lack of success. Rotter, however, realised that he was wasting his time. So, when Ewing was absent, Rotter tried to see if he could work out the cipher key. Clarke says that he later came across a cupboard stuffed with nonsensical jottings and that these turned out to be the direct code translations that Rotter had written down at Ewing's bidding.

It must be said that Clarke was particularly contemptuous of Ewing and his account may well be neither a fair nor an accurate one. For example, Ewing would have known about the work done by the French in breaking the German military cipher and it seems odd that he should rule out a similar process being involved in the naval messages. Also, he had of course long had some familiarity with codes and ciphers, so it seems unlikely that during all that time he would not have realised that the intercepted messages could be enciphered as well as coded. However, Clarke's is one of only two accounts that we have of Room 40's first breakthrough.

Denniston, who gives us the other account, recalled how the atmosphere at the Admiralty changed towards the end of October following some visits by a Russian military man. An unknown person – now known to be Rotter – was then noticed working in a small room that became out of bounds. 'Then one fine day [Ewing] remarked that it was blowing hard in the German Bight and in reply to direct questions explained what was afoot.'[4]

The details of the wind flow in the Bight came from a weather report that had been decoded and deciphered. Rotter had concentrated his efforts on these weather reports and German intelligence messages sent out by the naval wireless station at Norddeich 'to all ships'. Once Rotter found out how to break the cipher keys, the naval codebreakers were able to start deciphering and decoding the German naval messages sent in SKM and other codes.

Although the naval codebreakers had learned from the French military success with German ciphers, they kept their own breakthrough secret even from the codebreakers in MI1(b). The acquisition of the code books was to be kept absolutely secret.

Ewing also wanted his staff back from the War Office. There was now plenty of naval work for them to be getting on with. So, when relations between the War Office and the Admiralty cryptographic units began to fray towards the end of the year, Room 40 and MI1(b) went their separate ways. As one of the naval cryptographers on loan to the War Office later commented, 'One is bound to admit that signs of jealousy were not absent even in this small section of men drawn from many branches of civil life.'[5] It was, said Denniston:

> … now clear that the Admiralty cryptographic section had found a task which concerned the navy alone and that there might be an enormous outlet for their energy … relations between the two offices were already somewhat strained and the new activities in the Admiralty were a closely guarded secret and a definite breach occurred.[6]

The military and naval cryptographic units hardly communicated at all until the spring of 1917. Denniston later commented, 'Looking back over those years, the loss of efficiency to both departments caused originally by mere official jealousy is the most regrettable fact in the development of intelligence based on cryptography.'[7]

It is possible that MI1(b) had some hint of what had happened at the Admiralty and wanted part of the action. Certainly, the Admiralty did pass on to MI1(b) some intelligence derived from its naval intercepts. For example, when it intercepted a message revealing the current key in use with German military cipher system on the Eastern Front, details of the key were given to MI1(b).[8] However, they did not give any hint about the source of the intelligence. General Anderson in charge of MI1(b) asked Room 40 how it had found out about the key, but got no answer.[9]

At that time, wireless traffic on the Western Front had dropped away, with mobile battles turning into static trench war. So, MI1(b) was looking for things to do. It asked Room 40 for closer co-operation several times and met with no success.

With access to the code books, and methods in hand to break the cipher keys, Room 40 was ready to become one more cog in the naval war machine. But it had to remain a highly secret one. Denniston recalled:

> Practically no one I met had any idea of the existence of such a cog, which was satisfactory to know, as we had tried to conceal our identity. I had to keep a straight face, and lie right well to many old friends from Osborne days whom I met up there, whom wanted to know what my job was.[10]

Codes and Ciphers

The German Navy, as well as the army and diplomats, used either a code book or a cipher, or both, to secure their messages, whether sent by wireless or cable. In this chapter, we will look at the three German Navy code books whose capture was recounted in the previous chapter and also at some of the ways in which messages were enciphered.

A key source for this chapter is a section on codes and ciphers in a large multi-volume secret history of the naval conflict written after the war by two members of Room 40, Frank Birch and William F. Clarke. Both men, this and their other writings show us, were rather arrogant and brimming with sarcasm. The codes and ciphers section is generally attributed to Birch, who was a historian (a 'rather dull' one, according to one writer). Unfortunately, Birch is at his most abstruse and opinionated in this document from which little insight can be gained. Someone in the Admiralty, commenting on it in 1921, wrote:

> I have read this chapter very carefully. It seems a pity that more has not been written on this subject, which would be of all absorbing interest to [a Naval Officer] engaged on ciphering duties. This particular work fails chiefly in that throughout ... it is written in a style which I feel sure no one except a super civilian will understand. ... As it stands this work is a danger if it can be understood at all. A detailed criticism would fill many pages.[1]

Fortunately, there are also several captured German documents, including the three main code books and other documents, among them the German instruction books for using the various cipher systems used with the code books, in the National Archives. From Birch's text and these German documents, as well as a recent academic study, it has been possible to put together a hopefully more comprehensible account of the German naval codes and ciphers.

★★★

The *Signalbuch der Kaiserlichen Marine* (SKM, Signal Book of the Imperial Navy) is an impressive tome. It looks like one of those oversized Bibles usually seen propped up on a lectern in a cathedral. It weighs much more even than a book of its size should as its covers are lead-lined to aid its sinking if thrown overboard. To the British observer, the likeness to a Bible is heightened by the Gothic script of the early pages. At the top left-hand corner of the title page, in small underlined Gothic font, is the word '*Geheim!*' ('Secret!'). Lower on the same page is the Kaiser's coat of arms and next to it an official stamp of the *Kaiserlichen Marine*, the Imperial Navy. On the next page, among a series of general instructions, one line is printed in heavy type: 'If the danger arises that the *Signalbuch* could fall into enemy hands, it must be thrown overboard or destroyed (by fire).'[2]

The comparison of the SKM code book with the Bible is not based entirely on its great size and old-fashioned typeface. Figuratively speaking, the SKM was the German naval signaller's bible. It was not just a code book. Indeed, it was not even primarily a code book. It was, as its title suggests, a book about all types of naval signalling. It dated from pre-wireless days of flags, semaphore and lamps.

The FT (*Funktelegrafie* – W/T or wireless telegraphy) section, although the biggest section in the edition used during the First World War, was added as an afterthought. In modern jargon, it was a 'bolt-on'. Even within the wireless telegraphy section there was not one code book, but several subsections. The main ones were a dictionary of words, lists of ship names and geographical place names, plus smaller code sections for compass bearings, map grid references and so on. This may have eased the task of designing the code book and integrating it with the existing signals book, but it introduced serious weaknesses by giving code breakers hints as to the contents of encoded messages.[3]

The basic system was quite simple. A three-letter code word – such as AAB or EVT or NLT – represented a plain-language letter, word, name or phrase. '*Sicherheit*' (security) was represented by RTL; '*Lebensfähig*' (viable) by MDJ; and '*Musterung auf Gefechtsstationen*' (muster at battle stations) by ODI. The dictionary of words was in alphabetical order so to code a word or phrase the user would look it up and read off the code word.

The three-letter code words were also in alphabetical order. To decode a code word, it would be looked up in the list of code words and the plain-language meaning read off. Some examples of SKM entries are given in Diagram 7.1 below.

AÄB	= a	[letter 'a']
AÄC	= ä	[letter 'a' with an umlaut]
AÄD	= ab	[a common German prefix]
AÄE	= abändern-ung	[alter/amend – alteration/amendment]
AÄF	= abgeändert	[altered/amended]
AÄG	= in Abänderung	[in amendment/in alteration]
[...]		
DOX	= Canadier	[Canadian]
DOY	= Cardiffkohle	[Cardiff coal]
DOZ	= Celsius-Grade	[Celsius/Centigrade degree]
DOα	= Cent	[cent (money)]
DOγ	= Chance	[chance, prospect]
[...]		
LYA	= Lage	[situation]
LYÄ	= augenblickliche Lage	[momentary situation]
LYB	= in der Lage	[in the situation]
LYC	= kritische Lage	[critical situation]
LYD	= politische Lage	[political situation]
LYE	= politische Lage hat sich gebesseert	[political situation has improved]
LYF	= politische Lage ist geclaert	[political situation has become clear]
LYG	= politische Lage ist gespannt	[political situation has become tenser]
LYH	= politische Lage ist ungewiss	[political situation is unknown]
LYJ	= Schwierige Lage	[difficult situation]
LYK	= Strategische Lage	[strategic situation]
LYM	= tactische Lage	[tactical situation]
LYP	= Lagern-ung	[store, storage]
LYR	= Lagune	[lagoon]
LYS	= lahm, -heit	[lame/tired, lameness/tiredness]
LYT	= Lage is gefaerlich	[situation is dangerous]

Example:
Plain-language message – *Political situation [of] mayor changed; prospect [for acquiring] Cardiff coal changed; situation difficult*
Coded message – LYD DOL AÄF DOγ DOY AÄF LYJ

Diagram 7.1 – Sample entries from the SKM code book dictionary section (*Worterbuch*) (source: ADM137/4156)

It will immediately be obvious that there are some special letters used in the code words, such as 'α' and 'γ' (the Greek letters alpha and gamma). This extends considerably the number of code words beyond what would be possible with just the basic twenty-six letters of the alphabet. More importantly for cryptanalytic purposes, both the plain-language entries and the code words are in alphabetical order. This means that only a single word list is needed for both encoding and decoding. A plain-language word or phrase beginning with 'a' is likely to have a code word beginning with 'A'. Similarly a coded message with a code word beginning with 'A' is likely to be a word beginning with 'a'. These are known as 'one-part' codes.

A basic technique for improving code book security would be to allocate the code words in random rather than alphabetical order (see Diagram 7.2 below).

Part 1 for encoding:

Arrange	= GHR
Arrange immediately	= AAC
Arrange on arrival	= RTL
Arranged	= WEF
[...]	
Motive	= WBV
Move	= AAD
Move as soon as feasible	= NAE
[...]	
Trade	= WWN
Trade embargo	= AAB
Trade note	= LRF

Part 2 for decoding:

AAB	= Trade embargo
AAC	= Arrange immediately
AAD	= Move
AAE	= Despatch
[...]	
LRF	= Trade note
[...]	
NAE	= Move as soon as feasible
[...]	

Diagram 7.2 – Two-part code example

This requires two lists, whereas the simpler structure adopted for the SKM requires only one list. Code books with randomly assigned code words are known as 'two-part' codes (also as 'random' or as 'hat' codes – as if the code word had been taken out, sight unseen, from a hat, or in German as '*Lotteriechiffre*' – lottery codes). Such two-part code books came into use later in the war.

Thus, the SKM is quite straightforward – an alphabetical one-part code book with alphabetical entries. However, the simple structure was complicated by the extra sections for ship names; code words for compass bearings were preceded by an X; times were always preceded by a Y; the grid boxes used to determine location at sea on German maps were prefixed with a Z. Thus, a very high number of code words within coded messages began with X, Y or Z.

Another useful aid to the codebreakers was the list of ship names. This assigned a two-letter code to each ship in the German Navy (including merchant ships). This two-letter code was preceded by a standard extra character, the Greek letter ß (beta). But the unprefixed two-letter code was also used as a 'call sign', used at the start of messages if a wireless operator wanted to call another ship, or a ship wanted to identify itself to others. Analysis of call signs – which were effectively the names of the user organisations – became a primary task of eavesdroppers. As Birch noted, 'These complications were all of a nature to puzzle the German coder and assist the English decipherer.'[4]

Another great weakness, however, was not a design flaw. It was that the code book was not changed often enough. Indeed, the copy captured in August 1914 stayed in use by the German Navy, despite their having some idea of its loss, until 1915. When it was updated, the code book's structural weaknesses were retained and British cryptographers were able to work out the new code from knowledge gained from the old.

★★★

The *Handelsschiffs-Verkehrsbuch für den chiffrierten verkehr mit Deutschen Handelsschiffen* (HVB – 'Merchant Ship Transport Book for the Coded Traffic With German Merchant Ships'), although primarily for use by merchant ships, was also used by warship and Zeppelin crews. Each entry is represented by a four-letter code word: '*Koenig*' (king) is represented by SCZR; and '*wie viel lokomotiven sind erforderlich*' (how many locomotives are required) by SPGC.

As with the SKM, the HVB code book was a one-part system and also had its own regularities built in. The book was alphabetical but started its code words with DABC (not AAAA or anything in between). The DA— code words all represented ship and squadron names of German and foreign navies (see examples in Diagram 7.3). Code entries with K---, L---- and M--- were devoted to proper names and letters or combinations of letters for spelling out words not in the dictionary section. The words and groups of words in the dictionary were given codes between OALB to PZWV, and RABC to VPKC. Code entries OABC to OAKN were assigned to grammar and grammatical descriptions, such as '*Punkt*' (full stop) or 'the next group is in plural'.

The use of four-letter code words meant that there were many more possible combinations than were needed. However, rather than allocate the prolific number of potential code words in random order, the complex structure described above was devised. No doubt it seemed very systematic and well ordered, but again it introduced severe weaknesses. Only seventeen of the possible twenty-six letters of the basic alphabet were used. More noticeably still, only twelve of them – D, G, K, L, M, O, P, R, S, T, U and V – would ever appear as the first letter in a code word.[5] These restrictions aided the breaking of the ciphers used with the code book.

Alongside the four-letter code words, the HVB also had a second set of code words, consisting of pronounceable nonsense words, designed for the sending of messages by telegraph cable. So that, as well as '*Koenig*' (king) having the code word SCZR, it also had a second option to code it as 'mukop emari'. This type of pronounceable 'word' was commonly used for telegrams as they were easy for Morse operators to deal with, being carefully designed not to be similar sounding and to exclude situations where a small error in tapping out the Morse code would send a quite similar set of letters but with a totally different meaning.

★★★

The third main German naval code, the *Verkehrsbuch* (VB), translates as the 'Transport Book', but this does not give a full impression of the way it was used. Submarines and small patrol boats at sea used it instead of the SKM for communications to shore stations. Also, it was used by the German naval and military attachés located at foreign diplomatic posts or posted alongside foreign military forces. Some standard diplomatic traffic was also communicated using the VB (such as between Berlin and Madrid),

Cable code word	W/T code word	Plain word	(Meaning)
babac igapo	DAKC	Gazelle	(ship name)
babac agefu	DAKF	Gefion	(ship name)
babac ihave	DAKG	Geier	(ship name)
babac ihebo	DAKL	Gneisenau	(ship name)
babac ihuli	DAKM	Goeben	(ship name)
[...]			
gosid ehige	MSZK	Vigholm	(place name)
gosid ehyra	MSZL	Vigo	(place name)
gosid ekica	MSZN	Vigsö Bucht	(place name)
		Dänemark	
gosid elavo	MSZO	vih	(syllable for spelling words)
gosid emari	MSZP	vik	(syllable for spelling words)
gosid emego	MSZR	Vikerö Fjord	(place name)
gosid enafy	MSZT	vil	(syllable for spelling words)
gosid eneci	MSZU	Vila, Port	(syllable for spelling words)

Diagram 7.3 – The HVB Code Book System

as was wireless communication between the German Imperial Navy and the army.

The VB differed from the other two main naval code books in that the code words were groups of five numbers rather than letters (known as 'code groups'). Thus, 'embargo' was represented by 38256. The code group 63389 meant, '*Telegram [nr] [vom] [betr] ist eingetroffen [im]*' (Telegram [number] [from] [concerning] has arrived [at]). The bits in square brackets are optional, meanings that will be obvious to the user from the context. It is important to note that the code groups were derived from the code book's page number (providing the first three numbers of the code group) and from the number on the page of the plain-language entry (each numbered 00 to 99). So, code group 63389 means page 633, page entry 89.

The code book started on page 100 with grammatical entries; pages 101–250 contained code groups for proper names and for combinations of letters for spelling out words not in the word list; pages 251–280 contained a list of ships, banks and their branches, telegraphic routes, cable offices and so on. Pages 281 to 712 (the end of the book) contained the main word list or dictionary. One section – that giving code numbers for single and pairs of letters – shows how the code book was also a signals book. The pairs of letters were primarily for use as recognition signals between ships at sea or ship and shore, and also for use with semaphore signals sent from one ship to another by flags.[6] The VB also had a set of the pronounceable nonsense words,

Note:

1) The page number gives the first three numbers of the code group and the individual entry gives the last two numbers. E.g. *alle* = 30059.

2) The section with examples from page 270 is for spelling out words with a single entry (so that A = 270 00 and B = 270 58). The double-letter entries are for use as recognition signals and with semaphore signals at sea.

Page 300

50	Alistro
51	alj
52	alk
53	Al–Kalah
54	Al–Khelb
55	Alkmaar
56	all
57	äll
58	alla
59	alle
60	allem
61	allen
62	aller
63	Allerheiligen B.	[All Saints' Day]
64	alles
[…]	

Page 148

11	Franz	
12	französisch	[French]
13	fras	
14	Fraserburgh (Scottl.)	[Fraserburgh, Scotland]
15	Fraternitö, Fort de la	
16	fray	
17	Fray Bentos	
18	fre	
19	fred	
20	Frederica	
[…]		

Page 257

60	Torpedoboat D3
61	Torpedoboat D4
[…]	
67	Torpedoboat D10

Diagram 7.4 – VB Code Book System

68	Torpedoboat S11	
69	Torpedoboat S12	
[…]		
Page 270		
(spelling code groups)		
00	A	
01	AÄ	
02	AB	
03	AC	
[…]		
57	ÄZ	
58	B	
59	BA	
60	BÄ	
61	BC	
[…]		
Page 302		
08	Artillerie	[artillery]
09	Schwere Artillerie	[heavy artillery]
10	Uberlegene Artilleerie	[superior artillery]
[…]		
12	Artillerieabteilung	[artillery detachment]
13	Artilleriefeuer	[artillery fire]
[…]		
28	Artilleristenmaat	[artillery trooper]

Diagram 7.4 – VB Code Book System (*continued*)

consisting of two groups of five letters that could be used instead of the five-figure code words.

Frank Birch commented that all three of the code books possessed many common features, 'great as were the single and especial disadvantages of each, the defects which they had in common were glaring'. The books were too large (not just physically but in the number of entries) to be used without difficulty. The SKM offered, for word and positional entries alone, some 300,000 three-letter code words but, reckoned Birch, probably not more than 5,000 were ever used. 'Helgoland' (Heligoland) was a very commonly used term in naval messages because it was a fortified base just outside the German Imperial Navy's North Sea bases. But as its code word was in the list of place names, it required two code combinations as its basic code word had to be preceded by a code word signalling a change of list from the preceding words in the message.

On the excessive number of useless entries, Birch exercised his full loquacious extravagance:

> The chief significance of this defect, of these albequestrian propensities, is one which may, perhaps, occur less readily to the layman than to the cypher expert. The expert knows that in such a book only a very few of the groups can be used and in guessing a [cipher] key on it, he knows that when he has [worked out] two letters he can guess with fair accuracy the remaining one [in a three-letter code word] … even if he has no knowledge whatever of the sense of a message or even the meaning of a single group in the book. It was indeed on this principle alone that the [cipher] keys on the successor to the SKM, the FFB, were originally solved.[7]

Ideally all the code words/code groups in a code book should be used a roughly equal number of times each (to foil codebreakers for whom frequency analysis was a key tool). Commonly occurring entries such as 'full stop', place names, ship names, naval unit names and so on all present severe challenges for the designers of effective code books. All three of the main naval code books were particularly ineffective in meeting these challenges. None of them made use of basic techniques such as employing 'dummy' groups (meaningless entries used to pad out the message and upset frequency analysis) or 'substitute' code words (offering several alternative code combinations for common plain meanings such as 'full stop'). 'These,' said Birch, 'afford the [cipher] key-guesser a considerable amount of difficulty.' But Room 40's 'key-guessers' were fortunate not to face such problems.

Birch roundly criticised the one-part nature of the code books:

> Yet of all the defects common to German codebooks the most striking and the least excusable consisted in the order in which the [code words] occurred. Early codebooks had never been formed with any great regard for cryptography. They never set out to defeat organised research. … The realisation of this defect came very late to the German authorities. They were slow to remedy it. It can easily be remedied by having two books, one for coding and one for decoding. … [otherwise] once the key is obtained and the sense of a few [code words] fixed, [the codebreaker] is able, with great ease, to fill in the remainder … Certain parts of the

alphabet occur more commonly than others; and in certain classes of messages the [code words] most commonly used will all occur on the same
page [of the code book].[8]

Birch concluded that the devising of German naval code book 'was bad,
unimaginative and lacking in the first essentials of secrecy, brevity and speed
of replacement'.

★★★

Once a message is coded, to make it more secure a cipher can be applied. But
the German naval ciphers were also often rather weak. Indeed, Birch drew
deep into his reservoirs of scorn when discussing the German ciphers. The
naval authorities:

> … decided to supplement such defects of existing [code books] … [But]
> the system of [ciphering] adopted was radically bad. … by its simplicity it
> helped the German as little as it hindered the British [cryptographer] …
> They caused little trouble to the expert English decipherer, sitting at ease
> with a number of copies of signals intercepted and forwarded by the most
> expert English wireless operators, [but] were a constant source of nuisance
> and confusion to a barely trained German depending upon the 'intake' of
> one wireless operator and lacking in time, ingenuity and skill to rectify small
> errors. … The actual method[s of ciphering] remained in use, though not in
> general use, to the end of the war.[9]

A 'cipher', in modern meaning, usually implies the use of a 'key' and a 'process' (or a set of rules) for using the key. Most often, we now think of the key
as a word or set of numbers. But some of the ciphers used in conjunction
with the naval code books did not bother with a keyword. The key, in these
cases, was a small printed booklet of only two or four pages. The main subject
matter in each booklet was a pair of tables – one for enciphering and one for
deciphering – with a set letter (or number) as a substitute for each code letter
(or code number) in a code word (or code group).

We will start with the *Chiffreschlüssel zum HVB* (Cipher key to the HVB).[10]
This is the simplest type of cipher imaginable with a straightforward substitution, character by character, according to a list or table with just two columns.
Using this table, every time the letter 'C' appears in a code word it is substituted with an allocated letter, say 'M'. The same set of substitutions is used

for every message until the table (or 'key') is changed. As the cryptographer's most important technique for breaking ciphers is a 'frequency analysis' of the number of times each letter of the alphabet is used in the enciphered message, this steady, unchanging system of substitution will not hide any pronounced frequency 'bulges' in the enciphered messages – the cipher letter for code letter 'E', for example, will appear with the same frequency as an unenciphered 'E' and thus be easily identifiable.

Diagram 7.5 shows an example of a message coded with the HVB and then enciphered with the cipher substitution table. In this example, the 'pronounceable nonsense' code words have been used. The enciphered message starts with a call sign or telegraphic 'address' (Elond Bremen), plus a regular HVB code entry (kisah aciba), which means, 'The contents of this message have been enciphered with the HVB key'. Neither of these parts of the message were enciphered (shown in square brackets in the enciphered message in the example).

The message is from the steamship *Neckar* to a wireless station (Elond, in Bremen), and is addressed to the German Admiralty Staff, informing it of the ship's expected arrival at Shanghai. The first code word to be enciphered is 'hanib ynixe'; this enciphered as 'zivol evora' by substituting each letter in the code word with the appropriate letter from the cipher table.

Elond Bremen HVB cipher For Admiralty Staff Arriving 15 June Shanghai Neckar

HVB coded message:

Elond Bremen kisah aciba – hanib ynixe – kukib uroli – mifob alyri – fysuc ixonu – bugik arecu

Enciphered message:

[Elond Bremen kisah aciba] – zivol evora – bybol ytuzo – comul ineto – mewyd oruvy – lyxob itady.

(Note: kisah aciba = code word for 'the contents of this message have been enciphered with the HVB key'. Elond Bremen is the call sign.)

German original	English translation	HVB code word	Enciphered word
Für Admiralstab	to Admiralty Staff	hanib ynixe	*zivol evora*
Bei eingetroffen	arriving	kukib uroli	*bybol ytuzo*
15, Juni	15 June	mifob alyri	*comul ineto*
Shanghai	Shanghai	fysuc ixonu	*mewyd oruvy*
Neckar	[sender's name]	bugik arecu	*lyxob itady*

Diagram 7.5 – Plain-Language Message (translated into English)

We saw in Chapter 1 that several German messages were sent out at the beginning of the war warning ships to use the SKM instead of the HVB, or to use the 'reserve' key with the HVB, as the usual key had been compromised. These messages tell us that the HVB key was not changed frequently. Indeed, at the outbreak of war there was one key for everyday use and another in reserve. In the case of the HVB, then, Room 40 was faced with a badly designed and insecure code book, a very simple cipher system and an infrequently changed 'key' (or table of substitutions).

The situation was only slightly more complex in the case of the VB. As we saw earlier, the VB used 'code words' with numbers instead of letters (known as 'code groups'). Code groups can be subjected more easily to complex cipher techniques than can those with letters. Addition and subtraction operations, for example, are easy to perform with numbers and were commonly used in ciphering operations (known generically as 'additive' ciphers).

One method used was to add or subtract three numbers, say 212, from all of the first three numbers in the code group (which was determined by the page number of the code word entry). The same three numbers were added to or subtracted from every code group. One method used by the codebreakers was simply to add and then subtract 000 to 999 to every enciphered word in turn in an intercepted message until recognisable code groups were encountered. It was a repetitive task, but an effective one.[11]

However, the German cipher designers failed to take any real advantage of the potential of numerical substitutions. Instead, the German Imperial Navy turned the code groups made up of numbers back into code words, this time using the ten-letter nonsense words. And, just as with the HVB, a one-for-one substitution table was effectively all that was provided.

We saw that the VB code groups were made up of a three-number page number ('*stammzahl*' – root number) and a two-number code-word entry number for that page ('*eindzahl*' – end number) giving a five-number code word. The cipher converted five-number code groups into ten-letter cipher words. The root number and the end number were separated, and each was given a five-letter nonsense word.

For example, a code word 36782 (page 367, entry 82) would be represented as (root number) 367 = 'evuet' and (end number) 82 = could be either 'iacus' or 'voval'. The decision as to which of the two end number options to use was left to the cipher clerk, '*nach wahl*' ('according to choice'). So, 36782 would be either 'evuet iacus' or 'evuet voval'. The substitution table was, in effect, a ten-page code book where the root numbers were listed first, then the end numbers.[12] This was essentially a pointless operation. And again, the booklet with the key was changed – but infrequently.

The absence of concern for security stands in sharp contrast to the considerable effort put into the core design principle of the system. The apparently nonsensical words – 'iacus' and the like – were in fact very carefully chosen so that errors in transmission could be corrected. The navy's instruction book for using the cipher points out that a fault can be generated either by the 'medium' – i.e. the cable or the ether – or by the operator. The annex to the code book contains half a dozen pages of instructions on how to correct transmission errors. Far less attention was paid in the instruction book to security.

★★★

The cipher systems we have looked at so far were 'substitution' ciphers, where another letter or number was substituted for the encoded letter or number. An alternative approach is the 'transposition' cipher, where the code word letters are not replaced but are jumbled up into a new order.

The transposition ciphers seem to take a seemingly big step up in extra complexity compared with the simple substitution ciphers described above. However, even the basic transposition system remains surprisingly simplistic. This transposition cipher technique was used by both the German Navy and Army – it was the ÜBCHI cipher used on the Western Front by the German Army discussed in Chapter 5. It is, however, slightly more complex to explain, so I have used a plain-language English message as an example in Diagram 7.6.

This transposition cipher system depended on a 'keyword'. This was derived from a standard book, according to a set of rules, or it was distributed by some, usually secret, method. It was not unusual for keys to be sent by wireless messages and they were thus open to being compromised. For the example, we will use 'FEZLNE' as our key. The example message reads, 'TO ARMY COMMAND LIÈGE ATTACK AT TEN TODAY'.

First, the keyword is written out in a row on a piece of paper. Then a number is written in the next row under each letter according to the following rules. The number '1' is written underneath the earliest letter in the alphabet in the message. In our example keyword, the earliest letter in the alphabet is 'E', appearing in second place, so '1' is written underneath it. There is another 'E' at the end of the code word, so '2' is written underneath it. The next letter in the alphabet, 'F', appears as the first letter in the key word, so '3'

F	E	Z	L	N	E
3	1	6	4	5	2
T	O	A	R	M	Y
C	O	M	M	A	N
D	L	I	E	G	E
A	T	T	A	C	K
A	T	T	E	T	O
D	A	Y	G	H	Q
Key = FEZLNE					

Diagram 7.6: Example of a plain-language English message.

is written underneath that. There is no 'G', 'H', 'I', 'J' or 'K' in the keyword, but there is an 'L,' so '4' is written underneath it; then '5' is written underneath the next letter in the alphabet to occur in the keyword, which is 'N'. Finally, the number '6' is written underneath 'Z' (see Step 1, Diagram 7.6).

The content of the message is then written out in horizontal rows, with each row consisting of six letters (i.e. the number of letters in the keyword) underneath the row with the numbers 1 to 6: 'TOARMY' in the first row, 'COMMAN' in the second row, 'DLIÈGE' in the third and so on (Step 2).

Then the vertical columns are written out in a single stream, starting with the column numbered '1' (OOLTTA), then column '2' (YNEKOQ), followed by column '3' (TCDAAB), and so on. This forms the message to be sent: OOLTTA YNEKOQ TCDAAB RMEAEG MAGCTH AMITTY (Step 3).

All the original letters in the message are there, but in a completely different order. It was standard procedure for all messages to be transmitted by wireless to be split into groups of five letters for transmission.

At the receiving end, the operator would reverse the process, by writing out the keyword and numbering the columns in exactly the same way as the enciphering operator. He would then write out the message, one column at a time, starting with the first set of letters under column '1', the next set under column '2' and so on. The plain (coded) message could then be read horizontally, row by row. It would be possible to put the transposed stream of letters through the whole process once again, creating a 'double transposition' to make the message much harder to crack if intercepted.

A weakness of single-transposition ciphers in general is that the original letters are all present, just jumbled up. If a way can be devised to unjumble them, the plain text will appear. A technique known as 'anagramming' is possible for single-transposition messages which have the same length and the same key. Diagram 7.7, Step 1 shows two intercepted and enciphered messages of thirty-two letters each. The two intercepted messages are written out on a number of cards as shown in Step 2 (in the example, only the first four pairs of letters are shown). The cards are then rearranged (anagrammed) until the two messages make sense in military German, as shown in Step 3. Step 4 shows the translations of the messages. As will be clear from the example, this technique is dependent on a good knowledge of military German and local geography.

A British intelligence report says:

> It is obvious that at least two messages are [initially] necessary as otherwise it would be impossible in the first message to tell whether 22, 12, 21, or 32 came in the third place. Two or more messages are also very valuable in building up the anagram as the end of a word in one will generally be in the middle of a word in the other and the next letter is more easily obtained.

Diagram 7.7 - Solving a transposition cipher using the 'anagramming' method

STEP 1 - Two intercepted German army messages each 32 letters long:

a) ISOSK INMED NAOTN IXTMR AAFNN TEXLT HA

b) NARSD KEKEI HRZKR IENKB DHKVW EKDII BE

STEP 2 - Both messages are written out on pieces of card in pairs

1	2	3	4	.....	32
I	S	O	S		A
N	A	R	S		E

STEP 3 - The cards are tried in different places until the two messages can be recognised

2	18	22	14	6	13	25	17	10	23	28	4	30	9	31	26	1	11	19	27	24	16	7	12	8	5	21	15	32	29	20	3
S	T	A	T	I	O	N	X	D	F	X	S	T	E	H	T	I	N	M	E	N	I	N	A	M	K	A	N	A	L	R	O
A	N	H	K	K	Z	W	E	I	K	D	S	I	E	B	E	N	H	K	K	V	I	E	R	K	D	D	R	E	I	B	R

STEP 3 - The messages are translated:

a) STATION XDFX IS IN MENIN ON THE CANAL ...

b) TO HKK TWO KD SEVEN HKK FOUR KD THREE ...
(HKK - Höhere Kavallerie Kommando - Cavalry High Command;
KD - Kavallerie Division - Cavalry Division)

Diagram 7.7

Some further steps are necessary to reveal the key that can then be applied to reverse the transpositions of other single messages sent using that key. For this type of cipher, only the keyword needs to be distributed, rather than the booklet of substitution tables needed for the other two ciphers. The keywords need not be printed in a booklet but could be, for example, drawn from something such as a book or directory held by both parties.

Many cryptographic experts insist that all codes and ciphers can be broken given enough messages to work with and enough time to work on them. If this is true, and it probably is, then encoded and enciphered messages can only be seen as secure for a finite time. What matters is how much time it takes to anagram the two messages. If a message says, 'Attack tomorrow', it is of little use if it takes a week to break the message. However, if the key is identified and remains in use for a month, then the original messages are worth breaking as the key can be used to decipher other messages enciphered with the same key. Thus, code books and cipher keys need to be changed frequently if security is to be retained.

On this, the German naval effort was hopeless. In the acid pen of Frank Birch:

> Even after four years' experience the German Admiralty got no further than devising a key which could be solved in three or four days but was kept in force for ten days or a fortnight, and allowed [code books] to remain in force for a year which could effectually be compromised in two months [and often less].[13]

The HVB was the first code book to be changed when a new edition was released in early 1916 (known as the AFB). The SKM was not replaced until May 1917 (by the FFB) and the VB was partly replaced in 1917 (by the 'Nordo' code). The success of Room 40 later in the war was built upon the lessons learned in the first two years of the war when the German Imperial Navy effectively overlooked the need to make a serious attempt to understand the nature of 'wireless war'. These shortcomings gave the British codebreakers just enough of a challenge to allow them to learn their new trade before the Germans introduced tighter security measures.

★★★

At the start of the First World War, the German Imperial Navy had a limited but powerful presence in the Mediterranean in the form of a large, modern battle cruiser *Goeben*, and a light cruiser *Breslau*, under the overall command of Rear Admiral Wilhelm Souchon. Although it was a new ship, which had only been commissioned in 1911, on the approach to the war in 1914 the *Goeben* was experiencing problems with its boilers that reduced its top speed. When Souchon heard about the assassination of Franz Ferdinand, he feared that it might lead to war, so he took his ship for repairs to the port at Pola in the Adriatic, on Austro-Hungarian territory. As the political situation deteriorated, Souchon took the *Goeben* out to sea even though the repairs were not fully completed, and headed towards the Sicilian port of Messina, where he ordered *Breslau* to join him. On 2 August, the day he arrived in Messina, Souchon received wireless messages informing him, 'War imminent', and later, 'Mobilisation ordered'.

Souchon realised that the state of the *Goeben*'s boilers meant it was unlikely he could get up enough steam to break out of the Mediterranean and dash through the North Sea home to Germany, so he decided to hang around and do what damage he could in the Mediterranean. 'The thing to do,' he later wrote:

> ... was to act quickly, before our unhappy plight became apparent, and to make the utmost of man and engine power as long as coal, water and ammunition lasted ... My plan of operations was rapidly conceived: to bombard the principal ports of embarkation of the XIX French Army Corps on the Algerian coast; the fortified ports of Bona and Phillippeville ... We got news of the outbreak of war with France through the friendly Sardinian wireless station of Vittoria [just before leaving Messina].[14]

At this stage Britain had not yet entered the war, but it had taken various preparatory steps, one of which enraged the Turkish Government and nudged it towards an accommodation with the Central Powers. In May 1911, Turkey had contracted British shipyards to build it two pre-Dreadnought-class ships for completion in mid-1914. On 28 July, Winston Churchill, First Lord of the Admiralty, sequestered the two ships to widespread anger in Turkey, where the money to pay for them had come in part from public subscription. The British action lubricated Germany's negotiations with Turkey.

British ships under Vice Admiral Milne spotted *Goeben* after it had bombarded Philippeville, but as there was no state of war between Britain and Germany at that time, he refrained from attacking it. Instead, he followed *Goeben* until it slipped away as it headed back to Messina. Then began a series of misjudgements by the British about where the German warships might head – back to Pola in the Adriatic or west to Gibraltar and beyond?[15]

In fact, after German diplomatic pressure on Turkey, it was decided that the two German warships should head east, for the Dardanelles and Constantinople (Istanbul today). The arrangements for coaling the ships, and the diplomatic toing and froing between Berlin and Constantinople, led to a flurry of wireless messages, many of which were intercepted by the British.[16] However, as the messages were encoded using one or other of the code books mentioned above and additionally were enciphered, they were at that time unintelligible to the British.

After war between Britain and Germany had been declared, a British warship picked up the trail of *Goeben* and *Breslau* and started to follow them as they headed, unexpectedly, east. An inconclusive exchange of shelling took place off southern Greece but interpreting ambiguous orders not to engage if outgunned, the British ship gave up the chase.

The Admiralty was outraged. Prince Louis Battenberg, the First Sea Lord, said, 'The escape of the *Goeben* must ever remain a shameful episode in this war.'[17] The damage to Vice Admiral Troutbridge's reputation had its effect on Admiral Sir George Cradock off the coast of Chile in early November at the Battle of Coronel, where hundreds of lives were squandered in an unequal clash between Cradock's squadron and that of Graf von Spee.

The two German warships steamed off to seek shelter in the Dardanelles and then on to Constantinople. There they were rebranded with Turkish names and became part of the Turkish Navy, although they were commanded and manned by German officers and men (who exchanged their German caps for fezzes).

In November, Turkey announced it had joined the side of the Central Powers and the two warships wreaked havoc on the Russians in the Black Sea. Russia was also unable to export wheat through the Straits and thus to earn income to fund its contribution to the war, or to import ammunitions.

Security concerns mean that the originators of enciphered messages, as a rule, do not keep copies of the enciphered versions after they have been sent and received, in case captured documents give hints to an adversary of how messages are enciphered. Similar issues mean that those who intercept enciphered material generally do not keep the enciphered intercepts either, only the decrypted versions. This means that it can be difficult to follow the full processes of encoding, enciphering and decryption. Just over 100 years after the beginning of the First World War, thanks to recent research, the *Goeben* incident now provides us with material with which to conclude this look at codes and ciphers.

The use of archival research and modern computer science by a team of Israeli and German computer scientists and historians located some encoded and enciphered messages in the General Consulate in Genoa relating to the *Goeben* incident and led to the unravelling of the full process of their encoding and enciphering.[18] These messages included nine messages that were encoded and enciphered in a ten-letter cipher.[19] By collating these ten-letter encoded messages with documents from the National Archives at Kew, it was confirmed that one of the messages, sent on 3 August 1914, had been encoded using the VB code book and then enciphered. Significantly, this message is one of very few in the considerable number of German naval messages intercepted by the British where the original cipher version of the text has been preserved.[20]

A security breach in some of the other messages (which were encoded in the 18470 German diplomatic code) gave away the identities of two cipher keys, 718 and 469. The 718 key was also mentioned in a post-war publication by a US codebreaker, Captain Charles J. Mendelsohn, who was discussing a key technique known as the *Schieber* (slider) cipher system.[21]

Further work in the National Archives located some captured German cipher documents, including a slider table with the key 528.[22] Using standard codebreaking methods and some reverse engineering with modern computer programs for confirmation, it has been established that the message sent on 3 August 1914 was encoded using the VB code book and enciphered using the slider technique with key 528. The process of encoding and enciphering is shown in the flowchart in Diagram 7.8c.

The message of 3 August was sent from Berlin to the *Goeben*. It reads:'*Bündnis geschlossen mit Türkei Punkt Goeben Breslau sofort gehen nach Konstantinopel bescheinigen*' ('Alliance concluded with Turkey Stop Goeben [and] Breslau proceed immediately to Constantinople Acknowledge'). It was first encoded using the VB code which, as seen above, uses code groups. For example, the phrase '*Bündnis geschlossen mit*' is found in the VB code book, to be encoded as 35159 (indicating that the entry is found on page 351, entry 59). It was then enciphered using the slider cipher technique, with the key 528. This gives the enciphered code group of 30720. A further step is to convert this enciphered code group into the ten-letter nonsense word 'bgefc amics' for ease of transmission in Morse code (see above in the section on the VB code book).

The term 'slider' does not indicate a mechanical sliding device (although paper strips could be slid to new positions to change the substitutions). Rather, the slider was a table of figures combined with a process that substitutes some of the numbers in the code groups. A variety of slider tables could be used, each identified by a three- or four-digit number or key. In the case of the message above, the identifier was 528 (sometimes called 5288, as digits 4 and 5 in the code group are both changed by the same column of numbers in the slider). In the National Archives document, the key is called VB99, although this is a name given by Room 40 as they did not know the German key number at the time.[23]

The slider table for this message is given in Diagram 7.8a. The enciphering of the complete message is shown in Diagram 7.8b and Diagram 7.8c is a flowchart of the whole process from plain text to encoded and enciphered message.

Diagram 7.8a

Original digit	2nd digit becomes	3rd digit becomes	4th & 5th digits become
KEY (528)	5	2	8
0	5	2	8
1	8	7	3
2	1	3	4
3	4	5	6
4	7	0	5
5	0	8	2
6	9	1	7
7	2	9	1
8	6	4	9
9	3	6	0

Digit 1 remains unchanged

Diagram 7.8b

[ADM 137/4065] Adm to Goeben, 3 August 1914

Plaintext	Encoded	Enciphered	10 letters
August 3	30845	35452	ESSUYEDUCT
Bündnis geschlossen mit	35159	30720	EGEFCAMICS
Türkei	23607	24181	COIFFEZORU
Goeben	25583	20896	BORGHIGAND
Breslau	25527	20841	BORGHAVIMU
sofort gehen nach	42404	41085	GAHICIBIAS
Konstantinopel	17066	12277	AFLUYEVETE
bescheinigen	33526	34847	ERRAVOZUBO

Diagrams 7.8 a, b, c

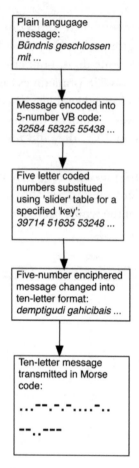

Diagrams 7.8 a, b, c *(continued)*

The use of the slider is to start by writing out the key as shown in the table in Diagram 7.8a. In the example, the second original code word 35159 is used.

Step 1: The first encoded digit, 3, is unchanged.

Step 2: The second encoded digit, 5, is enciphered as 0 (locate 5 in the first column and read the number in the same row from the second column).

Step 3: The third encoded digit is 1 and is enciphered as 7 (locate 1 in the first column and read the number from the same row in the third column).

Step 4: The fourth encoded number, 5, is enciphered as 2 (locate 5 in the first column and read the number from the same row in the fourth column).

Step 5: The final original encoded digit, 9, is enciphered as 0 (locate 5 in the first column and read the value in the same row again from the *fourth* column). Note that the fourth column is used to encipher both the fourth and fifth encoded numbers (which is why the 528 key is sometimes known as 5288).

Result: The substituted version of the code group now reads 30720. The VB code book would then give the ten-letter nonsense code word for this code group ('bgefc amics' in this case).

The process is repeated for each code group in turn. The stream of all the ten-letter nonsense words in the messages would then be transmitted using the Morse code. At the receiving end, the stages involved in enciphering the message would be reversed (with a deciphering table) to reveal the plain-language text.

Sliders were used fairly widely in German ciphers but were easily broken by repetitive work. The reader may note that the two ships' names, *Goeben* and *Breslau*, are, respectively, encoded as 25583 and 25527 using the VB code book, then using the slider enciphered as 20896 and 20841, and then substituted as 'borgh igand' and 'borgh avimu' in the enciphered ten-letter word version. This reveals weaknesses in both the code book (having a special section for ship names with the same initial number 255) and the cipher (reproducing these regularities in the enciphered versions as 208 and 'borgh').

To conclude this chapter, we can note that the First World War German codes and ciphers methods were quite simple, even the double transposition ciphers and the slider cipher technique, especially when compared to the complex cipher machines, Enigma and *Geheimschreiber*, used by the Germans in the Second World War. The techniques used in the First World War by the German Imperial Navy presented British codebreakers with only a few unsolvable codes or ciphers from the end of 1914 right through to the end of the war.

Early Days

At the outbreak of war the Admiralty had only one station working at intercepting German naval wireless traffic. This was Stockton, and it was really supposed to be doing something else. Then, shortly after war broke out, a barrister and amateur wireless enthusiast, Edward Russell Clarke, contacted the Admiralty to report that he had been picking up German messages on his private wireless set at home and volunteered his services.

What Russell Clarke had been doing was actually illegal. At the start of the war, the Defence of the Realm Act made it a crime to operate a wireless set to transmit or receive signals. All operating licences were suspended, and sets were ordered to be dismantled. Alistair Denniston commented:

> It is not clear why the Police or Post Office had not sealed up [Clarke's] apparatus, but it can well be imagined that some rash official had tried his best on Russell Clarke and had been forced to retire the worse for wear.[1]

So, at least, goes the legend. As with the overall cover story about Room 40, this one has aspects of the truth, yet it hides reality in significant aspects – once again pushing the role of amateurish good luck.

Documents at the National Archives and the General Post Office archive tell a quite different story. Russell Clarke's involvement with wireless began before the war when he served as a member of the War Office Wireless Committee and during his six years as a commissioned member of the Electrical Royal Engineers Volunteers. Professionally, too, as a barrister, he was an expert on wireless technology and patent litigation. In late August 1914, he arranged to meet Alfred Ewing to voice his concerns that German agents might be sending illicit wireless messages to Germany from within Britain. He offered 'to undertake a search' for any such transmissions. He could 'use his own appliances, making use of an existing mast at Devizes or elsewhere'.

Ewing reported on his meeting to the head of Naval Intelligence, Henry Oliver, 'I have known him personally since about 1891 when he was a pupil under me at Cambridge. His notion is clearly worth carrying out as he proposes.' Oliver recommended:

> The W.O. [War Office] and G.P.O. [General Post Office] should be written to as to the employment of Mr Russell Clarke in the manner suggested by the D of E [Director of Naval Education]. Mr Russell Clarke is acquainted with the latest German developments in W/T [wireless telegraphy].

Additionally, before the end of August, Ewing was already taking steps to arrange interception (by Marconi Company's long-range receiving station at Towyn in North Wales and at government facilities in Canada) of German wireless and cable messages that were being transmitted from the German wireless stations at Sayville and Tuckerton in the north-east of the United States to Berlin.[2]

The Admiralty and the War Office already worried about illicit German wireless transmissions and even about a secret telegraph cable laid before the war from British shores to Germany. The fears were part of the general panic about German spies in Britain. Among the panic mongers were two novelists, William Le Queux (author of *The Invasion of 1910*) and Charles Cutcliffe Hyne, who both contacted the Admiralty even before the war began.

The subject was broached again in late 1914 in an article written by Cutcliffe Hyne and published in the nationalist magazine *John Bull*. When prompted into action on 16 December, the War Office Intelligence Department enquired of the GPO, 'Can you trace a file which was sent to you some months ago [by Cutcliffe Hyne] concerning different methods likely to be adopted by Germans in this country endeavouring to communicate with Germany?'

The GPO, which was experienced in the hard realities of laying submarine cables, was sceptical: 'It seems improbable that a cable suitable for working across the North Sea could have been laid and landed at any point on this side without detection.'[3] But the War Office was taking no chances and asked the novelist for further ideas.

Cutcliffe Hyne replied eagerly with a long speculative list of possible ways of hiding wireless antennae and cables:

> I should say it is highly likely that they are doing this by ordinary cable. Seeing the state of their *ante bellum* preparation in other countries, it is not hard to believe that they already had their cable laid before the war. If this had not been done, they have probably laid it since ... The shore end would be made to look like an ordinary derelict mooring wire, with a little dressing of broken ends, etc. could easily be made to look too antique for even the dockside loafer to steal. ... The men who are using them at this end are probably not Germans, and almost certainly do not speak with a German accent. Some may be American, many probably Scandinavian, the majority almost certainly British or Irish. A spy would look upon the risk as practically nil. To start with he takes his precautions against being found out. If these fail what has he to face? Not being shot out of hand, as would be the case elsewhere, but a solemn trial, with a sporting chance of being let off on some legal technicality.[4]

The concerns dragged on for a while until all but tiny traces disappear from the archive files.

With hindsight, it never seemed to have been realistic, except as a plot in one of Cutcliffe Hyne's novels. Nor did Russell Clarke discover any illicit transmissions. Instead, his attention turned to more fruitful airwaves – abundant wireless messages that were transmitted, not to Germany, but from within it, to German Imperial Navy ships and distant German colonies and diplomatic missions.

★★★

As war approached, several wireless stations started intercepting material at both naval and Marconi Company sites. For example, a message on 3 August was intercepted at 'the Admiralty, Chelmsford, Stockton, etc'.[5] German messages were also picked up by a wireless station at the Admiralty in London and another at Dover, as well as aboard several British warships.

At the start of the war, the Marconi stations were taken over and formed the basis of a much-expanded interception service.[6] Marconi Company had devoted significant resources to training amateur Morse code operators in the years before the war and these trainees became available for employment in the services.[7]

Another private wireless owner, Baynton Hippisley, had dismantled his set at his home in Stone East immediately war had been declared, faithfully following the instructions from the GPO. But he was then invited by an acquaintance, Sir Henry Norman, the Assistant Postmaster General, to visit his home where he also had a wireless set and 'write down anything sent in by W/T [wireless telegraphy] in Morse Signals, Norman having I presume by reason of his position of Assistant Postmaster General managed to keep his station in commission'. A few days later, 'Russell Clarke turned up with a request that I should return home and put my own station in commission again. This was done at the request of ... Sir Alfred Ewing.'

Hippisley set up a directional aerial pointing eastwards:

> ... and some stuff obviously of Hun origin was taken and sent to [the Admiralty] from our local village post office. After a short time Sir Alfred came down to see how we got the stuff, telling us that what we were sending up was of the greatest importance. He asked if we could suggest any improvement.[8]

Hippisley and Clarke told him that they would really like to set up a station on the east coast where it would be easier to pick up German wireless signals. With Ewing's agreement, they moved their wireless sets and antennae to Hunstanton. Hippisley recalled that Clarke was 'too short-sighted to be any good aloft', so he and another recruit, C.P.O. Marshal, had to raise the antenna.

They then settled down to keep a permanent watch. 'It was a killing job but we kept it up till the folk at the Admiralty took pity on us and sent a relief crew.' A party of GPO telegraphists was dispatched to help and 'things became a bit easier after that'.

It was the start of a long journey. Hippisley recalled that by the end of the war there were sixteen fully staffed stations in operation, 'most of them of my own construction in what was then the United Kingdom [including Ireland] and two in Italy and one in Malta'.

Clarke and Hippisley decided that a useful addition to their team would be Leslie Lambert:

> [Clarke] and I used to work wireless telegraphy with [Lambert] long before the War from our home stations. It struck us that he would be most useful to us when we started up at Hunstanton. [Clarke] tried to get hold of him, but he was already serving on a ship.

Clarke referred the matter upwards and got his man:

> Lambert was of course socially a cut above some folk I have to deal with.
> … He was a clever conjuror and used to give shows to the Royal chil-
> dren … [one day at Hunstanton] I received information that some people
> had broken through the sentries and on arrival I found a party from
> Sandringham with Her Majesty Queen Alexandra who looked through the
> window and was surprised to find Lambert sitting writing at a desk. She
> called out, 'Why Lambert what on earth are you doing here?' The dear lady
> being stone deaf did not get his answer. This episode was not entered in the
> log nor was it reported to the Admiralty. I had a few words with the Corps
> of Sentries about the break in. He smiled at me and said they all knew her
> and the party were Home Guards raised from Sandringham Staff.[9]

Lambert became a key figure in the interception of German naval and diplomatic wireless transmissions. He also had another occupation under a different
name. As A.J. Alan, he was a popular broadcaster on the BBC. He wrote his
own crime and ghost stories, which he then read over the air with the aid of
his monocle – dressed always in a dinner suit. His was the classic 'BBC accent'
of the inter-war period. A.J. Alan's true identity was kept secret until after his
death. This second occupation allowed Lambert to bring together his two
passions – entertaining and wireless technology.

A not untypical story of his, called 'My Adventure in Chislehurst', is about
how the narrator, at an exhibition of wireless equipment, meets an old friend
– a wealthy stockbroker – who is suffering from a cold. The friend invites
the narrator home for dinner, to see his new wireless set imported from the
United States and to meet his new wife. When they get to the house, however,
there is a phone call from the young wife saying that she cannot get home
as her car has broken down many miles away. His wife also tells her husband
to make sure he takes some aspirin for his cold before retiring. All this the
narrator infers from listening surreptitiously to one side of the telephone conversation. Anyway, the pair of wireless buffs enjoy a lavish dinner and listen
to the US 'super-het' wireless. The patriotic narrator is scornful about the
foreign gear:

> Needless to say, the tall-boy [screening the radio from view] was far and
> away the best thing about it. When he switched it on the volume of dis-
> torted noise was so appalling that I can't think why the ceiling didn't
> come down.[10]

After downing some brandy, the narrator makes his way home. Later that night the stockbroker is found dead – the result of poisoning. It is clear that the culprit is the wife but there is no evidence to prove it.

The narrator gives evidence to the coroner's inquest, although he does not tell us whether he reported having listened in to his friend's telephone conversation. At first it looks as if the wife will get away with murder, but a final (and unconvincing) twist to the story ensures that justice will be done.

The style is now rather dated (it is assumed, for example, that you will realise that someone who is a stockbroker is sure to have a team of servants on hand at home to prepare dinner). Of interest for our story are two points that reflect aspects of the social and cultural background. First, the fashionable subject of wireless technology among the moneyed classes. Second, the natural acceptance by an upper-class gentleman that it is not shameful to listen in on one's friends – as long as one does not admit it.

Lambert's expertise was technological and intuitive, not scientifically based. Trial and error, combined with long hours, made his work a great success. A report written at the end of the war recommended that he be kept on the staff. Among his many creditable points, it noted, 'Lieutenant Lambert has a wireless telegraphy station at his private house in London at which he keeps watch for some hours every day and is in constant touch with International wireless telegraphy arrangements'.[11]

From 1914 through to 1918 Lambert was to make a considerable contribution, along with Russell Clarke and Hippisley, to improving the technical performance of the British naval wireless interception service.[12] Later in the war, he made advances such as discovering a method used by the German wireless engineers to evade interception.

The interception station at Hunstanton was mainly concerned with picking up the signals transmitted by the high-power German naval wireless station at Norddeich. Two types of message were regularly broadcast 'to all ships': weather reports and intelligence on the movement of Allied shipping. The capture of the German code books and the breaking of the cipher keys meant that Room 40 could decipher and decode these messages, but their content was of limited intelligence value.

However, some time that autumn, Russell Clarke visited Ewing at the Admiralty to discuss his work. When Clarke was shown some of the naval messages that Room 40 was dealing with, he realised that there were many other naval messages in similar form being sent by the Germans on lower-power transmitters. He told Ewing that he could get hundreds of such messages, 'which if read would give the daily doings of the German fleet'.[13]

However, Ewing had few wireless sets available and he was unwilling to give up intercepting messages that he could already decipher and decode. There was:

> … only one aerial at Hunstanton which was doing good work on military interception and [Ewing] was a little loath to lose good stuff for a pig in a poke. However he agreed to a weekend trial which was of course conclusive. From what we could read of the stuff intercepted at Hunstanton alone it was clear that we should from now onwards be able to follow every movement of the enemy provided always that they used the same key, call-signs and book.[14]

The number of sets and operators at Hunstanton was increased and the promised hundreds of daily messages were intercepted and despatched to 'Ewing, Admiralty'.

★★★

We left Sir Alfred Ewing and his small team of cryptographers towards the end of 1914, shortly after they took delivery of captured copies of the Imperial Navy's code books. During November, Assistant Paymaster C.J.E. Rotter broke the key for the cipher used with the SKM at that time. Russell Clarke and his colleagues were now feeding scores of intercepts to Ewing's office in the Admiralty building.

Ewing needed several more cryptographers, some clerical assistants and more space. He had to give up one of the perks of his post as Director of Naval Education – his office, with its fine view over Horse Guards Parade where, in more peaceful times, he would take his children, or associates he wanted to impress, to witness such flamboyant demonstrations of imperial martial pride as Trooping the Colour. The move to more spacious accommodation, out of the way of any nuisance from chance visitors, also gave the team (properly known as ID 25, for Intelligence Department 25) its identity – Room 40.

With the move, Ewing lost more than just his view of the parade ground. As the organisation grew it needed people who were skilled in the intricacies of the German language and naval matters, as well as cryptography. The demands of the work imperceptibly began to leave Ewing lagging behind his own increasingly specialised staff. Forceful and ever more experienced codebreakers and intelligence experts stepped in to fill the vacuum and

Ewing's role seems to have diminished in inverse proportion to the organisation's expansion.

He was 59 years old in 1914. His first wife had died in 1908 and he married a younger woman in 1911, but his energy was far less than it had been during his prime. His favourite holiday pastime was mountain climbing, and he regularly visited the Alps. On a trip in 1908 he contracted a sickness and wrote home:

> I am in pretty good walking form now. It is when I try to climb boulders that, like the sailor in the story, I feel all of a tremble. We found some boulders on the way home yesterday and I played on them enough to show me my incompetence. I am now more than ever certain that a Swiss holiday is just the thing to set one up. I already feel seven years younger, and next week hope to pull in my waist band as far as they can go.[15]

A few days later, while Ewing and his party crossed the Theodule Pass to Breuil, they encountered a violent hailstorm and were repeatedly blown off course and 'covered with ice like armour'. After the ordeal was over Ewing said, 'The experience was more enjoyable after the event than at the time.'

Although he continued to climb in later years, Ewing was much less adventurous than he had been in his younger days when he had to continually prove that he was better than other men. Climbing at the extremes is a young man's game. Older climbers have to watch others coming along behind them climb rock faces far smoother and ice falls far more intimidating than ever they did. Cryptographers, like climbers and mathematicians, often do their most outstanding work when they are fairly young.

Subordinates and rivals began to be seen by other members of staff as the real managers of Room 40, and Ewing is portrayed in the accounts that survive as more and more marginal and jealously protective of the way he had set up his organisation. Ewing's organisational skills brought Room 40 into existence as a cryptographic bureau, but his temperament proved inadequate for turning it into an intelligence centre – even if his boss, Henry Oliver, had wanted such a thing.

★★★

The budding organisation won vital support from the government's navy minister, First Lord of the Admiralty, Winston Churchill. On 11 November 1914, Churchill addressed a memo to Ewing and the navy's newly appointed

Chief of Staff, Henry Oliver (previously Director of Naval Intelligence and the man who appointed Ewing). It read:

> An officer of the War Staff, preferably from the ID [Intelligence Division] should be selected to study all the decoded intercepts, not only current but past, and to compare them continually with what actually took place in order to penetrate the German mind and movements and make reports. All these intercepts are to be written in a locked book with their decodes, and all other copies are to be collected and burnt. All new messages are to be entered in the book, and the book is only to be handled under direction from COS [Chief of Staff, Oliver]. The officer selected is for the present to do no other work. I shall be obliged if Sir Alfred Ewing will associate him-self continuously with this work.[16]

This document is often called Room 40's 'Charter', but this is a misreading. On one level it is simply a note instructing Ewing to appoint someone to handle and assess the intelligence that was being revealed by the decrypts. On another level, the memo may well have been a way for Churchill, sensing Room 40's potential and ever conscious of his image in the eyes of history, to lay a clear documentary mark in the records, showing his intimate involve-ment with the organisation from its earliest days.

From a different perspective, far from being a charter of rights setting Room 40 free to acquire and assess intelligence, the memo actually shackled it, creating a restrictive framework and limiting how the intelligence could be used – even to the extent of specifying exactly how decodes should be written out and secured for storage. Churchill's big fear was giving away the secret by misusing intercept intelligence. This was a source too important to squander. But his rules were too tight.

Both Churchill and First Sea Lord 'Jacky' Fisher were clever, ambitious and determined men. Both also were moody and impulsive, reacting to things too quickly. Churchill was domineering and determined never to lose an argument, and Fisher had an explosive temper. Churchill's memo created an organisational problem that was to plague the way Room 40's intelligence could be exploited by placing the cryptographic team under the overworked and unable-to-delegate Chief of Staff Henry Oliver, rather than the Director of Intelligence.

Oliver, on his promotion, was succeeded by a ruthlessly go-ahead new Director of the Intelligence Division, Captain William 'Blinker' Hall. He became one of the few in the Intelligence Division who were allowed to know the secret of Room 40. None of his staff could be told, nor was he allowed to be in charge of Ewing, who was supplying such important intelligence.

Instead, Ewing continued to report directly to Oliver, even after his promotion to Admiralty Chief of Staff. But Oliver was too busy, working twenty-one hours a day, and Hall, who had the energy and ideas necessary to make effective use of the intelligence bonanza, was side-lined by Oliver. It was Oliver who controlled what intelligence was used and how.

Room 40 became, in the words of Patrick Beesly (a Second World War Naval Intelligence officer), 'Oliver's private cryptographic bureau'.[17] He would receive the intelligence, assess it and then draw up orders for the navy to act, involving Fisher and Churchill in major events but not seeking advice from the admirals in charge of the fleet.

When the commanders at sea saw things with their own eyes that clashed with the intelligence they had received (such as being told incorrectly that only a minor German force was at sea), they began to doubt the value of Room 40's intelligence generally. Churchill, who was obsessed with security and controlling as much as possible himself, failed to see that this new intelligence source was being badly handled.

★★★

Yet, for all his failings, Churchill was also a doting stepfather to his infant cryptographic organisation, giving it support and encouragement as well as providing the sustenance needed to ensure rapid early growth.

However, growth meant more staff. Those who had been lent to the War Office were brought back and others brought in. From the end of 1914 until the end of the war, Room 40 underwent a slow but steady expansion. According to Denniston:

> In the earlier stages of development new men were sought who had but two qualifications, a good knowledge of German and a reputation for discretion. Cryptographers did not exist, so far as we knew. A mathematical mind was alleged to be the best foundation but it must be noted that except for [Ewing], Russell Clarke and Henderson, no one had such a reputation and in fact the majority of those chosen had actually had a classical training.[18]

This is rather different from what happened during the Second World War at Bletchley Park. Then, it was indeed mathematicians and chess players who were recruited to tackle complex mathematical types of cipher. But the German reliance on code books and simple ciphers during the First World War meant that cryptography was then often more akin to translating text on fragments of ancient papyrus.[19] People who were skilful with words were needed.

Late in 1914 and early in 1915, more potential cryptographers were recruited. One of them, joining in December 1914, was Herbert Morrah, a well-known writer and literary critic. His novels included such forgotten titles as *A Serious Comedy* and *The Faithful City*. Morrah was an Irishman and, according to William F. Clarke, 'a rabid Home Ruler'. This brought him into frequent conflict with a bellicose clergyman, Reverend W.H. Montgomery, who joined Room 40 a few days after Morrah. He was 'an Ulsterman who had to be kept on peaceful terms with Morrah'.

Before the war, Montgomery was a 'lecturer and writer on Historical subjects at Cambridge, being an MA and resident member of St John's College'.[20] He had also spent time in Germany and was the translator of a chapter on the 'Teutons' in the *Cambridge Medieval History*. He was very good with languages. According to William F. Clarke, Montgomery 'died learning to drive a motor in 1926'.[21] As a cryptographer, he earned Denniston's highest acclamation: 'very sound'.

Two other early recruits were Lord Monkbretton and H.W. 'Harry' Lawrence, both of whom seem to have been recruited for their social background. Monkbretton was a former private secretary to Joseph Chamberlain. Later, with two other socially elevated members of Room 40, Norton (one of the original team members) and Edward Bullough (who joined in September 1915), they formed what became known as the 'Gentleman's Watch'.[22]

Lawrence's occupation sounds an odd one for a potential cryptographer – he was an expert on furniture and art. William F. Clarke felt he needed to record only two other items of information about Lawrence: first, he was the brother of the actor Gerald Lawrence, and second, he was 'one of the most popular of our staff ... one of our most loveable members'. Unfortunately, neither snippet adds anything to our knowledge of his cryptographic or linguistic contribution.

If German-language experts were needed to decode and decipher, a naval eye was required to assess what the intercepts could reveal. The messages transmitted by the German naval command seldom spelled anything out in obvious form, such as 'leave harbour at 05.00 to reconnoitre in the area of Dogger Bank, returning the following morning'. Rather, there were orders to switch on harbour lights or to make wireless contact at a certain time. It took naval experience to work out what a set of messages implied.

The first man appointed to fill this post was Assistant Paymaster Rotter, but his cryptographic skills were wasted in spending time dealing with the translated intelligence and so he was transferred back to work on ciphers. Blinker Hall, rather than Ewing, was responsible for finding someone else for the job.

Captain Herbert Hope was working in the Intelligence Department, all the while dreaming of getting sent to join the crew of a warship, but was assigned in fact to compiling charts and records of German ship movements. 'Our duties,' he recalled, 'were not arduous, nor did they call for the exercise of any great intelligence ... I continued at this dull occupation, cursing my luck at not being at sea, all through August, September and November.' Then he was summoned to see Hall:

> When I first went to Sir Reginald Hall, he first impressed on me the need for absolute secrecy and then informed me that German naval wireless telegraphy messages were being decoded in the Admiralty; the First Lord (Mr. Winston Churchill) had decreed that an executive naval officer was to be appointed to sift messages and I was detailed for the purpose.[23]

The new job was initially just as disappointingly tedious as had been the work tracking German ships, and Hope sat on his own in an empty office waiting until someone brought him a few decoded messages. At first, these numbered just half a dozen a day. Hope wrote:

> These messages were not, in themselves, of great importance and in some cases were not very intelligible. I quite realise now that at that early stage my remarks were very amateurish and beside the point, and must have added to the worries of the COS [chief of staff], who by that means got prejudiced, in addition to other reasons, against my work and myself.

Hope told Hall that he needed to see the original decodes and speak directly to the cryptographers and translators, if he was to draw real intelligence from the intercepted messages. But Hall explained that, as the production of the decodes was not under his control, he was unable to authorise closer contact. This impasse was broken thanks to the irascible First Sea Lord Jacky Fisher. One day in November, Fisher came across Herschell wandering round the Admiralty looking for Hope to deliver some decodes to him. Fisher took Herschell to Hope's office, went in and questioned Hope about his work.

Hope grabbed the chance and explained his difficulties to Fisher. The First Sea Lord wasted no time and instructed Ewing to initiate Hope into the 'Holy of Holies…':

> … I was introduced into the Mystery on 16 November 1914. This was the beginning of a sphere of work which was probably unique, was absorbingly interesting and which threw me into a close relationship with probably as fine a set of fellows as it would be possible to meet.[24]

Hope won the respect of the cryptographers and became, in their eyes, 'Our beloved chief', according to William F. Clarke. He saw Hope as 'the hub of Room 40 … mainly responsible for its success'.

Until then, the full set of raw daily decodes had been sent to the privileged inner circle who were allowed to receive them. Hope realised that this was becoming impractical as too many messages were now being decoded. Someone had to assess and filter them, 'that is to say, to decide what type of message should be sent in, as with the increasing number of them it was clear that a selection on these lines must be made'. He also kept a copy of all messages, compiling a database of intelligence about the 'organisation and economy of the German fleet'.[25]

This was helped by the systematic use the German Imperial Navy made of wireless. Vessels at sea in and around the German Bight regularly transmitted details of their position by reference to a secret grid system. The documents captured from the *Magdeburg* included maps of the grid system and the SKM included the code words used for transmitting them. So, once the cipher key had been broken these messages could be decoded and the positions of enemy vessels established.

This intelligence was not of much immediate tactical use – it was not feasible to rush off and attack ships or submarines based on such intercepts. But the messages provided good medium-term intelligence about German naval operations, especially the many minor ones by submarines and minelayers. According to Hope:

> Whenever any of their vessels was at sea, she was continually signalling her position by saying what [grid] square she was in. By plotting all these positions on a chart we were soon able to establish clearly defined channels, and furthermore, it was soon seen that there were a large number of squares in which no ship ever reported herself and which remained conspicuously blank on [Hope's plotting] chart: it was only reasonable to suppose that

these blank spaces were mined areas. As soon as sufficient information was obtained, a chart was made out and circulated.

Hope learned how to use both the routine and the unusual:

> Experience showed that the Germans were exceedingly methodical in their methods and a large number of signals were made day by day which were of great assistance in solving the new 'key' to the code when it was shifted … [but it was also found that] any messages which were not according to routine were to be looked upon with great suspicion' as possibly indicating the start of a German naval operation.

Rotter's key-breaking skills were called on again at the beginning of December. An error was made by a German wireless operator. A message was despatched from Norddeich to all ships and was broadcast in two different forms. In one, the message was coded using the standard SKM code book, but in the second form the message was partly in the VB code and partly in the SKM. 'This enabled the VB key "A" to be quickly determined [shortly after] the VB came into our hands.'[26] 'Quickly', in this context, means about two weeks, for it was on 15 December that it was broken.

But the cramped system of not passing on intelligence to those who needed it (such as fleet commanders) still prevented the best use being made of the intelligence that Hope extracted from the decodes:

> In a very few months we obtained a very good working knowledge … of the German Fleet. Had we been called upon by the [Admiralty] Staff to do so, we could have furnished valuable information as to movements of submarines, minefields, minesweeping, etc. But the Staff was obsessed by the idea of secrecy; they realised that they held the trump card and they worked on the principle that every effort must be made to keep our knowledge to ourselves so as to be able to keep it up our sleeves for a really great occasion such as the German Fleet coming out in all their strength to throw down the gauntlet in battle … In other words the Staff was determined to make use of our information *defensively* not *offensively* [emphasis in original].[27]

★★★

The German Imperial Navy was slower than the Royal Navy to intercept wireless messages. Before the war, bureaucratic struggles hindered developments and it was only late in 1914 that the navy adopted this form of intelligence. It was prompted by a German cavalry unit in north-western France which began picking up Royal Navy messages when Allied army wireless traffic reduced after the 'race to the sea'.

The High Seas Fleet Commander Friedrich von Ingenohl ordered three battleship squadrons to collect British wireless traffic for the *Admiralstab* to decrypt, although with little success. British signals were intercepted during the German raid on Yarmouth on 3–4 November, but without being decrypted. However, traffic analysis was used to recreate British actions during the incident.

The first break of British naval traffic took place in November, when the '*Admiralstab* forwarded a single-page report to the High Seas Fleet containing the cryptographic solution for a British cipher used by army wireless stations and for traffic between the British army and Royal Navy stations'.[28] A wireless station in Cologne also intercepted British naval traffic and passed on encrypted messages to the navy.

The Admiralstab did not want a centralised decryption unit and so, when the army captured a French naval code book, copies were sent to 200 ships and squadrons throughout the fleet for them to do their own codebreaking. This suggests that, unlike the British Admiralty, which saw codebreaking as a strategic tool, the Imperial Navy thought of it as a tactical one, where local units would break local signals in short timescales in minor operations. This view was perhaps influenced by the fact that the British naval traffic that was being intercepted came from small patrol ships on the English coast rather than the British Grand Fleet.

Ships' commanders gave a lower priority to intercepting enemy traffic than handling their own wireless messages within the Imperial Navy. And there was also, initially at least, a lack of German naval wireless stations on land dedicated to interception. A station set up near Antwerp after the German capture of that city only intercepted Royal Navy signals when it was not otherwise busy with its work for the independent Marine Corps:

> This lack of dedicated North Sea-based listening stations delayed German decryption efforts and directly impacted the success of operations later in the war. ... [the] lack of a unified centralized command would later result in a degree of friction (lack of co-ordination and efficiency) in the dissemination of intelligence.[29]

The German Army broke a couple more British naval ciphers in early 1915 and by mid-1915 the German Navy decided to set up a *Nachrichtenabteilung*

(Intelligence Section) at the army wireless station in Lille. Towards the end of the year, this developed into a fully independent decryption service, *Entzifferungs Haupstelle* (Main Decryption Centre), based at the existing naval wireless station at Neumünster, near Kiel. It provided expertise to three new subordinate centres at Tøndern (modern Tønder) near the German–Danish border, covering the North Sea; at Bruges, intercepting Channel traffic; and at Libau (modern-day Liepāja), covering the Baltic.

However, these stations were also responsible for monitoring German fleet traffic, again making the interception of British wireless traffic a subordinate task. This was especially critical during sea battles when the stations concentrated on tracking large volumes of German signals as well as trying to intercept British ones. As a result, their success was limited. Although the army unit:

> … [in] Lille had achieved near-total penetration of the simpler codes used by British patrol and coastal forces, the encryption used by the Grand Fleet was much more complex, especially the most critical signals, making their signals more difficult to decrypt.[30]

In July 1917, the French recovered documents from a German U-boat, UC-61, which was grounded on the French coast. These showed that the Germans had been reading encoded Admiralty warnings to British ships about the location of British mines. Vice Admiral Bacon observed, 'This shows that the auxiliary code or vocabulary signal book is useless as a code. I have given orders that the fact of any area being declared *clear* is not to be passed by W/T [wireless telegraphy].'[31]

On the other hand, the German Imperial Navy never seriously considered the extent to which their own codes and ciphers had been penetrated. German admirals expressed exasperation at the way in which the British fleet appeared whenever the German High Seas Fleet left harbour on a sortie into the North Sea. After one incident, where the British knew about German minesweeping operations in the Bight on 17 November 1917, Admiral von Hipper observed, 'The war at sea made it absolutely obvious that some secret power was working against us.'[32] However, he failed to join the dots.

★★★

At the start of the war, both naval officers and the general public in Britain and Germany expected an early and decisive clash of the naval titans. But it was not to be.

The Grand Fleet was moved a few days before the war began to the relative safety of Scapa Flow. It provided a natural harbour, large enough to provide sheltered moorings and plenty of room for manoeuvring. Smaller detachments were based further south at Rosyth, Harwich and Dover. Winston Churchill later wrote:

> The strategic concentration of the fleet had been accomplished with its transfer to Scottish waters. We were now in a position to control events and it was not easy to see how this advantage could be taken from us … If war should come, no one would know where to look for the British fleet. Somewhere in that enormous waste of waters to the north of our islands, cruising now this way, now that, shrouded in storms and mist, dwelt this mighty organisation. Yet from the Admiralty building we could speak to them at any moment if need arose.[33]

The German Imperial Navy adopted a defensive posture too, waiting for the Royal Navy to come to it, to venture a long way from home with a prolonged voyage back to safety. The main German naval bases at the outbreak of war were Kiel in the Baltic and ports in the German Bight (an old English word meaning 'bay'). The newly opened (and enormously expensive) Kiel Canal allowed ships at Kiel to reach the Bight, the section of German coast between Denmark and the Netherlands where the coast turns from trending roughly north-east to north. The coastline is like a reverse L-shape, with the main base of Wilhelmshaven and secondary bases at Cuxhaven, Bremerhaven and Emden all nestling in the corner where the horizontal and the vertical sections meet. This was an excellent set-up for defence, with few prominent landmarks, plenty of shifting sandbanks, plus shallow, narrow channels and myriad opportunities for defensive booms and gun positions.[34]

But, the very factors that made the Bight a good place for defence also made it a poor site for launching offensive operations. At low tide, the High Seas Fleet could not cross the shoals and sandbanks that gave access to the North Sea and it took two tides for the full fleet to put to sea.[35] Sorties along the coast were at risk of being spotted from the Dutch or Danish coasts. The German fleet commanders convinced themselves that Dutch trawlers (and British trawlers disguised as Dutch ones) were watching them and passing on intelligence about German fleet movements to the Royal Navy (when, in fact, it was their own wireless transmissions that were revealing the German fleet's sorties).

The German expectation was that the British would conduct a 'close' blockade, aiming to prevent any ships – military or commercial – from entering or leaving German ports. They hoped their navy could sally forth and attack small squadrons of British blockading ships, whittling away its superiority until the Grand Fleet could be destroyed in a final conflagration. When this did not happen, and the British instead imposed a distant block-ade, German naval strategy was scuppered.[36] German commanders came to realise they were in fact cooped up in their secure bases with nothing for the bigger ships to do except accompany minelayers and minesweepers on their duties. In any event, the Kaiser refused to allow the High Seas Fleet to risk major offensive operations, which meant that there was little alternative but to conduct a naval *Kleinkrieg* – 'small war' – deploying mines, torpedo boats and submarines.

The sinking of the Royal Navy warship *Hawke* by U-boats on 5 September, and three more cruisers on 22 September, led Jellicoe to withdraw the Grand Fleet from Scapa Flow, even further out of danger, to waters around Northern Ireland. By mid-September, the British commanders were coming to realise that the main enemy of their warships was not the High Seas Fleet. A warship that could take two or more years and vast sums of money to build could be sent without warning to the bottom of the sea in a few minutes by a comparatively cheap torpedo. In October 1914, Jellicoe informed Churchill and Fisher at the Admiralty that in any conflict with enemy warships he would turn his ships away at the first sign of enemy submarines. Churchill and Fisher both backed his stance, recognising that, as Churchill put it, Jellicoe 'was the only man who could lose the war in an afternoon'.

However, this small war generated lots of wireless signals. As a Room 40 cryptographer noted after the war:

The strategic position of the German fleet, assembled as it was in the different anchorages of its North Sea and Baltic ports, all of which must have been in [landline] telegraphic communication with each other, would, it might be imagined, have enabled the use of W/T [wireless telegraphy] to be reduced to a minimum … [however] staff work was bad … [and] the volume of W/T traffic was enormous. Important details of intended operations, dispositions of battle squadrons, cruisers and flotil-las, the ordering of lights, etc. were conveyed by this means, with the result that very definite news of contemplated movements was given to the enemy.[37]

And, significantly, the German Imperial Navy used unnecessarily high-powered radio transmissions, so 'it seems doubtful whether the Germans were aware of the wide range of their wireless'. Additionally, wireless traffic between ships in the North Sea and Wilhelmshaven was relayed via the wireless station on Heligoland, 'owing to the belief of the sender that his W/T installation was not powerful enough to communicate directly, whereas as a matter of fact, these messages were easily picked up by British stations much more remote'.[38]

This is not to say that the German naval authorities took no precautions against interception. They believed that technical innovations in transmission (such as the rapid switching of wavelengths) would keep their communication safe.

However, another factor helped to convince the Germans that their messages were not being decoded. The material intercepted by the German interception and codebreaking centre at Neumünster gave no indication of a leak of German communications.

★★★

To break the stalemate in the North Sea, the German Imperial Navy's commanders sought a way around the Kaiser's ban on offensive naval operations. Wilhelm's orders left room for operations aimed at 'trying to damage the enemy'.[39] Von Ingenohl sanctioned a sortie on 4 November to shell the English east-coast town of Yarmouth. Churchill later claimed that when the Admiralty first received reports of the bombardment it was assumed it must be a precursor of a more major operation elsewhere:

> The last thing it seemed possible to believe was that first-class units of the German fleet would have been sent across the North Sea simply in order to disturb the fisher-folk of Yarmouth. ... Several hours of tension passed; and then gradually it became clear that the German battle cruisers were returning home at full speed and that nothing else was apparently happening.[40]

The attack was rationalised by the German Imperial Navy as having the 'strategic objective of luring the British fleet out into newly laid minefields, but for some Germans at home it was their retributive function that was important'.[41]

Despite the venture's minimal success, Ingenohl soon planned another attack. Morale in the German Imperial Navy was suffering from inactivity, so on 16 November he sought the Kaiser's permission for another sortie. The plan was for Rear Admiral Franz Ritter von Hipper, commander of the German fleet's battlecruiser squadron (which served as the scouting force of the High Seas Fleet), to take four battlecruisers, several cruisers and some destroyers to bombard Scarborough and Hartlepool, and lay mines in shipping lanes.

Ingenohl was forbidden to take his main battle fleet to sea, but without telling the Kaiser, he did send his big ships out. They were to wait just east of Dogger Bank, to attack any British forces and draw them onto newly laid German mines. In total, 112 German vessels put to sea, the greatest German naval force to sail up until then.

But here the events we have been discussing in this book intervened. Room 40 decoded warnings of the second raid. At 3.27 a.m. on 14 December, an order was intercepted asking for 'extreme reconnaissance' by airships and aeroplanes to the north-west and west 'as German forces will be at sea'.[42] A little later, another message gave away the timing of the departure of Hipper's battlecruiser fleet – it would leave the River Jade at 3.30 a.m. and pass Heligoland at 5.30 a.m. After that, apart from a couple of messages ordering transfer of control of torpedo boats, no further signals were intercepted until 3.23 a.m. on 15 December (when a message transferring wireless control was intercepted) and then there is another gap until the following morning.

Meanwhile, the Royal Navy readied itself to respond to this intelligence windfall. There was insufficient information about the planned target for the raid to be prevented, but the intercepts should have given enough time for British warships to sail into the middle of the North Sea, get to the east of the German ships and cut off Hipper on his way home. However, the intercepts did not reveal that the High Seas Fleet would also sail.

Churchill and the Admiralty wrongly concluded that it was definitely not going to leave port. So, only Beatty's battle cruisers, with light cruisers and destroyers, and a single squadron from the Grand Fleet, were ordered to sail and intercept the German forces. Jellicoe, with the main part of the Grand Fleet, was ordered to stay in port. The order, drafted by Oliver, told Jellicoe:

> Good information just received shows that the German First [Battle] Cruiser Squadron with destroyers leave the River Jade on Tuesday morning early and return on Wednesday night. It is apparent from information that [Ingenohl's] battleships are very unlikely to come out.

Jellicoe would have preferred to put all his ships to sea, believing that the power of the fleet should be used in a concentrated form and not in a way that risked defeat of isolated portions of it. His appeal to the Admiralty to revise its decision was rejected. Beatty set to sea to rendezvous with other forces east of Dogger Bank – just 30 miles from where Ingenohl, with his much bigger and more powerful force, would be waiting.

The first German ships to leave port were Hipper's raiding force. They hit bad weather as they sailed east. So Hipper sent his light cruisers and destroyers back to Ingenohl and the main fleet near Dogger Bank. With his remaining ships, he continued with the raid and successfully bombarded the two towns and Whitby too, then turned east to head home.

The British fleet had put to sea shortly after the German fleet and had steamed well to the east of the German ships then turned west, hoping to intercept them. For some hours the two fleets steamed towards one another. The first sighting was made about 4.20 a.m. when a German submarine reported seeing the British ships. The first clash occurred at about 5.15 a.m. between advance ships 'screening' the main fleets.

For two hours, in the dark, a scrappy battle took place between a few British destroyers and a superior German force of cruisers and destroyers, with the British ships suffering badly. During the fighting, one British ship fired a torpedo towards a German cruiser. Although the cruiser managed to avoid the torpedo, its firing was reported to Ingenohl. About this time, the first smatterings of light began to appear in the sky. This revealed to both sides that they were facing much bigger forces than they had so far realised.[43]

Ingenohl, who had been worried about the threat from submarines and mines, had been growing concerned as reports of the battle came in. Convinced that the whole British Grand Fleet was at sea, he decided to turn back to avoid risking damage to his ships and incurring the wrath of the Kaiser. At 5.30 a.m. he ordered the High Seas Fleet to turn and return to port. He did so shortly before Beatty's smaller force sailed to nearly the same spot. Here was the chance German strategists had dreamed of – an outgunned, isolated squadron of the British fleet that could be destroyed, reducing the overall balance of naval forces between Britain and Germany closer to parity. But, as the author of the official British Naval History put it, the German admiral 'knowing nothing of the presence of our squadrons, fairly turned tail and made for home, leaving his raiding force in the air'.[44] Fortunately for Hipper, the British made just as big a mess of the opportunity that Ingenohl's flight and Room 40's intelligence had provided.

By 11 a.m., after Ingenohl's High Seas Fleet had left the scene, extra British forces had been ordered to sea (including, too late, Jellicoe's Grand Fleet). But, at this point the morning's clear weather disappeared and cloud and rain moved in, making sighting of the enemy difficult. One British admiral said, 'They came out of one rainstorm and disappeared in another.'[45]

Beatty, seeing some firing in the distance, thought that it involved only one German ship and did not give chase. Then Beatty's signals officer, not for the last time, sent an ambiguous message to the light cruisers engaged with the German ships. This led to several cruisers also calling off the chase. After that, the British lost sight of the Germans. Hipper and his raiding fleet escaped.

By this time, Room 40 was intercepting more messages. One message sent by Hipper at 12.45 gave his position, but by the time the message was deciphered, decoded and sent out to Beatty, at 2.50 p.m., it was already too late. Another message caused some alarm at the Admiralty, giving the first indication that the High Seas Fleet was at sea. In fact, the message recorded the position of the High Seas Fleet on its retreat, but this was not understood at the Admiralty. They feared that it was setting out to catch Beatty's battle cruisers unawares.

The first set-piece action to take place with the help of Room 40's decodes had been a failure. Room 40's intelligence was misused and communications between ships at sea had been atrocious. An opportunity to engage the German fleet had been squandered. Perhaps it is understandable. It took British generals on the Western Front some years to work out how to beat the German Army, so it was probably too much to expect that the Royal Navy could get everything in order for its first encounter.

There was public anger at the outcome in Britain. The seemingly unchallenged raids on the British coast led to hysteria. After the raid, 'the mayors [of Scarborough, Whitby and Hartlepool] demanded coastal artillery and dreadnoughts anchored off the beaches'. This was not feasible as it would have invited attacks on isolated ships. Regardless of the urging of the mayors, the Grand Fleet had to be kept concentrated. The panic spread wide and far: 'The Indian Government telegraphed that Madras must be protected.'[46] Churchill later wrote:

> Dissatisfaction was widespread. However, we could not say a word in explanation. We had to bear in silence the censures of our countrymen. We could never admit, for fear of compromising our secret information, ... [the one] comfort we had.[47]

Churchill and the navy got their next opportunity to make something of Room 40's remarkable output of intelligence very soon, little over a month later, in January 1915.[48] The German Imperial Navy suspected that the British

Navy must have had some advance warning of the German fleet's movements during the attack on Scarborough, focusing their suspicions on British and Dutch trawlers who plied the area around Dogger Bank, reckoning these spies were sending details by wireless to the British. A plan was conceived to set a trap. But Ingenohl, unusually, on this occasion actually sent orders for the operation to Hipper by wireless.

At 10.04 p.m. on 22 January he ordered a reconnoitre of the Dogger Bank area. 'They are to leave this evening during darkness and return during darkness tomorrow.'[49] At 11.54 p.m. on the same day, instructions were sent by wireless for Buoy 8 and the Alte Jade to be lighted before dusk, and for the outlier lights of the River Jade to be switched on between 5.45 p.m. and 7 p.m., for ships to leave the port.

The Admiralty first learned about the new German operation at about midday on 23 January. It took Churchill, Fisher and Oliver until 2 p.m. to work out their response. It was not until 2.10 p.m. that Jellicoe and Beatty were given their orders.

Beatty's battle cruisers, sailing from Rosyth, were the first to arrive and encounter the German ships. Jellicoe's Grand Fleet was still 140 miles away when the fighting took place, and his ships missed the battle. But at least this time Room 40's intelligence had been successfully used to engineer a meeting of big warships and the British fleet outgunned the German ships.

Room 40 later decoded a message from Hipper reporting his position, speed and course, adding, 'eight large ships, one light cruiser [and] 12 destroyers in sight'. At 9.37 p.m. he reported, 'Seven light cruisers [and] 26 destroyers following me. Behind them further clouds of smoke. Propose to attack ships, keeping in touch when in inner German Bight.'[50] In the mêlée that followed, Beatty's flagship took a battering and had to retire from the fight, but two German ships were badly damaged. One of them, *Blücher*, eventually turned sideways and sank. The images of German sailors sliding down the great hull of the ship as it finally went under are some of the most famous photographs of the war and offered the Royal Navy a propaganda coup.

A short time later, Beatty thought he saw a submarine mast in the water and ordered his ships to turn away, allowing space to build up between the British and German ships. In fact, Room 40 knew there were none in that area. However, Oliver had chosen not to inform Beatty of that.

Then there was another ambiguous ship-to-ship signal sent from Beatty's flagship. Thus, the German ships escaped. At 11.41 p.m. a wireless message was sent from the high command to the High Seas Fleet, which was idling in port 'to get up steam in all boilers'. But this was a gesture; it would be impossible for the fleet to get up steam, wait for the tides, file through the shallows and sandbanks and get to Dogger Bank in any useful time. More helpful was an order sent at 4.40 a.m., telling the port-bound sailors to line up on deck and give the returning ships three cheers.[51]

Room 40's intelligence had been handled better on this occasion than during the Scarborough raid. The encounter had been engineered based on intercepted orders, and it was incompetence in the Admiralty and at sea that led to the German escape. If Jellicoe had received information about the German operation immediately Room 40 had decoded it, the Grand Fleet could have got up steam and sailed almost two hours earlier. That would have given Jellicoe adequate time to get to Dogger Bank to take part. If Beatty had known that there were no German submarines in the area, he might have pushed his pursuit.

In retrospect, however, the main issue was not what the British thought about the Battle of Dogger Bank. Rather, it was the effect the battle had on the German Imperial Navy. The fleet hardly left the Bight to venture into the North Sea until the middle of 1916. In the first half of 1915 it made the occasional foray but sailed no further than about 120 nautical miles from home, where it was certain not to meet a sizeable British fleet. The German Imperial Navy conceded control of the surface of the North Sea to the British, who were left free to enforce their blockade. As a result, German interest in the North Sea turned below the surface.

Blockade

In the years running up to the First World War the British developed far-reaching plans for extensive 'economic warfare' against Germany. A legal innovation, 'Predelegated Directives', gave the government the power, if the need arose, to bring an enemy economy to its knees within weeks or months.[1] The strategy exploited London's role as the financial capital of the world – 'the world's bank, the world's clearing house, the world's greatest stock exchange, the only free market for gold, the chief source of money and credit to facilitate international exchange, and hub of the global communications network'.[2]

The economic, financial and communications strength of the British Empire would enable it to choke the German economy, leaving it with little choice but to seek peace. In 1904, an Admiralty report noted:

> Out of a total trade of about [£] 572 millions (exports plus imports) carried on by Germany in the year 1903 it would appear that about 60 per cent is sea borne ... In view of the geographical conditions (the British Isles lying like a breakwater athwart the path of German trade) ... there would be no practical difficulty in proclaiming and maintaining an effective blockade of the entire German seaboard.[3]

However, the outbreak of the war, regardless of policy, was accompanied by economic dislocation of unparalleled severity. The Vienna stock exchange began to fall as early as 13 July,[4] but the real trigger for collapse was Austria-Hungary's ultimatum to Serbia on 23 July. When the European stock markets opened on the Monday morning, 27 July, prices dropped across the board as panicked investors sought to liquidate their holdings. Within hours, trading in Vienna was suspended. That afternoon the shock reached New York. Before the end of the week every stock exchange in every major country (including Wall Street) had been forced to close its doors.[5] Interest rates jumped upwards, and gold and sterling became unavailable. The world's foreign exchange system effectively closed down:

> Only after the Bank of England announced, on 13 August, that it would discount any and all bills of exchange drawn up prior to the declaration of war did the wheels of international commerce begin to turn again – very slowly.[6]

This was not the best environment in which to tighten the economic screw by bringing the German economy to its knees. A split opened in Whitehall between the Admiralty on the hawkish side, and the Foreign Office and Board of Trade on the dovish side. The Board of Trade feared the damage that economic warfare would do to British manufacturers and financial companies, while the Foreign Office worried about damage to relations with neutral countries – especially the United States. As a result:

> The objective was progressively downgraded from precipitating a total downfall of the German economy to mere trade restriction … By the end of 1914, the last vestiges of economic warfare had been abandoned in favour of what was termed the 'blockade', an entirely distinct strategy of economic coercion whose methods, goals, and underlying assumptions differed fundamentally from those of economic warfare.[7]

★★★

Even the blockade as implemented by the Royal Navy from the end of 1914 was a controversial policy in itself, requiring its own legal innovation – or just plain old disregard of the law. In the words of the First Sea Lord, Jacky Fisher, 'Might is Right and when war comes along we shall do just as we jolly well like!'[8]

Traditionally, blockades had been placed just outside enemy ports. However, developments in naval technology – submarines, mines and torpedoes – made this militarily impractical. The astounding growth and interdependent complexity of modern trade also made it logistically impracticable. A vital port for Germany was Rotterdam in the neutral Netherlands. Traffic along the Rhine to and from Germany had risen by a massive 800 per cent between 1898 and 1913.[9] Additionally, the geography of Britain's position in relation to the European mainland – that 'natural breakwater' – favoured a distant blockade, closing off the Channel at one end of the breakwater and the seas between Scotland and Norway at the other.

While international law permitted close blockades, it did not recognise the innovation of the distant blockade. The British ignored the law and directed ships to ports to be searched and perhaps for goods to be seized – a policy that naturally enraged neutrals. An Order in Council, issued by the British on 20 August 1914 and strengthened by later orders, gave the Royal Navy the power to seize any goods that were due to be delivered to a neutral port if it was suspected they might be forwarded to an enemy country. Smaller countries were caught up in the whirlwind, becoming, against their will, pawns in the strategic military calculations of imperial conflict. Many European countries were desperate to keep out of the war and to remain neutral.

The Netherlands, Sweden, Denmark and Norway had all championed peaceful international relations. But with the outbreak of the First World War their shared view of peaceful international relations had to adjust to the demands of their bigger neighbours. Norway 'felt safe so long as Britain controlled the seas'[10] and so was pro-British. Denmark was also sympathetic to the British, but shared a land border with Germany and exported much agricultural produce to Germany. It had to continue to do this, but insisted on sending food to Britain as well to underline its neutrality.

Sweden was the most inclined of the Scandinavian countries to favour Germany.[11] It had close economic ties with Germany, supplying iron ore and advanced engineering products. It also feared that if Russia defeated Germany, then Sweden would be dominated by its large eastern neighbour, perhaps losing its independence.[12] The Russians intercepted a Swedish Government telegraph that was sent to Vienna complimenting Austria-Hungary on the ultimatum it had sent to Serbia (which sparked off the war): 'The [Swedish] King gave the German representative to understand that, in the event of a conflict, Sweden's position would undoubtedly be with the Triple Alliance.'[13]

As was said of the Netherlands, 'The Dutch may have wanted to ignore the war, but the war did not ignore them.'[14] Located on Germany's north-western border, it seemed an obvious target for a German invasion and indeed figured in some German war plans.[15] In the end, Germany's military strategists decided that, although the Dutch Army could certainly be destroyed, an invasion would slow down the attack on France. Also, the Netherlands had its uses as a neutral. If it were taken over by Germany, its ports would be blockaded.

By leaving the Netherlands unoccupied, and with the British expected to enforce a close blockade of German ports, neutral Dutch ports could serve as a source of blockade-busting supplies.[16] However, the distant blockade and British attempts to prevent supplies passing through neutral territory, and especially Rotterdam, meant that Dutch trade was subject to British scrutiny and control at sea.

Initially, the north European neutrals did well out of the war, as Germany was willing to pay high prices for supplies. But, as the British tightened the blockade, the neutrals suffered deprivations. The blockade eventually affected the Dutch economy badly, as its entrepôt trade – a major part of its economy – was severely disrupted and so were its own imports (leading to severe shortages of food in the later years of the war).[17]

On 26 August 1914, the British Government ordered the Royal Navy to stop all ships carrying food to Rotterdam on the assumption that, unless guaranteed to the contrary by the Dutch Government, the cargo was destined for Germany. The Dutch Government and Dutch industry decided it was best to submit 'voluntarily' to Britain controlling its imports. The Nederlandsche Oversee Trustmaatschappij (NOT – the Netherlands Oversea Trust) was set up to manage trade in accordance with British demands.[18] The Foreign Office wrote to the Dutch Government on 26 December 1914:

> His Majesty's Government is ready to accept the consignment of cargoes to the Netherlands Oversea Trust as a guarantee that these cargoes are destined for home consumption in the Netherlands ... His Majesty's Government hopes that the Netherlands Government will find it convenient to send the earliest possible information concerning each individual consignment addressed to the Netherlands Government to His Majesty's Legation at the Hague so that the unmolested passage of such consignment may be secured.[19]

The NOT was formed on 23 November 1914 and had its first cargo approved in January. By March 1915, some 5,000 contracts had been successfully delivered.[20] Officially it was a private concern, not part of the government, so it could be claimed that it did not affect Dutch neutrality.[21] Those Dutch entrepreneurs who complained about the restrictions were told by their compatriots, 'England can do what it wants and if we do not fit in with it, the whole sea could be closed to us and we would [also] be denied access to the [international] telegraph network', something that would seriously damage trade.[22]

The Germans grudgingly accepted the situation – not least because a lot of goods, illegally or semi-legally, did find their way over the border. Indeed, smuggling goods and supplies across the Dutch–German border became a major activity for many people who lived close to the border, as well as owners of Rhine barges – despite the intense efforts of the Dutch Government to control illicit trade by imposing fines and even jail sentences for those caught.[23] British Intelligence gathered reports of smuggling – from the motor boat *Geertrude Margretha* caught at Rotterdam with around 60,000kg of copper on board, to the small-scale smuggler who was apprehended on the border near Tiel attempting to export six sacks of peas and who was fined 50 guilders.[24]

The British were still prepared to bully the Netherlands if it was thought necessary. As the war went on, the rules were extended and toughened. The Dutch, for example, exported pigs to Germany. This was, according to one Dutch historian, a 'thorn in the eye' of the British. As the pigs were fed on imported maize which could not be re-exported, the British insisted that pig exports should also be forbidden as they were in effect 'maize on trotters'.[25]

In 1917, a dispute arose over the alleged Dutch supply of building materials to Germany for use in the construction of the 'Siegfried' defensive line. The 'sand and gravel question' led to the British blocking Dutch access to cable and postal communications in October (while the Germans threatened an invasion if the Dutch did not deliver the demanded supplies, and massed troops on the border to give weight to their threats).

It was only from 1916 that the blockade had any real effect in hampering the German war effort and damaging civilian morale. At least, this is the accepted view of many historians. Eric Osborne, for example, argued that the blockade was 'the greatest factor behind the Allied victory over Germany'. It was, he writes, an amalgamation of military and diplomatic means 'to form one of the greatest weapons in the Entente's arsenal against Germany'.[26]

But this is a controversial opinion among historians, some of whom argued that the blockade had little material effect. Paul Kennedy put this view in strong terms: 'In sum, all assertions about the grand or cruel effects of the Allied maritime blockade are mythological. None the less, it remains one of the greatest myths in naval historiography.'[27] Another historian, Nicholas Lambert, observed, 'Though the effects of the blockade and its importance in Germany's defeat have been much discussed, unfortunately there is little hard evidence against which to test such statements.'[28] Be that as it may, Alexander Watson wrote:

The blockade did more than any other action to radicalize the conflict. While the act of restricting access to the entire North sea, and therefore to both enemy and neutral ports across northern Europe, was drastic, most damaging was the blockade's erosion of the distinction between combatants and non-combatants.[29]

Views on both sides at the time were certain about the effects of the blockade. Sir Edward Grey, the British Foreign Secretary during the early years of the war, later wrote, 'The blockade of Germany was essential to the victory of Allies.'[30] The German Government also certainly did not think that the blockade was unimportant. Its reaction has been described as apoplectic, with the British being denounced for waging a 'starvation war'. Initially, the blockade was fairly ineffective with food shortages actually caused more by German Government incompetence and chaotic domestic policy making:

> While the Central Powers' propaganda blamed the deprivation on a ruthless British 'starvation war', the causes were thus more complex. Britain's naval blockade did not cause the shortages so much as force Germans and Austro-Hungarians back on their own ever shrinking resource base.[31]

However, Germany's perception of the blockade became the central dynamic of action and reaction that was eventually responsible for bringing the United States into the war. Britain and its allies could import food and munitions from the United States, but Germany could not. The German high command bridled at this imbalance and came not to care what neutrals would think about the introduction of retaliation against the British by unrestricted submarine warfare.

★★★

The British blockade on maritime trade with Germany through neutral ports was enforced by converted liners armed with guns powerful enough to sink U-boats but little else. They had to spend day after day at sea, whatever the weather, patrolling the seas between Scotland and Norway. Boarding parties would be cast to sea in small rowing boats, even in the roughest conditions, when a mistake in approaching the suspect vessel could mean destruction of their fragile boat and certain drowning. Once on board, they would search the ship's papers for details of potential contraband goods bound for Germany and decide whether to send them to port for inspection.

This is the story that has been well covered by generations of historians since the end of the war.[32] But behind the storm-battered ships lay a substantial intelligence operation that has attracted rather less attention.

An operational command centre, known as the War Room, was set up and enabled the Admiralty to direct global operations by wireless. Winston Churchill ordered it be put into operation on 1 August 1914, some seventy-two hours before the start of the war:

> The core of this organisation was the oceanic shipping plot, very secretly developed some seven or eight years previously, which tracked on gigantic wall-mounted charts the movement of every warship in the world plus merchantmen of special interest such as colliers and large, fast merchant vessels with the potential to be converted into commerce raiders. The system represented a huge investment in intelligence and communications technology ... By this means observers could see that 'within a week of the outbreak of the war the German mercantile flag has been driven from the high seas'.[33]

As well as government intelligence, Lloyd's of London contributed information, especially on British-registered shipping and on foreign vessels insured through Lloyd's. It also passed on details of any applications for insurance that it considered to be 'suspicious' and vessels leaving ports such as New York that Lloyd's thought were intended for Germany.

An early sign of friction between Britain and the United States arose over US plans to sell German merchant ships that had taken refuge in US ports at the outbreak of the war. British Intelligence intercepted a cable from the US State Department in Washington to the US legation in Denmark about secret negotiations to broker the sale of more than 1 million tons of German shipping capacity which was holed up in US ports between Boston and New Orleans.[34] The British saw the sale as an attempt to find a way around the blockade. For our purposes, it is worth noting that the intercepted cable was among the first of many US State Department cables that the British came to intercept.

To be effective, the blockade required careful examination of the documents that were found on searched ships, from official bills of lading to private correspondence in post sacks, as well as many thousands of intercepted commercial and neutral government cables. This required a substantial amassing of data and a structure of bureaucracy to trawl through it for clues of blockade-busting activity:

Wartime experience also demonstrated that administration of the blockade required a level of information gathering and processing that far outstripped what was available to the British state. Incomplete, conflicting and faulty information inhibited the implementation of strategy. Not until much later in the war, after the government had overcome internal political opposition about the power and size of the state, and after the adoption (and invention) of more advanced information management techniques, were blockade officials finally able to achieve something approaching the necessary degree of coordination. Until such time the effects of the blockade could not be measured with reasonable accuracy and directed accordingly.[35]

A section of Room 40, known as Room 37, examined intercepted documents or cables that were thought to be in code or cipher. In addition, a lot of the information that was of use to the blockade enforcers was picked up from German wireless messages sent from Nauen to Madrid and arranging onward despatch to South America. These cable and wireless intercepts revealed the cover ruses (such false names and addresses and the setting up of shadow neutral-registered companies) that were used by Germany to acquire goods. Only by following up as much of the intelligence as possible could the stranglehold on supplies be applied.

An intercept of 14 July 1916, between Berlin and Madrid, indicates the problems the Germans had to face. The German Embassy in Spain had located some much-needed animal hides and enquired how to get them to Germany. The reply pointed out that this would only be possible by transporting them to 'Rotterdam in transit [and] … assigned to the [Netherlands] Overseas Trust. This is probably impracticable, as the English control is particularly rigorous with regard to hides and leather.'[36]

Intercepts also revealed details of routes that had so far escaped British attention. Madrid urgently requested photographs for propaganda purposes and advised they should be sent from the Netherlands to New York 'with the express instructions that the pictures should be forwarded from there on Spanish steamers. These have hitherto not been searched.'[37] Following the decoding of the telegram by Room 40, it is unlikely that these ships continued to enjoy the freedom from being stopped, boarded and searched by Britain's blockading forces.

Much intelligence was derived from cable traffic between the United States and Europe. An intercepted cable message from a US purchaser explained to a German exporter that only goods that had actually arrived were being paid for. Thus, the exporter, Albrecht Bonitz of Annaberg, 'will know that any goods for which he has not been paid have been seized'. This information was filed away by the British for recovery 'in case a claim is put forward that the goods are American property'.

Other cables gave details of payment transfers, often in the region of tens of thousands of US dollars, from banks such as the Deutsche Bank transferring cash to the Guaranty Trust in the United States.[38]

Another example comes from intercepted cables that passed through London en route from the United States to the Netherlands. The International Harvester Corporation, a manufacturer of agricultural machinery and trust fund, cabled William Conchon at the Amstel Hotel in Amsterdam on 30 October 1914, stating, 'Holland America Line state shipments for delivery [to] Germany must be consigned [to] Holland Government [.] request officials authorise shipment [of] Sisal fibre and malleable castings.' The next day, the Admiralty Trade Department noted:

> It will be recollected that the Holland America Line arranged that provided their vessels were not searched a) they would only carry Cargo consigned to the Dutch Government b) and that Cargo consigned to the Dutch Government would not be allowed to leave Holland. The two telegrams attached throw a lurid light upon the proceedings being carried on by this Company and by the Dutch Government. Should not the *Martynsdyk* be stopped?[39]

The Admiralty was overwhelmed by information. It had neither the technology nor the organisational infrastructure to handle it. Data-handling machinery was limited in those days to 'punched-card' machines (also known as 'tabulators') or required 'hand processing' (i.e. pen and paper). Although some tabulator installations handled large amounts of data, the challenges presented by the volume and complexity of blockade information were too great in the days before the advent of the electronic data-handling machines we nowadays know as computers. Instead, the Admiralty had to focus on subsets of blockade information, squeezing out infractions in important areas.

★★★

The European neutral countries resisted such Allied measures, not just because they wanted to trade and make extra profits, but also because they feared retaliation from Germany. The US Government was less easily influenced by Germany's threats. It was, however, seriously upset by the British

blockade measures. Although the United States often pres'
back its stopping and searching of ships and seizing what
contraband, the Wilson administration repeatedly declin
European neutrals to join with them in making diplomatic rep..
the British. The United States lacked a sense of solidarity with the small sta..
of Europe and did not want to become their champion. This fitted the US
President's view of the war and the United States' neutrality.

Woodrow Wilson was committed not just to a formal neutrality, but to
neutrality 'in fact as well as in name'. The United States, he said, must be
'impartial in thought as well as action'. But, as one writer has pointed out,
'Such impartiality was not … generally held to exclude sympathy for one side
or the other: the idea of neutrality in thought was a novel one'.[40]

Wilson wanted to remain aloof from the Europeans' imperial conflict. He
saw himself as an impartial party who could bring about peace between the
warring sides; he did not want either of them emerging victorious. Initially,
the US Government was angered by the British seizing US goods bound
for Germany. However, the United States did not push their outrage too
far as the war became an economic bounty. While US trade with Germany
dropped substantially, trade with the Allies increased even more, increasing
by approximately 184 per cent in 1915 – a trebling of trade that was already
ten times as great as that with Germany.[41] On the other hand, US exports
of iron ore, wheat and cotton were politically important for electoral reasons. And cotton exports were especially sensitive as they were a key part of
the southern economy still (and Wilson being a southerner was alert to the
continuing sensitivities about the Civil War). As one US historian puts it, as
tension between the United States and Germany grew:

> A crisis with Britain came and went in midsummer [1915] as cotton grow-
> ers in the South began to fear that the British might not continue to support
> the price of the staple. Wilson warned the British, who secretly bought
> enough Southern cotton to keep the price high, notwithstanding the cutoff
> of American cotton to the German market by the British blockade.[42]

While the British blockade prevented any arms getting from the United
States to Germany, President Wilson approved arms sales to the Allies (in
accord with the law on neutrality).

Woodrow Wilson often silently accepted British behaviour, but at other
times he and many other Americans resisted it. In September 1914, Britain
captured US tankers that were delivering petrol to Germany. Intercepted US

lomatic cables also revealed to the British how the 'State Department was allowing itself to be used as a conduit for communication between US businesses and their customers in Germany'.[43]

The British and United States were annoyed with each other, and British policy was to push the United States as far as they could be pushed without going too far. By early May 1915, Wilson was reaching the end of his tether.

On 5 May, Wilson instructed his diplomatic agent, Colonel House, to emphasise to the British Foreign Secretary that there was a serious change under way in US sentiment towards Britain 'because of the needless delays and many willful interferences in dealing with neutral cargoes'. And a pro-entente member of Wilson's Cabinet was moved to exclaim, 'Each day ... we boil over somewhat at the foolish manner in which England acts'.[44] Then, at this potentially dangerous time for the British in their relations with the United States, just two days later, on 7 May, a German submarine sank a British oceangoing passenger liner, *Lusitania*. Not for the last time, German submarine warfare saved the British.

10

Counter-Blockade

In late 1914, the German submarine U-18 sailed right into Scapa Flow, the base of the Royal Navy's Grand Fleet. A British Intelligence account tells the story:

Scapa Flow was at this time the Mecca of ambitious [German] submarine officers; all their hopes had turned in that direction, no place was so much discussed and so far no submarine had succeeded in penetrating its defences.

When U-18 and another submarine, U-16, sailed on 11 November:

They appear to have been much worried by the presence of the Fishing Fleet off the Dogger Bank and the watch-keeping officer of U-18, Lt. Neuerburg, … advocated their being all sent to the bottom by mines, as it was obvious they were on look-out duty.

U-18 made it all the way to the entrance to Scapa Flow with:

[the] crew strung up to the highest pitch of excitement, with the firm intention of attacking the Fleet and if possible [Jellicoe's flagship] *Iron Duke* or of perishing in the attempt. The boat rounded the point, proceeded close up to the boom, till a view could be obtained of the whole harbour.

A diary kept by a crew member records what happened next: '… and then came disillusionment. All had gone! The nest was empty! There was not a single large vessel in the harbour.'

U-18 withdrew, heading for Moray Firth and hoping to locate the Grand Fleet. Just south of Hoxa Sound, it was rammed by British destroyer *Garry* and the periscope ripped off. The damaged submarine started to sink, 'The boat rose and sank at steep angles up to 30°. The men were ordered to run forward, then to run aft.' The submarine hit the bottom and started to rise. On surfacing, it was rammed again and then started to sink once more:

> Thank heaven no water came through. The same terrifying business we had just been through re-commenced. The boat shot upward and downward. The men rushed fore and aft … we stumbled over loaves of bread, kettles and cooking pots from the galley.

The submarine then fell to the bottom again and with no engine or steering the crew used compressed gas to send it up to the surface, where they surrendered.[1]

★★★

At the start of the war, German submarines were limited to patrolling the German Bight and nearby areas looking for Royal Navy ships to sink. The submarine gave the Imperial Navy its only early successes.[2] On 22 September, U-9 sank three Royal Navy cruisers, *Aboukir*, *Cressy* and *Hogue*, in the Channel.

The *Aboukir* was torpedoed first. The captain thought his ship had struck a mine, so the other two ships came close to pick up the wounded. This made them easy targets for more torpedoes. Dutch and British trawlers rescued 837 men but 1,459 were lost. The sinkings came as a deep shock to the Royal Navy.

When the German Imperial Navy realised that their submarines could stay at sea for longer than expected they sailed further, pushing northwards up to the Norwegian coast, and venturing westwards, too, crossing the North Sea to Harwich, the Firth of Forth, Cromarty Firth and Scapa Flow in search of British blockading lines and warships. The issue of how they should be deployed became a key question for German policy makers. For most of the rest of war they would struggle with the strategic implications of this question.

Most German naval commanders remained unimpressed by the performance of the submarines. A report from U-21, transmitted by wireless on

8 February 1915 and intercepted by Room 40, indicates the limited military value of an average submarine voyage in that period.

The commander reported that he set out on 2 January from the Belgian coast, via Varne Bank in the Channel, heading towards Barrow-in-Furness and fired, 'without success', on an airship shed, attracting immediate return fire. He then moved on to near Liverpool and sank a steamer. In St George's Channel, the submarine was fired on by a patrol yacht, but was not hit. Sailing further south, to near the Lizard, U-21 spotted a merchant ship with a gun and flying no flag.

The submarine headed east towards Le Havre, where it hung around for twenty-four hours without seeing any steamers. Three mines were spotted, as were British destroyers on blockading duty between Dover and Calais. Finally, a report of difficulties locating a German buoy on the return journey was sent in.[3]

The net result of the trip was a couple of sunken merchant ships and some pretty unexciting intelligence. It was hardly a great revelation that the Royal Navy had destroyers protecting the cross-Channel shipping lanes.

However, following the Battle of Dogger Bank in January 1915, German naval strategists were left with little other choice than to turn to the submarine.[4] 'Naval commanders swung over to advocating a U-boat campaign largely because the inability of the High Seas Fleet to wrest maritime control from the British had been demonstrated in the course of 1914.'[5] The naval commanders also came under pressure from the German Army, which was now dug into static trench lines in northern and eastern France. 'What,' they wanted to know, 'was the navy doing? … month and month goes by and nothing is done.'[6]

The idea of a submarine blockade of British merchant ships found increasing support in policy-making circles. There was also growing anger at the British blockade and what was seen as US participation in it. Britain had swept the sea clear of German warships as well as German merchantmen. So the British could import as much grain as they needed from North and South America and buy as many munitions as they could afford from the United States.

The German Ambassador in Washington, Albrecht Count von Bernstorff, complained that the United States sold arms to the Allies and, while it said it would be prepared to sell arms to Germany, the blockade prevented Germany from buying such arms. This US attitude was seen as 'un-neutral'. According to Bernstorff:

If it is the desire of the American people to maintain an honorable neutrality, the United States will find the means to stop this one-sided traffic in arms, or at least use it for the purpose of protecting legitimate commerce with Germany, particularly in respect of foodstuffs.[7]

In Germany, diplomats and statesmen pressed their case on the United States Ambassador in Berlin, James W. Gerard:

In the autumn of 1914 Zimmermann [the Undersecretary of State at the German Foreign Office] showed me a long list sent him by Bernstorff showing quantities of saddles, automobiles, motor trucks, tires, explosives, food stuffs and so on, exported from America to the Allies and intimated that this traffic had reached such proportions that it should be stopped. ... Nothing, however, would satisfy the Germans. They seemed determined that the export of every article, whether food or ammunition, which might prove of use to the Allies in the war should be stopped.[8]

According to Gerard, 'the Germans [failed to] consider that America could not vary its international law with the changing fortunes of war and make one ruling when the Germans lost control of the sea and another when they regained it'.[9]

In effect, the United States was telling Germany that the imbalance of trade with Britain on the one hand and with Germany on the other was a matter of *realpolitik*. If Germany could reverse the equation and control the seas, it could buy food and munitions from the United States. But, under the existing conditions, Germany could not do that, and it was not the United States' job as a neutral to do anything about it.

For Imperial Navy officers it seemed there was nothing they could do in retaliation against the British. 'It was in this state of embarrassment and frustration that the German navy and government considered proposals for a submarine campaign against merchant shipping.'[10] The Imperial Navy argued that Britain was even more dependent on overseas trade for food and other supplies than Germany. Thus, Britain would find itself unable to maintain its war effort within weeks of a counter-blockade being carried out from beneath the surface of the sea.

For the first six months of the war, Germany had done little to antagonise the government of the United States, 'where indignation was accordingly directed against Britain'.[11] The decision taken on 4 February 1915 to attack both enemy and neutral merchant ships risked changing that. It was a big gamble, justified, the German authorities thought, by its expected effect of frightening away neutral ships. According to the German announcement:

> The waters around Great Britain including the whole of the English Channel, are hereby to be included in the zone of war, and after 18th inst. all enemy merchant vessels encountered in these waters will be destroyed, even if it may not be possible always to save their crews and passengers. Within this war zone neutral vessels are exposed to danger since, in view of the misuse of the neutral flags ordered by the government of Great Britain on the 31st ult., and of the hazards of naval warfare, neutral vessels cannot always be prevented from suffering from the attacks intended for enemy ships.[12]

A message transmitted on 7 February from Norddeich 'to all ships' and intercepted by Room 40, informed them of the 'proclamation of [a] military area around England, Scotland and Ireland. All merchant ships within the area will be destroyed.'[13]

★★★

While Germany had insufficient submarines to make its economic blockade effective, it did have enough to sink sufficient neutral vessels, and drown sufficient neutral citizens, to ensure that it would eventually upset the United States. But the hawkish faction in Germany had insisted that an effective blockade would precisely depend on terrorising neutrals so that they would shrink from venturing into danger zones.

The submarine was not an ideal blockading vessel. The accepted (and legal) practice of 'cruiser warfare' consisted of stopping and searching a suspect vessel and then, if it was trading with the enemy, putting a crew on board to pilot the seized vessel home as a 'prize'.

However, this was difficult when using submarines. They did not have room to carry enough sailors to provide crews that could take several ships back to Germany, let alone take the ships' crews on board. This meant that they had to sink intercepted ships. This, in turn, meant that they had to give the ship's crew time to lower their lifeboats. This required them to surface to give the necessary warning, thus making the submarines vulnerable to being shot at or rammed.

The British Royal Navy exploited this. It employed decoy vessels, converting merchant ships to carry guns that were hidden from view until a marauding submarine made itself vulnerable. Soon, however, the Germans became wise to these tricks and the submarine commanders started sinking ships without warning. This was 'unrestricted submarine warfare'.

At the start of the submarine campaign, Room 40 was getting fairly good intelligence on the overall state of readiness of the submarine fleet. For example, an intercept of 9 March 1915 from the commander of a U-boat 'half-flotilla' reported its situation: U-24 was ready for service at Emden, while U-28, also at Emden, was only ready for limited service in the Bight; at Wilhelmshaven, U-21, U-22 and U-30 would be ready by 27 March, the situation with U-33 was 'uncertain'; at Kiel, U-32 would be ready on 11 March and U-19 on 1 April; and U-20, U-23, U-27 and U-29 were already on 'distant mission'. Room 40 put a question mark in their transcript of the decode after U-23, presumably because it was garbled in transmission and this was a guess – a reminder that the quality of transmission affected the quality of the decodes.[14] Also wireless messages sent during submarine voyages, picked up by British direction-finding stations, gave rough indications of where the U-boats were and their route over time.[15]

From March to May 1915, the German Imperial Navy kept, on average, six submarines at sea, sinking twenty-nine merchant vessels in March, thirty-three in April and fifty-three in May. (To put that in context, there were over 1,000 sailings of merchants to or from British ports every month.) Three U-boats patrolled the Western Approaches and the Irish Sea, covering the routes to Liverpool and the Bristol Channel (with its vital coal ports on the South Wales coast). One submarine each was stationed off the Thames Estuary, the Tyne and the north-east coast (covering routes between Britain and Scandinavia).

Vessels from the Netherlands, Norway, Spain and Greece all became victims of the submarines. Germany achieved a propaganda defeat on 27 March 1915, when a U-boat stopped the liner *Falaba*. The submarine commander ordered the ship's crew and passengers to take to their lifeboats but allowed insufficient time for everyone to get into a boat. After just five minutes, the U-boat fired upon the liner and sank it, killing 104 people including one US citizen.

The Germans were encouraged by the apparent acceptance by the US Government of the loss of this one American and a few other US citizens in the first few months of the submarine campaign. However, the furore following the sinking of a Dutch steamer that was bound from Rotterdam to Baltimore led the Kaiser to declare, on 2 April, that no neutral vessels should be attacked. The neutrals' anger had achieved its first rollback of the terms of the German submarine blockade.

However, this compromise still left open the problem of neutrals travelling on British ships. On 10 March 1915, Room 40 intercepted a typical intelligence report sent from Norddeich 'to all ships' (a euphemism for submarines) informing them of potential targets. These were a 'large' British merchant ship, *Khim* and another merchant, *Omrah*, which were to leave London on 12 March. The second report in the message mentioned that a 'fast steamer *Lusitania* leaves Liverpool 13 March'.[16] Further intelligence reports named the liner, as well as other ships.

★★★

Germany put more submarines to sea from the summer of 1915 onwards and sinkings increased sharply – 114 in June, 86 in July, 107 in August and 58 in September. And the 'strike rate' improved too, rising from ten ships sunk for every one submarine lost between March and May, to thirty-five victim vessels for each submarine sunk.

Room 40 could pick up the signals sent when the U-boats left port, when they were out on duty and when they returned home, but there was little good use they could make of the intelligence. Any systematic attempt to warn the hundreds of isolated ships of the potential presence of submarines would soon give away the source of the intelligence and could lead to the loss of all the intercepts Room 40 was picking up.

Intercepts revealed the wireless station at Norddeich informing 'all ships' that British grain ships were expected to leave South Atlantic ports for London, Hull, Liverpool and Leith in mid-March 1915, providing plentiful opportunities for German submarines to undermine Britain's fairly precarious food supply. The German intelligence operation also watched Belgian and Dutch ships closely, feeding back information that was then broadcast by the German Imperial Navy and picked up by Room 40.

The Marine Corps at Bruges was informed on 1 March that Rotterdam Harbour was expecting the steamers *Elisabeth van België*, *Baron Baeyens*, *Hainault* and *Prasident Bunge*, all flying Dutch flags and with Dutch masts. Two days later, further intelligence from the German Consul in Rotterdam claimed that the steamers *Hainault*, *Prasident Bunge* and *Leopold II* were preparing to sail in a convoy – while flying a Dutch flag, with over 1,000 Belgians on board intending to travel to Britain to join the British Army – and were due to leave the Dutch port on Thursday to go to Hull.[17]

As Room 40's network of direction-finding receivers expanded, location information about German submarines improved. In March 1915, for example, a direction-finding station picked up 'suspicious' wireless signals, thought to be German submarines, located at 56 degrees 16 minutes north and 4 degrees and 45 minutes east at 11 a.m. By 6 a.m. the next day, the source of the signals had moved to another location. Several other reports the same day, from the direction-finding stations, provided evidence of other submarines in and around the waters surrounding the British and Irish isles.[18]

All this great variety of intelligence about submarines was pouring into Room 40. But even if this intelligence could have been used to influence the outcome of the submarine assault, it was, in fact, hardly used at all. Just as naval historians have, by and large, concentrated their writings on the big battles, most particularly the Battle of Jutland in 1916, so the navy's senior commanders overlooked the chance of using Room 40's intelligence offensively against the submarines because they wanted to keep it all secret until the day when the two big fleets would meet and blast one another to smithereens.

The problem was the now familiar one – the ineffective use of Room 40's output in the Admiralty. The officer responsible for plotting U-boat positions in the Naval Intelligence Division was not allowed to see the product of Room 40's work (indeed, he did not know of Room 40's existence). Conversely, Room 40 was not allowed to know the locations of British warships and merchants:

> Although by the spring of 1915 at least some of the staff of [naval intelligence division, German Section] E1 were doing their best to follow the movements of U-boats, it must have been a case of the blind leading the blind so far as any advice which they could give … In any case, with so few merchant ships equipped with wireless and no convoy system, the problem of controlling the hundreds of ships sailing independently and diverting them from known danger areas was well nigh insuperable.[19]

The logbook of telegrams sent out by Section E1 giving naval units warning of sightings, confirmed and unconfirmed, of German submarines contains a pretty wide variety of sources of information. Most came from naval or merchant ships, coastguards and the like. But some members of the general public also kept the Admiralty informed.

To quote one example, in early February 1915, Mr Thomas Glen of Prestatyn, North Wales, reported having seen several times lately submarines off the coast near the holiday resort of Rhyl. He also reported having observed 'powerful searchlights'. The senior naval officer at Liverpool was asked to investigate, although it seems unlikely that German submarines would use searchlights to advertise their presence.[20] Unfortunately, the logbook contains no messages of the sort that we have seen Room 40 decoding and that gave reliable and reasonably up-to-date reports directly from the enemy.

★★★

However, it seems that Henry Oliver did use Room 40's decodes to protect certain cargoes. For example, holding a special ship back in port until the coast was clear, so to speak, or re-routing them away from danger spots.

The liner *Lustitania*, however, was not considered special enough to be warned that a German submarine was possibly lurking around the approaches to the coast of south-west Ireland as the liner approached the area. The *Lusitania* was a well-known ship and, as one of the fastest ships on the Atlantic, an icon of the age of the oceangoing liner.

It had eight decks, was 250m long and displaced over 30,000 tons. Its four turbine engines consumed 1,000 tons of coal a day and powered the liner through the Atlantic seas at an average speed of 20–25 knots – as fast as the most advanced warships. It was truly luxurious, with 'gold and white, glass-domed, Louis XVI dining salons and mahogany-panelled lounges and smoking rooms with huge marble mantlepieces'.

On 7 May, the *Lusitania* was torpedoed as it approached Ireland from the west near the end of its Atlantic crossing. It sank with the loss of 1,201 lives – including 128 US citizens.[21] Its sinking was bound to attract enormous publicity in the United States, even without the American deaths.[22]

In the United States and Allied nations, the sinking of the liner was seen as an outrage, an act of barbarism. According to one writer, 'A flame of indignation swept across America … It shattered the universal approval of neutrality … which was the mood of the nation on the outbreak of war.'[23] It also diverted the US mood of anger from Britain and directed it instead towards Germany.

However, the authorities in Germany did not understand the outrage. Bernstorff wrote, 'Accustomed as we have been to daily reports of battles and casualties, [we] were little impressed by the destruction of a solitary passenger ship.'[24] Indeed, in Germany there was jubilation at the sinking of the liner. Its demise was seen as striking a blow against the 'starvation blockade'. There, the hypocrisy of an outcry of concern at causing the deaths of women and children by drowning at sea, but not at the barbarism of starving women and children to death in Germany, was as strikingly obvious as that hypocrisy was wholly invisible to the Allies and to the United States.

Under pressure from President Woodrow Wilson, the Kaiser decreed that large passenger liners, even if flying an enemy flag, would not be attacked, rolling back a bit further the effectiveness of the submarine blockade. Germany also suggested marking US ships in specified bright paint patterns. The United States rejected this particular offer, but President Wilson seemed otherwise to accept the situation, clinging to his determination to keep out of the war.

On 10 May, he undermined the effectiveness of any response with an injudicious comment in a public speech. 'The example of America must be a special example,' he said:

> The example of America must be the example not merely of peace because it will not fight, but of peace because peace is the healing and elevating influence of the world and strife is not. There is such a thing as a man being too proud to fight. There is such a thing as a nation being so right that it does not need to convince others by force that is right.[25]

Wilson sent three diplomatic 'notes' – a relatively mild form of diplomatic protest – to Germany (on 13 May, 9 June and 21 July) that achieved a slight rollback of the German submarine campaign.

It should be noted that, in addition to the submarine attacks on Allied and neutral vessels, Germany was conducting a sabotage campaign – today it would be called a terrorist campaign – on US soil against US economic targets, as well as placing delayed-action incendiary devices on Allied and neutral vessels sailing from US ports.[26] Wilson resolutely downplayed and ignored this provocation for fear it would damage his objective of keeping the United States out of the war and undermine his hopes of mediating a peace settlement.

After the sinking of the *Lusitania*, the submarine offensive continued, but under slightly stricter rules, forbidding the sinking of passenger ships and neutral merchant vessels. Yet, even then the rules were not always followed.

On 19 August, a German submarine sank a British steamer, *Arabic*, causing the death of forty-four passengers and crew, two of them US citizens. This led to more anger in the United States and more diplomatic notes from President Wilson. The Kaiser hoped to find a solution by forbidding the sinking of passenger liners unless the passengers and crew could be saved.

A Room 40 history, written at the end of the war, observed:

> It must have been particularly galling to the [German] naval authorities to be obliged from political considerations to curb the activities of the submarine

commanders who had been exhibiting the greatest prowess during August. … Apart from all other considerations, the sinking of the *Lusitania* came to be generally regarded by the German navy as a capital political error. … it was received with extraordinary rejoicing by the German public at large and was an endless source of encouragement to those who suffered most from the Allied blockade.[27]

Even after the sinking of the *Lusitania*, the German authorities remained carelessly antagonistic towards the United States, remaining convinced it would not join the war – and even if it did, it would not be capable of making an effective military contribution to the Allied side. The Undersecretary of Foreign Affairs, Zimmermann, in discussion with the United States Ambassador, James W. Gerard, told him:

The United States does not dare do anything against Germany because we have five hundred thousand German reservists in America who will rise in arms against your government if your government should dare to take any action against Germany.

According to Gerard, Zimmermann:

… worked himself up into a passion and repeatedly struck the table with his fist. I told him we had five hundred and one thousand lamp posts in America, and that was where the German reservists would find themselves if they tried any uprising.[28]

The first chapter in the history of German 'unrestricted submarine warfare' closed in spring 1916 when, on 23 March, the passenger ship *Sussex* was sunk with eighty fatalities, including four US citizens:

This produced from Wilson what was tantamount to an ultimatum, a statement that unless the German Government abandoned 'its present practices of submarine warfare', America would sever diplomatic relations altogether … This secured on 5 May 1916 the *Sussex* 'pledge', whereby Germany suspended unrestricted submarine warfare. But she made the suspension conditional upon American efforts to compel the British to abandon their blockade and reserved her rights if those efforts should fail.[29]

A new chapter in the unrestricted submarine warfare saga was not ruled out. In the meantime, the Imperial Navy decided on one more attempt to catch the Grand Fleet unawares.

★★★

A British Intelligence account says, 'From numerous articles appearing in the German press at the beginning of 1916 it is evident that disappointment with the results of submarine warfare was widespread in Germany.'[30] With the scaling down of submarine warfare, the German Imperial Navy sought again to find a role on the surface of the seas and attention turned again to the idea of drawing the Royal Navy into a North Sea clash.

The battle of warships at Jutland, at the end of May 1916, is one of the most celebrated incidents of the First World War. Hundreds of books have been written on the subject and there seems to be no stemming the flood of new ones. Here was the big chance that Oliver and the other senior Admiralty figures had been waiting for, holding back on their use of Room 40's intelligence, for the day when the German *Hochseeflotte* ventured out of its lair.

The first indication to reach Room 40 that some move was planned by the German Imperial Navy came from intercepts ordering the despatch of a small flotilla of submarines. Initially, there was nothing to suggest a special sortie, but a couple of days after they had left port the U-boats had not shown up on any of the usual trade routes, nor had they been spotted searching for British warships. 'In the absence of any signs of activity, it became obvious that they had been sent out on some particular service, in all probability connected with some operation by the German fleet.'[31]

The codebreakers then started to pick up other signals indicating that an operation was in the offing. Scheer sent ahead a 'scouting' squadron of some forty ships to draw any British ships on to the main German fleet. In all, over 250 ships put to sea. When Hipper's scouts and Beatty's battlecruiser squadron first met, Beatty was indeed drawn, unawares, towards the bigger, more powerful *Hochseeflotte*. But, just as Hipper was drawing Beatty, so Beatty turned and started to draw the German fleets towards Jellicoe's even bigger ships – except that Jellicoe was slow in arriving, even taking time to stop and search some merchant ships.

The battle truly took place in the fog of war, with both sides mistaking the enemy ships they glimpsed momentarily in the mist for isolated parts of the enemy fleet. The usual British inter-ship signalling problems and inability of the commanders to communicate with one another about intentions and orders ensured that the conflict did not turn into a great conflagration. However, three British warships, *Indefatigable, Invincible* and *Queen Mary*, were blown apart (the latter was Hall's old ship until his appointment as Director of Naval Intelligence).

The ships' demise was the result of shaving their armour plating to a minimum (in order to give them more speed) and the demands of upholding the navy's tradition of fast gunnery. This required keeping open the flash doors for speed of supplying shells to the gunners but which, if closed, could have stopped shell hits on the gun deck from spreading down to the arsenals. Beatty commented, 'There seems to be something wrong with our bloody ships today.'

Without Jellicoe's delayed arrival, the battle may indeed have been more violent. Instead, it gave the German fleet the time to turn for home. The escape was successful because the Admiralty failed to pass on to Jellicoe Room 40 intercepts which would have allowed him to know which route the German ships were taking back to the Bight. Jellicoe was sent one intercepted message that should have alerted him to the German route home, but he did not really trust the intelligence. Later messages that would definitely have pointed him in the right direction – such as asking for airship reconnaissance – were not passed on.

German propaganda was quick to paint the battle as a great victory for the Imperial Navy and an unmitigated disaster for the Royal Navy. It was true that Britain suffered more casualties (6,954 compared with 3,058) and lost a greater tonnage of shipping (111,980 to 62,233 tons). And, indeed, this view was widely accepted at first, both in Britain and abroad in neutral countries where the great battles were eagerly followed for hints of who would be the likely winners of the war.

At home, Jellicoe was criticised for showing inadequate aggression and determination to engage with the enemy. The attitude persists. Jellicoe, in the words of a naval historian writing ninety years after the battle, was a worrier and 'great worriers are rarely great warriors'.[32]

In Germany, Kaiser Wilhelm was ecstatic: 'The English have been beaten. The spell of Trafalgar has been broken. You have written a new chapter in world history.'[33]

Soon, however, sentiments began to change. Intercepts of German diplomatic messages between Berlin and Madrid illustrate what happened. Immediately after the Battle of Jutland, the German Ambassador in Spain had been quick to report back to Germany, 'The Spanish press, including papers not specially friendly to Germany, recognise that Germany has had a great victory at sea … [with one paper declaring] the end of the 400-year supremacy of England'. However, the effectiveness of the propaganda waned as the implications sunk in of the German fleet having fled the battle scene. The ambassador lamented:

> Considerable harm has been caused by concealment of the loss of *Lutzow* and *Rostock*. The unofficial report [of the sinking] created a bad impression in German circles and, unfortunately, especially so in Spanish circles friendly to us. … The first impression of a great German victory has been entirely destroyed.[34]

Within a month of the battle, Scheer told the Kaiser:

> Even the most successful outcome of a fleet action in this war will not force England to make peace … [because of] the disadvantages of our military/geographical position and the enemy's great material superiority … a victorious end to the war within a reasonable time can only be achieved through the defeat of British economic life – that is by using the U-boats against British trade.[35]

'For You the War is Over'

Captain Malcolm Hay joined the Gordon Highlanders at the start of the war. He was among the first of the British Expeditionary Force (BEF) to land in Belgium in August 1914. His first few days were spent marching 'along pleasant country roads through a country of hedges and orchards, very like central and southern England', but also on tiring cobbled roads.

On Sunday, 23 August his unit was ordered to march off to a peaceful rural scene and dig a trench. After some cavalry passed, heading rearwards, it dawned on Hay that his unit's trench must now be the front line. After a day of fierce fighting, where they held off the advancing German troops, Hay received orders to retire. On pulling back, he learned that other units had suffered badly and the whole British Army was retreating. As they withdrew, Hay and his men came back into contact with the German forces near a village called Béthencourt. A machine gun began to play up and down the trench they had dug:

The bullets began to spray too close to my left ear, and laying my glasses on the parapet I was about to sit down for a few minutes' rest, and indeed had got half-way to the sitting position, when the machine gun found its target. Recollections of what passed through my mind at that moment is very clear. I knew instantly what had happened. The blow might have come from a sledge-hammer, except that it seemed to carry with in an impression of speed. I saw for one instant in my mind's eye the battlefield at which I had been gazing through my glasses the whole day. Then the vision was hidden by a scarlet circle, and a voice said, 'Mr. H. has got it'.[1]

Hay had been hit in the face and was helped back by his troops, but eventually he had to be left behind when further retreat was necessary. He was expected to die, but against the odds he survived, ending up as a prisoner of war in a Belgian hospital. There, he recovered slowly.

In his account of his experiences, Hay does not tell the reader the exact nature of his injuries. But he indirectly lets us know what happened when he records the later arrival of a wounded French soldier, Jean:

> His wound in the head was on the left side, almost exactly in the same place as my own – the bullet had made the same furrow, all the symptoms were identical, the right leg dragging, the right arm hanging, the slow elephantine movement; but there was a difference … between the two points of impact. In the case of Jean the impact of the bullet was a hair's-breadth more to the front of the head, only the difference of perhaps a tenth of a millimetre. And so it was that poor Jean had not only lost the power of motion on the right side, but also speech, memory and understanding.

Fortunately for Hay, while he did indeed have much trouble in moving, his power of speech and thought were unimpaired.

As he got better, he was transferred to a prisoner-of war-camp in Germany where he met both brutal Germans and kind Germans and on a long train journey witnessed Germany's impressive massing of men and materials for the front. Eventually, in January 1915, Hay was one of a number of badly injured officers and men exchanged for German prisoners on the Dutch–German border. The extent of his injuries meant he would not make any further contribution to the war effort, so it was safe to send him home. As he was about to leave the prison camp in Würzburg, he was told by one German, 'For you the war is over'.

★★★

The territory of north-western Europe, from the Netherlands to northern France, is marked by a series of frontiers, tide marks left by incursions of war, religious strife and rebellion into these lands. Going south from the province of Holland, the first frontier to be crossed is a religious one, between the Protestant north and the Catholic south. The next frontier on the journey south is the political border between the Netherlands and Belgium. This border has some highly unusual aspects. There are some small enclaves of Belgian territory entirely enclosed within the Netherlands. Even today, a

Dutch police officer cannot arrest a suspect who flees – or just steps – into part of 'Belgium'.

The largest enclave, Bar-le-Duc, proved rather useful for a while to Allied Intelligence. A wireless transmitter was erected in what was sovereign Belgian territory and used to transmit intelligence gathered in France and Belgium to the Allied military authorities (until the Germans learned how to feed in disinformation).

Further south comes the linguistic border between Dutch (in its Flemish dialect) and French (with its local Walloon usages, such as '*septant*' for seventy in place of the '*soixante-dix*' in *French* French). This boundary is the oldest and stretches back to the times of the Roman Empire, which brought Romance language into the lowlands of north-western Europe. It has moved very little in the last 2,000 years (one modern exception being when, in the nineteenth century, Brussels became a Francophone enclave in Flemish-speaking territory).

A short way further south there is another political boundary, that between Belgium and France. (The situation is actually a bit less regular than implied, for the language boundary crosses into the far northern corner of France where there are about 100,000 Dutch speakers.)

In late 1914, a new frontier was carved into the soil of the French and Belgian borderlands – the trench systems that divided Germany's armies from those of the Allies. After Germany's attempt to knock out the French Army was defeated on the Marne in September 1914, the British and German armies launched a series of attempts to outflank each other, eventually reaching the sea near Dunkirk, in what became known as 'the race to the sea'.

An order on 15 September to the BEF said, 'The commander-in-chief wishes the line now held by the Army to be strongly entrenched, and it is his intention to assume a general offensive at the earliest opportunity.'[2] The first part (and similar orders to the French and German armies by their commanders) was fully implemented by 14 October and trenches ran from the shores of the Channel to the Swiss border. The second part took longer to achieve.

There was an immediate consequence. As Denniston recalled, 'When the Armies settled down to trench warfare, the number of messages intercepted, and the number of stations heard, gradually diminished until about April 1915 when work had practically ceased.'[3]

All the same, some German Army wireless sets clearly remained in situ. One day, after a successful German attack on the French Army, a message from the German HQ was sent out by wireless congratulating all the units involved in the assault. Each station replied in turn, in the traditional manner, with its own call sign acknowledging receipt of the message.

This was an unusual break in the near overall silence in the ether on the Western Front in late 1914 and throughout 1915, except for in mid-1915 for air-to-ground encoded wireless messages sent from aircraft acting as spotters for artillery targeting. Two wireless stations remained in use and were thought to be armoured trains that could not readily link up to the telephone and telegraph networks that increasingly provided for military communications on both sides from November 1914 onwards.[4]

The BEF eventually laid some 400,000 miles of telegraph and telephone wire, erected 90,000 telegraph poles, dug in 47,000 miles of specially designed 'trench cable', and deployed 40,000 trench telephone sets, 36,000 telephone switchboards and 10,000 portable exchanges.[5] The trench war was primarily an artillery war (artillery – not the machine gun, gas, rifle bullet or bayonet – was the single largest killer of soldiers). Artillery could damage cables, unless they were laid at least 2m below the surface. The networks were 'meshed' so that if one link was damaged, communications could be switched to another link.

However, while landline communications were fine for those on the defensive, they had limited utility in offensive operations. This did not matter so much to the German Army, because after the onset of trench warfare Germany would, in general, remain on the defensive in the west (until the Battle of Verdun in 1916 and the Ludendorff Offensives of 1918). But, time and again, the British and French attacked into a communications void, sending troops blindly into the killing zones.

The state of military technology and tactics at the time favoured defence over attack. One reason for this was precisely the problem of communication during an attack. Commanders, even if they were not ensconced safely some way from the front, could give middle-ranking and junior officers precise and detailed orders before a battle started but once an offensive began communications were severed.

It could take a messenger (optimistically dubbed a 'runner') hours to negotiate a passage through the battlefield and get back to unit command, and for reports from all units to be gathered and passed on to HQ, and new orders to make their way out. However, the situation had already changed by the time the reports reached HQ, let alone when the runner returned – if they returned. As one British officer later wrote about the battle for the Belgian town of Charleroi as early as mid-August 1914:

It was the same old story, the divisions, fully engaged, were evidently finding it hard to give a precise account of themselves. We were up against one of the great difficulties of modern warfare. There we were, in a friendly country, with all the equipment of a modern state at our disposal, yet the Army Commander was without news of a battle in which two of his corps were engaged less than ten miles away.[6]

The most important category of intelligence needed at the front was the detail of the army units ranged on the other side of no man's land – the enemy's 'order of battle'. It was also vital to know if the enemy was planning any attacks and, if so, where they would fall. In the absence of German wireless messages to intercept, this information had to be found in other ways.

Networks of spies and agents were a potential source of intelligence about troop movements occurring some way behind the lines, but it was hard to recruit a network of agents, harder still to find a way of getting information out of the occupied areas, and hardest of all to sustain the network in operation in the face of determined counter-espionage efforts by the enemy backed up by the tactics of terror. Agents and spies thus provided a fitful source of intelligence.

The German Army was even more severely disadvantaged in this respect, as few French people were prepared to risk their lives to aid an invading army, while the Allies found a somewhat more plentiful supply among civilians in occupied Belgium, Luxembourg and northern France and a conduit for intelligence out of the occupied zone through the neutral Netherlands. By 1918, there were 4,350 agents in 130 networks supplying information to the British Army in Belgium, engaged mainly in train watching, but also observing airfields.[7] Finding ways to get their information out of the enemy zone and across to the Allies presented a major challenge.[8]

★★★

As new technologies were adopted and adapted, wireless communications and the use of codes and ciphers grew in importance. Improved artillery aiming, air reconnaissance, relatively portable wireless sets, and 'earth-telegraphy' systems all depended on coded or enciphered communications. Air and ground 'forward observers' needed to inform artillery batteries where to point their guns and then guide them precisely to the target.

Special codes were devised for aerial target spotting (the breaking of which became a key task for army codebreakers). Similarly, codes were developed for use with earth telegraphy (also called 'power-buzzer' or 'Morse-buzzer'). A standard telegraph tapper key and a battery to provide power could be taken forward with troops and used from anywhere without a wire back to HQ. It was light in weight, easy to use and needed only one person to carry and operate it. A short length of wire from the battery was attached to a rod that was plunged into the ground.

However, the signals tapped out on the key were conducted by the earth and could be picked up by anyone with a similar rod connected to a receiver. It was first introduced by the Allies, and the German Army became aware of the system in 1915 but did not make use of it themselves until late 1916 (during the Battle of the Somme). Depending on the soil and the underlying geology, transmissions could be detected over distances of 4,000m, although often much less. But, like wireless, it was open for all to listen in to, so codes were essential.[9]

On the Allied side, communications for a long time depended on telephone and telegraph lines. British Field Service Regulations specified that orders should preferably be given in written form – by telegraph or by runner carrying a piece of paper – so that misunderstandings could be minimised. The telephone, however, became the preferred means of communication, allowing questioning and discussion to eliminate misunderstanding. However:

> Unfortunately, the mud, damp and shell fire made the laying and maintenance of telephone lines particularly difficult and the reliable communications seemingly offered by the telephone often failed at critical moments … [All the same] because the telephone seemed to offer an answer to all the army's communication needs, other forms of communication were ignored, shelved or dropped and the undue reliance on the telephone began to produce real problems.[10]

These problems were caused by the ability of the German signals corps to intercept British telephone conversations and power-buzzer messages from late-1915.

The German Army developed a listening device called the Moritz, which was widely used to intercept and amplify weak signals. Each German listening post was staffed by a sergeant major, two interpreters, two Morse operators and two 'linesmen'. The system involved, somewhere or other, making a direct contact with an Allied telephone wire. This gave access to any calls on any wire connected to it.

A British Intelligence report noted, 'Instructions issued by various formations, regarding the use of the telephone and the danger of interception of telephone messages, together with threats of disciplinary action if such instructions were disobeyed' had little effect.[11] While conversation is useful for communicating orders and reports with great understanding, it is hard to devise – and harder to enforce the use of – a coding system for spoken language, especially in rapidly developing situations. So, telephone conversations were inevitably in plain language.

The German Army intercepted orders being sent to British units on the front line, heard returns on battalion strengths, and listened as units moved in and out of the line, thus building up a picture of the British 'order of battle' and detecting planned assaults. The first hint that the Germans were tapping telephone calls came from a prisoner of war in March 1916, but nothing effective was done to prevent the security breach.

The lack of telephone security allowed the German Army to know when and where the first day of the Battle of the Somme would be launched. Late on that fateful day, 1 July 1916, a German listening post was discovered in a dug-out by advancing British troops. They found wiring in place and documents which showed that calls had been intercepted for some time, including details of conversations from telephone links far back from the front line, such as between division and corps headquarters.

When the documents made their way back to the intelligence section, some were in for a dreadful shock. 'One of the intelligence officers was able to recognize some of these notes as being conversations in which he himself had taken part, whilst others contained copies of orders issued by his Corps.'[12]

Renewed efforts to convince commanders and junior officers to use care began to take effect and from late 1916, 'the regular and uninterrupted stream of intercepted English gradually ceased, any signal successes being sporadic and due to local indiscretion or carelessness on our part'. Later on, a 'scrambler' telephone was introduced, the Fullerphone, which secured calls effectively by transforming the electric currents, turning the call into an unintelligible mess unless you could unscramble it.

★★★

The attention of MI1(b) in London was steadily drawn away from the Western Front towards the widening war, including the Caucasus and the territories of the Ottoman Empire. Decrypted intelligence was passed to London by the

Russians, who had gained access to telegraph messages between the Austrian Ambassador in Istanbul and the Austrian Foreign Office in Vienna.

At first, the War Office in London did not realise the value of the information they received from Russia until, on 20 October 1914, they learned the identity of the source of the intelligence that revealed that war with Turkey was imminent.[13] And by capturing code books belonging to the Grand Vizier as well as the Ottoman War Minister, MI1(b) was being drawn outside of strictly military cryptography and ushered into the unfamiliar world of diplomacy.[14]

The first capture of documents by the British on the Turkish front seems to have taken place early in 1915 (or perhaps late in 1914). News reached MI1(b) of the acquisition of a Turkish spy along with his code book in Egypt. The code book was sent to London, but there was little expectation that it would stay in use for long because details of its capture were revealed during a court case. However, a fortnight later, photographic copies of the code books used by Enver Pasha, the Turkish War Minister, and by the Grand Vizier of the Ottoman Empire, were delivered to MI1(b) in London. A week after that, the cryptographers were also provided with information about the call signs used by Turkish wireless stations to address one another. A few days later, on 29 January, a translation of the instructions for using Enver Pasha's code book also made its way to London.

However, if the documents were coming in, the same could not be said about actual Turkish messages. When MI1(b) asked the intelligence unit in Egypt if they had translated any messages using the captured code books and instructions, they were told that no messages had been intercepted.[15] Looking for something to do, MI1(b) had its attention diverted to cable messages of neutral governments.

Britain was the global hub of the world's cable networks and most transatlantic traffic between the United States and Europe had to travel via Britain to get to neutral Europe. When the war started, the legal constraints on intercepting telegrams were lifted and a strict censorship imposed. Private codes and ciphers were banned and all telegrams examined by the censor's office.[16] Neutral governments could continue to use codes and ciphers, but there were no longer any legal reasons why such diplomatic messages sent in code or cipher could not be subject to close scrutiny – and by codebreakers rather than just censors.

On 11 January 1915, it was agreed that MI1(b) should take over all duties connected with the supervision and attempted solution of suspected codes and ciphers in letters intercepted by Postal Censorship.[17] Later, the same was applied to Cable Censorship. An official historian at GCHQ (the post-1945 successor to Room 40 and Bletchley Park) later wrote, 'There is no evidence on the reason for this switch to cable, though it may be relevant that Anderson had worked on such intercepts during the South African [i.e. Boer] war.'[18] A new front in the intelligence war was opening up.

★★★

This chapter started with an account of how one soldier had experienced the start of the land war, how he was injured and how he was extremely lucky to survive. More luck came his way when he was sent back to Britain in a prisoner exchange programme. Captain Malcolm Hay was fairly wealthy and would be able to live comfortably. He had done his duty and sustained serious injury, so his illustrious family history could record another glorious chapter.

Hay's grandfather, Lord James Hay, was the 7th Marquis of Tweeddale and an experienced soldier, having been aide-de-camp to Wellington at Waterloo, a century earlier. His son, James Gordon Hay, lived in splendour at the family home at Seaton, near Aberdeen, but did not have children until quite late in life. He was 65 when his son, Malcolm Hay, was born, and he died a couple of years later.

Hay's mother also died when he was still young, just 11 years of age. Hay was brought up for much of the time by a part of the family who lived in France, where he was well educated in modern and classical languages. At the age of 21, he inherited the family estate at Seaton where he lived the leisurely and seemingly unambitious life of the Scottish laird, walking the local hills, rooting around in local archives, getting involved in local politics. This seemed likely to be the pattern his adult life would follow until, in 1914, the war started. Hay immediately volunteered, only to be wounded before the end of August and back home on his estate by the beginning of 1915.

After a few months' convalescence, Hay was itching to do something for the war effort. So he went to London and, hauling himself along on two sticks, turned up at the War Office, demanding to be given a job. He was effectively bilingual in English and French, and had good Italian, as well as a 'reading knowledge' of German and Spanish. He also had a fair acquaintance with Greek and Latin. So, although he had difficulty getting around, he could surely make a contribution.

In December 1915 he was appointed to MI1(b), where some efforts were being devoted to looking at diplomatic telegrams. But, it was a small-scale effort and there was much more diplomatic traffic passing through British-controlled cables that could be exploited. Hay's second wife later wrote that the injured soldier:

> ... at once saw the possibilities and potential value of information available in the central control of the world-wide cable service, and the network utilising the then recent invention of wireless transmission. He therefore protested at the waste of existing opportunities to procure valuable intelligence in this field, and eventually secured permission, on his own conditions, to re-organise and re-form the department.[19]

For Hay, the war was just beginning.

'The Pillars of Hercules Have Fallen'

One of the murkiest incidents in English history is that of Titus Oakes and the 'Popish Plot' of 1678. An outcast and a misfit, Oakes was nevertheless at the centre of a national panic over an alleged Catholic plot to murder King Charles II and place his brother, the Duke of York (later James II), on the throne. The allegations were lies and half-truths but gained momentum in the febrile times. Several innocent people were executed, and old political scores were settled. Even Samuel Pepys, Secretary to the Navy and its most formidable administrator, was sucked up into the whirlwind of fear, suspicion and violence because of his closeness to the Duke of York. Pepys was lucky to escape with his life.

Some of the evidence used to convict some of those who suffered the agonies of execution – as traitors, by hanging, drawing and quartering – was made up of intercepted letters, one with passages in cipher. It was found in the possession of an English Jesuit priest, Edward Coleman. He had been secretary to the Duke of York and at the time of the uproar was secretary to the Duke's wife. As one writer commented, 'The only legitimate evidence against [Coleman] is that provided by his own correspondence; this is written for the most part, in language so obscure that it can be twisted as much or as little as the historian desires.'[1]

The letters, from the Papal Nuncio, were not very convincing evidence of anything. Yet, in the temper of the times, with an economic downturn and high unemployment in London adding to the volatile emotions of the crowd, fear of a reversion to Catholicism drove the frenzy of paranoia and suspicion. The fact that one letter was partially encrypted was obvious proof that there was something amiss. It has also been taken as such in many historical accounts of the furore surrounding Oakes and the plot since then.

The incriminating letter had been written by the Papal Nuncio on 12 January 1675 and contained various passages where some of the plain language is replaced by series of numbers. The key section reads:

> What you propose touching 51666279669961 which is, 66717576661676676 cannot be put in execution 566662516756665667 but with the 7776999166996167976669961 of all 516791776662966499671919 and only 667191776691 comprising 96669991516791947151416791 you may then consider if the terms wherein at present are 51679166545666462679196880204 it would be for the interest of the Duke to produce unto light an affair of this nature. That which I can with truth assure you, and whereof the Duke may be persuaded is that 669977669 16564519167627664617199647671625167976664916162679663204 will employ 6681272 and 5108126 and 516777626796646 for 5166919164916 167626662679161669451646451665166812666679981204.

All attempts made at the time by a House of Commons special committee of investigation to break the cipher and reveal its contents were failures. Indeed, the cipher remained unbroken until 1934 when a retired army captain published a book entitled *The Jesuits and the Popish Plot*. The author had written other books on Catholic history, setting the record straight on a number of issues where the rough and tumble of the life-and-death struggle between adherents of Protestantism and Catholicism in Britain had led to a besmirching of the reputation of British Catholics.

Of interest to our story is an appendix to the main text, where the author provides a solution to the cipher that, for over 250 years, had defied decryption. The cipher, he pointed out, was in fact a straightforward substitution cipher (in effect, a simple code) with code words (using numbers rather than letters) of two or three numbers replacing the plain-language letters. The author noted that only seven numbers were used. He also pointed out:

> The number 8 or any two-figure group containing that number, seems to have been used as an indication of change to another table, a code of three figures which was used for names of persons, places and words used frequently in the correspondence.

The 'cipher' was, he said, 'extremely simple' and was defeated by frequency analysis.

The newly decoded letter did not provide any conclusive evidence to the historical dispute. The Papal Nuncio was no doubt a very wily politician and knew how to write a letter without giving much away. The section of the letter cited above reads:

> What you propose touching the money which is in the castle [i.e. Castel S. Angelo where the Pope was supposed to keep a stash of treasure] cannot be put into execution by the Pope [except] with the consent of all the cardinals, and then by means of a Bull; you may then consider if the conditions, where are at present the affairs of England, it would be for the interest of the Duke [of York] to bring to light an affair of this nature. That which I can with truth assure you, and whereof the Duke may be persuaded is that, should he happen one day to become the master of England, they will employ at Rome both money and credit to assist him to restore the Catholic religion in England.[2]

No doubt it would in fact have made little difference to the case against Coleman, even if the letter had been decrypted and the suspicious cipher sections been shown to be less damaging than expected. Still, it must have been very satisfying for the author, a non-academic historian, to crack a code that had stymied so many for so long.

He did, however, have an advantage over those who had attempted to solve the cipher in earlier times. He had been the beneficiary of an ideal opportunity to learn a lot about codes and ciphers, for he had spent nearly three years as the head of the War Office's decryption unit, MI1(b). He was none other than Captain Malcolm Hay – whom we first met in the previous chapter, being wounded in the retreat from Mons in August 1914 and then again when he dragged himself along Whitehall on two walking sticks to the War Office to demand a job at the beginning of 1916.

★★★

Hall later wrote:

> Before my appointment some progress had already been made by Messrs. Strachey and Pletts with the American diplomatic code. I am not able to say definitely how this code was first broken. I was told that some clear texts

were obtained which facilitated solution. Until the beginning of 1916 the work of the War Office cryptographic section was limited to investigation, with intermittent success, of German [army] field ciphers, and to the reconstruction of the American Diplomatic codebooks.[3]

A post-war intelligence account suggests, 'The work was entirely fresh to all members of the staff, there were no past records as guidance, and the problem of how to solve large codebooks had to be thought out *ab initio*.'[4] This is a somewhat misleading claim.

Work on the US code book began when a known plain-language text was to be transmitted in the code and could be intercepted. A surviving MI1(b) file of 15 February 1915 says, 'It is suggested that we should try to get hold of American code – an opportunity arising from the impending transmission of a [diplomatic] note to America which of necessity must go verbatim.'[5]

A report noted that on 17 February the plain-language text was received in MI1(b) and on 22 February, 'the same note [was] received in a five-figure code'. Unfortunately, we have no details of the planted text. Probably some diplomatic issue was to be put to the US Embassy which would have to be transmitted word for word to Washington for a response. The codebreakers could then look for the planted text in the coded message, thus enabling them to start breaking the code.

All or part of three different US code books were reconstructed by mid-1916 and several cipher tables were also broken, and some evidence suggests that some US codes were broken from 1914.[6] The first surviving copy of a decoded US State Department telegram dates from 3 May 1915 and is a report from the US Ambassador in Berlin, James Gerard. Like all the surviving copies of MI1(b) decodes, it begins with the statement, 'MI1 has received the following reliable information'.

The scant evidence suggests that several sections in Military Intelligence, the Naval Intelligence Division, the Foreign Office and the prime minister's office would have received at least some decoded messages. The copies of the decodes that have survived (with a few exceptions, such as the intercept of 3 May 1915) are held within Admiralty files, so they appear to have been the copies sent to Hall as Director of Naval Intelligence.[7]

Hay's second wife, writing in the 1970s, said that Hay 'at once' saw the value, if used properly, of MI8's censorship of cable traffic and negotiated for complete independence so long as he 'produced the goods'.[8] According to Hay:

In the spring of 1916 I began to realise the potential value of the enormous mass of encoded messages from all over the world ... About this time I had an interview with the [Deputy] Cable Censor, Lord Arthur Browne, who arranged for copies of all diplomatic cables to be sent to my office. In 1916 information was badly wanted about what was going on in Greece and I decided to make a start with the Greek code. No one in this country had hitherto succeeded in breaking a diplomatic codebook without what we used to call 'a crib' [such as the diplomatic note of which a plain language copy was available when breaking a US diplomatic code book]. The problem was undertaken and solved by Mr. John Fraser, who [later became] Professor of Celtic at Oxford.

Fraser had joined MI1(b) in February 1916 and was to prove to be a prolific codebreaker and an accomplished linguist, having knowledge of some twenty-one languages at the end of the war. He broke or helped to break Greek, Spanish, Argentine, Uruguayan, Turkish, Swiss, Swedish, Norwegian, Brazilian, Dutch and Vatican codes before he left in 1919, going on to become a professor in 1921.

The Greek code book was to be his first major achievement. Hay recalled:

The chief difficulty was [that ...] we had no means of knowing in what language the messages were written. The natural hypothesis was that they were written in Greek. After working for many weeks on this assumption Fraser concluded that the text must not be in Greek but in French. In June when I was home for a few days leave, Fraser sent me a telegram: 'Pillars of Hercules have fallen'. It turned out that the Greeks used a number of different code-books, some in Greek, some in French. All these were reconstructed.[9]

The diverse patchwork of states in the Balkans and south-eastern Europe was to be a focus of much diplomacy by both sides in the war. Each alliance sought to turn neutrals into allies, or at least to make them into 'benevolent neutrals'.

In 1915, the Serbian Army had been driven out of Serbia by Habsburg and German forces. The Allies asked Greece for the expelled Serbian troops to be evacuated to Salonika (present-day Thessaloniki). By September 1915, the king had agreed to the Allied request, but this led to the collapse of the government. In early November, the new government declared itself to be a 'benevolent neutral', favouring the Allies. Details of the intense political and diplomatic negotiations behind this move were revealed to MI1(b) by its breaking of the Greek code books. According to a MI1(b) document, 'The solving of the code in which [very long Greek] messages were sent proved of the very highest importance.'[10]

Given the high volume of neutral traffic carried over telegraph cables, there was plenty of material to work on. In fact, with Strachey and Pletts successfully reconstructing code books and cipher tables, more members of staff were needed to handle the repetitive task of decoding messages. Several more wounded officers joined the team for this work.[11] By the autumn of 1916, MI1(b) had ten cryptographic staff, although it is impossible to be certain whether they all worked on diplomatic codes. In July 1916, a new section was split off from MI1(b) to handle intercept intelligence about German air raids on Britain, initially with a staff of just four officers (see Chapter 19).

MI1(b) moved to new premises in Mayfair as it expanded. A tall, burly, no nonsense non-commissioned officer stood guard and made sure no one wandered into the building. However, Central London street life could still impinge on the codebreakers. On one occasion, a passionate letter to the police pleaded for help. Hay wrote:

> One of my sub-Sections located at 5, Cork Street complains constantly of the nuisance caused by the large number of itinerant musicians constantly parading that street. This sub-Section is now engaged on important work for which quiet is essential. If you could see your way to prohibiting street noise in the immediate vicinity … I should be extremely grateful.[12]

★★★

Back in the Admiralty, Room 40 was also expanding its sphere of operations into diplomatic codebreaking. But it was not a move that had been co-ordinated with MI1(b). The two organisations' activities did in fact turn out to be complementary, but that was by chance. The frosty relations between them endured throughout 1915 and into 1916. All the same, changes were occurring that would end the disconnect.

As a newly acquired task, Room 40's diplomatic work slipped out of the control of Sir Alfred Ewing and came under Blinker Hall, the Head of Naval Intelligence. It was Hall, the navy career officer, who provided the driving force behind the shift of attention from purely naval intelligence into the systematic operations in the diplomatic sphere, not Ewing, the career academic administrator. Hall also started the process of fostering co-operation between the two organisations.

Frank Birch commented acidly that, although Britain had constrained Germany's communications with the outside world, any future 'historian will wonder whether any cause save the most crass habitude prevented the full utilisation of the favourable situation in which the Allies found themselves'. Between August 1914 and May 1915, some 170 German diplomatic telegrams were transmitted as neutral traffic via cables that passed through Britain on their way to the Americas, containing information about negotiations with the US Government and German sabotage and espionage efforts in the Americas:

> Owing to the deficient coordination of British intelligence none of these telegrams ever reached a decyphering bureau. ... The main cause was that the various intelligence services departments were compelled to work in 'watertight' compartments, a radically false system by which deciphering departments, censorship, press reading departments etc., had no knowledge of each other's intention, and received no news of each other's activities, or of the problems on which they were engaged, and which they were capable of assisting each other to solve.[13]

Another important factor that edged Room 40 towards diplomatic surveillance was the volume of wireless traffic between Berlin and Madrid, coded with the *Verkehrsbuch* (VB) naval code book. Madrid was of great importance to Germany. Here was its most important European embassy and its centre for communications and trade with the rest of the world. It became a prolific source of diplomatic intelligence (see Chapter 15). So, Room 40 became involved in the interception of transmissions of German diplomatic messages by wireless or over cables, while MI1(b) specialised in the cable traffic of neutrals (except the United States and Spain).

★★★

At this point, a small diversion and a short step backwards is necessary to review some events in Persia in early 1915. Germany and its new ally, Turkey, wanted to stimulate disaffection for the British Empire among its millions of Muslim subjects. Early in 1915, the highest religious figure in Constantinople, the capital of the Islamic Ottoman Empire, declared a jihad on the rule of Muslims by foreign infidels.

Turkey would attack the Russians in the Caucasus and assault the British in Egypt and Suez, hoping to raise a popular rebellion and sever Britain's lifeline to its empire through the Suez Canal (and also to secure the recovery of Egypt as a subject territory of the Ottoman Empire). German diplomatic, military, sabotage and espionage teams were to be infiltrated into Persia and Afghanistan.[14]

Arthur Zimmermann, Undersecretary for Foreign Affairs in Berlin, was in overall charge of planning for jihad in the east – the so-called Zimmermann Plan. He chose a fit, young, brash German Foreign Office staff member and intelligence officer, Wilhelm Wassmuss, to lead a team whose job it would be to stir up anti-British rebellion, first in Persia and then in Afghanistan.

No sooner had Wassmuss arrived in Persia than his plans started to go awry. He fell out with his colleagues and abandoned them, starting his own guerrilla war against the British in Persia. He knew local languages and some of the tribes.[15] Wassmuss's campaign almost came to an early end in March 1915 when he was captured by British-funded local forces near Bushire. However, he escaped and for the rest of the war caused minor damage to British interests, raided British-owned banks, committed acts of sabotage and even held a few British citizens as hostages.

When he fled from capture in Bushire, Wassmuss left behind two German companions, all their arms and ammunition, quantities of propaganda material (aimed at stirring up revolt in India) and various papers. These documents were sent back to India House in London and found their way into a basement storeroom. The legend, put about by Hall, is that he had a chance meeting with a young naval officer, not long back from Persia, who recounted various daring ventures, including the story of Wassmuss's capture and his escape.

Hall's attention was captured by the mention of the documents.[16] He made enquiries as to their whereabouts. When the documents were brought to his office ('within hours'), it was discovered – according to Hall – that they included a copy of a German diplomatic code book known as '13040' (later to become a key to the uncovering of the Zimmermann Telegram – see Chapters 16–18). However, the claim is disinformation, as we shall see.

A British civil servant, C.J. Edmonds, based in Persia at the time, later wrote an article entitled 'The Persian Gulf Prelude to the Zimmermann Telegram', which appeared in the *Journal of the Royal Central Asian Society* in 1960. According to this account, shortly after Wassmuss's escape, the German Consul in Bushire was arrested by British troops. 'Two dictionary ciphers' were discovered 'wrapped up in several pairs of long woollen underpants'.[17] Some writers have suggested that Wassmuss deposited his code book(s) with the consul before his arrest. Others point to the repeated concern that Wassmuss expressed for his lost papers. Support for the Wassmuss connection comes from the diary of one of his abandoned colleagues, Dr Oskar von Niedermayer. He claimed that 'after Wassmuss's narrow escape from capture the British had found his baggage ... all his papers, including his code'.[18]

Importantly for the later story of the Zimmermann Telegram, historians now accept that the two code books captured from the German Consul in Bushire were known as '89734' and '3512', and came from a quite different 'family' of codes to '13040'.[19] Whatever the precise details, Denniston has left us with the brief comment, 'One day in April [1915, Hall] produced a fresh line of goods – treasure trove in Persia it was said'.[20] Certainly Hall admitted to having invented the capture of the 13040 code book as a cover story when these matters were first made public after the war (as a result of claims in 1926 made in US courts for damages caused by German saboteurs in the United States).

The Wassmuss story is one of several false leads laid down by Hall about the Zimmermann Telegram.[21] The 3512 code book was used by German consuls in the Ottoman Empire and by a key figure in German intrigues in Persia, Niedermayer, 'whose telegraphic communications from Tehran were now regularly intercepted by British intelligence'.[22]

★★★

George Young was a Foreign Office diplomat and an expert on the Near East, who was serving in Lisbon when the war started. He resigned his post to seek 'active employment' and came to the notice of Hall. He was seconded to Room 40. Young, however, was unhappy to have an office job and still hankered after action. He left Room 40 in 1917, gaining a commission in the Royal Marines.[23] In between, he made a major contribution to Room 40's codebreaking work.

A letter dated 28 September 1916 from the Admiralty to Ewing informed him that 'Their Lordships' approved the:

> ... proposal that Mr George Young ... should be definitely reorganised as supervising under you the branch of your special work dealt with in Room 47 OB, together with the Ladies Section. ... The work of this Section should be, as is the case of Room 40, be kept in touch with the Intelligence and Operations divisions, and the DID [director of naval intelligence] is to be consulted with regard to it in the same manner as hitherto. The intelligence division is to continue to be the connecting link between this Section and the Foreign Office.[24]

Young recalled that in accord with these instructions:

> Sir Alfred Ewing gave me leave to organise the political work as a separate
> branch ... the results subsequently reached in the political region were very
> largely made possible by the partial separation from the naval work.[25]

Hall's intrusion into diplomatic codebreaking has been presented as an uninvited one into affairs that were properly the concern of the Foreign Office.
But Hall was specifically appointed as the connecting link between the new
diplomatic section and the Foreign Office. He certainly took charge of the
new 'Research Section', edging it away from Ewing's purview.

The two men did not get on. Oliver later recalled that Hall 'was always
trying to boss Sir A. Ewing and he would not put up with it, he was not
that sort of man, and when he [joined] the First Lord had promised him a
free hand.'[26]

Young recorded that it was only when a separate system of 'files, registra-
tions and indexes etc' for diplomatic work was set up that real progress began
to be made. The new section consisted of Young, Benjamin Faudel-Phillips,
Nigel de Grey (a recruit from the world of publishing) and Montgomery (the
belligerent Ulster clergyman).

Faudel-Philips was a 'city' man with family connections to London's
financial centre. Both his father and his grandfather had been a Lord Mayor
of London and that became his nickname. De Grey had studied languages
and tried to join the Foreign Office as a diplomat. Although his German
and French were good, he did less well in Italian and was turned down. In
August 1915, he joined the Royal Naval Volunteer Reserve (RNVR) and
was appointed as an observer in the Royal Naval Air Service in Belgium,
ending up in Room 40. Hall thought highly of him and put him in the
Research Section.

We have already met Montgomery as antagonist of Herbert Morrah over
the latter's support for Home Rule in his native Ireland. Montgomery at one
stage told Hall, 'He was not one of those [clergymen] who believed that clerics should not take part in war and that his only regret was that he could not
get to sea'.[27]

The Research Section – also known as the diplomatic or the political
section or Room 45 – started life in possession of the VB, along with
knowledge of the cipher systems used with it and the two German Foreign
Office diplomatic code books: 89734 and 3512, captured – somehow or
other – in Persia. These two code books turned out to be very similar

to one another. They were, in fact, reshufflings of the same sets of printed pages.

Within the code books, the individual numerical code words were made up from the three-figure page number and a two-figure page entry number (with 100 entries on each page). The pages were printed in double-sided pairs, so that there were four pages on a single sheet. The order of the sheets could be changed (i.e. being given a new page number), but the entries on each sheet stayed the same. It was then discovered that several other code books were also reshufflings of the same sets of pages. This meant that, when a new code in this family was introduced, and once one code word had been worked out, it revealed the meaning of all the other code words on the same sheet – some 400 meanings in all.

As a British Intelligence report observed:

> A large quantity of very secret negotiations travelled in codebooks easy to reconstruct. [Details about the] methods of cyphering or 'keying' these books were sent in telegrams that at some stage passed over British wires and were easily decipherable. Nor was it until 1918 that the wireless messages to Madrid proved any serious difficulty to anyone who cared to read them.[28]

According to Young:

> These gave immediate admission to the very secret wireless correspondence between the [German Navy ministry] and the Madrid naval attaché, the semi-secret wireless correspondence between Berlin Foreign Office and Madrid and Lisbon and occasionally North and South America. ... [the VB was] an integral and indispensable part of the general diplomatic correspondence with Madrid. From the beginning it has been in the hands of Lieutenant Faudel-Philips who can best report on its technique of 'sliders' and 'keys' [see Chapter 7] and on the knock-outs it has administered to various German coups.

Unfortunately, as far as is known, Faudel-Philips left no such account.

Solving the cipher keys revealed a significant amount of intelligence about German activities in the Middle East, such as details of strategic agreements between Germany and Turkey, approaches to the Afghan Government, and the hoped-for uprising in Persia. From then on, 'German political and military dispositions both Persian and Afghan were known with a few hours in London'.[29]

Frank Birch, in a humorous account of Room 40, *Alice in ID25*, calls Room 45 the 'Mansion House' after the Lord Mayor's grand residence, and describes the work of the section as 'the Lord Mayor's Show'. Dillwyn Knox contributed a short verse about the section:

> It is commonly thought we derive
> Great blessings from Room 45
> Our courtly Lord Mayor,
> By his party there,
> Has rescued the Empire alive.[30]

★★★

Room 40's naval section found itself stretched in this period. Early in 1916, the AFB (*Allgemeines Funkspruchbuch* or 'General Wireless Code Book'), replaced the HVB. However, the expert cryptographers knew enough about the old code book and German telegraphic habits that they could start to 'reconstruct' the new book from scratch. All the same, this took time and for a while messages were only partially decipherable.

A copy of the code book was eventually recovered from the crashed Zeppelin L-32 on 27 September 1916. Room 40 could then decode entire messages again. Zeppelins were a handy source of cipher keys too, with ciphers being recovered from L-32 on 24 September 1916 and L-48 on 17 June 1917.[31] U-boats also provided useful material, such as U-109 in 1918.[32]

A major change occurred in May 1917 when the FFB (*Flottenfunkspruchbuch* or 'Fleet Wireless Code Book') replaced the main naval signal book, the SKM. The FFB was a two-part code, the only one introduced by the German Imperial Navy during the war.

The introduction of the new code book was accompanied by the German Navy's first complete change of call signs, the introduction of daily key changes and a new system of map grid squares 'disguised by a transposition code'. However, by then Room 40's knowledge again gave it the means to break the new code book, the daily keys and so on, despite the difficulties of breaking a two-part code book. Room 40's output in terms of naval intercepts reached its peak in the second half of 1917 – in the months after the new code book and security measures had been introduced.

A number of factors helped the reconstruction of the new code book from scratch, such as the fact that submarines were compelled to use 'spelling-group' code words to spell out the names of steamers they sank and whose names had not got a specific code word – and, of course, the British knew which vessels had been sunk, thus giving reliable 'cribs'.

The FFB was also compromised by uncoordinated wireless operations. The old SKM code book was kept in operation in the Baltic, while the new FFB book was used in the North Sea. Another factor helping to beak the FFB was that it had far too many entries, so only a few were used. When key-finder found the first two numbers in a cipher they could easily guess the last one (in the case of FFB, which had three-number code words). 'It was indeed on this principle alone that the keys on the successor to the SKM, the FFB were originally solved.'[33] The key used for ciphering the code was first known as Gamma Alpha, and from 21 April 1918 as Gamma F.

Intercepts also showed Room 40 that some British naval codes were being broken by the German Navy at its codebreaking unit at Neumünster. However, the intercepts of the German messages confirmed that Room 40's activities remained unknown to the Germans. As a British Intelligence report noted:

> The very serious error was made by the German authorities of using and publishing freely to the fleet by wireless signals the results of Neumünster's researches. Thus the English and Russian authorities could often be aware of the failure of their efforts to secure secrecy by the use of a code. The climax was reached in 1917 when decypherings of the English [naval] code were sent unencyphered alongside the equivalent [code word] in the German codebook which had then only lately come into force: Not only was it evident to the English authorities that great progress had been made in the decypherment of one of their codes, but also the sense of certain yet unresolved meanings of German codewords could be ascertained on this side merely by looking them up in an English decode-book. The apparent failure on the English side to act on intelligence received must have lulled the German Admiralty into a false sense of security.[34]

★★★

By accident, Room 40's and MI1(b)'s diplomatic work meshed quite well at this stage and there was little overlap. This was fortunate, as there was still little communication between them, let alone co-operation. However, as MI1(b) had concentrated on cables – and as Germany was largely cut off from the cable network – it was only picking up the traffic of neutrals. Given its experience with German naval intercepts, Room 40 came to handle the German traffic that did manage to leak out to the wider world, whether by cable or wireless.

We will look at the fruits of this naval and military foray into the world of diplomatic surveillance in subsequent chapters. At this stage, it must have appeared to the codebreakers that they had Germany well penned in. It was cut off from the world's cable network and all its wireless transmissions could be intercepted and, by and large, decoded. But this complacent attitude was to be shaken by the discovery of two separate channels of communication that Germany had found to circumvent Britain's communications stranglehold.

From the beginning of the war, the Swedish Government allowed the German Foreign Office to send messages between Stockholm and Washington bundled up with Swedish diplomatic traffic. This leak was reported to the British Foreign Office in May 1915 and British diplomats then delivered a protest to Sweden. The Swedish Government was appropriately embarrassed and promised that no more German messages would be sent on the Stockholm to Washington route. They did not add that instead the German messages would be sent to Stockholm and then on to Buenos Aires for forwarding to Washington (and by reversing the route for return traffic). So, the British Foreign Office's reaction in complaining to Sweden had simply shifted the link out of sight, not stopped it from working.

Exactly what happened between May 1915 and September 1916 is unknown, but for all that time Germany was sending its messages over the Swedish routing, according to the standard story, without anyone being alerted to the fact. In September, Room 40 received an intercepted coded letter (probably seized during a search made by a blockade-enforcing ship) sent from the German Minister in Mexico to the German Chancellor Bethmann-Hollweg, recommending that the Swedish Chargé d'Affaires in Mexico City should be awarded a German honour. 'He arranges the conditions for the official telegraphic traffic with your Excellency. In this connection he is obliged every time, often late at night, personally to go to the telegraph office to hand in the [German] dispatches', the German minister explained.[35]

Hall later recalled:

> It was clear that steps would have to be taken to have all Swedish Foreign Office cipher telegrams brought to us for examination … In many cases it was found that after a few Swedish [code words], our old friend [German diplomatic code book] 13040 would appear. Our excitement, moreover, may be imagined when through this means we discovered the route by

which Bernstorff [the German Ambassador in Washington) was communicating with his government ... In this way we found ourselves in
full possession ... of the enemy's every move in the diplomatic game of
the moment.[36]

The route was dubbed the 'Swedish Roundabout'. This time, there was no
protest. Hall was firmly of the view that a communications link, once uncovered, should not be broken but observed. 'Once across it, let it run,' he said.[37]
Thus, if this account is correct, from 14 September 1916, Germany's supposedly secret communications link was exposed to Room 40's scrutiny.

One of the new recruits, de Grey, who had been found to have a 'great
talent' for cryptography, was put on Research Section work looking at
messages sent in code 13040 that had been accumulating.[38] De Grey soon
reconstructed enough of the code book for the general sense of messages to
be clear. Soon after the Swedish Roundabout had been uncovered, intercepts
were supplying good diplomatic intelligence, also about purchases of goods
and setting up lines of credit to pay for them.[39] Hall recalled, 'We knew from
the [German] ambassador's admirably clear dispatches the points of greatest
importance in [President] Wilson's fluctuating policy.'[40]

The German Ambassador in Washington found the 'circuitous route ...
extremely slow', but it worked after a fashion.[41] Certainly, Sir Roger Casement,
the Irish nationalist who went to Germany in 1914 to gain German help for
an Irish uprising (see Chapter 15), had little problem getting messages back
and forth to Washington, even if they took a long time. A colleague of his
wrote on 12 November 1915:

Through the courtesy and goodwill of the German Embassy in America, we
have, since the outbreak of the war, been able to keep up unrestricted communication with Sir Roger Casement [in Germany], though the process is
necessarily and regrettably very slow, and I have during all that time been
able to hand to Colonel von Papen, the Military Attaché, such communications and suggestions as we wished to reach the German Government.[42]

Room 40 also uncovered (perhaps from intelligence picked up by British
agents in the United States or prompted by the discovery of the Swedish leaks
to take a closer look at other neutral cables) that Germany had yet another
hidden outlet. This time it was with the help of the United States – and on the
orders of President Wilson. The German Foreign Office would take telegrams
to the US embassy in Berlin, from where they would be transmitted to the

State Department in Washington – via Copenhagen, London and the transatlantic cables – before being handed over to the German Embassy. According to the former official historian at GCHQ:

> This practice is generally considered to have begun on 2 June 1915 when the German ambassador in Washington, Count von Bernstorff, agreed it with President Wilson to facilitate negotiation during the crisis following the sinking of the *Lusitania* by a German submarine and it is not clear why MI1(b) had not already spotted it.[43]

When the furore over the liner receded in the spring of 1916, the link was temporarily closed and the speed of German communications between Washington and Berlin slowed down as the Swedish Roundabout had to be used again.

The US channel was again opened for German use in September 1916. Nigel de Grey wrote to Hall on 21 September:

> I append a list of Buenos Aires telegrams received giving the number of cablegrams between certain dates. May further search be made for these please. It is now abundantly clear that telegrams are passing to Washington not intercepted by us [as postal mail] and not transmitted via Buenos Aires [in the form of Swedish telegrams]. Neither can the telegrams omitted from our series be fitted into the wireless messages from Sayville or Tuckerton – their number is by no means large enough. I consider it likely that they are sent via the State Dept. and the USA Embassy and might consequently be interceptable [*sic*] there.[44]

A decrypt of an intercepted message from Gerard, the US Ambassador in Berlin, to the State Department in Washington revealed what was afoot. Wilson was at this point pursuing peace proposals and getting negative responses from the Allies. But in Germany he found an apparently more positive attitude. Gerard reported:

> Germany is anxious to make peace. I can state on the best authority that if the President [of the United States] will make an offer of mediation in general terms … that Germany will accept in general terms immediately and state her readiness to send delegates to a peace conference. Today [German Foreign Minister] von Jagow will ask me to forward a cipher message to Bernstorff [the German Ambassador in Washington] through the State

Dept. ... Of course the utmost secrecy is desirable for if any hint is given that the suggestion came from Berlin and not as the spontaneous act of the [US] President the whole matter will fail and be denied. I desire to know whether the message may be forwarded for delivery to Bernstorff.[45]

We will return to this subject in Chapter 16.

★★★

It was becoming increasingly obvious that Room 40 and MI1(b) needed to communicate more than they had done since the autumn of 1914. Some neutral cable messages contained information about matters discussed in German messages, so co-ordination was vital both to improve cryptographic success and to ensure the best evaluation of the intelligence uncovered. For example, Room 40 received letters and messages seized by the blockade-enforcing ships from neutral vessels that might reveal the names and addresses of agents or companies willing to supply goods in South America or the United States. It would be vital to work with MI1(b) to ensure that any cable telegrams between neutral countries sent to these addresses and companies were intercepted wherever possible.

In October 1916, Ewing effectively left Room 40 to become Principal of Edinburgh University. This was not his choice. He would have preferred to remain where he was, but the official view of his contribution had soured. As a post-war internal account put it, 'The officer in charge of Room 40 from October 1914 to [October 1916] was a civilian – Professor Ewing. He would not regard his section as part of the Intelligence Division and its work was severely handicapped in consequence.'[46] Having gained control over Room 45, the Research (i.e. political/diplomatic) Section of Room 40, Hall, seeing the potential more clearly than Ewing, became aggrieved at Ewing's lack of initiative.[47]

Nigel de Grey, who was to become a key figure in Room 40 (and at Bletchley Park in the Second World War), recalled that Hall mistrusted Ewing and 'made a compact with the "research party" that if ever we dug out anything of importance we were to take it direct to him without showing it to Ewing', whom he saw 'as a chatter-box (rightly)'.[48] Oliver recalled how the irritation that existed between Hall and Ewing eventually exploded into a row. Oliver and the Secretary to the Admiralty, Sir Graham Greene, held an enquiry and 'spent a long afternoon restoring peace'. The peace did not hold and in May 1916 Ewing was approached with the offer of the principalship of Edinburgh University.

This was a significant offer, the capstone to an outstanding academic career, and in normal circumstances he would have jumped at the opportunity. However, Ewing was reluctant to let go of his 'baby' and told the university that he was busy on 'secret war work' that he could not possibly afford to give up. In October 1916 the offer was repeated, this time in an interview with Balfour, then First Lord of Admiralty, who made it clear that Ewing was no longer needed full time in Room 40. This time, Ewing recognised that he was being sacked and accepted the job in Edinburgh. He was supposed to retain his title of Director of Naval Education and a supervisory role in Room 40, but this was a face-saving gesture.

When Hall was awarded a knighthood in October 1917, Ewing graciously wrote to him to say that he was:

> … glad to see that your work as Head of the Intelligence Division is receiving special recognition. Anyone who knows how good it has been will feel, as I do, that the recognition is well deserved. I hope that my baby prospers.[49]

It is no coincidence that shortly after Ewing departed, Room 40 and MI1(b) started to communicate again. In fact, Hall and Hay were already co-operating informally before Ewing left the Admiralty. The archives show, for example, that in August 1915 Hall gave MI1(b) information about a German cipher and in May 1916 he sent the Director of Military Intelligence translations of correspondence between the German Ambassador in Washington and the Chancellor Bethman Hollweg in Berlin.[50]

Hay respected Hall, realising that he was intent on exploiting interception for all its worth. Yet Hay, who was a man who liked to get his own way, also recognised that Hall had a streak of ruthlessness about him that he lacked. Hall would stop at nothing to achieve his tactical goals, such as deceiving and misinforming both the enemy and, if necessary, his colleagues. Hall delighted in subterfuge and sleight of hand in his dealings with the Germans, but he respected few rules at home either. All the same, he worked well with Hay, realising that gathering more intelligence was more important than inter-departmental rivalries. When MI1(b) moved to Cork Street in Piccadilly in mid-1917, Hay had a private telephone line installed to connect him with Hall's office at the Admiralty.

The archives contain some correspondence between the two units, with the earliest dating from 15 October 1916, discussing technical issues about Greek and Spanish code books. A letter sent in Ewing's name in September 1916, shortly before his departure, illustrates that he was being forced to

Geheim!

TITEL A 20

№ 151

1

Signalbuch

der

Kaiserlichen Marine.

(Entwurf.)

Herausgegeben vom Admiralstab der Marine.

Berlin 1913.

Title page of the *Signalbuch der Kaiserlichen Marine*, SKM, the main German naval codebook.
(National Archives)

Zahlen-Signal	Buchstaben-Signal	Bedeutung	Zahlen-Signal	Buchstaben-Signal	Bedeutung
527 96	C G M	Beobachtungsperſonal ＊＊	528 51	C I J	bergen ⸗ung [s. Sonnensegel, Torpedoſchutznetz]
97	C G N	Beobachtungspunkt	52	C I K	ift (ſind) geborgen
98	C G O	Beobachtungsſtand	53	C I L	was iſt geborgen (von)?
99	C G Ö	Beobachtungsſtand befindet ſich (auf, bei, in)	54	C I M	Bergerolle ＋
528 00	C G P	wo ift der Beobachtungsſtand?	55	C I N	Bergungsdampfer [s. Hilfe]
01	C G Q	Beobachtungsſtand zerſtören	56	C I O	Bergungsgeſellſchaft ＊
02	C G R	Beobachtungsſtation	57	C I Ö	Bergungsgeſellſchaft Neptun, Stockholm
03	C G S	Beobachtungsſtation errichten (auf, bei, in)	58	C I P	Switzers Bergungsunternehmen, Kopenhagen
04	C G T	feindl. Beobachtungsſtation (bei, in)	59	C I Q	Nordiſcher Bergungsverein, Hamburg
05	C G U	feindl. Beobachtungsſtation (bei, in) beſchießen	528 60	C I R	Bergwerk
			61	C I S	Bericht, berichten [s. Havarie]
06	C G ü	feindl. Beobachtungsſtation (bei, in) zerſtören	62	C I T	Bericht abſenden (an)
			63	C I U	amtlicher Bericht
07	C G V	Beobachtungsſtation meldet	64	C I ü	authentiſcher Bericht
08	C G W	Beobachtungsübung	65	C I V	Bericht einreichen (über)
09	C G X	Beobachtungsuhr	66	C I W	eingehenden Bericht einreichen (über)
528 10	C G Y	beordern (für, nach), Beorderung	67	C I X	fälligen Bericht einreichen (über)
11	C G Z	Beplattung	68	C I Y	kurzen Bericht einreichen (über)
12	C G α	Beplattung iſt unverſehrt	69	C I Z	verantwortlichen Bericht einreichen (über)
13	C G γ	Beplattung iſt weggeriſſen (durch)	528 70	C I α	Bericht erſtatten (über)
14	C H A	bequem ⸗lichkeit	71	C I γ	mündlicher Bericht
15	C H Ä	beraten ⸗ung	72	C J A	ſchriftlich berichten (über)
16	C H B	Beratung abhalten (über)	73	C J Ä	fortlaufend ſchriftlich berichten über die Lage (in)
17	C H D	nach eingehender Beratung			
18	C H E	zur Beratung	74	C J B	telegraphiſch berichten (über)
19	C H F	berauben ⸗ung	75	C J D	fortlaufend telegraphiſch berichten über die Lage (in)
528 20	C H G	berechnen ⸗ung			
21	C H Ï	berechtigen ⸗ung (zu)	76	C J E	Berichterſtatter (B. E.) (Nr. n in) [s. Hauptberichterstatter]
22	C H J	berechtigt			
23	C H K	Bereich [s. Station]	77	C J F	B. E. i. V. M. = (B. E. [V. M.]) (Nr. n) in
24	C H L	außer Bereich			
25	C H M	außer Bereich der Geſchütze	78	C J G	B. E. (B.E.[V.M.]) (Nr.n) abweſend (von, ſeit)
26	C H N	im Bereich			
27	C H O	im Bereich der Geſchütze	79	C J H	Adreſſe des B. E. (B. E. [V. M.]) (Nr. n) (in)
28	C H Ö	bereit (zu)			
29	C H P	ſich bereit halten (zu) [s. Abgabe, Abreise, Arbeiter usw.]	528 80	C J Ï	B. E. (B.E. [V.M.]) (Nr.n) (in) hat Amt niedergelegt, (wegen, weil)
528 30	C H Q	ſich bereit machen (zu)	81	C J K	nach Angabe des B. E. (B. E. [V. M.]) (Nr. n) (in)
31	C H R	bereit ſein (zu)			
32	C H S	wann können Sie bereit ſein (für, zum)?	82	C J L	B. E. (B.E. [V. M.]) (Nr. n) (in) iſt angewieſen (zu)
33	C H T	bereiten ⸗ung			
34	C H U	bereits	83	C J M	B. E. (B.E. [V. M.]) (Nr. n) (in) iſt ausgefallen
35	C H ü	Bereitſchaft			
36	C H V	1. Bereitſchaft	84	C J N	(weitere) Auskunft durch B. E. (B. E. [V. M.]) (in)
37	C H W	2. Bereitſchaft			
38	C H X	3. Bereitſchaft	85	C J O	B. E. (B.E. [V. M.]) (Nr. n) (in) benachrichtigen (daß, von)
39	C H Y	in Bereitſchaft ＊			
528 40	C H Z	Bereitſchaftsmunition	86	C J Ö	habe B. E. (B.E. [V. M.]) (Nr.n) (in) benachrichtigt (daß, von)
41	C H α	Bereitſchaftsmunition an die Geſchütze mannen	87	C J P	Briefadreſſe des B.E. (B.E.[V.M.]) (Nr. n) (in)
42	C H γ	Bereitſchaftsſtellung	88	C J Q	Briefadreſſe des B.E. (B.E. [V. M.]) (Nr. n) (in) iſt geändert u. lautet
43	C I A	bereitſtellen (für, zu)			
44	C I Ä	bereitwillig ⸗keit	89	C J R	folgendes iſt Briefadr. eines neuen B.E. (in) (Name bzw. Deckname, Ort, Straße uſw.)
45	C I B	bereuen			
46	C I D	Berg ⸗ig			
47	C I E	＊ verſchärfte Bereitſchaft			
48	C I F	＊ gewöhnliche Bereitſchaft	528 90	C J S	＋ Bergungsarbeit
49	C I G	＊＊ Beobachtungsposten	91	C J T	＊ Bergungsverſuch
528 50	C I H		528 92	C J U	

30＊

Sample page from the SKM. Example: CGR is the codeword for *Beobachtungsstation* (observation station). (National Archives)

Time of Origin.	MESSAGE.
113	From X haven 1.35 a.m. Aug. 4 S. from Berlin No. 15 to Cruiser Goeben. Original cipher text. | Duigarbel velocisla 51 essugedal eyefcamics coiffezore komma borghigand borghaoimen gohicibies ofluyevele essaoozubo demptigudi Deciphered :- No 51. August 3rd Alliance concluded with Turkey, Goeben (and) Breslau to proceed immediately to Constantinople. Acknowledge. From Admiralty — staff of the navy.
114	From Berlin Aug. 4 12.25 p.m. to "Eber Lüderitzbucht No. 15 3rd August. From the Admiralty Staff of the navy. Attitude of Great Britain still hesitating. Nevertheless great caution is called for. Acknowledge.

Intercepted and decoded message, recorded by Room 40 in a log book, on 4 August 1914, instructing the German warships *Goeben* and *Breslau* to head for Constantinople. Unusually the record includes the original German cipher text (see Chapter 7). A second decoded message informs German ship commanders that Britain was still undecided about whether to declare war, adding, 'Nevertheless great caution is called for'. (National Archives)

00	Gniben	50	gorod
01	gno	51	Gorontalo (Celebes)
02	gns	52	gos
03	gnu	53	Gosport (Engl.)
04	gny	54	Gosport (Virginia)
05	go	55	got
06	Goa	56	Gotha
07	god	57	Gothenburg
08	Godavari	58	Gothenburg Sund
09	Godnatt	59	Gotland I. (Schwed.)
10	Godrevy Id.	60	Goto In.
11	Godrevy Head	61	Gotska-Sandö In.
12	goe	62	gou
13	Goedereede I. (Holld.)	63	Gough I.
14	Goeland	64	Gourock
15	Goeree I. (Holld.)	65	Goury (Frkr.)
16	Goeren Seegatt	66	gov
17	gog	67	Govens, St. —, Head (Engl.)
18	Gogo I.	68	govia
19	gol	69	gow
20	Goldküste	70	Gozo I. (Malta)
21	Goldnes Horn	71	Gozo I. (Candia)
22	Goletta	72	gr
23	golf	73	gra
24	Golfo nuevo (Patag.)	74	Graadyb
25	Golfstrom	75	Grabow
26	gom	76	grac
27	Gomani B. (O.-Afr.)	77	Gracias à Dios K.
28	Gomera I. (Canarische In.)	78	Graciosa B.
29	gon	79	Graciosa I. (Azoren)
30	gona	80	grae
31	Gonaives (Haiti)	81	Graesholm I.
32	Gonave In. (Port-au-Prince)	82	Grafton I. (S.-Am.)
33	gonia	83	Grähara
34	good	84	Grain I.
35	Goodwin Sds.	85	gram
36	Goodwin, East —	86	Grämsay I.
37	Goodwin, North —	87	gran
38	Goole	88	Gran
39	goon	89	Granada (Niagara)
40	goos	90	Granada (Span.)
41	gor	91	grand
42	gör	92	Grandcamp
43	Gorda Sound (W.-Ind.)	93	grande
44	gordon	94	Grande, Porto —
45	Gore B.	95	
46	Gorée (Senegal)	96	
47	Gorey	97	
48	Gorgona (Panama-Kan.)	98	
49	Gorinchem	99	

Sample page from the *Verkehrsbuch* codebook used by the German Navy and diplomatic service. Example: 15235 (i.e. page number 152 and entry number 35) is the codeword for *Goodwin Sds* (Goodwin Sands). (National Archives)

Admiralty Building, London. (Author's collection)

„Blücher" nach siegreicher Seeschlacht auf der Doggerbank 24.1.16.

W. Kruger, Rüstrieg..

Sinking of the German warship *Blücher* during the Battle of Dogger Bank in the North Sea, 24 January 1915. (Public domain, author's collection)

Guerre 1914-15... LES ALLIÉS EN ORIENT
SEL-DUL-BARR - Bombardement du 15
Juin 1915. Au premier plan le poste de T. S F.
63me Série

War 1914-15 .. THE ALLIES IN ORIENT
SED-DUL-BAHR — Bombardment of
June 15th 1915. In the foreground a wireless Post
Visé, Paris No 1317

British Army field wireless station in the Dardanelles. (Public domain, author's collection)

THE END OF THE "BABY-KILLER."

British propaganda poster about the Zeppelin bombing raids on Britain. Room 40's wireless interception service was a major tool for countering the air raids: 'End of the Baby Killer.' (Public domain, author's collection)

Wireless operator receiving a message on board a Royal Navy warship. (Public domain, author's collection)

Admiral Jellicoe, Commander of the Royal Navy's Grand Fleet during the Battle of Jutland, North Sea, 1916. (Public domain, author's collection)

overcome his antipathy to co-operation by the needs of his staff. 'Enclosed is an example of a kind of message we occasionally get. It looks like it might be giving a bearing from a Directional station. There are no calls. Do you recognise it as military?' he asked MI1(b).[51]

Some letters to and from Denniston and Lord Lytton in Room 40 to Crocker in MI1(b) illustrate the intensifying level of co-operation. In December 1916, Denniston wrote, 'I am very glad this opportunity of avoiding duplication of work has arisen and hope it may be carried through successfully.' On 13 February 1917, he told Crocker:

> Herewith some more Spanish work and one small Chi [a type of military cipher message]. Touching the Turkish question I wonder if Strachey would like to see some intercepts of a year ago when Constantinople and Berlin were only joined by W/T [wireless telegraphy]. As there is now an expert in this language something might in time be made of them which would throw light on subsequent events.[52]

On 21 March Crocker wrote to Lytton:

> Many thanks for the two telegrams you have just sent over. I suggest that the missing words in the second telegram are 'three hundred'. Very few messages in this code are received here but I will see that copies of everything I get are sent over to you.

On 24 March Denniston was informed:

> I have complained to the Censors about the gaps in the serial numbers of the Chilean telegrams and hope they will retrieve those missing. The Greek telegrams you kindly sent over are proving most useful in providing examples of some of the rarer varieties. I am sending you all the Bulgarian stuff we have … With regard to the Swedish telegrams, we are not entirely convinced there is really more than one code. When we get a little bit further I will let you know.[53]

There were still tensions, but the two teams were able to get together to ensure that they complemented each other rather than engaging unaware on the same codes and ciphers.

The year of 1917 saw a dramatic expansion of MI1(b). Codes were broken belonging to Argentina, Brazil, Denmark, Italy, Japan, Netherlands, Norway,

Persia, Sweden, Uruguay and the Vatican. By the end of 1917, forty-three members of staff out of a total head count of fifty worked on diplomatic codes. Room 40 also expanded its Research Section, but to no more than ten people.

Once the United States joined the war, there was less diplomatic interception done by Room 40. Only the Berlin–Madrid wireless link and German cable messages to South America then remained a fruitful source of diplomatic traffic for Room 40.

The Foreign Office also began to appreciate the sort of intelligence it was receiving from intercepts. A letter to the War Office of 23 August 1917 noted:

> It would be of the greatest use if we could collect gradually the personal factors of Allied and Neutral Diplomatists all over the world, especially of course of Ambassadors, Ministers and Chargé d'Affaires. Do you think it would be possible to initiate the collection of such exceedingly valuable information?[54]

Diplomatic interception was establishing itself as a central part of the war effort, just as had already happened with military and naval interception.

13

Inside Room 40

A visitor entering the rooms grouped around [Blinker Hall's] office at the Admiralty or being granted the rare privilege of passing through the door marked 'No admittance' which led to the cluster of rooms in the old building, known as Room 40, was at once struck by a change of atmosphere. On his way through the long, bleak corridors he had passed some elderly messengers, leisurely delivering papers to rooms from which there came no sound but the scratching of pens, and had caught a glimpse of some solemn-looking officers, talking in whispers, and he now found himself in an atmosphere vibrating with excitement, expectation, urgency, friendship, and high spirits … There was much to astonish a visitor to those rooms, and some excuse for his believing that he was a victim of hoax. In Room 40 he would be introduced to a number of officers in RNVR [Royal Naval Volunteer Reserve] uniform, and some, over military age, not in uniform, and told that in real life they were Fellows of Colleges at Oxford and Cambridge, Professors with a galaxy of academic distinctions, a Director of the Bank of England, a famous music critic, a well-known actor, a publisher, an ex-President of the Oxford Union, an art expert, a world-famous dress-designer. Perhaps his greatest surprise would be when he was introduced to a Professor of Divinity and a Roman Catholic priest in clerical garb … If he was lucky, Hall himself, would come in like a tornado, and in his inimitable staccato way tell his staff, eagerly awaiting his return, what he had been doing … A visitor entering the watchkeeper's room, in 1916, about 11.30 a.m., would either have seen three or four men, very tired and drawn, who had for the last eight hours been straining their brains to discover the cypher key, which changed a midnight, and had been defeated, or he would have seen these same men looking very cheerful and waiting to tell their reliefs, with a little pardonable pride, that they had nothing to worry about for the rest of the day. If he had entered one of the adjacent rooms, occupied by the men wrestling with unbroken cyphers, he would have seen two or three sphinx-like figures, who had perhaps been torturing the medley of figures or letters in front of them for several months, but had never relaxed their efforts, though it had often seemed that no progress was possible.[1]

This account of an imaginary visitor's likely reaction on entering Room 40 was written by Captain William 'Bubbles' James in his biography of Blinker Hall. James took over from Captain Herbert Hope as head of Room 40's naval section in the spring of 1917. Perhaps James is recalling his own reactions when he first went to Room 40 to be initiated in what his predecessor called the 'Holy of Holies'. There were few visitors to Room 40 who were not already intimately connected with it. So, it seems a fairly inappropriate device for James to deploy to describe Room 40 in his biography of Hall, his old boss and hero.

Interestingly, the other account of inside Room 40, written by Frank Birch, is also set around the same device. This time, the visitor is not male, as James assumes his imaginary visitor would be, but a young girl. She ends up in Room 40 by some fantastic imaginings and proceeds to meet the weird and wonderful denizens of the cryptanalytic world. Is it coincidence that both writers, in telling us about a place that was carefully guarded to prevent visitors getting inside, should choose this narrative device? Does it tell us something about a suppressed desire to tell the world about the secret?

For the insiders, such accounts are evocative of what for them was a strange interlude in their normal academic or business lives. However, as one code-breaker noted, 'So much is missing. Of the hurried consultations, the notes or slips of paper, the one hundred little details that are so vital to [the secret] side of this subject, there remains no trace.'[2]

Birch's privately published booklet is entitled *Alice in ID 25*[3] and tells the story of a young girl walking along Whitehall with her nurse, when a slip of paper falls from an upper window to land at her feet. She picks it up and starts to read it: 'Ballybunnion – Short begins – vd – sn – dd – um – um – v.v.v. – depresses key – fierce x's and wipers'. As she reads the text, she starts to feel herself getting smaller and smaller, then a White Rabbit appears dressed in:

… Sunday best – spats, spectacles and a little back coat, and he kept doing up and undoing its buttons with nervousness. 'Dear me, dear me' Alice heard him say as he passed her, 'it's past ten. I shall be late for the DIND'.

Of course, 'DIND' is a code word standing for Director of Naval Intelligence Division, Blinker Hall. The White Rabbit may represent Frank Adcock, a Cambridge ancient historian who played a significant role in both the First and Second World Wars identifying suitable academic recruits for Room 40 and, twenty-five years later, for Bletchley Park (where he recommended, among others, Alan Turing).

Alice follows the White Rabbit hoping to see this DIND, only to fall into a hole, and she tumbles for some time down a twisting and turning tube before dropping into 'a sort of cage of golden wire'. She looks around and sees a large room full of big creatures, all fast asleep. Someone picks her up and asks where she came from and what was her 'time-group', to which she has no answer. The creature says, in that case she must be either 'N.S.L. or Baltic'. At that, everyone in the room wakes up and 'howled in chorus, "We *don't* do Baltic. We *won't* do Baltic. We *have* never done Baltic. It's a tradition".'

Birch was in charge of the Baltic Section from 1917 and is reflecting the attitudes he met when it suggested mid-war that Room 40 should tackle intercepted messages from the Baltic, which had been previously discarded as unimportant. In fact, decryption of messages from the Baltic proved to be of use in a number of ways (such as when new code books were used elsewhere in parallel with old ones in the Baltic).

Clearly Birch has exaggerated for comic effect. Also, his pen portrays only a handful of the inhabitants of Room 40. It seems likely that he only wrote about people who he was sure would not be upset by his caricatures. Two of those mentioned by name in *Alice in ID25*, Morrah and Knox, certainly contributed to the project. As long as we allow for a suitable degree of over-egging of the pudding by Birch, the booklet surely does give us a glimpse of some of the characters who made up Room 40.

No doubt there are many in-jokes which pass over our heads. The tea party of the better-known Alice story is replaced by a 'key party', and when a key arrives some of the staff jump up and demand their beds because 'they go to bed for the next 48 hours'. No doubt those who lived through it would know what little joke is here. 'The Little Man' is probably Denniston, who was indeed short of stature; the Dormouse may be Nigel de Grey; Grumbling Willow could be historian Leonard Willoughby; and the Chief Clerk is probably William F. Clarke. As Alice wanders around, one creature she meets is described as 'like something between a Labour Member [of Parliament] and Sir Frances Drake'. He kept on turning out his pockets, poking into dark corners and counting beds. He finds that one is missing. Here, it is difficult to know who this is or what the joke is.

Captain William 'Bubbles' James makes several non-appearances in *Alice in ID 25*. Quite a few times Alice asks questions to which she is told she will have to ask James, whose 'hours are 7 to 10 and 10 to 7', yet he is apparently never there. It transpires that he is actually present from seven minutes to ten until ten in the morning and from ten minutes to seven until seven in the evening. The joke here is that James did not spend too much time at his desk in Room 40, in contrast to his predecessor, Captain Hope. The creature poking into dark corners and counting beds underlines the point by telling Alice, 'Nice chap, Captain James, knows 'is place. Mind you, I '*ave* known owners as couldn't leave you alone, but 'e ain't there more 'n' 'e's wanted. 'E leaves it to me.'

James's 'Bubbles' nickname was due to a portrait of him as a baby, blowing bubbles, which was used for advertising Pears soap. He was cast in a very different mould from Hope and set about the job in his own fashion, putting the eccentric academics and wealthy gentlemen into naval uniforms – sometimes to almost comic effect, as in the case of the classically unmilitary body and demeanour of Dillwyn Knox.

James saw his task as more an administrative one than being part of the team analysing the decodes. For this sort of task, James had no feel. Hope's paternalism was swept overboard and replaced by a 'brisk and breezy quarterdeck manner'. The term 'breezy' is indeed the most common description of James's approach to his colleagues and is clearly a euphemism. His first few weeks left not a few of Room 40's cryptographers feeling a little bruised.

If it took time for the codebreakers to adjust to the new captain of their ship, it also took James a while to get used to his most unusual of naval crews. And even if James did not become part of the team working on the decrypts, he did give the unit more weight when it came to putting their views to the naval staff as he was recognised as a good seaman, one who might make the senior ranks.

Under James, Room 40 gradually adopted more responsibilities. Staff numbers grew in 1916 and 1917 as the war effort on both sides was intensified. Room 40 started its transformation under the leadership of blustery Blinker Hall and breezy Bubbles James from a cryptanalytic bureau into an intelligence centre.

Alfred Dillwyn (Dilly) Knox, who appears often in Birch's tale, was widely said to be the most gifted of Room 40's codebreakers. Birch had first met Dilly in 1910 when they were both at Cambridge (where John Maynard Keynes was also a friend of Dilly's). Dilly is teased unmercifully in Birch's tale, but he must have enjoyed it as he contributed the verses that are included in the booklet.

He was the second oldest of four brothers, all of whom went on to become well known in their own fields (their two sisters, however, are less famous). One brother, Ronnie, also became a codebreaker, joining Room 40 briefly. After the war, he became a Catholic priest and, as Monsignor Ronald Knox, was renowned in religious circles as a writer on Catholicism and as translator of the New Testament. Wilfred was an Anglo-Catholic priest and a social worker in the East End of London. Edmund, the oldest of the four, became the editor of *Punch*. The boys' father had been Bishop of Manchester, but Dillwyn became an atheist.

In 1916, when he joined the staff of Room 40, Dilly was a lanky, socially awkward intellectual with an interest in some of the more obscure aspects of ancient languages and was a true eccentric. Birch describes him in *Alice in ID 25* as 'Dilly the Dodo'. Alice, he writes:

> … thought he was the queerest bird she ever had seen. He was so long and lean, and he had outgrown his clothes, and his face was like a pang of hunger. … Alice thought him a very hard man to please … he handed her a sheet of very dirty paper on which a spider with inky feet appeared to have been crawling … [Dilly the Dodo] began fumbling in his pockets. 'What's the matter?', asked Alice. 'I've lost my spectacles', cried the Dodo angrily, as he turned up the chairs and table. 'Where are my spectacles?' and he glared angrily at the secretary. 'I expect they are in *that*', jerked the secretary pointing to a tobacco-pouch on the table.

Dilly the Dodo, it turns out, keeps his glasses in the tobacco pouch, so that when he finds them, he knows where his tobacco is, namely in his glasses case. However, when the glasses case is actually opened it contains a ham sandwich. Dilly the Dodo observes:

> 'Now this serves to remind me that I'm hungry.' Poor Alice was now completely bewildered, but she managed to ask, 'Can't you remember when you're hungry?' [to which Dilly the Dodo replies] 'I'm always hungry but I can't always remember it'.

A while later, Alice observes that Dilly the Dodo, 'who had been stuffing silently all the time, suddenly jumped up and doddered past her crying, "I must go to Room 40 and find fault with things"'.

Knox also targeted himself in one of the verses he wrote for *Alice in ID 25*:

The sailor in Room 53,
has never, it's true, been to sea
But though not in a boat
he has yet served afloat –
in a bath in the Admiralty.

Knox had indeed persuaded the authorities to install a bath in his room and said it was in the hot steaming tub that he did his deepest thinking and made his cryptographic breakthroughs. Knox did not look too impressive, however, in the military uniform that he and the other codebreakers were required to wear after Bubbles James took charge. His brothers, Ronnie and Wilfred, were one day walking along Whitehall and when they saw 'Erm' (as they nick-named him in recognition of his persistently hesitant speech) 'coming out of the Admiralty, all dressed up, as Wilfred put it, like Lord Nelson. Both were too overcome to ask him what he had done with his telescope'.[4] One of Knox's biographers put it thus:

> Dilly himself conspicuously failed to look naval, long thin wrists stretched out from the cuffs of a uniform that hung on him like a sack. His work was presented, as it had been in his Eton days, in inky scribbles on sheets of dirty paper, frequently mislaid. … [But] there was a certain art, a certain flair with which Dilly was born, for the shadow patterns of groups of letters, no matter in what language, revealing themselves, like a secret dance, only to the patient watcher.[5]

In 1908, Dilly had taken on the completion of an edition of the 'mimes' of Herodas, a 2nd/3rd-century BC Greek poet, recorded on battered papyrus dating from about AD 100 which had survived in the dry desert conditions. The academic who started the edition died and the young Dilly was the obvious person to finish the job. He set about the task with gusto. 'He intended to be not only linguist, palaeographer and papyrologist but to understand the whole world of the ordinary Greek people depicted by Herodas.'[6]

The verses he translated could be rather rum, concerning:

> … the pander [pimp] who sues for assault because a girl has been stolen from the brothel; the mother with a delinquent son; the woman whose slave has proved an unsatisfactory lover, and wants him whipped, but doesn't

want anyone else to see him naked; the woman who complains about servants, visits the temple, can't wait to see the expert leatherworker in the sex
shop ... The mimes provided an intensely difficult game in which nearly all
the rules were missing, but Dilly intended to win.[7]

Probing the seedy verses about the daily lives of ancient Greeks would seem to
be rather a different task from studying the operations of the German Navy's
mine-laying vessels or the ambiguous diplomatic telegrams emanating from the
German Foreign Office. But Dilly's focus was on the intellectual excitement of
solving the translation/cryptographic puzzle, not the content of the messages,
whether titillating or terrifying. In his academic work he would have to deal
with fragments of writing on fraying pieces of papyrus, filling in the gaps from
insight and intuition – not so different from his task as a cryptographer.

Dilly was the classic socially inept academic, with an inability to convey
his ideas easily. Keynes wrote of him that his work was always submitted
'in a most loathsomely untidy, unintelligible condition', forgetting to write
down the necessary steps, and 'even in conversation he is wholly incapable
of expressing the meaning he intends to convey'.[8] One biographer wrote of
his rather cold, utilitarian personality that elevated intellectual pleasure above
human relations:

> Dilly had eaten cold porridge at Aston [public school], because the pleas-
> ure of eating consisted of the pleasure of filling your belly, so now [at
> Cambridge] he declared that one should drink only to get drunk, and that
> women (to whom he was always timidly and scrupulously polite) existed
> only for sex. True pleasure came from solving problems.[9]

However, at the end of 1917 he was given a new secretary, Olive Roddam,
from a wealthy Northumberland landowning background. As Roddam
worked in the room equipped with a bath, Knox had to finish with his soak-
ing before she arrived in the morning. From someone used to the all-male
environment of the common rooms at Cambridge this was an unsettling
intrusion into a settled way of life. It was probably the first time he had been
in such close contact, for hours each working day, with a woman. He was
overwhelmed, and immediately after the war Knox and Roddam were married – to the surprise of everyone, from friends and colleagues to family
members on both sides.

Their marriage took place a couple of weeks after that of Frank Birch and
Vera Gage, daughter of Henry Charles, the 5th Viscount Gage. The Knoxes

and Gages at first attempted to live in the same house, but this was soon abandoned, with Dilly and Olive moving to rural High Wycombe.

Dilly so much enjoyed the intellectual challenge of codebreaking that he stayed on after the war. He also continued to work on the edition of Herodas, spreading the fragments of papyrus on his knees on the train to London each working day, trying to divine the order of the poems from the surviving text. He had finished the edition by 1922.

Dilly was offered the professorship of Greek at Leeds University, but turned it down, preferring to exercise his skill and intellectual delight in secret on puzzles in diplomatic codes and ciphers. At one point, he was solving Hungarian codes without having bothered to learn any of the Hungarian language.[10]

With another cryptographer, John Tiltman, Dilly also broke Communist Party messages sent on the Comintern (Third Communist International) network of wireless transmitters, leading to the identification of Russian spy networks. In the Second World War, he played a major role in the breaking of the German Enigma cipher.

Details of some of his achievements in that war remain secret even today, officially because to release such details would give away information about cryptographic methods that are still relevant today. The author of a biography of Dilly, who worked with him at Bletchley Park, was allowed to see the relevant file to refresh her memory but was told which sections of the file she could not mention.[11] She claims that there is nothing in the file that needs to remain secret. His contribution, however, was cut short by stomach cancer that had been diagnosed in 1938. He spent his last few months working on German ciphers from his bed at home, dying there in 1943.

★★★

Another member of Room 40's staff, William F. Clarke, was closely associated with Frank Birch, helping him at the end of the war to compile a history of the naval war with Germany based on intercepts and other intelligence. He also left some more or less useful material about the staff of Room 40.

Clarke was a 33-year-old barrister in 1915:

> I had always had a sneaking desire for the sea … When war broke out I used all my ingenuity to get into the Naval service, all in vain for a time at least; I was too old. However, my brother, eleven years older, was also trying and got accepted, dropping ten years of his age which nearly made us twins.

I pursued the same tactics, secured an interview, went through an amus-
ing medical only to hear that my defective eyesight disqualified me [for
active service].[12]

This imperfection did not prevent him being of use to the navy and Clarke
became a paymaster, handing out cash to about 1,000 servicemen each week.
'Later I took over the job of supervising all the disciplinary work, for which
my eight years at the Bar had fitted me.' In early 1915 he was summoned,
unexpectedly, to see the Director of Naval Intelligence, Blinker Hall:

I was then told that I would be transferred to HMS *President* for duty outside the Admiralty. What this meant I had not the faintest idea. Early in
March I reported for duty. Then at last my eyes were opened; our task was
cryptography, of which I had never heard.

Clarke was told to work alongside Captain Hope, handling the decoded intelligence. He was, however, not much of a cryptographer and did not work on
breaking codes or ciphers.

In an account that was slightly reminiscent of Birch's version, Clarke
described the kerfuffle whenever there was a change in cipher key: 'When
it changed the experts were called in, retired to the other room whence
they emerged after a short or long interval with the solution to the amazement of us, ordinary folk.' For the non-experts, the night watch, in particular,
was fairly relaxed: 'In 1916 one generally slept half the night, only one of us
remaining to deal with traffic.' This arrangement, however, did not suit all.
'Some fellow watchkeepers like Fremantle were either too fussy or too noisy
to allow anyone to sleep in the adjoining room'.

This was in early 1916; however, after the Battle of Jutland in the late spring
of that year, the key changed every twenty-four hours. From then on, it was
the job of the Night Watch to break the new key. Clarke recalled, 'In normal
conditions, coming on at 10 a.m. we found the night watch had already
solved the problem unless one had the ill fortune to relieve the so-called
Gentlemen's Watch, Norton, Lord Monkbretton and Morrah.' All the same:

The work was quite easy for anyone with reasonable common sense and a
good knowledge of German; things were to be very different in later years
when new codebooks were frequently introduced, reciphering [*sic*] tables
lasted but a short time and became more complicated and the volumes
increased enormously.

Clarke has left us short comments on many of his colleagues. Unfortunately, they are not always very revealing, all too often only giving us a name and a note of when they died. It is social chit chat and gossip about one's colleagues and tends to be either dismissive or fawning. He records, of Herbert Morrah, he had 'quite inexplicably from what we know of him and his capabilities, been President of the Union [at Oxford]'. On the other hand, Lord Lytton, later Viceroy of India, is 'a most charming and modest personality and a very good cryptographer who solved the hardest problems we ever had to tackle'. On Rotter, he says, 'The great success that we achieved, in spite of the idiosyncrasies of his chief [Ewing], was due to his indomitable patience.'

Captain Hope was the best member of staff. 'To him, more than to anyone else, the credit of [Room 40's] achievement must be assigned. Modest, retiring, he exercised a control over all its operations with unfailing skill and understanding.' Elsewhere, Clarke wrote of Hope:

[He was] the hub of Room 40. Was mainly responsible for its success. Our beloved chief, this appellation applied to someone else in 1945 by de Grey caused no end of amusement. Left us in 1917 much to the country's loss and did most valuable work in the Adriatic. Came back in 1939.

However, Bubbles James, Hope's replacement, was obviously inferior, but he came too late to do any real harm:

He was a very different type to Hope, very pushing, very self-confident. He had been a remarkable success as a Commander at sea but he came to a job which required other qualifications which, in my opinion he did not possess. But luckily by then everything was so organised that we required little but a figurehead and for that he was admirably suited.

Even his success in persuading the Admiralty to increase staffing levels to cope with more intercepts is cast in an unfavourable light. Clarke suggests that James's motive was to gain influence and power by having a bigger organisation under his control. James wrote a biography of Blinker Hall in 1955 and during his researches he saw Clarke's papers. On reading these comments on himself and others, he observed that Clarke 'seemed to dislike a lot of people'.[13]

Clarke leaves us with two snippets on George Young. First, he informs us that Young 'made a claim to Inventions Board for devising a system of solving German FO [Foreign Office] cyphers'. Unfortunately, there seem to be no more records of this (although he is possibly referring to the machine devised to guess code words in two-part or 'hatted' codes – see the next chapter). Second, he coldly states:

> There died the other day Sir George Young and got published a note making the remarkable and quite false claim that he was sent to the Admiralty 'to reorganise Room 40'. He was in it, it is true, for some time but he was never employed on its most important work.

This last comment seems rather unfair as Young set up Room 40's political/diplomatic section when he joined in May 1915. There is no doubt that his section – in the decoding of the Zimmermann Telegram, the breaking of numerous German Foreign Office codes and ciphers, and the development of machines to guess code words – did some of Room 40's most important work and Young surely deserves some credit for its success.

Sir Alfred Ewing was very definitely at the top of Clarke's list of people he disliked. When acting as the Admiralty censor in the 1930s, Clarke objected to some of Ewing's claims about Room 40 in a book he wanted to publish. Clarke wrote to the Attorney General, 'Sir Alfred Ewing, as far as I know, never solved any cryptographical problems himself – he only hindered others.' In another document, he wrote that Ewing:

> ... had been titular Head of Room 40 on its inception in 1914 and was technically over Captain Hope. In fact, i.e. in actuality he never was, he never really understood the problems and wasted more valuable time of his subordinates than can be imagined.

This outburst followed a post-war incident when a letter was sent out to Room 40 staff inviting them to a reunion, in which it was implied that Ewing had been Hope's subordinate, rather than the other way around. Clarke was the author of the offending document, but denied blame when Ewing reacted angrily. Clarke claimed:

> The letter asking him to [the reunion] was a multiple one, drafted by me but sent out in my absence in Germany on Armistice business by Denniston. It contained the phrase 'who worked under Captain Hope'. This upset [Ewing] and he wrote in answer that he had not worked under Capt. Hope but that the latter had worked under him and he advised me to consult others who knew the facts before I took on the job of secretary. It was not

until many years later that I was able to put matters right with an abject apology for something for which I was not really responsible.[14]

Clarke's memory provided us with a peculiar mix of gossip and name dropping. Edward Bullough, a professor of Italian, it is noted, is married to the daughter of Eleanora Duse, but we are told nothing of Bullough's cryptographic service. Duse was a famous actress, then about 60 years of age, who had been the most notable of the many lovers of the Italian poet, war propagandist and ideological fount of Italian fascism, Gabriele D'Annunzio.[15] Of Harry Lawrence, one of the early recruits, Clarke observed that he was 'one of the most popular of our staff ... one of our most loveable members. Expert on furniture and art. Died soon after the war. Brother of Gerald Lawrence, the actor.'

Other famous or wealthy people Clarke admired included Lieutenant Commander F.C. Tiarks, RNVR, who was a city broker. According to Clarke:

[He] had been in the navy for a few years. Ran our D.F. [direction-finding] section – interspersed with his purchase of Anglo-Persian shares. Shocked Admiralty messenger who came from 1st Lord to summon him, by looking at his watch and saying he would come in three-quarters of an hour.

An unpaid member of the team was Ralph Vaughan-Williams. William F. Clarke's only comment was that he was the son of Lord Justice Vaughan-Williams, 'whom WFC knew', though he is rather better known today as a composer. Lieutenant J. Beazley RNVR was a Fellow of Christchurch Oxford, 'Great authority on ancient pottery. Called "kingo" as dealt with the German "Ingo" code. One of the few employed in Room 40 who did not advertise the fact in Who's Who.'

Lieutenant Benjamin Faudel-Phillips RNVR was the son of the former Lord Mayor of London. According to Clarke, he was a 'Serocold "find" ... He succeeded Young as head of Diplomatic section. Wealthy, generous and popular. Entertained members of Room 40 OB at his lovely house, Balls Park.'

Mr Harold E. Boulton was known as 'Daddy', says Clarke, adding, 'As far as I know no particular but a charming character. I think he died some time ago.' R.P. Keigurn, a schoolmaster in Room 40, was a 'good cricketer'.

Fortunately, Clarke left us with a few comments on some of the women who worked in Room 40. Some were cryptographers, such as Miss Hannam, who knew French and German and had served in France at GHQ on German field codes, and Miss Haylar, who worked on 'current Italian non–alphabetical' codes. Denniston, recommending that they be kept on after the war, later commented, 'Re: Hannam, Watkins, Spurling, Marreco, Anderson, Haylar: The services of these ladies are invaluable. They are experienced in the working out of all kinds of codes.'[16]

June Spurling joined MI1(b) in 1918, having been transferred from GHQ in France where she had worked on German field codes. Unfortunately there is no hint about how she got to France to do codebreaking work in the first place, but she must have been very good to have earned the transfer. Also, she was one of the handful of cryptographers kept on at the end of the war when only the very best were offered a post.

Clarke tells us little about the women's cryptographic skills but was keen to list their social pedigree. Miss Joan Harvey was daughter of the Secretary of Bank of England, 'returned for WW2', comments Clarke. Miss R.M. Welsford was a university graduate who 'in 1939 insisted on coming back uninvited'. Miss Violet Hudson was the 'daughter of soap magnate'. She acted as Clarke's secretary and 'used to arrive at unearthly hours in the morning. Very nice child,' but 'used to embarrass us by her early arrival (when the night watch was still bathing)'.

Miss Catherine Henderson, Clarke informs us, was the 'daughter of 'Billie Willie' Henderson, Admiral, later one of the organisers of the convoy system'. And Mrs Margaret Bayley, who only joined in November 1917, was the 'wife of city doctor. Her love affairs with W.L. Fraser and Russell Clarke caused some trouble. … Curtiss who in my view was the most useful of them all.'

By 1916 there were twenty women working in Room 40. The secretaries and typists were kept in hand by Ebba Hambro, wife of Sir Everard Hambro, the merchant banker. Lady Hambro amazed some of her more staid male contemporaries when she smoked a cigar at a social function.

There were less fortunate colleagues too. Lieutenant K. Marlowe, son of Marlowe of the *Daily Mail*, 'committed suicide when off duty'. G.H.M. Haggard was 'a regular naval officer who had lost his leg as a result of a misfire. Strange creature [who] went to Cambridge after the war and married a girl who was in the family way to save her name.' Captain Ralph George Barnes of the Canadian Engineers was a 'tubist [handling messages] from 5/12/17 to 4/3/19'. Clarke's only observation was, 'one-eyed, called The Ghost'.

Major James Dubuisson was an 'Army cavalry officer who had lost his legs. Charming fellow.' Fremantle, a royal naval officer 'of a famous family … was for some time my follow on the night Watch and he created some amusement by asking for the day off as he was to be divorced'.

With these short glimpses into the people of Room 40, we come to the end of Clarke's post-Second World War recollections. In his words, 'So much for personalities. I am afraid my memory may have led me into a few errors, but it is the best I can do after these long years.'

★★★

According to an internal assessment written at the end of the First World War:

Recruits [to Room 40] were chosen rather on the grounds of military inca-
pacity than for aptitude at research and in the main, the lack of foresight
at the beginning of the war – the failure to obtain the services of a sufficient number of suitable men – embarrassed and curtailed the efficiency
of the section throughout. Almost to the last, there was an inner body of
some half-a-dozen officers attempting the impossible. They were experts
and as such solved all the enemy codes and ciphers; they were intelligence
officers engaged in continuous research for supplying operations division
with a summary of the daily situation; and until 1917, the whole routine
of watchkeeping, copying and circulating signals as they arrived fell on
their shoulders.[17]

Another assessment noted:

The very greatest difficulty was experienced throughout in finding individuals with the necessary 'flair' for cryptography. This was equally true of
the purely military as well as of the diplomatic side of the work. Really
expert cryptographers can never be found ready made: only experience can
make 'expert' the individual who possesses the necessary mental qualifications and aptitude for the work. In the majority of cases it was found
that the most likely source of technical experts lies amongst those trained
in scientific and linguistic work. For the work of decoding messages and
amplifying diplomatic codebooks already solved, the personnel was mainly
drawn, irrespective of sex, from the members of the Universities possessing
high linguistic qualifications.[18]

An aptitude test was devised in 1918.[19] An important point must be made
here. In the Second World War, many of the best cryptographers were mathematicians, but in 1914–18 the cream of the codebreakers were people like
Dilly Knox with a flair for words and language. This was not, as often implied,

some sort of shortcoming, but a wise approach as the First World War codes were word based and needed linguists (whereas the Second World War cipher machines, Enigma and *Geheimschreiber*, were mathematical challenges).

In addition to Birch's and Clarke's sharp pens, there are also a few documents that shed a light on some of the cryptographic work of individual codebreakers. These come from CVs compiled at the end of the war by those wanting, or who were asked, to stay on in the post-war cryptographic successor to Room 40 and MI1(b). These CVs show us how the codebreakers moved from one job to another, expanding all the time their ability to cope with a wide range of codes, ciphers and languages. The selection of those asked to compile their CVs is obviously biased towards those with the greatest range of experience – we are dealing here with some of the half a dozen or so star cryptographers of Room 40 and MI1(b) – but they can usefully illustrate the sort of work that a cryptographer would do over a period of several years.

★★★

The most detailed account of cryptographic activities comes from the clerical warrior, William Montgomery. As we have seen, Montgomery was no mild, peaceful clergyman. His CV also shows that he was not in the least modest or humble. Like most new recruits, his first spell of duty in Room 40, beginning in April 1916, was on the watch decoding naval messages in SKM and VB. In September 1916, he was transferred to the political/diplomatic section, dealing with cable messages sent to and from Washington, Mexico, Argentina, Brazil, Chile, Peru and other South and Central American states.

He worked on code 13040 and claimed a significant contribution to decoding the Zimmermann Telegram. Montgomery also informs us:

> Half a dozen other ciphers were dealt with by this sub-section including the 'hat' cipher 7500, to the early stages of which I made some useful contribution. At this time I discovered independently the 'sliders' used to disguise messages passed on from Washington to Buenos Aires and vice versa, and (later) the 'slider' used to disguise VB messages sent to the German forces in East Africa.

From March 1917 he was back on naval work and 'I was practically in charge of the sub-section dealing with American ciphers'. The code then in use, 26040, had daily changing keys 'which had to be discovered from the message itself. This was regularly done with success'. He also worked on 'odd' or occasional ciphers including a 'multiple alphabet cipher with certain curious features used by the Germans in Morocco', a complicated multiple alphabet cipher used by a German agent in India, and many others:

> ... by recognising the connection of certain messages submitted to us by the Americans with the old HVB, I was able to supply evidence which secured the condemnation in the American Prize courts of a vessel which had acted as a supply ship to the *Dresden*. In decoding a Buenos Aires message, I conjectured the phrase 'spurlos versenkt' [sunk without trace] (not then in our reconstruction of the codebook) which was afterwards so useful for propaganda purposes [see Chapter 19].[20]

'Later when the American material stopped owing to the publication of certain telegrams' – i.e. the Zimmermann Telegram, but referring to the United States' entry to the war as a result of its publication – Montgomery was 'entrusted' with going back to US cables from before the first decipher:

> If prompt use was to be made of the valuable material which it contained, it was impossible to wait till the whole was decoded. A rapid survey and selection had to be made dealing with newspaper and political intrigues, supply ships, firms deserving to be blacklisted, dangerous persons, agents, etc. The Americans, to whom the results were generally communicated, made a special acknowledgement of their value.

From February 1918, Montgomery was in charge of Room 228. The first cipher he tackled there was a 'hatted' or 'two-part' cipher used for communications between Berlin and Madrid, 'in which their most important material was sent out'. He recorded:

> The cipher was already in a workable stage, but as it was not very advanced, and as there was a considerable amount of daily material, I had little time for any other research ... I did however during this time discover a dictionary-code used in Morocco, build up to a workable point the 'Delmar' cipher, of which the beginnings were given to us by the French, get out a Spanish alphabet cipher, etc. besides keeping up the general direction of the work on the old American material ... In conjunction with Miss Robertson, the very efficient head of the lady decoders in Room 229, I worked up from an early stage another 'hat' cipher containing much important political

material, which it was thought at the time might be wanted for publication. This involved constant overtime work for six months.

This work would undoubtedly have brought Montgomery into contact with the machine techniques used to reconstruct the 'hatted' codes by guessing code words at a far more rapid rate than could be done by human codebreakers:

> I also at various times, by orders of the late Director of Naval Intelligence, prepared dossiers of cipher material on various subjects. The most important of these was commended by him as 'good staff work'. I have a considerable facility in acquiring a working knowledge of a language, e.g. I can read Dutch without having studied it, and lately got up enough Polish for certain practical purposes.[21]

This is truly a formidable list of achievements.

★★★

Another codebreaker who left us with a good account of his work was Mr C. Somers-Cocks. He joined in June 1916 and worked on the watch until:

> … transferred by Sir A. Ewing to political side; assisted for two months in getting current messages out in cypher 9972 and its variants, of which a portion had been made out … and also Madrid messages 89934 … Beginning of 1917 Washington, South and Central America, 13040, 5950 and their variants (which had been partially made out) until the messages stopped about the end of the year. Examined American messages in commercial code, then 'back numbers' of same cyphers. About April 1918 current messages in 92700 (Arab or Persian cypher) variant of 13040, made up a more complete edition of this for sending abroad.[22]

He later worked on 6400, an incomplete 'hatted' code, and a code known as 'Delmar', as well as others, including German–Bulgarian codes and ciphers. Little else is known about him except comments left by Clarke, who observes a couple of times that he was 'celebrated for his spats'.[23]

★★★

John Fraser of MI1(b) was also a cryptographer with a long record of achievements. He later became Professor of Celtic at Oxford. He joined in February 1916 and made an immediate contribution by breaking the French-language Greek code books (see Chapter 10). He was familiar with twenty-one languages and broke or helped to break Greek, Spanish, Argentine, Uruguayan, Turkish (Army Field Code), Swiss, Swedish, Norwegian, Brazilian, Romanian, Dutch and Vatican codes and ciphers.

★★★

Lieutenant John Hooper was a modern languages teacher at the Royal Naval College, Osborne, who joined Room 40 on 17 November 1917. As with all new recruits, he started as one of the people keeping the watch, working on German naval codes, 'consisting in decyphering messages from the German High Sea Fleet and "getting out" the daily key'. Denniston gave him his highest accolade: 'very sound'.

Despite his obvious skill, he had to be returned to Osborne in January 1918:

> The authorities at the RN College Osborne having refused to release me
> for work in ID25 I resigned my appointment there, but as a term's notice
> was necessary, I was compelled to proceed for one term to the RN College
> Dartmouth to which I had previously been lent.[24]

He returned to Room 40 in April and from then until June resumed watch-keeping duties in Room 40. He also handled German political/diplomatic ciphers and the translation and summarising of plain-language wireless news. From June until July 1918, he undertook 'research work in connection with the new German naval cypher'. Then he was appointed as an intelligence officer, keeping the Operations Division supplied with information about the distribution and movements of the German High Seas Fleet.

After the war ended, he stayed on and acted through December 1918 as an interpreter at Scapa Flow, where the German fleet was ordered to be laid up. In January 1919, he worked on the compilation of a daily 'Summary of Wireless News', derived from reading and summarising all '*en clair*' messages from all parts of Europe:

> The knowledge of contemporary political events thus acquired should be of
> considerable assistance in cryptographic work. When time permitted I have

also been engaged during this period in familiarising myself with the various German diplomatic cyphers e.g. German FO book, 'Satzbuch', naval cypher between Madrid and Berlin, Austrian cypher, etc.[25]

★★★

We have been able to gain a few impressions of what it must have been like inside Room 40 and we have made mainly brief acquaintances with the foibles, pedigree, personal charm or otherwise, injuries, date of death and even cryptographic skill of a few of its inhabitants. There were many more members of staff of both Room 40 and MI1(b) about whom we have no more than a record of their name on a 'tea-list' or in a staff address book. Often, where names occur on more than one list, there are spelling differences, so that it is not always possible to be precise about exactly all the details. It is even less clear when it comes to assessing who did what and how well. Apart from the handful of end-of-war CVs, we have only a few hints.

14

Codebreakers

In the early years of the war, the German Army in the field commonly used transposition ciphers (which moved the letters in a message around before transmission). But, from the middle period of the war it increasingly used codes, rather than ciphers, for field communications (although many times both codes and ciphers were used). Well-designed codes were quicker to use, less prone to error, made messages shorter (by replacing a phrase of several words with a single code word) and, if used properly, could afford greater security. As a captured German Army instruction noted in July 1918, information:

> … can be transmitted considerably quicker than it would be in 'clear' by using the phrases and words in the code book, because for each of the phrases or words, only one code-word consisting of only three figures or letters can be employed.[1]

The instructions from a German Army code book, the *Schlüsselheft* ('Key Book' – see Chapter 19), reminded users:

> In front line positions the coding of messages is rendered more difficult by the battle conditions (hostile fire, exposure to weather, moral[e] influences). Experience shows that the troops are inclined to use 'clear' without considering that this may often have serious tactical consequences. This must be avoided at all circumstances.[2]

According to a British Intelligence report:

> From the evidence now available, it seems clear that during March 1917, the Germans realized the value of the information which could be obtained by us from their wireless signals and messages. At this period a radical change was made in the system of aeroplane and field station calls, so as to make it much more difficult to obtain information from them, while at the same time the use of a cipher for wireless messages was abandoned in favour of codes.[3]

Coincidentally, in the middle period of the war, some of the captured German naval code books that had been in service since the start of the war (or even earlier), were replaced by new ones. Room 40 was suddenly blinded to the plain-language meaning of the new code words. Some of these new code books were later captured (for example, from downed Zeppelins), but not all. The messages sent in codes that had not been captured could only be read if the code book was 'reconstructed' by intellectual effort. A few German diplomatic code books were also captured, but others were literally a blank book as far as the British codebreakers were concerned and, like those facing MI1(b) and the army field cryptographic units, had to be reconstructed from scratch.

So, from the middle of the war, in the British Army, navy and diplomatic cryptographic sections, the art of reconstructing a code book more or less purely from intercepted coded messages became a vital skill. Unfortunately, we lack good narrative accounts of the codebreakers working on mundane daily messages to reconstruct code books. However, a few working documents, such as training manuals, provide detail of the techniques of code book reconstruction. The techniques were applicable whether the code book was military, naval or diplomatic code, but the examples are mainly drawn from army documents.[4]

The biggest difference between an army field cipher and a diplomatic cipher was the number of code words each contained. An air-to-ground communications code would have only a couple of hundred code words and an army field cipher around 2,000, but there would be at least 10,000 in a diplomatic code. Field codes may be easier to break as the smaller number of code words means that each code word is likely to reappear more frequently. However, this could be offset by more frequent changes of the code book (smaller ones being easier to update).

A good, secure code book would ensure that all code words were used and that all were used a roughly similar number of times. But, in real life, codes did display noticeable differences in the frequency of use of code words. The codebreakers discovered that they needed to know the meanings of about 20 per cent of the code words in a code to be able to decode messages more or less effectively and to know about 50 per cent to be able to decode nearly all messages.[5]

For field codes with about 2,000 code words, the codebreakers would concentrate on working out the meaning of code words until they had gathered about 300 meanings. Then they would turn to attempting to decode as many as possible of the messages they had accumulated.[6] This would then provide a lot more useful solutions and allow more messages to be decoded.

★★★

Codebreaking required persistence, lots of repetitive and tedious work and only a few brief glorious moments of insight. As one codebreaker observed, 'It is necessary to dig deeply as well as widely in the process of code solution, and one message, if worried as a dog worries a bone, will sometimes yield more marrow than several pages discursively scanned.'[7] The War Office concluded:

> Research of this kind requires an active, well-trained and scholarly mind; not mathematical, but classical … When once you have got together two or three men of the right class, they will soon map out the work [for] themselves.[8]

The universities were the obvious places to find such people, but many were drawn from the ranks of wounded officers.

Codebreakers 'certainly tested the limits of military tolerance'.[9] One officer described those he had to liaise with in northern France as:

> A rummier set of fellows I never came across in all my born days. It was not in the smallest degree possible to teach these wonderful fellows a scrap of discipline. You had to treat them as geniuses, and to expect from them the most erratic behaviour. … They were men of all ages, one of them had been a schoolmaster, another was a stockbrocker, a third was a designer of ladies' hats – a very rum bird – and the fourth was a solicitor's clerk. They lived together in a dirty little rabbit hutch, smoking pipes all day and all night, the hut being frightfully untidy, like themselves, and I don't think they looked upon washing or shaving as part of their day's serious work. But they were amazingly brilliant fellows – both as linguists and as mathematicians. As

soon as a new code came along they pounced upon it like vultures on their prey, and stuffing their pipes with tobacco, and muttering new letters over and over again as they felt in their pockets for a match, they would wrestle with that new problem until they had made it clear as daylight.[10]

The codebreakers would seem to have had an impossible task. They were presented with a page of jumbled, apparently meaningless numbers or letters and had to derive some information with no idea of the meaning. In fact, this is an exaggeration, for no Allied codebreaker was ever confronted with an utterly new phenomenon. There was always some background information with which to make a start. The codebreakers had some knowledge of the German Army or Imperial Navy units ranged against them, and their communication networks. Also, they had some awareness of the structure, and thus the content, of the messages. This background knowledge gave the first insights into a 'blank' code book.

Codes had the effect of guiding the user towards building messages constructed from the stereotyped language of the code words for phrases. This structure was then accentuated by individual users who referred to a subset of familiar phrases remembered from the full range of those provided by the code book. So, the same code words appeared frequently and often in some sort of ordered relationship. Even where the code explicitly provided several code words for a very common single plain entry, such as '*punkt*' (full stop), operators would restrict themselves to using just two or three of the multiple options provided. The British codebreakers also noticed that German operators had a preference for code words that were pronounceable and thus more easily remembered, for example 'KAD' rather than 'DKA'.

The codebreakers were also aided by errors of all sorts. A British Intelligence report observed:

> Experience shows that no cipher or code can be completely 'Fool-proof'. This is especially true of field ciphers and codes, owing to the very large number of people to whom the enciphering and encoding are entrusted, very few of whom have had any previous experience of the work. Regulations and instructions, however detailed they may be, and however carefully worded, are bound to fail somewhat in practice.[11]

Many more mistakes were made whenever a new code or cipher system was introduced. This was useful as it undermined the effectiveness of a change of code.

In March 1918, the German Army introduced what could have been a very effective system. However, a message sent in both the old and new systems helped the Allied codebreakers to start the recovery of the new code book, showing them its structure (see Chapter 19). But the German operators, probably trying to recover the time taken in using an unfamiliar code book, did not bother to encipher the coded messages. As a result, about half of the messages in the early days were sent unenciphered.[12] As one British Intelligence officer concluded:

> Mistakes have never been completely eliminated. Whether they can be so eliminated by means of an efficient system of control remains to be proved. Numerous as the mistakes are, they can generally be traced to lack of discipline and care on the part of the encoder.[13]

Errors could also affect an entire system. Of major help to the codebreakers was the fact that many of the new code books – and this was particularly true of German diplomatic code books – were 'reshufflings' of existing code books. So many 'new' codes were really members of a 'family' of code books with shared characteristics. Diplomatic code 18470, for example, spawned a number of reshuffled codes: 2310, 2815, 80574, 12444 and 1777.[14]

Once the cryptanalysts had made a start on cracking a reshuffled code book, and guesses made as to the nature of the reshuffling, some of the content of an earlier code book might be recovered in large chunks. This could happen, for example, if the reshuffling was simply a rearrangement of the pages, with the entries on each page unaltered. This was common with German diplomatic code books which used code words made up of numbers, with the first three numbers derived from the code book page number and final two numbers from the entry number on the page. The pages were printed double sided with two code sections of 100 words on each side – a total of 400 code words per printed sheet. When one code word was worked out, all 400 were compromised.

★★★

However, the codebreakers could not depend entirely on errors to deliver easy results. They needed skill, too. As one expert put it at the time:

> The would-be solver must possess a thorough knowledge of the language employed, not only from the point of view of vocabulary but also from that

of a knowledge of all the peculiarities of its grammar, syntax and idiom and the peculiar phraseology, diplomatic, commercial or military, in which the messages are likely to be couched … a highly trained visual memory which will help him to remember the look of a code group, to recognize it on its reappearance, and to remember where he has seen it before, what its sequences were, and what theory, if any, he had formed about it each time it occurred. … [the codebreaker] must possess the faculty of keeping anything from a dozen to twenty theories in his mind in order to build up a chain of coincidence and reasoning until each link fits into its place and forms a coherent whole.[15]

The theory has it that once a cipher key has been broken, all messages enciphered with that key can be worked out, but on the other hand, working out the meaning of one code word in an unknown code does not help to solve the meaning of any other code words. Practical experience with German codes soon disabused the codebreakers of this asserted security advantage of codes:

It is astounding to anybody who has not actually worked on the solution how the discovery of one code [word] will lead to that of numerous others. One apparently insignificant word discovered in a practice message, and applied to other messages from different parts of the front, may yield between ten and twenty-five [other code words].[16]

The key reason for this is that reconstructing a code is based on close analysis of the relationships implicit in strings of adjacent code words.

The codebreaker would start by gathering all the messages coded in the new code book. Records were typed out so that the maximum amount of material could be 'brought under the eye' at any one time. The codebreakers' main tool was an index recording every time a code word was used in any message sent in a particular code and the code words (solved or not) it was used in conjunction with.

Here is a sample of a plain-language German Army field message (based on an army battalion's morning report, taken from an Allied training document) and its translation:

An Division 105 Punkt Abend Meldung 18-2-17 Punkt (1) von 10 Uhr 25 Morgens bis 3 Uhr 30 Nachmittag 40 Schuesse schweren Kalibers auf Kartenpunkt M2 Planquadrat 5209 Punkt (2) Fiendliche Flieger Taetigkeit gering Komma 5 Flieger ueber Abschnitt 7A Punkt (3) Wetter gut Komma sicht klar Punkt (4 bis 7) nichts Punkt (8) 2 Unter-offiziere und 7 Mann schwer verwundet Komma 10 Mann leicht verwundet Punkt (9 bit 10) nichts Punkt Gezeichnet Bataillion II/316 [end-of-message code word]

To Division 105 Stop Morning Report 18-2-17 Stop (1) from 10 hours 25 am to 3 hours 30 pm 40 shots heavy calibre on map point M2 grid-square 5209 Stop (2) Enemy aircraft activity low Comma 5 aircraft over Section 7A Stop (3) Weather good Comma visibility good Stop (4 to 7) nothing [to report] Stop (8) 2 non-commissioned officers and 7 men seriously wounded Comma 10 men lightly wounded Stop (9 to 10) nothing [to report] Stop Signed Battalion II/316 [end-of-message code word]

The first step was to identify certain code words from their position in the message. Messages usually ended with sequences such as 'Stop, sender's name, end-of-message code word'. They often started with sequences too, such as 'message number, date and addressing information'. The German for 'to' ('*an*') commonly appeared at the start of the name of the person or unit to whom a message was sent.

There were various types of opening and addressing used by different operators or units and it took time to become acquainted with the full range of possibilities. Again, some existing knowledge was useful here. For example, knowing how particular units used letters or numbers to spell out names and addresses, or knowing how different users such as divisional commands or wireless administrative units formatted their messages.

If a unit always started its messages, 'To commander 4th division', or 'To commander 5th division', etc., even when the code was changed it was likely that the code words for 'to', 'commander' and 'division' would remain in the same place in new messages (unless a systematic restructuring of the format of messages accompanied the new code). In the example message in Diagram 14.1, some of the start-of-message ('To Division 105') and end-of-message ('Signed Battalion II/316 end-of-message code word') material could soon be identified if they were known entities.

The codebreakers also learned that comparison of initial and final code words often showed that the same code words occurred at the beginning of some messages and at the end of others. 'This will point fairly conclusively to the fact that these groups represent the units or persons sending or receiving the message.'[17]

The next step was to start looking at the text of the message, trying to identify code words representing very common phrases, words, spelling groups, numbers, punctuation marks and grammatical signs. Frequently used words would be searched for in recognisable combinations or places. '*Punkt*' (stop) was the most commonly used code word, appearing at the end of sentences, but also in formatted reports, and appearing with numbers and names, as in the example message. '*Komma*' (comma) was also very frequent, often appearing with numbers, but not at the end of sentences. The example message shows a typical formatting of a regular situation report with specific items being mentioned in specific order in every message (probably sent in identical format by several different units). But, to go beyond such opening moves, it was necessary to start a much deeper analysis of the relationship between code words in a message.

The sequences in which code words appeared took on overriding significance. Numbers were particularly important in this sort of analysis. '*Bis*' ('to' in number sequences, but not 'to' in the addressing sense) could not end a message and was nearly always between two groups of numbers, such as 'four to five'. '*Und*' (and) was frequently used with numbers on each side but could not begin a message and was sometimes followed by '*bis*'. '*Uhr*' (hour) sometimes occurred among numbers but at other times was preceded, but not followed, by numbers (distinguishing it from '*bis*').

Other useful terms, such as '*von*' (from) and '*zwischen*' (between), have similar restrictions in their use. Such words and numbers were often used together in common sequences, such as 'from 8 hours 40 to 10 hours 45 and between 11 hours 10 and 12 hours 20'. This initial assessment of a new code would reveal several sequences of code words that probably represented numbers or the words frequently used in conjunction with them ('*Uhr*', '*von*', '*bis*', '*Division*', '*Bataillion*' and so forth).

Further logical analysis can help work out the code words representing numbers. For example, in specifying times of the day, the number before 'to' or 'between' will be lower in numeric value (in most situations) than the numeric value of the number that comes after it. The numeric value of a number preceding 'hour' must be between 1 and 12 and if there are two numbers in front of it, then the first must be 1 and the second must be 0, 1 or 2 (although clock times in many codes were given using twelve different code words to prevent this particular type of analysis). All the same, from long practice it was realised that if there were any numbers after 'hour' then they were practically certainly 5, 10, 15, 20, 30, 40 or 50, and by far the most frequent was 30. If there were two code words, then the first ranged from 1 to 5 and the second invariably represented 5.

The lower numbers, especially 1 and 2, were the most commonly used numbers in messages. A frequent message sent by wireless stations when they needed to order new batteries was: '*Bitte* [number] *Akkumulatoren*' ('please send [number] batteries'). The helpful aspect was that the number required was always very low, just one, two or at most three. Another common message was: '*Sofort einen Mann nach KW schicken*' ('Send one man to KW immediately').

The example message also shows how formatted reports often gave section numbers in sequence, i.e. starting with 1, then 2, and so on, and used in conjunction with surrounding brackets or other grammatical symbols, so giving a conspicuous set of code words that revealed the plain meaning of several numbers. Weather reports, where observers sent in details of atmospheric pressure, temperature, wind, humidity and visibility, contained lots of formatted numbers often within specific ranges (e.g. atmospheric pressure would range at the most between about 950 and 1040 millibars). Casualty reports could also be put to use. At one stage, when the Italian Army was reeling from a German attack in northern Italy, the German Army transmitted information about the numbers of Italian soldiers who had been captured. These numbers were correlated with the numbers of losses known to the Allies and the code words for several numbers were worked out.

Having accumulated this mass of logical relations between sequences of code words and any assistance offered by past knowledge of division names and the like, the cryptographers could then use logical reasoning, experience and intuition to work out what actual numbers were represented by what code words. Knowledge of, say, the army divisions known to be in an area could give some numbers away. For example, if two code-word sequences – 'RQD–RIM–MFR' and 'ADR–MFR–SXG' – were found in two messages next to another code word that was thought to mean 'division' and it was known that Divisions 245 and 356 were in the area, it could be guessed that 'RQD' = 2, 'RIM' = 4, 'ADR' = 3, 'MFR' = 5 and 'SXG' = 6, even though there was only one code word, 'MFR', in common.

By this stage, the codebreaker had worked out a number of code words that represented certain known numbers, identified code words that represented unknown numbers, and identified several basic words such as '*punkt*', '*komma*', '*und*', '*von*', '*bis*', '*zwischen*', '*uhr*' and so forth. The next step required from the cryptographer agile leaps of the mind based on a deep

understanding of German military (or diplomatic) language and an apprecia-
tion of the subconscious logic of language:

> It is at this stage of solution that the faculty mentioned above of being
> able to keep a dozen or twenty groups in one's mind at a time, with their
> sequences and context whenever known, and any theories that may have
> been formed about them when first encountered, will be most invaluable.[18]

★★★

Another useful way of reconstructing a code was 'spelling-group' code words.
Very few codes could provide sufficient code words to cover all situations and
words. In such cases spelling-group code words would be used to spell out the
word in syllables or (if unavoidable) letter by letter.

For example, a code might spell out syllables with three-letter 'spelling-
group' code words, so that 'AWN-ZNH-KDR' spelled out 'El-ber-feld' (a
place name) with 'AWN' being the spelling-group code word for 'el', 'ZNH'
for 'ber' and 'KDR' for 'feld'. These same code words would reappear in different strings depending on the word being spelled out. So, *'Felderwirtschaft'* (crop
rotation), could be 'KDR-BUL-SOM-MFZ-PYQ', representing respectively
'Feld-er-wirt-sch-aft'. Or, *'bereit'* (ready) would be 'ZNH-JGY', representing
respectively, *'ber-eit'*.

The codebreakers learned to spot spelling-group code words in coded messages by the same sort of analysis of code word combinations as they used to
identify numbers. It was found, for example, that when the same code words
often appeared in sequences of two, three or four, although not always in the
same order, they were most likely to be numbers. But, if sequences appeared
in exactly the same order, it was almost certain that they would be code words
for spelling groups.

The idea of using spelling-group code words representing groups of two
or three letters was intended to offer a more secure method than a simple
letter-for-letter system. Having a variety of spelling-group code words was
intended to hide frequency information. But, in fact, the new type of code
simply introduced a new set of combinations of frequencies and contextual
positioning. Once a few spelling-group code words were broken, decoding
became a sort of giant crossword puzzle. Context, frequency and background
knowledge provided the clues.

Spelling was supposed to be used solely for those few words within a message that could not be expressed by the use of the code words provided. If

used with abandon, spelling groups became a highly vulnerable part of any code book. But, as with so many rules, this one was regularly disregarded.

Operators often found it easier to spell words out rather than search for individual entries for whole words. Excessive use of spelling groups was common when codes were changed. According to an intelligence report, 'To the person who has been accustomed to encipher his messages, the search for code groups representing words may seem tedious. He will therefore prefer to spell out his message.'[19] The German cipher authorities were powerless to prevent this practice.

In the following examples, for ease of reading the sequences within the text I have used a single letter to represent the three-letter spelling-group code words. So that in the first example, 'X' stands for a code word of, say, 'XHW', 'Q' for a code word of 'QVU', and so on. It's worth quoting here the 'cryptographer's golden rule', according to a US codebreaker, Charles Mendelsohn: 'Guess a word.'[20]

The codebreakers often depended on some inspiration to start the reconstruction of spelling-group code words. An intelligence report noted, with aid of the message's context:

> It would, for instance, be fairly simple to spot the translation of the sequence [of spelling-group code words] X Q V P Q V as L-o-n-d-o-n, of W B Z Z B D L B as C-a-r-r-a-n-z-a, of L J C F Q C F M as T-h-o-u-r-o-u-t, of X Q S SY AY ZY as Z-o-n-n-e-b-e-k-e, of M D Q Q HY A D Q Q M I Q Y Z as D-r-o-o-g-e-b-r-o-o-d-h-o-e-k, etc. etc., if these were likely to be referred to in the text.[21]

Carranza was the Italian Army's psychopathic Chief of Staff; Thourout, Zonnebeke and Droogebroodhoek are Belgian place names.

This skill had to extend beyond single letter-for-letter substitutions to where groups of letters or syllables were coded, such as 'el', 'ber', etc. It was difficult, however, to design a system that provided a random set of code words.

The underlying plain language has its own regularities, even at syllable level. A glance at a German dictionary will show that many words begin with common groups of letters: '*sch-*', '*schr-*', '*ver-*' and '*vor-*'. There are also many common word endings, such as '*-eck*', '*-lich*' and '*-keit*', '*-lichkeit*' and even '*-ecklichkeit*'. Indeed, the German word '*Schrecklichkeit*' (beastliness) combines '*schr*', '*eck*', '*lich*' and '*keit*'. There are also many frequent pairings of letters in plain-language German words, such as '*au*', '*ei*', '*eu*', '*ie*'. These features could have worked to hide word or phrase frequencies, but instead often offered useful answers.

Abbreviations, too, were a good source of ways into unravelling the spelling-group code words. Close study of words thus became important in working out the meanings of these types of codes.

One Germany Army field code seemed to the codebreakers to make frequent use of spelling-group code words to spell out commonly used abbreviations (rather using specific code words for them). Sequences of code words such as 'B W R W B' and others were quite frequent. At first, it was thought that these sequences must be words such as '*neuen*', '*neben*', '*stets*', etc. (new, beside, always). But then longer sequences were identified, such as 'W B W R W B W', etc.

One anonymous codebreaker had the hunch that 'W' meant either '*Punkt*' (stop) or '*Bindestrich*' (hyphen) and 'B R B' stood for an abbreviation and meant either '*r i r*' (reserve infantry regiment) or '*k t k*' meant '*kampf truppen kommander*' (battle troops commander). As was observed shortly after:

> This was a very slender thread with which to unravel a whole code, but in codes it must be remembered that '*c'est le premier pas qui coûte* [it is the first step that counts]' and upon this slender foundation the whole code was eventually reconstructed.

All the occurrences of the '*Punkt*' or '*Bindestrich*' code word were identified and the message texts were broken into blocks separated by these code words. This, it was hoped, would indicate sentences or phrases. These chunks of code words were then analysed, as described above, to identify likely features such as numbers, common words, names and spelling-group code words. If several different wireless stations sent in short coded messages with the same stereotyped messages – such as '*25 Schuesse auf Abschnitt*' ('25 shots on Section') or '*Waerend der Abend Stunden Flieger Taetigkeit gering*' ('during the evening hours little aircraft activity') – it became possible to start cracking the spelling system.

This process was aided by a serious failing in the code system. A number of commonly used spelling groups – such as '*in*', '*an*', '*ich*', '*ist*', '*es*', '*da*', '*ein*', '*acht*', '*und*' – could form individual words on their own, or they could be used as part of a longer word. The same code word, for example, for '*acht*' was used to mean 'eight' as well as being a spelling group for '*acht*' in longer words (such as '*acht-ung*' [attention], '*acht-en*' [respect]).

Its meaning was first revealed using the techniques to work out logically the numerical value of code words identified as numbers. From this start, the word '*W-acht-me-ist-er*' (sergeant) was then worked out. Others, such as '*Es-t-am-in-et*', '*L-am-p-e*' and '*Fl-an-der-n*' followed. Having already worked out the spelling-group code words for '*k*' and '*t*', strings of letters such as '*--kt----*' or '*-----kt*' were revealed. The codebreaker with good knowledge of German and military communications would soon conclude that these words were '*taktisch*' (tactical) and '*kontakt*' (contact):

> One of the most interesting words which helped in beginning to get out the spelling words in a new code was a sequence of groups in the order Q W X Q W X W. This turned out to be *B-a-r-b-a-r-a*, used as the codename of a certain unit. The fact that the same word was spelt out in a succeeding message as *B-ar-b-ar-a* gave us [as well] the group for *ar*. Having got a possible *s* in the word *P-o-s-t* in another part of the code, we were soon able to identify another group as *S-a-tz-b-u-ch* (sentence book). From this point on all was plain sailing.[22]

Some further examples have been recorded of the sort of guesses that were involved in breaking codes using spelling-group code words. The meanings of the code words for spelling groups '*el*', '*ber*' and '*feld*' are, in the earlier example, given as AWN, ZNH, KDR respectively. However, below I substitute with single-letter code words, A, Z and K.

These code words were recovered when a codebreaker was trying to complete the decode of the following two-word sequence: '*W-lue-N-A*' and '*W-ie-Z*'. Noting that the two words both started with the same spelling-group code word, '*W*', the codebreaker hazarded a guess that this might well be '*sch-*' and that the meaning of the words then might be '*Sch-lue-ss-el*' and '*Sch-ie-ber*' ('key' and 'slider') and therefore a means to work out the cipher settings. This gave the meanings of rare code words '*A*' and '*Z*', respectively '*el*' and '*ber*', as well as the more common ones for '*sch*' and '*ss*'. From '*el*' and '*ber*', the codebreaker went on to guess that the code word sequence, '*A-Z-K*' was '*El-ber-feld*'. This gave the meaning of another code word, that for '*feld*' (field). This then helped work out the meaning of other code words.

This crossword-like skill could reach dizzying heights. It could even defeat instances where alternative code words were available for commonly used plain meanings such as vowels whose repeated appearances would soon show up in frequency analysis. For example, in one code, two different code words, '*X*' and '*W*', could both be used for '*a*'. So, when presented with two sequences 'X K K X Q X T' and 'X K K W Q W T', the codebreaker guessed that the word was '*apparat*' (apparatus), helped no doubt by the knowledge that the unit sending the message was connected with the signals service and frequently had to mention machines and apparatus – but it was nonetheless an inspired guess. Similarly, one codebreaker was presented with a partially decoded word, '*--st---a-ast*', and guessed that it would be '*Justizpalast*' (Court of Justice).

Once a few spelling groups had been filled in, more and more code words fell to the players of this gigantic crossword puzzle. As one codebreakers' training book observed, 'When one clue seems likely to be a fruitful one, everybody should work at it until it either proves to be the right one or is definitely discarded as leading nowhere.'[23] One military historian concluded, 'Successful codebreakers combine the pedantry of the grammarian with the logic of the linguistic philosopher and the flair of a chess grandmaster.'[24]

★★★

Various techniques were developed to make codebreaking more difficult, such as 'dummy' code words. These have no plain-language meaning. They are intended to disrupt frequency counts and also to hide the relationships between code words. But this required tight discipline over their use. Instead, many operators simply chose to insert dummy code words into messages with great regularity – such as every fifth code word – or they simply used far too many:

> It is a mistake to think that excessive use of dummy groups will hinder solution … Even if there is no regularity in their position in the message, their excessive use betrays their presence and does not hinder solution.[25]

Some operators even copied whole columns of code words out as dummies. 'These hindered us for some time, but, as soon as we found out what was the matter, we derived great benefit from this practice' as the order of code words and the structure of the code book was revealed.

False messages, sent to deceive the enemy in some way or other, and test messages, sent by wireless engineers for example when introducing new code books or wireless systems, could also betray a code. There was a natural tendency to use the text of well-known poems, songs or sayings in such messages, a habit derived from the exercises they would have used in training and as civilian telecommunications engineers in peace time. In the case of messages sent as part of a deception operation (for example, by sending lots of wireless traffic to give the impression that an army unit is based at one place, when in reality it has been moved elsewhere), if the code is broken then the whole deception scheme is blown. So, for the deception to work effectively, it would have been essential to create 'real' text for the imaginary army unit – no easy task.

As a US intelligence report from the Western Front in 1918 concluded:

> No code ought to be insoluble, given a sufficient quantity of material, a proper method of work, the necessary qualities in the would-be solvers, and sufficient time between changes of the codebook to admit of the reduction reaching such a stage as to yield information even if only fragmentary. In code as distinct from cipher a certain length of time must elapse before complete or even partial reduction is possible. The time taken is directly proportionate to the amount of material to work on, to the amount of outside information or of analogy with previous codes available, and to the number and experience of those engaged on it. ... A code is not solved in a day, nor even in a week, not even by a miracle.[26]

★★★

Codes could be made much more secure if they were 'two-part' codes with alphabetical listings of plain words/phrases and a random or 'unsystematic' allocation of code word. This type of code was considerably more difficult to reconstruct than one-part codes, which had both plain entries and code words in alphabetical order. A two-part code was also sometimes known as a 'hatted' code in British cryptographic jargon – as if the allocation of code words to plain meaning was done by picking the entries out of a hat. The German name was '*Lotteriechiffre*' (lottery cipher). They were 'the most confidential class of German diplomatic codes'. When they were first introduced, it took some time for the British codebreakers to work out their nature:

> [It] was ascertained by means of messages duplicated in readable codes and discovered by the system of registration and cross-referencing [i.e. indexing] and the preliminary work done by Fleet Paymaster Rotter on code 64, that these codes were unsystematic ... so each group had to be separately resolved [and had no connection] other than its context to other groups.[27]

The only means of reconstructing such a code was by logical analysis and repeated trial and error. No doubt there were many inspired guesses, such as those we have seen above, but most of the work was wrong guesses which were discovered to be wrong only after a lot of effort. This required start-ing again, and systematically analysing an unsystematic code. Given enough messages to work on, an expert cryptanalyst could perhaps work out the meanings of about five code words of a hatted code in a day. Given that the diplomatic code books contained 10,000 or more code words, it was essential to have worked out at least 2,000 code words before messages could be read with good effect, and preferably to have 5,000. But, as the life of a diplomatic code was on average about eighteen months before it was replaced, this could hardly make for any practicable break.[28]

We have seen above that the way language is structured means that only certain types of code word can follow or precede others. These rules can be built into logical equations: 'If A follows D and F comes before T, then A and F must be numbers and A must be greater than F.' The codebreakers were the sort of people who could juggle in their minds such comparatively com-plex strings of logical conditions and spot sequences that did or did not fit the rules. But, even for brilliant linguists, the number of such conditions that could be handled soon became too complex, even with the aid of scribbling on scraps of paper. This was the limiting factor – the time it took the bright-est brains of British universities to plod through trial-and-error assessment of guesses until either a condition was not met and the assumption had to be discarded or all conditions were met and a code word was solved.

Today, such operations are of course performed for us with ease by elec-tronic computers. A codebreaking machine, Colossus, was the world's first large-scale electronic machine and was developed during the Second World War and long assumed to be the first such machine.[29] Just a few hints have now been uncovered in Room 40 files at the National Archives to show that machinery was actually first employed during the First World War.

The Research Section first set about decoding the considerable accumula-tion of material that had been gathering. The shortage of staff available for this work led to the development of machines that helped with the decoding task (after the code book had been broken or reconstructed). Young recorded, 'The deficiency of staff being to some extent made good by labour saving devices, such as the "pianola" a mechanical means for making troublesome group transpositions.'[30] This meant that the machine would have been a 'punched-card' machine, similar to the continuous run of punched card that is used to control a pianola. With the help of such machinery, the accumulated material from the three reconstructed code books was decoded.

But then the section took a major step forward to creating codebreaking machinery. According to a history of Room 40's Research Section:

It was not realised that this form of [i.e. hatted] code required special treat-
ment until May 1916 when leave was granted to set up a special staff of
educated women to work machinery by which the guessing process
could be accelerated. By this method the [number of] guessed codewords
rose at once to twenty daily and by the law of increasing returns grew
mechanically to a maximum of 100 per day by which time the [code] was
approximately readable. In fact the reading of messages in such codes, which
resemble those used by our Foreign Office, proved to be merely a matter of
tedious drudgery for one or two experts and the staff of ladies trained by
Miss Robertson.[31]

Their task was described as 'grinding groups out of the hat machine'.

This is the most important discovery from Room 40 files released in recent
times. Unfortunately, there are very few other details, and no other references to these machines in any other documents that I have seen. There are a
few references in documents to 'machinery' (for example, a reference to the
'machinery set up' by Ewing) but these are figurative uses, in the sense of 'the
machinery of government' or the 'civil service machine'.[32] The 'hat machine',
however, was an actual, and not a metaphorical, machine and would certainly
have been a 'punched-card' machine, like the decoding pianola device.

Punched-card machines (also known as tabulators) had become common
in administrative, commercial and, to a lesser extent, scientific applications
and could store data and handle repeated, elementary, logical processing steps
within limits. Indeed, in 1916 British Intelligence attempted to create a massive database of killed and wounded German soldiers by deriving information
from German newspaper reports. However, the complexity of the application
and concerns over the accuracy of the data led to the system being abandoned
in 1917. All the same, it shows that there was a willingness to experiment with
punched-card machines.[33]

The job the 'hat machine' had to do was a complex one, working out possible code word meanings. Such a machine might have to check all occurrences
of that particular code word in all messages received to ensure that it met
the appropriate logical rules about its appearance in sequences with other
code words. The punched-card machine was thus being used as a prototype
computer, performing logical processes that could be also be carried out by
humans with pen and paper, but on quite a different timescale.

This machine accelerated the process of codebreaking of hatted codes ten-
fold, from one person guessing ten code words a day to one machine guessing
100. Suddenly, it was possible to reconstruct hatted codes in a practicable

timescale. This revelation brings the birth of mechanised codebreaking forward to 1916.

The first hatted code to confront Room 40 came into use in March 1915, with code number 6400. Rotter started work and this was carried out 'on the ordinary lines' (i.e. without the aid of a machine), over the winter of 1915–16, but progress was slow. From May 1916, code 6400 became the first hatted code to be worked on with the aid of the codebreaking machine and was soon readable. After that, breaking it 'proved to be merely a matter of tedious drudgery for one or two experts and the staff of ladies trained by Miss Robertson'.

When the German Foreign Office took the code out of use in the winter of 1916–17, Room 40 and its machines had worked out 5,000 of the 10,000 code words. Code book 6400 was followed by 5300. Material sent in the code began to accumulate in the autumn of 1916, with messages being sent between Berlin and Greece, and Berlin and Madrid.

The German operators did not make the mistake this time of transmitting messages in both old and new codes, so the early stages were hard work. The code was used with a subtractor cipher, adding to the difficulty of breaking it. According to Young, the combination of code and cipher was so difficult to break that it would have remained unreadable had it not been for the earlier break of 6400. Other hatted codes included 53, 39, 42, 2700, 7600, 9751, 6937, 9972 and 9572, but again a lot of these were variations of the same basic system.[34] Another important hatted code was number 7500. Young reckoned that some 13,000 German code groups had been correctly guessed by the diplomatic section in the first year and a half of its life. Each word involved an average of three guesses. 'This implies a missing word competition for a year and a half with an average of 70 guesses daily.' Code 7500 was the one used to transmit the famous Zimmermann Telegram.

★★★

The women and their machinery, housed in Room 229, also dealt with neutral messages. By 1918, they were handling German, Austrian (with Room 57), Turkish, Bulgarian, Spanish (with Room 47) and other codes. US codes were the province of the team working in Room 54. Room 47 was set up under Lord Lytton to tackle items such as intercepted mail from neutral countries that was suspected of being in code or cipher.

Within eighteen months, Hall and Young had turned the Research Unit into a sophisticated diplomatic codebreaking organisation. The material they worked on was all plucked out of the airwaves, while the diplomatic messages being intercepted by MI1(b) were all taken while they were being transmitted over cable. Room 40's diplomatic work uncovered German espionage and sabotage plans. The machine breaking of Code 64:

> … made it possible to defeat German intrigues in Spain, Portugal, Ireland and Morocco, including a series of risings in the latter country; and to keep His Majesty's Government in touch with their diplomatic activities in North America and south-west Europe.[35]

★★★

A fearsome new weapon was unveiled in the middle of 1916 on the battlefields of north-west Europe: the tank. Around the same time, another new tool of war was also first deployed – mechanised cryptanalysis. Both tank and decrypting machine are symbols of the intensified prosecution of the war by the Allies and their determination to find ways round the stalemate of the war on all fronts.

Ironically, it is possible that the codebreakers of the time did not see this machine as a great advance, merely as a drudge. Some indeed saw such machines as a drawback. One First World War cryptographer, in the interwar period, observed:

> Quite early on tabulating machines had been brought into use and while in certain circumstances they were of great use, they did, in my opinion, a great deal of harm as many idle people thought they relieved them of personal indexing; this, I think, led to failure to solve many of the hand codes as contrasted with machine types.[36]

It is also noticeable that no one added their experience of working with machines to the CVs discussed in the previous chapter, yet from his work it is certain that Montgomery must have been closely connected, and probably Nigel de Grey, too. The CVs were designed to show how essential their authors were to the post-war successor to Room 40 and MI1(b); how intelligent and skilful they were at devising means of breaking codes by the dedicated application of their brain power. To be associated with the simplistic mechanistic plodding of machinery was hardly conducive to achieving that aim.

Today, in the light of the remarkable invention of the ultimate fast, plodding machine, the electronic computer, we attach more credit to those who conceived and built such machines. But that is with the benefit of hindsight. In an address to the British Association in 1931, Ewing said:

> More and more does mechanical production take the place of human effort, not only in manufactures, but in all our tasks … Almost automatically the machine delivers a stream of articles in the creation of which the workman has had little part. He has lost the joy of craftsmanship, the old satisfaction in something accomplished through the conscientious exercise of care and skill.[37]

One wonders if Ewing was thinking here, in part at least, of the machinery that started to change the workshop codebreaking unit he had set up into a faceless bureaucratic section of a bigger operation in which the individual counted for little as they mindlessly churned out guessed code words – instead of sweating over them like some gigantic crossword puzzle.

Another explanation for the reticence may be security. In the file in the National Archives containing a typewritten copy of George Young's history of the section, in which he does mention the machinery, he notes that the German hatted codes were very similar to those used by the British Foreign Office. Someone has added a couple of exclamations marks in pencil beside this observation. Maybe this is a clue as to the need to keep quiet about this development.

The great secret in cryptography is not so much that a code or cipher can be broken, but how long it takes to break it. Machinery may be plodding, but it is relentless and comparatively fast. The machinery allowed hatted codes to be reconstructed in a practicable timescale. It is possible that all mention of machinery was considered too dangerous. Whatever the reason, we have very little information about this machine-based codebreaking operation. Who conceived it, set it up and ran it? What processes did the machine follow? Was it especially built/adapted for the purpose, or was it a standard punched-card machine with an innovative program of commands? These questions, unfortunately, remain unanswered – perhaps because no one was very proud of this aspect of their work, or maybe they feared its consequences.

The Spanish Interception

William Reginald 'Blinker' Hall has often been compared with Queen Elizabeth I's fearsome intelligence chief, Francis Walsingham, who tricked Mary Queen of Scots into sending coded messages to plotters. Walsingham's codebreaking expert, Thomas Phelippes, decoded the messages that led Mary to the executioner's block.

Both Walsingham and Hall were extremely energetic intelligence chiefs and consummate plotters. Both were ruthless men determined to make use of the intelligence they gathered to attack and confuse the enemy. Both were also good administrators. Walsingham set up an almost recognisably modern intelligence organisation with spies and interception of communications as well as Phelippes's codebreaking activities, and even a 'special operations' branch. Hall turned Ewing's cryptographic unit into an intelligence centre, integrating it with the Naval Intelligence Division to very good effect, and he was not averse to carrying out some dirty deeds.

Hall was born in 1870. His father was a Royal Navy officer and became the very first Director of Naval Intelligence.[1] The family's link with the navy stretched back to the end of the eighteenth century, so it was little surprise that Hall found himself joining the navy – as was the fashion – at the age of 14. He was promoted to sub lieutenant by the time he was 20. Family connections and hard work earned Hall useful promotions. He received his first command in 1901 and became a captain in 1905. He developed a reputation for running a smart, efficient and disciplined ship, but he also showed a progressive side to his character, opening the first cinemas, bookshops and chapels to appear in navy ships (all of which became accepted features).

Some of Hall's exploits have been frequently recounted in books over the past few decades, often based on his own unpublished 'autobiography'.[2] This was written with the help of a ghost-writer, who told Hall, 'You may not have realised yet how much embroidery there will have to be. I shall of course supply this, but equally of course only after I have got the framework from you'.[3] It is not clear how much of the detail is true and how much was made up.

Hall left us a few hints as to how he had disinformation planted. He claimed that one navy agent was employed to go to lunch with neutral diplomats at a 'gentleman's club' in St James's and quietly pass on snippets of information. According to Hall, those deployed in this task were 'men who in more normal times would have laughed at the idea that they could ever be of any conceivable use to a branch of our Intelligence service'.[4]

One incident that is reasonably well documented illustrates Hall's ruthlessness and his willingness to abuse his position in pursuit of his personal views. During 1916, Room 40 intercepted messages between Berlin and Washington concerning German support for nationalists in Ireland, although most were not decrypted until after the rising and probably only one message, sent on 18 February 1916, gave timely warning that an uprising was planned for April. This read:

> The Irish leader, John Devoy, informs me that rising is to begin in Ireland on Easter Saturday. Please send arms to [arrive at] Limerick, west coast of Ireland between Good Friday and Easter Saturday. To put it off longer is impossible. Let me know if help may be expected from Germany.[5]

Closer to the day itself, Room 40 started to intercept naval messages about the delivery of German arms for the planned rising.[6]

The war had put a stop to all political developments in Ireland, especially any discussions of Home Rule. But some currents within Irish nationalism saw in the conflict an opportunity to accelerate independence through an armed rising. Some, such as the US Clan na Gael, which funded Sir Roger Casement's trip to Germany to garner support for the rising, saw Britain as Ireland's enemy, rather than Germany: 'England's difficulty is Ireland's opportunity.'[7]

Casement thought that an Irish revolt could only succeed if it was supported by the Germans. He went to Germany a fortnight before the beginning of the war. He backed Germany when the war broke out, proclaiming, 'We feel that the German people are in truth fighting for European civilisation at its best ... We recognise that Germany did not seek this war, but that it was forced on her.'[8]

In Germany, Casement negotiated for arms and ammunition. A treaty was drawn up in 1915 promising material support. Casement also backed setting up an 'Irish Brigade', drawn from Irish prisoners of war, to fight the British. Only a handful volunteered to join the brigade and German faith in Casement, and in the potential of the Irish to inflict damage on Britain, dwindled.

Casement also lost faith in the Germans and turned against them, sharply changing his tune from adoration to hatred:

> Oh Ireland – why did I ever trust in such a Govt as this – or think that such men would help thee! They have no sense of honour, chivalry generosity ...
> They are Cads ... That is why they are hated by the world and why England will surely beat them.[9]

As 1916 drew on, the Germans scaled back their support, initially promising 100,000 rifles but in the end actually only despatching 20,000 (and they were captured Russian rifles in poor condition). The rising was due for 23 April, Easter Saturday.

Close to Easter, Room 40 intercepted messages indicating that Casement was soon to set out for Ireland. The rifles and ammunition were shipped separately on a converted German steamer disguised as the neutral merchant ship *Aud* due to arrive on Good Friday. It set sail on 9 April from Lübeck. On 15 April, Room 40 intercepted a message from Nauen enquiring 'whether German auxiliary cruiser vessel, which is to bring weapons to Ireland has actually ...'[10] The message was garbled, but its meaning was clear.

The *Aud* arrived on 20 April but failed to make contact with rebels and was found by a British warship.[11] The German commander scuttled the ship as it was being escorted to harbour.

A submarine with Casement and his colleagues as passengers set out on 12 April, but it was damaged en route and a wireless message said that it would turn back to Heligoland.[12] This gave Room 40 an indication that Casement was on his way. Another intercepted message on 16 April reported that U-19 was 'proceeding out to the north'. On 22 April, a message said, 'Landed Sir Roger Casement and Bailey.'[13] Casement was arrested within hours:

> ... in Ballyheighe Bay with two revolvers, ammunition, ciphers and maps ... their mission being to warn the Sinn Fein element to get ready to land the cargo from the *Aud* and to make all arrangements.

Among the materials found was a 'Secret Code on a single sheet of paper consisting of a series of numbers having a fixed meaning opposite them in English, thus 987643 = "Send more guns"'.[14]

Casement wanted to postpone the rising, but it took place and failed to capture widespread support. It was brutally crushed by the British Army. Casement and many other rebels were condemned to death.[15]

There is a coda to the story involving Hall. A widespread campaign took place in Britain and the United States for Casement's death sentence to be commuted. He had been a British Consul in Africa and South America for nearly twenty years. During this period, he campaigned against the abuse of native labourers, earning his knighthood for his work informing the world of the mistreatment of Amazonian natives in Peru. He was well known in the United States as a campaigner for human rights.

As the campaign gathered force, it looked possible that he might escape the noose. This angered Hall, who saw Casement as a traitor, plotting with the enemy while tens of thousands died in the trenches and at sea. Hall had the means at hand to sway opinion against Casement. In the words of William 'Bubbles' James, 'For some years Casement had been addicted to unnatural vices and had recorded his experiences in a diary'. The diary was among the papers seized when Casement was arrested.

Hall saw to it that Casement's homosexuality did not remain secret:

> Typewritten copies of pages of the diaries and photographic reproductions of specimen pages were circulated in London clubs and the House of Commons, and were seen by journalists who were known to be sympathetic to Casement and by signatories of the appeal for Casement's reprieve, whilst the appeal was pending.[16]

Support for Casement drained away and he was duly executed.

★★★

In Walsingham's time, England's main enemy was Spain. In the First World War, it was Germany that was the foe, not Spain. But Spain's role as the major neutral European country and as the hub of wireless and cable communications for Germany ensured that it became a focus of operations both for Room 40 and Hall's espionage adventures. Each side in the war wanted Spain's support in one way or another, so they cajoled and bullied the Spanish Government. Each side saw Spain as a vital theatre of 'special operations' (espionage, counter-espionage, sabotage, illicit propaganda, etc.), so tensions were imported. As one historian wrote, 'Internal dissensions intensified and became increasingly intertwined with disputes over Spanish policy towards the contending alliances, leading to constant political crisis.'[17] In some respects, the war was good for neutral Spain. Short supplies of Welsh coal meant that Spain's domestic coalfields were developed. Mineral mining and steel manufacture were also stimulated. Limited supplies and high prices paid for Spanish produce by desperate buyers in other countries meant that profits boomed.

However, inflation took off and, overall, industrial production went down. Some regions did better than others, and in the regions that suffered badly industrial militancy increased and parliamentary government became ever more precarious. On top of that, between 1914 and 1918 sixty-five Spanish ships were sunk by German submarines.

Some Spanish factions, especially the army and conservative 'Carlists', were pro-German.[18] Some others, such as the 'liberals' (representing business interests), tended to favour the Allies, including Conde (Count) de Romanones, leader of the liberals and, from late 1915 to 1917, prime minister. His policy was to be as helpful as possible to the Allies, but to keep that secret from public opinion and to make out that he was pursuing a policy of strict neutrality.

This made him the object of hate in the German Embassy in Madrid. Germany helped to sustain a vicious campaign against Romanones, aiding his many enemies in Madrid. The period of Romanones's premiership roughly coincided with the months when Germany was planning a new round of unrestricted submarine warfare during 1916 and early 1917. Room 40's intercepts illustrate how this wider issue entangled itself with Spanish politics.

During 1916, Germany toughened its attitude to Spain, engaging in sabotage and propaganda activities aimed at influencing public opinion. Some 70,000 Germans lived in Spain, but Germany's most useful tools were its Spanish supporters. On 27 January 1916, intercepts revealed that 'representatives of all those institutions assembled at the German embassy in Madrid to celebrate the Kaiser's birthday and express their sympathy for Germany at that critical time'.[19] The conservative Carlists and army officers were encouraged to rebel or to disobey orders if Spain took any action in favour of the Allies.[20]

★★★

The British window on German activities in Spain was provided by the wireless link between Berlin and Madrid. However, this was a public station and German messages had no priority. In one telegram to Berlin the

German Embassy bemoaned the fact that the wireless station had 'thousands' of messages waiting to be dealt with. Despite this, the Berlin–Madrid link was Germany's most important communications channel with the outside world. Messages could be sent in cipher without the need to provide a copy of the code book to the Spanish authorities. This was unusual, and illegal under international law, but Britain did not complain as they could break the ciphers and read the contents of the messages.

When the Spanish Government under Romanones began to make noises about restrictions on codes, the Germans, as revealed by Room 40 intercepts, countered by saying that they wanted only the same rules applied to their wireless transmissions as were in force for British cable messages sent over submarine cables that could not be tapped. On 22 May 1916, Room 40 intercepted a message from the German ambassador in Madrid, Prince Ratibor, to the German Foreign Office. He reported:

> England and, especially, France have been recently making a fresh propaganda by means of journalists, clergymen and professors travelling in Spain. The Spanish government is giving support to this … but without exposing their sympathies. In the end this propaganda cannot fail to have an effect, especially in political circles that have already been prepared for it. Since this form of propaganda is closed to us, we can count, on our side, upon the King and public opinion as our sole security against Romanones and the enemy's schemes.[21]

Ratibor suggested that as a countermeasure, the heir to the Spanish throne and a delegation of prominent politicians should be invited to visit Germany. Room 40 annotated the transcript of this message: 'This cipher is only lately readable, and the general sense of the last paragraph [dealing with the proposed visits] cannot be guaranteed.'

The intercepts revealed how the German Foreign Office had set up a *Zentralstelle für Auslandsdienst* (Central Office for Overseas Service) run by Matthias Erzberger. It distributed books, pamphlets, films, poetry, and photos as well as funding newspapers and magazines. Plenty of German money was paid to sympathisers and to pro-neutrals – so long as they were against the government. Some 500 local and national newspapers were influenced or controlled by Germany, thanks to its distribution of generous funding for sympathetic press coverage.

During 1916 a publicity campaign was launched to prepare public opinion for the reintroduction of unrestricted submarine warfare. Germany even funded Spain's anarcho-syndicalists, hoping a militant working-class audience would be influenced by propaganda against pro-Allies capitalists, accusing them of being responsible for the 'orgy' of exports which was the 'real cause' of workers' impoverishment. The attacks on Romanones intensified in December 1916, shortly before the fateful decision was taken by the Kaiser and his closest policymakers to risk renewed submarine attacks.

The intercepts revealed the full extent of German activities in Spain, ranging from political propaganda to sabotage and even the landing of phials of anthrax spores for use in South America to poison mules being bought by the Allies. One useful feature of the intercepts was the way they gave details of German spies and agents. For example, in June 1916 the German Embassy in Madrid was informed of an agent, Arnold, who was on his way to Spain to organise the destruction of ships transporting iron ore from Spain to Britain. A perplexed embassy queried in reply that the ores were always carried on neutral Spanish ships, so did the agent's instructions mean that the ban on attacking neutral ships had been lifted?[22]

Another example, from 4 October 1916, revealed that a German agent, known as South III, was:

> … quite reliable [and] he has been since May in Spain where he directs an intelligence service in France. He is 1.79 metres in height, slender (brown-haired and brown-eyed), twenty-fours years of age and speaks the Berne dialect. You should instruct him to come here [Berlin] if possible for fresh instructions, via Holland, as he is compromised in Switzerland and Italy.[23]

The intercepts often gave details such as the address of family or espionage contacts in Spain or other countries.

The intercepts also revealed information about sabotage that was planned to be carried out in France and Portugal. On 31 May 1916, Room 40 decoded a message from the General Political Staff of the German Foreign Office in Berlin that was sent to the German military attaché in Madrid. It reported the arrival in Spain of an agent who was instructed to organise 'further undertakings' against Portuguese factories and French hydroelectric plants, French roads in the Pyrenees and iron-ore shipments from Spain to Britain: 'You should apply for such moneys as are required for these enterprises; [Agent] A will travel further after three or four weeks.'[24] Madrid enquired of Berlin, 'Please give further particulars as to the waterworks in the Pyrenees whose destruction would be most important and whose surroundings make such an undertaking possible.'[25]

A plan to equip a group of North Africans with boats and arms to raid Morocco was uncovered by the intercepts, giving advance warning of the raid and its personnel. In June 1916, an intercept revealed that a German agent (of unknown nationality) had gone to Morocco. The local stationmaster who was supposed to introduce him to people who were interested in insurrection proved not to be of much use. Of his contacts, 'some of them were entirely unknown, some of them quite unusable and some of them unwilling to accept the Agent's proposals'. The mission soon ended as the agent was arrested after fourteen days.[26]

Another intercept revealed that the Germans had 'given up on' another local agent, Muley Hafid, who had taken money but done little to fulfil his promises. Instead, other agents, Abd El Malei and Raisuli, were recruited to lead an action planned for October to land a party on the North African coast and damage French-owned property. Details of the financing and agents were revealed.[27]

The plot's ups and downs were traced over the months. On 7 October 1916 the embassy in Madrid reported to Berlin that 'all is ready'. The decode revealed that the raiders had plenty of rifles but were short of cartridges. They also needed to be sent a copy of cipher 604 for communication with Madrid.[28] Three weeks later, another intercept revealed that seven men, four machine guns, 1,000 rifles plus ammunition and 50,000 francs were about to be sent to North Africa, but:

> We have got the impression from Hiba's communication that the enterprise has been betrayed ... In order to mislead the French, we suggest that without betraying the present change of plan, a message should quietly be sent to Hiba to inform him that the enterprise has been postponed until a better season.[29]

Portugal began the war in turmoil, with the ruling classes divided over which side to support. A military coup in January 1915 put a pro-German ruler in charge, but he was ousted by a democratic rebellion in May 1915. Fearful that if it did not ally with France and Britain, it would lose its colonies in Africa in a post-war peace settlement, the new government veered towards the Allies. In February 1916, the government seized German and Austrian ships that had taken refuge in Portuguese ports at the beginning of the war, so in retaliation Germany and Austria declared war on Portugal in March 1916.

In early June 1916, a message from Ratibor, in Madrid, to Berlin, proposed a form of extreme sabotage:

In order to close the Spanish-Portuguese frontier and make communications difficult between Portugal and the Allies, I suggest contaminating at the frontier with cholera bacillus rivers flowing through Portugal. Professor Kleine of the Cameroons considers the plan to be perfectly feasible. It is necessary to have two glass phials of pure culture, which please send when a safe opportunity occurs.[30]

The idea was dismissed by the German Foreign Office in Berlin. However, poison plots were undertaken by the Germans to damage the trade supplying ponies to Britain from South America and the United States.

The intercepts also revealed regular German intelligence reports from agents in Spain. A typical example comes from 6 October 1916, when it was reported that 116 steamers left Huelva with an average cargo of 2,700 tons of copper ore pyrites; fifty-eight of the ships were British, twenty-nine Spanish and were mainly destined for Britain and France.[31] Such intelligence reports were intended for onward transmission to German U-boats, which would then attack the shipping if possible.

Room 40 was also able to pick out useful information about German plans for acquiring and transporting supplies, discovering the names of companies set up to buy or ship goods anonymously and the routes they used. There was also plentiful information uncovered about the German financing of Spanish supporters and some deserving impecunious Germans stranded in Spain without income. One message, on 25 May 1916, revealed that Berlin was in the process of setting up a line of credit for 6 million pesetas with Spanish banks to be guaranteed by the Deutsche Bank.[32] In October, Undersecretary Zimmermann at the German Foreign Office in Berlin was demanding economies and care with spending as it was proving difficult to acquire pesetas.[33]

This sort of information, about sabotage plots, agents, purchasing, transportation and financing, could be used to take counteraction – having spies and saboteurs arrested, thwarting purchases of supplies and seizing goods en route. But, in the political and diplomatic arena, measuring the effectiveness of intelligence is harder.

Whether things would things have turned out any differently in the political sphere without Room 40's access to intercepts is uncertain. The reports of the political situation submitted to Berlin by the German Embassy in Madrid tended to be hyper pessimistic, occasionally hyper optimistic and seldom realistic. Clearly, the people behind these telegrams were intensely wound up, only too ready to burst into a rant. According to one historian,

Ratibor's attitude 'was one of imperiousness toward Spain and of personal vindictiveness toward liberal politicians such as Count Romanones ... The ambassador apparently was somewhat lazy, arising only at noon, and he suffered from arthritis.'[34]

It is also clear from German messages that Ratibor often misunderstood the situation, having a strong tendency to take anything other than whole-hearted support as an expression of outright antagonism. In these reports, whatever happened in Spain was caused by Allied or German manipulation. Thus, when railway strikes broke out in Spain in mid-1916, the German Ambassador reported that they had been instigated by the British, who were supposed to want a political crisis which would allow them to present an ultimatum to the Spanish Government demanding more concrete support.[35] No doubt Allied intelligence agencies also interpreted the intercepts according to their own prejudices, but at least they were presented with unequivocal evidence of the nature of German activities.

An intercept of 12 September 1916 made the German position clear:

[The] danger lies in the personality of Romanones. His removal however from the Spanish ministry by regular means is all but impossible. The clipping of his wings would have to be done through the King, but with the utmost prudence, as otherwise consequences are to be feared.[36]

The complex diplomatic balance between the Allies, the Central Powers and Spain is illustrated by the after-effects of a visit by the German submarine U-35 to the Spanish port of Cartagena in June 1916 and again four months later. The German Ambassador reported to Berlin that the visit 'has had a most excellent effect on public opinion in Spain'.[37] But it was not entirely successful, because the submarine did not bring the promised new cipher material that was desperately wanted in Madrid. Room 40 was no doubt relieved by this news.

It was also a propaganda trip and a possible way of delivering various materials needed for sabotage – including the phials of anthrax intended for poisoning operations in South America. It is known that anthrax was landed in February 1918 by two agents who were put into a boat not far off the coast, but it is not known for certain that it was delivered by U-35 on the earlier visits.

However, poisoning operations did take place before 1918 and the chemicals somehow or other got to Spain and then Argentina. Hall's agents in Spain arranged with the Spanish Police for the chemicals to be seized and one box to be handed over to the British. Herschell then took the phials personally to the Spanish King, who was suitably upset. The incident may have contributed to Ratibor being expelled.[38]

Returning to 1916, the visit of U–35 was a blow to the British and they protested long and loud to the Spanish Government. They threatened to torpedo the vessel if it should move out of the harbour, even while it was still in Spanish territorial waters, declaring the visit to be a breach of Spain's neutrality. Any further submarines could expect to be attacked, even in harbour. This led the Spanish King to enquire whether German support might be forthcoming were the British to carry out such threats, but he got no reply.

Then, on 16 July a message from Alfonso to Germany requested that no more submarines visit Spain.[39] In response, Germany was spurred into action and offered to protect Spanish harbours – but only if it was allowed to use Spanish ports as bases for its U-boat operations.[40] This would, of course, be seen as a declaration of war by Spain on the Allies.

The German Foreign Office did not want to accede to Spanish demands that no more submarines should be sent to Spain. On the other hand, it had little real choice but to act in accordance with Spain's wishes. The German Foreign Office sent Ratibor an explanation of its diplomatic balancing act on 5 October 1916. Germany 'never agreed not to send' submarines to Spain because it reserved its position in international law, but would quietly refrain from doing so.[41]

As the German high command moved steadily towards the resumption of unrestricted submarine warfare in the Atlantic, the opportunities for direct conflict with Spain grew. The propaganda war became more vital. An intercept from September 1916 reported how Ratibor believed:

The enemy's propaganda is succeeding in convincing wider circles of the inevitability of our defeat. In consequence there is a great depression and even partial defection in circles friendly to us … The success is generally attributed to the abandonment by us of the submarine campaign.

Previously friendly merchants shunned German clients. 'Military circles, which formerly spoke openly of refusing to act against Germany, now say that they will do what they are told in a case of conflict.'[42]

Ratibor reported to Berlin in early October that Romanones was making every effort to influence national sympathies against Germany's submarines because of their effect on trade. Germany needed to blame the Allies for leaving it with no choice but to sink neutral ships, convincing neutrals that the sinking of Spanish ships was the fault of the British and greedy ship owners.

The situation facing Germany was different to that facing the Allies. The British could still trade across the seas and oceans. Spanish ships could, for example, sail to Britain with Spanish fruit, but could not supply Germany or its allies. So, Germany saw it as only fair that it should be able to prevent ships – any ships – from delivering oranges and other fruit to its enemies. And, if the threat to Spanish trade with the Allies led to terror and fear among the population, so much the better. 'Public opinion is much alarmed. Our campaign in favour of neutrality is prospering,' read one intercept from Madrid to Berlin.[43]

The fruit trade was critical for the economic survival of many small farmers and fruit trading and processing businesses as well as shippers. The Spanish Government tried to persuade the Germans to allow safe passage to Spanish fruit ships sailing to Britain. Germany's response was to offer immunity from submarine attack – but only on condition that Spain negotiate with Britain to permit an equal number of fruit ships to sail to Germany.[44] No doubt the German Government knew that the British would not agree to such an arrangement, but it thought that it had neatly pushed onto the Spanish the task of approaching the British for permission to allow ships to take fruit to Germany and thus shift the blame for the final refusal of safety for Spanish fruit ships onto the British.

The negotiations dragged on. The Spanish evaded an approach to the British, while the Germans nagged on at them to demand British acquiescence.[45] At one point Ratibor, passing on an enquiry from the Spanish, asked Berlin whether 'onions will count as fruit for the purposes of safe conduct, but not raisins, almonds or dried figs?'[46] But Berlin was not in the mood for expansive gestures:

> In consequence of the war on commerce which England began ... Spain must see in our concession regarding fruit-ships an act of exceptional friendship and of consideration for its poorest classes. It is impossible to go further out of consideration for our own people.[47]

As the year ended, the momentous decision was taken by the German military high command (which had become the effective government of Germany) that unrestricted submarine warfare would be reintroduced in early 1917.

The beginning of that year was fateful for Spain, too. Romanones offered the king his resignation as prime minister, but the king refused to accept. This was a manoeuvre designed to strengthen Romanones's position as the choice of the king on his reappointment. On 11 January, the German Naval Attaché in Madrid sent a report – using a private code that could not be read by the German Ambassador, but which could be read by the British – to Henning von Holtzendorff, Chief of the *Admiralstab*. Holtzendorff was one of the strongest proponents of using submarines to attack neutral and enemy shipping. The attaché told him, 'The ministerial crisis is treated by the [Spanish] press as a farce … The result of this is that we cannot in any early future expect a ministerial change. A distinct cooling off is noticeable among our partisans.'[48]

The German concerns about Romanones's bias towards the Allies reached a crescendo around this time. The German Foreign Office feared the consequences of neutral reaction when the decision on submarine warfare became known. Some of Romanones's alleged misdeeds seem pretty petty – such as banning a German film but allowing the showing of a French one. And others seemed simply to reflect the reality of British domination of the surface of the seas and the need for Spain to earn foreign currency.

Romanones, complained Ratibor to Berlin, was 'allowing a steadily growing quantity of war material and raw material to be exported [to Britain] to compensate for exports [to Germany] which he has embargoed'.[49] The fear was that the announcement of unrestricted submarine warfare would give Romanones the opportunity to abandon Spanish neutrality, so ideally the Germans wanted to see him go immediately. As long as he remained prime minister, they would remain fearful.

However, Ratibor did not want to use force to overthrow the Spanish premier. 'So much has been gained by the wrecking of prestige of Romanones that the taking of any violent measures might be too much risk.'[50]

Romanones's premiership was to stagger on, pressed in on all sides by conflicting domestic and external interests, until June when an unholy alliance of leftist workers and rightist army officers, clerics and Carlists led to his downfall. He was replaced by a series of short-lived administrations that were inclined to be rather more sympathetic to the German position than he had been. But in the longer run, as the Allies started to clearly win the war, Spain swung more to supporting them.

★★★

Before leaving Spain, on the eve of the renewed campaign of unrestricted submarine warfare, it is worth noting some intercepts relating to cryptographic matters. A note added by Room 40 to message number 1016, sent on 22 May 1915 from Madrid to Berlin, read, 'Telegram 1060 is a fictitious telegram', adding that telegrams 1061 and 1079 were also fictitious. Room 40 commented, 'These refer to messages to be sent in [cipher] 064, a partly readable cipher, containing false news and intended to deceive the French who are supposed, probably erroneously, to be able to read it'.[51]

The intercept revealed that the Germans had become aware that the French knew that instructions had been sent to the German Naval Attaché in Madrid to set in motion plans to prepare to destroy German merchant ships that had been stuck in Spanish ports since the start of the war (for fear of Romanones giving in to Allied demands to seize them). Also, the French appeared to know something about the 'Cartagena affair' (the visit of submarine U-35 to the Spanish port) and about some of Germany's intrigues in Morocco. At first it was feared that the cipher – which had been in use continuously since April 1915 – had been compromised.

In an attempt to fool the French and trick them into some pointless action or put them off the scent, the German Embassy sent the fictitious messages to Berlin, hoping that the French would intercept them.[52] On 29 May, Room 40 intercepted a message from Berlin with a sternly worded reply to Madrid's report of a possible compromise. 'If the French government,' spluttered the German Foreign Office:

> … has obtained a knowledge of your ciphers it can only be through treachery or through insufficient precautions. Your Excellency will receive three new keys, which are to be employed in turn. … Your Excellency should keep the new keys in your personal charge, in your pocketbook or purse, and on the despatch or receipt of telegrams should supervise the ciphering yourself or through your deputy, and then resume possession of the keys. All telegrams received by you should be burnt immediately after deciphering. Ciphered secret correspondence should be kept in your personal charge.[53]

The intercepted message then gave the three new keys: 'Key number 11: 371, 107, 416, 923 514, 235. Key number 12: 237, 916, 721, 184, 352, 618, 531. Key number 13: 614, 247, 814, 324, 657, 347, 506, 134.'[54] These were keys for use with a '*Schieber*' (slider) substitution cipher (see Chapter 7). The sender of the message was right, the breach of security was due to a lack of sufficient precautions. But he was wrong about the sort of precautions that were missing. The breach was actually caused by his action in sending out the new keys by wireless.[55]

Madrid replied in an equally terse vein, 'In the opinion of my informant the leakage has taken place in Berlin.'[56] Ratibor said that the compromise must have occurred in Paris because the information was known there at the same time or even before the German officials in Madrid had been informed:

> We must in my opinion consider the auxiliary personnel concerned with general papers and to whom the secret papers are not accessible, but who, owing to their temporary employment in the office, are in a position to get an insight into what is going on and obtain possession of bits of messages … The fragmentary and partially false information of the French secret services strengthens the suspicion that the traitor is a subordinate and is himself an incompletely informed person.[57]

All the same, even though the ambassador did not think that the cipher itself had been compromised, he proposed some changes to the way the '*Schieber*' was used to encipher the most sensitive of coded messages by reversing the order of the numbers on each of the three slider positions. The telegram even went on to explain that this meant that 'the first row would read 457, the second row 665 and so on'. A code wording at the beginning of a message would indicate that this reverse technique was employed on a particular message. The intercepted message also (helpfully for Room 40) provided the proposed code wording: 'Is Considered Secret.'[58]

Not only did Room 40's codebreakers get access to useful cipher material, they were also able to watch German Foreign Office officials getting themselves into a completely unnecessary panic about the possible compromise of the cipher to the French. There was another cipher scare concerning the French just a few months later in October 1916. The embassy in Madrid reported that a French agent 'informs me definitely that particulars have been obtained from Berlin which enable them to get knowledge of our cipher communications', although apparently the current cipher used between Madrid and Berlin was not yet compromised.[59] But this concern did not stem either the flow of secret messages or the supply of code and cipher details over the airwaves. Over the following weeks, several more messages were decoded by Room 40 giving details of ciphers.

'Most Secret: Decipher Yourself'

Towards the end of 1916 and the beginning of 1917 Britain came very close to having to withdraw from the war. The reason was a threat from the United States to stop arms sales and to refuse new loans – loans on which Britain and the Allies now depended to carry on the war.[1] In conversation with his ambassador in London, Wilson was blunt:

> The Kaiser's U-boats were an outrage. But British 'navalism' was no lesser evil and posed a far greater strategic challenge for the United States ... the atrocious war was, Wilson believed, not a liberal crusade against German aggression but a 'quarrel to settle economic rivalries between Germany and England' ... Wilson spoke of 'England's having the earth and Germany wanting it'.[2]

According to economic historian Adam Tooze:

> Since the beginning of the nineteenth century the British Empire had been the largest economic unit in the world. Some time in 1916, the year of Verdun and the Somme, the combined output of the British Empire was overtaken by that of the United States of America.[3]

Britain lost its sovereignty by squandering its wealth on the war. Now the United States could end the war by enforcing a 'peace without victory' on both sides – although this would leave Germany with its territorial gains in Belgium and northern France.[4]

Yet, while this crisis between Britain and the United States was reaching boiling point, Germany threw away its opportunity to hold on to its conquests. According to one US historian, 'Unwittingly, the Kaiser [on 9 January 1917] made the decision which would lead to the destruction of the German war effort, the Second Reich and the Hohenzollern throne.'[5] The fateful decision was to resume unrestricted submarine warfare. Thanks to intercepts of US diplomatic communications, the British Government was able to watch the diplomatic struggle between Germany and the United States develop until the German Government made that gross mistake.

★★★

One of only very few hints as to the circulation of Room 40's diplomatic intelligence within the British Government comes from a diary entry made in early 1916 by Maurice Hankey, the Cabinet Secretary. Significantly, after the war Hankey marked the entry as not suitable for disclosure when his diary was being edited for publication. He wrote:

> I saw Captain Hall again first thing this morning. He showed me more of Colonel House's telegrams sent from Berlin … I found that Hall has not shown these telegrams to the First Lord [Balfour]. This information is of course priceless.[6]

Colonel House was Wilson's personal envoy, sent to Europe to seek peace. Unfortunately, we have no hard evidence of how the British inner circles of policy-making used – or did not use – this 'priceless' intelligence. We do know, however, from the files of intercepts, that full, detailed transcripts of the diplomatic rumblings became available as they were copied at the Censor's Office at the Central Telegraph Exchange in London as they travelled between US embassies in Europe and the State Department in Washington – including German messages sent between Copenhagen and Washington by the State Department on Germany's behalf.

The US Ambassador to the Court of St James's, Walter Hines Page, was a firm supporter of the Allies and repeatedly argued for US involvement on the side of liberal parliamentary democracies against the autocratic regimes of Germany and Austria (the autocratic member of the Allies, Russia, is conveniently not mentioned).[7] An intercepted despatch of 25 January 1916 is typical of many of his reports – which show little difference between Allied representations and his own views. He argued that a 'draw' – that is, with Germany remaining in possession of its conquests – would not bring a stable peace, as both sides would remain armed in readiness for renewed war:

> Permanent peace depends on the two great English-speaking nations … we [in the United States] are the larger in white population and potentially the stronger of these nations and peace cannot be obtained without our active sympathy with the smaller empire which is spending its resources fighting the assault of a military monarchy on a free Government. If we accept the forthcoming blockade, as England accepted our weaker blockade of the Confederate states [in the US Civil War], we shall save the world from the aggressive ambitions, both of Germany and Japan.[8]

During the US Civil War, Britain, despite backing the southern states in the war, had stepped back from trying to breach the Unionist blockade of Confederate ports. Now was the time to return the favour. Page backed Britain's approach to the distant blockade of the Central Powers, despite its breaches of international law and the consequences for Germany:

> If we insist on technical [i.e. legal] objections in order to build up a code of Naval and Marine Law, one, or both, the aggressive military monarchies will smash [international rule of law] … The only hope of permanent peace lies in such a decisive defeat of Germany as would prevent a new era of armament.[9]

Many such missives were sent to Wilson from Page during 1916, but Wilson was not listening. Once he had set his policy, he did not want his advisers putting forward contrary views and in 1916 he was turning against the British. As historian and diplomat George F. Kennan wrote:

> Wilson was largely his own Secretary of State in so far as the formulation of policy in major questions, [and] he shared with many other American statesmen a disinclination to use the network of America's diplomatic missions as a vital and intimate agency of policy.[10]

The messages from the US Ambassador in Berlin, James Gerard, have a different tone.[11] The German Chancellor, Bethmann-Hollweg, in an interview in March 1916, had told Gerard that peace could only come about under certain conditions:

Germany must have back all of her Colonies and an indemnity for the sur-render of northern France. About the Belgians he was vague but Germany would probably consent to give up most of it ... [but before that was pos-sible] he said he hoped America would do something against the English blockade and so create a better impression in Germany. The Chancellor seemed in favour of good relations with America and for a reasonable sub-marine war but he will have great trouble.[12]

In fact, there was very little prospect that the civilian Chancellor Bethmann-Hollweg could have delivered such a peace. He played along with Wilson's preference for a negotiated peace, but the objective was to win Wilson over to imposing restrictions on the Allied blockade so that Germany could fight on.

In May, Gerard reported on a talk over lunch with the Kaiser. Wilhelm had been in an angry mood, asking Gerard, 'Do you come like a Roman pro-consul bringing peace in one hand and war in the other?' Gerard replied that any differences between the two countries could be sorted out. At this the Kaiser 'began a speech' and accused the United States of a 'rough and uncour-teous tone'. He took objection to Wilson's description of Germany's method of warfare as 'barbarous'. As:

> ... Kaiser and Head of the Church in his country he had endeavoured to carry on war in a knightly manner ... [but] the opponents of Germany had used weapons and means which had compelled him to resort to similar means ... [the British starvation blockade] justified any methods of subma-rine war and that before he would permit his wife and little grandchildren to die of hunger he would utterly destroy England and the whole English royal family.[13]

An interesting side note comes from another intercept which revealed that Germany's position won support from the Vatican according to US sources. Gerard reported:

> The Vatican states that America can stop the war in twenty-four hours if it would act as it professes with complete neutrality and stay all trade with the Allies. This would seem to confirm the opinion frequently stated that the Vatican sympathises with the German position.[14]

A long, intercepted message sent in September 1916 from Bethmann to the urbane and Americanophile German Ambassador in Washington, Count

Johann von Bernstorff, illuminates the evolving discussions in Berlin. Despite victorious battles against the Russian Army:

> It is, however, still doubtful if we shall succeed here [in Central and Eastern Europe] in attaining a success which would terminate the war in the course of this year; we must therefore reckon for the present with a longer duration of the war. In connection with this the Imperial Navy promises itself by a ruthless resumption of the avoided submarine [warfare] in view of the economic position of England a rapid success which will make the arch-enemy England in a few months more inclined to thought of peace. For this reason the High Command of the Army has had to include a ruthless submarine warfare in its measures, [with a view] among other things also to relieve the position on the Somme ... the whole situation would, however, be changed were the President [of the United States] ... to make a proposal for peace ... [but this must happen soon if Britain was not to] improve her military and economic position at our expense.[15]

The bloody stalemate on the Western Front, strengthened by the catastrophic German attack at Verdun and the equally catastrophic Allied assaults on the Somme, combined with the German inability to sail the surface of the North Sea following the Battle of Jutland, diverted German attention to taking the struggle to below the sea surface. Although influential circles in Berlin were determined to resume full submarine warfare, in Washington Bernstorff was keen to avoid war with the United States, which he thought would be a disaster for Germany.[16] He could see that the German military high command failed to understand the potential of the United States if roused to war.

Bernstorff worked hard to avoid a breach in relations. He argued against military and commercial sabotage operations carried out in the United States and Canada by German agents, organised and paid for through the German Embassy. But he was overruled, and a number of bombs were set off in US factories and other sabotage actions carried out.

The German military attachés in Washington had their own code books, which were different from the diplomatic code books used by the ambassador. This meant they could communicate with Berlin about their planned operations without letting Bernstorff in on the secrets – although as the British could decode them, the intercepts revealed much about these sabotage operations to Germany's enemies.

Bernstorff's popularity with the diplomatic and fashionable circles of Washington and New York made the German military commanders contemptuous of him. But for the time being, his favour among the Americans served to string them out, making them think that Germany was seriously considering Wilson's search for a peace settlement – and encouraged Wilson to allow the use of the US State Department cable links to Europe.

'Germany is anxious to make peace,' said an intercept of 25 September 1916 from Gerard to Wilson. 'I can state on the best authority that if the President will make an offer of mediation in general terms … that Germany will accept in general terms immediately.'[17] But this was a bluff, to throw Wilson and the Allies off balance. The pleas were followed by threats. Bethmann-Hollweg told Colonel House and Gerard on 22 November:

> If his suggestion that Germany wanted peace should be continually ignored, Germany would be forced in response to adopt hard measures, but this would not be Germany's fault … What do these matters in Belgium [i.e. forced deportation of Belgians to work in Germany] matter compared to the hecatomb of [German] lives lost on the Somme since last July?[18]

The Foreign Minister, Gottlieb von Jagow, a firm opponent of unrestricted submarine warfare, was sacked in November 1916. His replacement was the first non-aristocrat ever appointed to the post, Arthur Zimmermann. Wilson, who was misadvised by Colonel House, thought the change of personnel actually signalled signs of compromise in Berlin. According to the historian Barbara Tuchman, House and Wilson:

> … believed they saw in the promotion of Under-Secretary Arthur Zimmermann the signal of an upsurge in liberal forces that would open the way to peace and the salvation of the world. … [Zimmermann] was a big, ruddy, good-humoured, square-headed bachelor of fifty years with blue eyes, reddish blond hair, and bushy moustache, the very epitome of the German middle class, although his middle-class origin he had contrived partially to remedy by an approved duelling scar on his cheek.[19]

In fact, Zimmermann got the job only because he backed the military, and he kept the job only as long as the military commanders were prepared to have him there. As the historian David Stevenson wrote, the 'context' for the decision on unrestricted submarine warfare 'was the growing ascendancy of Germany's high command, as part of the war's broader metamorphosis into a contest between autocracy and democracy'.[20]

Gerard was advised by Zimmermann to go home and speak to Wilson directly to convince him of the need for a change in US policy. While he was in Washington delivering that personal message, the British intercepted a German message sent to Wilson which effectively told the president that he must make peace – or else.

Wilson put off making any serious peace moves until later in the year, after the presidential election was out of the way, and Wilson did not notice Germany's increasingly shrill tone. Bernstorff, under pressure from the military, begged Wilson to respond to Germany's expression of support for a declaration of peace 'in general terms'.

When he had been safely re-elected, Wilson finally asked the belligerents for declarations of peace on 18 December. But, by then it was too late; the German decision had already been made (although it was not formally approved by the Kaiser until early January 1917).

Nine days after receiving Wilson's peace proposals, Bernstorff met Colonel House and asked him for a favour. To help him communicate in detail about Germany's response to Wilson's initiative, Bernstorff said it would be helpful to have access once again to the US diplomatic telegraph channel. Bernstorff told House that he was reluctant to put his proposals through the State Department because the Secretary of State, Robert Lansing, was biased towards the Allies and was prone to leak information to the disadvantage of Germany. It had already been made plain that Germany would have to disown the peace initiative if it became public. But, if a secret channel could be used to Berlin, Bernstorff would facilitate direct communication between Kaiser Wilhelm and President Wilson.

The president agreed – on condition that it was only for communication about the peace initiative. Lansing objected strenuously. He would have to suffer the indignity of having German messages coming in and out of his department in a code that he could not read. At one point, Bernstorff even had to complain directly to House about the obstacles erected by Lansing. Germany, he threatened, would not be able to pursue the peace initiative 'if the State Department takes this attitude'.[21]

Lansing was told to facilitate the channel. However, by then the German military leadership had already decided that it was ready to risk war with the United States. Hindenburg said:

We are counting on the probability of war with the United States and we have made all preparations to meet it. Things cannot be worse than they are now. The war must be brought to an end by all possible means.[22]

The newly reopened US communications channel would be very handy for sending out instructions to German embassies to prepare for this dramatic step – and its implicit intensification of the war – rather than messages about the peace proposals it was supposed to carry.

This was, of course, not the only communications route open to Germany. The Swedish Roundabout could get messages to the Americas and in some cases this route was used. But it was slow – taking as long as a week or two. The State Department channel, by contrast, could carry messages between the German Foreign Office in Berlin and the German Embassy in Washington within two or three days. It was an attractive and secure proposition to carry Berlin's orders for harsher war.

★★★

In mid-January 1917, German Foreign Secretary Arthur Zimmermann drafted a telegram that was to be sent to German ambassadors in neutral countries informing them about the resumption of unrestricted submarine warfare. It was not the first time Zimmermann had had to draft an important diplomatic telegram. In the crisis days of July 1914, in the absence of the then Foreign Secretary, von Jagow, Zimmermann had the job of drafting the telegram sent to Austria promising Germany's full support for whatever action Austria took over the assassination of the archduke in Sarajevo.[23]

This promise of unqualified backing from Germany is often blamed for propelling the world into the war – although of course Zimmermann did not decide the policy. The same was true in 1917. He gave support to the reintroduction of unrestricted submarine warfare, but he was not among the decision makers. His telegram would again be expressing his masters' orders.

It was a long telegram – consisting of 856 code words in all. Bernstorff and the other ambassadors were not to tell neutral governments until the day before the campaign was launched so as to ensure the maximum shock.

Drafting this telegram was Zimmermann's main task, but he also had to draw up a second telegram. The idea for this arose in the German Foreign Office but was approved by Ludendorff. It is this second message that has become known to history as the 'Zimmermann Telegram'. It was addressed to the German minister in Mexico. It instructed him, in the event of war between Germany and the United States, to offer the Mexican President an alliance, making joint war on the United States with the objective of recovering for Mexico its lost territories of New Mexico, Arizona and

Texas. It also suggested that the Mexicans should attempt to bring Japan into the alliance.

On the surface, it must have seemed like a good idea. Historians have tended to downplay the official support for this second telegram, treating it as an idea that slipped past the policy-making circles while they were distracted by the submarine warfare question. But the proposal to Mexico was not out of line with long-standing German policy towards Mexico and the United States. The German Foreign Office had more or less friendly relations with Mexico, where it had involved itself in intrigues since 1910 hoping to diminish US influence and boost its own:[24]

[The] German national leadership made it a priority to promote the already-existing US-Mexican tensions. With the provocation of a military engagement in Mexico, German officials wanted to divert US President Wilson's attention from the European theatre of war, halt arms suppliers to the Allies, and reduce the risk that the United States would enter the war on the side of the Allies.[25]

Mexico had friendly relations with Japan. Both Mexico and Japan had frictions with the United States. If this triangle could be exploited, then the United States would have its attention drawn away from Germany's renewed submarine warfare in the Atlantic and directed instead towards its southern border and eastern coast.

As one historian wrote:

On the international level, Zimmermann's telegram was a spontaneous and rather unsophisticated attempt to exploit American-Mexican tensions on the cheap, and not the product of long-harboured German designs to gain a foothold on the southern border of the United States. To Berlin, Mexico was never remotely as important as, say, the Balkans or Italy before it entered the war on the Allied side.[26]

And another historian concluded that the idea of an alliance with Mexico 'was more likely intended for use in the political struggle between government and military in Germany rather than as a serious treaty proposal to Mexico'.[27] But the idea fitted in with the mood in German military circles, which already saw the United States as an enemy.

The draft of this second telegram went through several stages, passing up and down through ranks of interested officials in the German Foreign Office.

The Zimmermann Telegram – only 150 code words in all – would be tacked onto the end of the much longer first telegram.

***

Much of what has been published about the sending, interception and decoding of the Zimmermann Telegram is misleading – with much of the blame being due to Blinker Hall. One of the two men who decrypted the Zimmermann Telegram, Nigel de Grey, later wrote, 'Many of the statements made by Admiral Hall are incorrect. Some were I think wilfully so.'[28]

Hall threw out misinformation to protect the real source of where the telegram was intercepted. His snippets have been widely repeated, building another misleading legend. In recent years, however, new documents have been released in Britain and research by historians has brought other information to light. The present view of events differs in several ways, some significant and some minor, from the previous standard accounts (provided by writers such as Barbara Tuchman and Patrick Beesly).

Zimmermann initially planned to deliver the two telegrams by submarine. U–35 was conceived as a blockade buster, a freight-carrying submarine rather than an attack vessel. It had already visited the United States twice, the second time as recently as 2 November 1916, partly to transport goods, but also as a propaganda exercise. Its westbound cargo was designed to show off Germany as a powerful and compassionate nation.

Its cargo of 750 tons of dyestuffs and medication for use against poliomyelitis bound for the United States was well publicised. No attention was given to the fact that the submarine also carried a new diplomatic code book, number 7500 (also known as 0075), for use by the embassy in Washington.

A third voyage of the submarine to the United States, named '*Deutschland*', was scheduled to leave Germany in mid-January. However, with the imminent announcement of submarine warfare this became awkward and the trip was cancelled.

Wireless was not a practical idea as any messages could be intercepted. So, contrary to the legend, the Zimmermann Telegram was not sent by wireless, nor was it sent by the delay-prone and circuitous Swedish Roundabout route. Nor, as is regularly claimed, were three copies sent by different routes. Instead, a single copy only was sent and that was via the US State Department channel.

Zimmermann also had to decide which code book to use. There were several different code books in use between Berlin and Washington, but the ones that interest us here are 13040 (sometimes known as 13042) and 7500.[29]

While the one-part 13040 had been in use for some time, the 'hatted' 7500 was comparably new, only being delivered to the German Embassy by U–35 in November 1916. As 13040 had been in use since 1907 and as the new code book had finally been delivered to the United States, it made sense to send the telegrams in the newer, and thus more secure, code.

But the German minister in Mexico City did not have a copy of 7500. So communications between Mexico and Washington still had to use the 13040 code book. This meant that Zimmermann's two telegrams – combined and sent as a single 'message' of just over 1,000 code words for the leg between Berlin and Washington – would be sent via the US channel coded in 7500 to cross the Atlantic. Once in Washington, Bernstorff or his staff would have to decode the long message and discover it contained one part for him and another part to be forwarded to Mexico. The shorter message would have to be recoded in 13040 for onward transmission to the German minister in Mexico.

★★★

The coded message was given by the German Foreign Office to the US Ambassador in Berlin on 16 January at 3 p.m. with the request that it should be telegraphed to the US State Department for forwarding to the German Embassy in Washington. When Gerard received the message, he asked what it contained. He was told that it concerned Wilson's peace initiative.[30] Gerard had it cabled on to the US legation in Copenhagen, who transmitted it in turn to Britain for forwarding via one of the transatlantic cables. It was soon in the United States and the Telegraph Office, and had arrived at the State Department in Washington by 7.50 p.m. Lansing objected to the unusually long telegram and declined to pass it on to the German Embassy until he received a direct instruction from the president. Colonel House explained to a frustrated Lansing that the German Government was talking to the president 'unofficially through me' and that the message must go through.[31]

The State Department forwarded it on 19 January to the German Embassy. There, seven clerical officers were set to work, each decoding a portion of the 1,000 code words of the combined messages using copies of the newly received 7500 code book. Once that had been done, two of the clerks then re-encoded the message to be sent on to Mexico in 13040.

It was taken to a Western Union office in Washington and sent on from there to Mexico City, arriving the same day. A message acknowledging receipt of the telegram in Mexico was sent on 20 January back to Berlin via the same route, arriving in the German capital on 27 January. The copies of both telegrams held in the embassy in Washington were burned.

It was expected that the declaration of unrestricted submarine warfare would at least lead to a break in diplomatic relations between Germany and the United States, and perhaps to war. So secret documents were destroyed to ensure no trace of incriminating or embarrassing information was left behind. Planning for the reaction of the United States to the announcement of renewed, unrestricted submarine warfare dominated attention at the embassy. The offer of an alliance to Mexico was only to be raised if the United States declared war.

97556 = Zimmermann

For the US diplomatic service to send a cable from Copenhagen to Washington it would travel first on the Danish domestic network to a landing point on the west Danish coast. There, a submarine cable would carry telegraph traffic to Newbiggin, about 10 miles north of Newcastle upon Tyne. From Newbiggin, landlines would transmit telegrams to the Central Telegraph Exchange in London for forwarding to Poldhu in Cornwall or to Ireland for one of the transatlantic cables.

As Zimmermann's telegram passed through London, a copy was made by the Censor's staff. It was telegraphed, on a direct line, to the Admiralty's own telegraph office. A copy of the incoming telegram was then sent by pneumatic tube to Room 40. The coded copy of the long telegram was thus received in Room 40 very early in the morning of 17 January, well before it had arrived at the German Embassy in Washington.

The officer receiving the telegram would make some notes on its time and date and probably classify it according to various characteristics. He might also perform some basic decoding work on simple parts of the message. It fell to two young codebreakers who were manning the night watch in the political/diplomatic section to begin detailed work on the two messages. They were Nigel de Grey and Dilly Knox.[1]

Nigel de Grey later recorded how he had 'begun work in [Room 40] in September 1915 under Sir Alfred Ewing. Was first instructed in the codes and cyphers used between Berlin and Madrid.' Some writers have suggested that he worked almost exclusively on 13040 code from the time that he joined the codebreaking team. However, it seems more likely (from de Grey's own account) that he was not kept in the Research Section permanently, for he tells us that he 'was then drafted to Room 40 where I did the usual Watchkeeping work, three-letter and four-letter Naval Signals, VB to the Naval and as used to America'.[2]

Hall, however, later recorded that de Grey showed considerable aptitude for cryptographic work, so he was moved to research, i.e. the political/diplomatic section. According to Hall:

> There had been a pile of uncyphered stuff to work upon, but nothing else. Yet by this time de Grey was rapidly reaching the stage where he could understand at any rate the general sense of nearly all dispatches sent in the 13040 code.[3]

De Grey's own account says:

> In spare time [I] worked also the [German Foreign Office] cyphers and codes as used to the Near East and generally wherever despatches or other material came to hand from other parts of the world. Shortly after the change of four-letter [code] book in 1916 was drafted to work out the new book. When that was solved was returned to Watchkeeping but in spare time worked alone on [German Foreign Office] code used to Washington and the South American states [i.e. 13040]. When this was solved it was discovered that constant traffic was maintained by cable through London between America and Berlin under cloak of Swedish [Foreign Office] and I then was instructed to form a small section for dealing entirely with American matters [plus the Far East] In all during this period some five or six analogous ciphers [were] solved; and one new [code]book was worked out in conjunction with Paymaster Rotter. After publication of the text of the Mexican Treaty [i.e. the Zimmermann Telegram, not a treaty], and the entry of the USA into the war, the section naturally came to an end and I returned once more to Room 40 naval work. On the change of [code] book in 1917 I was given the submarine section to work out and was engaged on that until the book was taken entire in July and August of that year. ... It is impossible to give exact details of all the odds and ends of cryptography that one did from time to time in [Room 40] nor a list of all the places to which the communications worked and solved were sent. In general, I think I used almost all the codes and ciphers in existence up to the time when I was sent to Rome [to expand operations in Italy in 1917]. It is not moreover that one wants to take the credit for the fact but merely

to state that one is fairly familiar with most branches of German cypher work performed by Room 40.[4]

De Grey did not stay on at the end of the war but returned to publishing. However, in 1939 he joined Bletchley Park, where he soon became deputy director responsible for the running of operations, security and machine cryptography.

In the introduction to this book I quoted de Grey's terse account of how he went to tell Hall about the first partial decode of the Zimmermann Telegram. Here we can indulge in Hall's rather more colourful account (thanks, no doubt, to his ghost-writer's fine embroidery work):

> I am not likely to forget that Wednesday morning, 17 January 1917. There was the usual docket of papers to be gone through on my arrival at the office, and Claud Serecold and I were still at work on them when at about half-past ten de Grey comes in. He seemed excited. 'D.I.D.', he began, 'D'you want to bring America into the war?' 'Yes, my boy', I answered, 'Why?' 'I've got something here which – well, it's a rather astonishing message which will do the trick *if* we could use it. It isn't very clear, I'm afraid, but I'm sure I've got most of the important parts right. It's from the German Foreign Office to Bernstorff.' I must have read through that imperfectly decoded message three or four times without speaking a word. I gave it to Claud, and he too read it in silence.

The partially decoded message read:

> Most secret, decipher yourself. We propose to begin on the 1 February unrestricted submarine warfare. In doing so however we shall endeavour to keep America neutral ...? If we should not (succeed in doing so) we propose (to Mexico) an alliance upon the following basis: (joint) conduct of the war; (joint) conduct of peace. (... An obscure passage ...). Your Excellency should for the present inform the President secretly (that we expect) war with the USA (possibly) (... Japan) and at the same time to negotiate between us and Japan ... (Indecipherable sentence meaning please tell the President) that ... our submarines ... will compel England to make peace in a few months. Acknowledge receipt. Zimmermann.[5]

The sections in brackets are marked as such on the archive copy of the files in the National Archive and indicate guesses as to a meaning. Elsewhere, there are wholly indecipherable parts indicated by '...'.

As can be seen, the general intent of Germany to seek a partner in war and peace is easily discernible in the partly decoded text. But it is not absolutely clear that Germany is encouraging war on the United States nor, crucially, is the passage promising Mexican acquisition of US territory in return.

There is a document which reveals that it was de Grey who actually recounted his story to Strauss, Hall's ghost-writer, when he was compiling Hall's autobiography. Strauss recorded that he had had:

> ... an entrancing evening last night ... Dinner at 8 and talked to 2 a.m.. Kelly, Mrs. K (who retired for one of the stories which will NOT appear in our book). I found I knew everybody there, Nigel de Grey, Lawrence, AEW Mason.

Strauss then notes the conversation recounted by de Grey that evening, including the first exchanges recorded in Hall/Strauss's account quoted above.

Before we get too attached to the idea that this charming account is wholly reliable, it is worth noting the next paragraph in Hall/Strauss's story:

> 'A cablegram', [Hall] said at last, 'sent, I suppose, through Stockholm? And will it go to Buenos Aires and thence up to Washington?' De Grey nodded. 'And they'll probably use other routes as well?' [asked Hall]. De Grey replied, 'Almost certainly they will.'

Hall adds the observation, 'At least two other routes were used'.[6]

As we now know, this bit of the story and the dialogue, including the claim that 'at least two other routes were used', are pure invention. They do not feature in the notes made by Strauss after his dinner with de Grey et al. The other important item of disinformation spread by Hall was that a diplomatic code book had been captured in Persia (from Wassmuss). As we have just seen, 13040 was actually reconstructed, largely by de Grey. Hall later explained:

> It was the official explanation which we had decided to give the American Government ... it would be much better from our point of view for the Germans to suppose that a copy of their 13040 codebook had come into our hands than that we were able to read their most secret dispatches.[7]

Even this claim is misleading. The misinformation was also designed to mislead the United States about where the telegram had been intercepted – in the 7500 code in US State Department messages.

De Grey's own account of those days is worth noting:

The telegram was sorted first to Knox whose business it was to fill in any
known [code] groups. His knowledge of German was at that time too
slender for him to tackle any difficult passages in telegrams (and German
diplomatic telegrams can be very ponderous) so that the procedure was
that if the telegrams appeared from what could be read to have any interest
he brought them to me for further study. We could at once read enough
groups for Knox to see that the telegram was important. Together he and
I worked all morning upon it. With our crude methods and lack of staff
no elaborate indexing of [7500 code] groups had been developed – only
constantly recurring groups were noted in the working copies of the code
as our fancy dictated. Work therefore was slow and laborious but by about
mid-day we had got a skeleton version, sweating with excitement because
neither of us doubted the importance of what we had in our hands. Was
not the American-German situation our daily bread? As soon as I felt suf-
ficiently secure in our version, even with all its gaps, I took it down to
Admiral Hall. ... I was young and excited [so incidentally was Dilly Knox]
and I ran all the way to his room, found Serocold alone and Blinker free.
I burst out breathlessly 'Do you want America in the war, Sir?' 'Yes, why?'
said Blinker. 'I've got a telegram that will bring them in if you give it to
them.' As may be seen I had all the confidence of my years. Then came
the job of convincing a man who knew no German with a half readable
text. And Blinker was no sort of fool. But he was patient with me and
was convinced.[8]

Although Hall added the imaginary part of the conversation about the use
of different routes, Strauss's dinner notes also offer a few interesting details
that did not make it into Hall's account for some reason or other. He wrote,
'The partially decoded telegram was "shadowy" and de Grey had to do some
explaining; you wanted to know exactly how it could be used ... You said you
must think things over by yourself.'[9]

Assessing the way the telegram might be exploited took Hall into
unusual waters:

It was the most anxious time, and from my point of view, a peculiar time,
for to the study of the enemy movements, which was our primary duty, was
added the necessity for an intensive study of American politics.[10]

Hall knew from the intercepted telegrams that unrestricted submarine warfare was soon to be resumed and there was a chance that this alone might bring the United States into the war. Also, the decode of the message in 7500 was only partial, and open to question indeed. Finally, there were the concerns about exposing the source of the information.

Hall decided to push de Grey, and later Reverend Montgomery, to work on the partial decode, and they did add a few code groups to their reconstruction but did not get very much further. Hall also decided to sit on the information, locking all papers up in his safe and telling de Grey that no one else must be told about the telegram. 'At that moment, nothing was to be done except to take all possible precautions to keep the news to our three selves.'[11]

The decoding was only partial because the message containing the two telegrams was coded in 7500 which was a new code book (delivered to the United States by submarine U–35) and was 'hatted' (i.e. it was a two-part code book with random allocation of code groups to plain entries). It had code groups made up of four numbers, although it was also possible to use a fifth number in a code group to signify the definite article or other grammatical signifiers.[12]

Room 40 had worked out a few basic code groups, but not much else. According to de Grey:

> 7500 had been too recently introduced for Commander Rotter to have progressed far in its solution. It should be remembered that he worked alone or nearly alone on a 10,000 group code which was 'hatted'. It was only in use to Washington and we had but few messages in it.[13]

As noted above, the draft decode taken by de Grey to Hall did not include the names of the states that Germany offered to the Mexicans. This was because at least some of them had to be spelled out using code groups representing one or two letters and these had not yet been worked out. So, for example, 'Arizona' was represented by four code groups representing the plain-language letter combinations, 'AR', 'IZ', 'ON' plus a single-letter code group representing 'A'. De Grey also recalled that the partial decode revealed that 'an alliance was being proposed with a country the code group (0979) for which was not positively identified but which might be Mexico. Negotiations were also mentioned.'[14]

In Chapter 14 we saw that the invention of machine methods by Room 40's political/diplomatic branch helped to speed up the reconstruction of hatted codes, where each code word had to be separately resolved, having no connection 'other than its context' within the coded message to the other code words.[15] There is no hint in the files whether the codebreaking machine was used on 7500, although it seems quite possible that it could have been. However, against this we must balance De Grey's account, cited above, which emphasises that the methods were unsystematic and there was no significant indexing (which was possibly key to the successful use of the 'hat machine'). Some questions thus remain. Was machinery used? Was it unsuccessful in the given time? Or, if it was not used, why not?

★★★

On 1 February, unrestricted submarine warfare resumed. President Wilson seemed unfazed. On 5 February, Hall went to see Lord Hardinge, permanent Undersecretary at the Foreign Office to request a meeting with Balfour, the Foreign Secretary.[16] The same day, he sent a telegram to the British Naval Attaché in New York saying that it was 'essential to try and get copies of all telegrams' since 18 January from the German Embassy in Washington to the German minister in Mexico, 'if procurable wire in original to me'.[17]

This appears to be Hall's first action in trying to obtain a copy of the telegram in Mexico. One reason suggested for his reluctance to act earlier was that, as the navy's Director of Intelligence, he had no authority to ask a Foreign Office official, Tom Hohler, the Chargé d'Affaires, to do something such as obtain, by what could only be illegal means, copies of communications from a commercial telegraph company under foreign ownership. Hall had probably acquired the authority from Balfour to send his message to Hohler.

Hall and Strauss have left us with an off-beat account of how the telegram was acquired through some good luck and some bad luck. The story concerns a British printer living in Mexico who was arrested for forging Mexican paper money and faced the death penalty. The honest printer was said to be a victim of a malevolent employee. A friend of the printer (in later accounts said to be his brother) knew a British diplomat, presumably Hohler, in Mexico City who was able to secure the printer's release. His friend (or brother) worked in the Western Union telegraph office in Mexico City and in return for saving the printer's life was only too happy to hand over some copies of telegrams.

In all probability this is another legend, perhaps with a grain of truth, perhaps not. The British diplomat, Tom Hohler, later claimed that he had already made contact with a telegraph office employee. Most likely the telegram was acquired for cash or under pressure of blackmail.

When the copy of the Mexico telegram coded in 13040 arrived in London it changed the entire situation. About 50 per cent of this one-part code book had been solved. It used three, four or five numbers to make up its code groups. The code book contained 19,200 words and consisted of five parts including a dictionary, personal and geographical names list, and grammatical indicators. It could be enciphered either using additive/subtractive or 'slider' ciphers. It was one of a family of code books, including 26040 and 5950, and was of pre-war origin, having been in service since 1907. As one US codebreaker said, 'A codebook is not like a wine that improves with age; it resembles a wooden ship which tends to develop leaks.'[18]

Here is a sample of a partially reconstructed 13040 code book:

15 – tyrann	40 – 300	65 – TT	90
16 – tyrannisier-en-t	41	66 – TU	91 – 299
17 – TZ	42 – U	67 – TUE	92 – truppentransport
18	43 – U	68 –	93
19	44 – U	69 – tüchtig	94 – TS
20	45 – U	70 – trotz	95 – TSCH
21	46 – U	71 – trotzdem	96
22	47 – U	72	97
23	48 – UA	73	98
24	49 – UB	74 – TRU	99

Note:
1) The three-figure page number would precede the two-figure page entry number to make a five-figure code group.
2) Blank entries are where Room 40 had not discovered the plain-language meaning.
3) There are several repeats of the plain-language letter 'U' (42–47) as an attempt to minimise code groups showing frequently used characters. However, this is partially undermined by using consecutive code groups.

Code book 13040 was the parent of several other code books (such as Nos 5950, 26040, 4401, 4631, 2970 and 'Arab' ['used chiefly in Persia']).[19]

Nearly all the plain text of the message became clear, critically revealing the offer of three US states to Mexico. Montgomery left us with a short comment on his central role in decoding the telegram in 13040. He claimed that the code book:

... had lately been discovered and brought to a workable point by Lt. Commander de Grey, but it was still in an early stage, and I believe that Lt. Cdr. De Grey would endorse the claim that my ['my' written in handwriting on top of 'the' in the typed original] careful linguistic work contributed to the result when the famous Zimmermann telegram to Mexico (in this cipher) was published, the decode was so accurate that the Germans thought it had been stolen and did not venture to disavow it.[20]

The full text of the telegram in English is:

Foreign Office telegram 16 January No. 1. Most Secret, decipher yourself. We intend to begin on 1 February unrestricted submarine warfare. We shall endeavour in spite of this to keep the United States of America neutral. In the event of this not succeeding we make Mexico a proposal of an alliance on the following terms: make war together, make peace together. Generous financial support and an undertaking on our part that Mexico is to reconquer the lost territory in Texas, New Mexico and Arizona. The settlement in detail is left to you. You will inform the President of the above most secretly as soon as the outbreak of war with the USA is certain, and add the suggestion that he should on his own initiative invite Japan to immediate adherence and at the same time mediate between Japan and ourselves. Please call the President's attention to the fact that the ruthless employment of our submarines now offers the prospect of compelling England in a few months to make peace. Acknowledge receipt. Zimmermann.

With the fully decoded telegram, Hall could now get to work using it. De Grey said:

I remember his saying to me, 'Our first job will be to convince the Americans that it's true – how are we to do that? Who would they believe? I've been thinking and the only person I think they would believe is Balfour.'[21]

The former First Lord of the Admiralty (following Churchill in 1915) was appointed Foreign Secretary when Lloyd George became prime minister at the end of 1916. Thus, Balfour already had an intimate knowledge of Room 40's naval work. Now, as Foreign Secretary, he was a recipient of diplomatic intelligence from Room 40 and MI1(b).

This point is of some importance as Hall has been accused of keeping this vital intelligence away from the politicians who were the people who should have seen it. But Hall decided early on to go to Balfour. As we have seen, Hall had been appointed to liaise between Room 40's diplomatic section and the Foreign Office. Yet, it has to be emphasised that Hall was running Room 40's political/diplomatic section as his own department and not keeping Ewing informed. Dilly Knox, writing in 1927, recalled that the 'material came from Hall; [the] messages [were] sent to Hall [and] action taken on messages by Hall'. The Room 40 staff:

> In so working on 13040 [cable intercepts] as against material coming from wireless they were acting without Ewing's knowledge and their activities were concealed from him. ... [intercept] material provided by Hall was worked on and returned to Hall by a staff appointed by Ewing; the staff was lent to or, more accurately, stolen by Hall.[22]

Now Hall had in his hands the potentially most explosive intercepted telegram of the entire war.

18

On Timing and Treachery

The last week of January was a sort of limbo. The inner policy-making circles of Britain (from intercepts) and Germany (from formulating the policy) both knew that submarine warfare was about to break out, but not the United States or other neutrals. The day before unrestricted submarine warfare was due to begin, they would be told, 'Neutral ships will sail in the blockade areas at their own peril'.[1] Also, any armed merchant ships outside the area would be treated as 'belligerent'.

Bernstorff made use of the last few days to plead with Berlin to change its mind. 'To begin the submarine war without first negotiating on the above proposals would in my opinion place us utterly in the wrong ... injury to Wilson's feelings would make the avoidance of a breach quite impossible.'[2] But nothing would now stop the orders to the German Imperial Navy.

On 31 January, the US Ambassador in Berlin, James Gerard, reported to Washington that Zimmermann had informed him that unrestricted submarine warfare would resume the next day. The British intercepted the telegram that Gerard sent to Washington. It revealed that Zimmermann said:

It was their last chance as Germany could not hold out a year on the food question ... he realized that it was a very serious step and would probably bring the whole world into the war, but that Germany had this weapon and must use it no matter what the difficulties were. ... Mr. Gerard considers that there is no doubt but that Germany believes that Americans are a fat, rich race without sense of honour and ready to stand anything in order to keep out of the war ... the Germans think and newspapers have stated that the US Government's peace moves are inspired by fear only.[3]

Wilson's reaction was indeed restrained, breaking off relations but not threatening war. Fear and uncertainty kept a lot of neutral ships in port, waiting to see how serious things would become.

On 13 February, Bernstorff informed Berlin:

> ... as since 1 February no incident has occurred which affected Americans the war feeling has considerably decreased. The country does not want war ... it should be possible to put off real war for some time if we do not proceed against the USA itself ... Wilson wishes under no circumstances to enter upon an alliance with our enemies.[4]

But once again Berlin was not interested in its ambassador's views. While Bernstorff had been pleading for moderation in attitude to the United States, Zimmermann was stirring the pot. Without the United States making war on Germany, his proposal would not get to the Mexican President. So, on 5 February, Zimmermann sent another telegram to Mexico, this time via the Swedish Roundabout. It instructed the German minister to present the proposal for an alliance to the Mexican President immediately. The telegram was intercepted on 8 February, well before it got anywhere near South or Central America. The message was coded in 13040 and was fully decoded by 10 February, revealing that the plain-language meaning of code group 0979 was indeed Mexico.[5]

The message read in part:

> Provided there is no danger of secret being betrayed to USA you are desired without further delay to broach the question of an alliance to the President [of Mexico]. The definite conclusion of an alliance, however, is dependent on the outbreak of war between Germany and the USA. The [Mexican] President might even now, on his own account, sound out Japan. If the President declines from fear of subsequent revenge you are empowered to offer him a definite alliance after conclusion of peace provided Mexico succeeds in drawing Japan into the alliance.[6]

★★★

With the United States showing little sign that the submarine attacks would push it into war, Hall decided the time had come to act. He showed a copy of the Zimmermann Telegram decode to Edward Bell, the contact for military and intelligence matters in the US Embassy in London, with a request to keep the information quiet for the time being. The following day, 20 February, Hall met Balfour, Hardinge and his private secretary. Balfour decided that Hall should handle arrangements with the US Embassy and then Balfour would formally hand it over to the ambassador, Walter Hines Page. Balfour is recorded as having said, 'I think Captain Hall may be left to clinch this problem. He knows the ropes better than anyone.'[7]

Page was presented with a translated copy of the decoded telegram and other background papers at the US Embassy on 23 February. He drafted a memo to Wilson that reached the State Department in Washington at 8.30 p.m. the next day. Page's memo said:

> Early in the war, the British Government obtained a copy of the German cipher code used in the above message and have made it their business to obtain copies of Bernstorff's cipher telegrams to Mexico, among others, which are sent back to London and deciphered here.[8]

Thus Page, unwittingly, passed on to Wilson Hall's false claim about the way the telegram was discovered and decrypted – and helped establish the persistent myth of the capture of the 13040 code book, rather than Room 40's reconstructing it.

The Secretary of State, Robert Lansing, was away, and the memo was received by his assistant secretary, Frank L. Polk. He informed Wilson, forwarding Page's memo to the president. It said, 'The receipt of this information has so greatly exercised the British government that they have lost no time in communicating it to me.'[9] The president, never a man to hurry, decided to wait until Lansing returned to Washington, which was not until the following Tuesday, 27 February, before deciding what to do.

On 26 February, however, Guy Gaunt, the British Intelligence agent in New York, heard about the telegram from US contacts and telegraphed Hall asking if he had any more information as this was the first he had heard of it. Hall replied the next day, 'Do not use till [Wilson] announces it, premature exposure fatal. Alone I did it.'[10]

Hall's 'Alone I did it' comment has been seen as a self-congratulatory claim underplaying the role of de Grey and others in decoding the message and of Hohler obtaining a copy from Mexico City. However, in his book on British Intelligence on the Western Front, historian Jim Beach reproduced a 1915 illustration of an internal Christmas card from BEF GHQ I Section with the same phrase, 'Alone I did it'. In the text, Beach pointed out that the 'I' was the 'contemporary abbreviation for intelligence'.[11] It is quite likely that Hall's use of the identical phrase has been misinterpreted and he meant that the revealing of the Zimmermann Telegram was entirely the work of Naval Intelligence. The former official historian at GCHQ says that Hall's actions were approved at the 'highest quarters', this being a two-word code word for the prime minister, Lloyd George. On 1 March, Hall sent another telegram to Gaunt in New York: 'It is imperative that knowledge of this affair shall never be traced to British source.'[12]

When Wilson and Lansing met on 27 February, Lansing, not surprisingly, pointed out that the telegram proposing war on the United States had been transmitted over a US State Department channel. A shaken Wilson exclaimed, 'Good Lord! Good Lord!'[13] The two men agreed that the telegram should be made public, but not before a copy had been acquired in the United States. They also agreed that it should not be published officially. That would make it look as if the government was trying to herd the American people into war or to put pressure on Congress where a vote was imminent on the arming of US merchant ships in response to sinkings by German submarines. Wilson also sent a note of thanks to Balfour for providing information of 'such inestimable value … [and for] so marked an act of friendliness on the part of the British government'.[14] A copy of the telegram was acquired, despite initial resistance, from Western Union. It was slightly edited by Lansing and then handed over to a news agency on 28 February.

★★★

The next day, 1 March, the story appeared in US newspapers. While there was much outrage, there was also a nagging voice of doubt about its authenticity. Pro-German newspapers and senators asserted that it was a British trick. *The Fatherland* newspaper declared it a 'brazen forgery planted by British agents … obviously faked'. Randolph Hearst instructed his newspaper editors to treat it as a forgery, even after Wilson had vouched for its authenticity. And several senators put down a motion asking the government to reveal the source of the telegram. Lansing replied:

> The Government is in possession of evidence which established the fact that the note referred to is authentic, and it is in the possession of the US, and that the evidence was procured by this Government during the past

week, but that it is in my opinion incompatible with the public interest at the present time, [to provide] any further information.[15]

It looked as if the release of the telegram might backfire.

★★★

One other piece of news management is worth noting. Stepping back to the beginning of February, following the breaking off of diplomatic relations between the United States and Germany, Bernstorff and his embassy staff, totalling 200 people including their families, left the United States on 9 February. They left New York aboard a Norwegian liner after receiving assurance of safe passage from the British.[16] However, on 16 February the liner was taken into Halifax for searching. The ship was held until 27 February before being allowed to cross the Atlantic, preventing Bernstorff getting back to Germany before the telegram had been handed over to the United States.

Laid up in Halifax, Bernstorff was out of contact with Berlin while the German Foreign Office and Eckardt in Mexico tried to ensure that blame for the leak of the telegram was not placed on them. Bernstorff's opposition to the resumption of unrestricted submarine warfare made him a handy scapegoat.

There was also a bit of a rumpus about the breaking of a seal on a Swedish trunk seized between New York and Halifax. Hall, it seems, put it about that German papers had been found in the trunk. The rumour reached Berlin so that the first official German reaction was that the 'treachery' – for such it must have been – took place on US territory and had happened under Bernstorff's watch.[17]

The first Bernstorff heard of the publication of the note, and how it was suspected that the telegram had come to US attention, was when he landed in Norway on 2 March. 'We have always refused to meddle' with US politics, he protested rather ineffectually. After his return, Bernstorff was subject to considerable criticism, with Ludendorff laughing at him to his face. He left the country in the 1920s. His son was later murdered by the Nazis.

Back in the United States, the growing wave of opinion which viewed the telegram as a forgery dissipated entirely on 3 March when, to the amazement of all involved, Zimmerman acknowledged that the telegram was indeed genuine. William Bayard Hale, a Hearst newspaper correspondent in Berlin and a German agent (having received $15,000 for propaganda work), tried to prevent him making the admission but Zimmermann said, 'I cannot deny it, it is true.'

Historian Barbara Tuchman wrote that Zimmermann's admission of authorship was even more effective in drawing the attention of the United States than the initial publication of the telegram. 'Nothing since the outbreak of war had so openly conveyed a deliberately hostile intent towards Americans, and nothing had so startled opinion across the country.'[18] Lansing, in his memoirs written in 1935, observed:

> I had expected Zimmermann to deny the message and to challenge us to produce proofs. That would have been the politic thing to do ... If we did not produce the evidence there would always be the charge that the whole thing was a fraud ... Thus the Zimmermann telegram resulted in unifying public sentiment throughout the United States against Germany, in putting the people solidly behind the government and in making war inevitable, if not popular, because the German Government's sinister intent toward the United States could no longer be doubted. The 'cold-blooded proposition' of Germany's Secretary of Foreign Affairs in one day accomplished a change in sentiment and public opinion which would otherwise have required months to accomplish.[19]

The story shifted from 'Germany against Britain' to 'Germany against the United States'. The papers labelled Zimmermann's proposal the 'Prussian Invasion Plot'. Pro-Germanism, neutralism and pacifism all lost their influence as the realisation dawned on the public that Germany had mooted a declaration of war on the United States. Newspapers – including German-language ones in cities such as Detroit, Chicago, St Louis and Cincinnati where there were substantial German-American communities – which had loudly asserted that the telegram was a fraud now took up an angry anti-German tone. Americans adjusted to the realisation that they would be going to war.

Wilson, however, was still reluctant to take the step into the abyss. On 18 March, German submarines sank three US merchant ships with heavy loss of life. Wilson's hopes that the Germans would be cautious were dashed.

The US conspiracy theorists' pendulum swung from an irrational belief in the telegram's lack of authenticity to the other extreme, with one senator proclaiming that the telegram contained unpublished sections about setting up German submarine bases in Mexico and amassing German reservists in Mexico to 'attack all along the border'. Lansing denied this, but the omniscient senator insisted 'that the denial was diplomatic but he believed that his information to be absolutely correct'.[20] The Zimmermann Telegram was shepherding the most determined neutral nation in the world into the fold of Germany's most determined enemies.

However, many historians argue that the Zimmermann Telegram alone was not the catalyst for the United States' entry into the war. David Stevenson, for example, says the telegram:

> ... mattered less than developments on the high seas ... the uproar proved a flash in the pan. By mid-March coverage had almost disappeared and in April few newspapers highlighted it as a reason for intervention.[21]

However, this is far from being a unanimous view. US historian Michael Neiberg accumulates several examples of newspaper commentaries on the subject of the telegram. To cite one example, the *Review of Reviews* in April said:

> Far more than the submarine policy or any of Germany's violations of neutral rights the Zimmermann Telegram had the effect of making the American people feel that Germany had put herself beyond the hope of keeping America in a non-combatant position.[22]

Neiberg concludes:

> By itself the telegram did not lead the United States into the war, but it certainly confirmed in the minds of many Americans, including those who had recently been ambivalent, that declaring war was the only remaining choice. ... A willingness to go to war was widespread by March. ... [Even] German-Americans also rallied to the cause, even though many of them had voted against Wilson just a few short months earlier.[23]

Also, in March, the Russian Tsarist Government was toppled by revolution. The Allies no longer counted a reactionary autocratic monarchy among their number, removing one of the factors that had held the United States back from earlier participation.

On 20 March, Wilson's Cabinet voted unanimously in favour of war. The following day, Wilson called a meeting of Congress for 2 April, two weeks earlier than had been planned. Even at the last moment, on the eve of the Congressional meeting, Wilson cried out, 'If there is any alternative, for

God's sake, let's take it'. At a packed joint meeting of both houses the next day Wilson said that the German Government 'means to stir up enemies against us at our very doors, the intercepted note to the German minister at Mexico is eloquent evidence. We accept this challenge of hostile purpose.' Wilson confided to a colleague that he was sure that 'Germany would be beaten and so badly beaten that there would be a dictated peace ... At the end of the war there will be no bystanders with sufficient power to influence the terms.'

★★★

The US reaction to the German offer of US territory to Mexico was painted by Zimmermann as validation of his sending the telegram in the first place. He said that taking into account US behaviour towards Germany and other facts:

> ... which everyone knows ... it is obvious that the consideration on our part was not frivolous as to what defensive measures we should take, if we were attacked by the United States. It was not only right, it was the duty of the leaders of the state, to make provisions for an eventual armed conflict with the United States.[24]

Never mind that those provisions brought about that very conflict.

The publication of the Zimmermann Telegram and the entry of the United States into the war must have been greeted with undisguised joy by those in the know at Room 40 and in the upper circles of the British Government. There followed for the British codebreakers what must have been an immensely enjoyable series of intercepts documenting German attempts to pin down the source of the leak of the Zimmermann Telegram.

As seen above, initially the blame was pinned on 'treachery' within the German Embassy in Washington. Zimmermann told the Reichstag that he had absolutely no idea how the United States got hold of the telegram, which had been sent in an 'absolutely secret code'. In an official statement it was claimed:

> It is not known in what manner the American government was made acquainted with these instructions, which were sent to Mexico by a secret route; but the act of treachery – one may assume it to have been such – appears to have been perpetrated on US territory.[25]

With Bernstorff's return to Germany, the search for the culprit switched to Mexico. On 7 March, Zimmermann telegraphed the German minister in Mexico City, Eckardt, via the Swedish Roundabout, instructing him to 'burn compromising instructions'.[26] In particular, the second telegram (sent on 5 March instructing immediate proposal of an alliance and believed still secure) was to be kept totally secret. Berlin also demanded to know what had happened to the telegram in Mexico. Eckardt reported how it had been:

> ... deciphered in accordance with my special directions, by Magnus [his personal secretary]. [It], as in the case of everything of a politically secret nature, [was] kept from the knowledge of the Chancery officials ... [the] originals were burnt and ashes scattered ... [and were] kept in an absolutely secure steel safe ... up to the time they were burned.[27]

Berlin was not satisfied. On 29 March a message to Eckardt warned him, 'Various indications suggest that the treachery was committed in Mexico'. A stung Eckardt responded:

> Greater caution than is always exercised here would be impossible. The text of telegrams which have arrived is read to me at night in my dwelling house by Magnus in a low voice. My servant, who does not speak German, sleeps in an annexe. Apart from this, the text is never anywhere but in Magnus's hands or the steel safe, the method of opening which is only known to him and myself.

He then pointed the finger of blame at the Washington Embassy, where 'even secret telegrams were known to the whole chancery' and two copies were regularly made of all telegrams for embassy records. Eckardt concluded, 'Please inform me at once, as soon as we are exculpated, as we doubtless shall be.' He received such an assurance on 4 April.[28]

An investigation by a cipher expert, Dr Goeppert, decided from the outset that 'betrayal had resulted from American not British action ... possibly by the treachery or carelessness of some member of the Chancery staff in Washington'.[29] Thus, three assumptions – that the British were not involved, that the Washington–Mexico message was not involved and that neither the 13040 nor 7500 codes had been compromised – led the German authorities away from the truth.

It is possible that behind these assumptions lay an unwillingness to face up to the consequences. If 13040 had been compromised, then confidential communications with Mexico would become all but impossible (notwith-standing German attempts to set up a wireless receiving station in Mexico, which came into operation in April 1917).[30] Hall later observed:

> The Germans actually thought that there had been leakage between Bernstorff and Mexico, which is what I wanted. Right to the end of the war, I do not think that the Germans suspected that we knew as much as we did about their intelligence service.[31]

Meanwhile, the German Foreign Office, army and navy bickered over the security of ciphers. The army's cryptographic section reckoned that German Foreign Office codes were not secure, although the diplomats disagreed:

> Your Honour's assertion that almost all cipher telegrams can be deciphered is untenable. If the matter were so easy, the German wireless stations would probably not fail to decipher Russian, English and French wireless messages. To my knowledge the German wireless stations have only succeeded in par-tially deciphering the Italian wireless messages; this may be explained by the fact that they had material supplied by Austro-Hungarian army to serve as basis. Without such an aid, the decipherment of an unsystematic cipher [i.e. a two-part or hatted code book], is out of the question. ... decipherment of these wireless messages is impossible even for the most clever specialists. It can only result if the entire [code book] is betrayed or essential parts and keys come to the knowledge of a foreign government.

The report also dismissed rumours picked up in the Netherlands that a lot of German codes had been broken. A dozen false messages were handed to the source, who was supposed to be able to get them to the Allies, but no signs had been seen at all that the messages had caused any response by the Allies. So, 'this shows the value of such reports'.[32]

As far as the German Foreign Office was concerned the only possible cause of the leak can have been human betrayal. But the army was not impressed by this line of reasoning. 'The art of decipherment has developed into a sci-ence during the war,' wrote one army official. He asked the German Foreign Office to think again. He offered some practical reasoning:

> Under the Chief of Field Telegraphy there is an office which is exclusively occupied with the decipherment of foreign systems and which has suc-ceeded in breaking all field and naval systems now in use as well as several

diplomatic systems. Even unsystematic [codes] with changing encipherment have been solved by this office without aid from other sources.[33]

A few days later, it was reported:

> With respect to the so-called *Lotteriechiffre* employed for some important matters, investigation showed that this did involve greater difficulty in solution but nonetheless would only assure adequate security if certain defects were eliminated and if a number of codes were available for use at the same time.[34]

But the diplomats were not having it. In August a memo insisted:

> The Foreign Office adheres, first and last, to the point of view that its new *Lotteriechiffres*, especially when re-enciphered, can only be regarded as not absolutely secure if betrayal or careless use of the ciphers or of the enciphered correspondence occurs.

In September, with the row still rumbling on, the army reported that it had taken four weeks for two of its cryptanalysts to reconstruct enough of such a code so that 'almost every telegram could be solved for practical purposes'.[35] At that point, sadly, the archive file of the correspondence ends.

★★★

Before concluding this chapter and the story of the Zimmermann Telegram, we need to step back slightly to observe briefly the reaction of the neutrals to the German decision to resume unrestricted submarine warfare. Reports from US ambassadors in various capitals, sent to Washington over cables passing via London and intercepted there, revealed panic in neutral countries. The fear was not just that their shipping and essential trade were at risk, but that there might be a ratcheting up of the war generally, dragging them further into the conflict.

Spain held back from reacting publicly because it wanted to know what the United States was likely to do. 'Spain desires to take identical action with the US if that is possible,' reported the US Ambassador in Madrid. Switzerland too wanted to know the US reaction:

The Swiss Government is anxious to know what attitude the Government at Washington intends to take about the German Note. Switzerland fears that her commerce with the United States and that her imports and exports will be ruined. Her position is precarious.

In Norway there was 'consternation' and desperate attempts were made to persuade Britain and the United States to give protection to Norwegian vessels. The US Ambassador in Copenhagen reported, 'Great depression has been caused in Denmark by the German Note. The [Stock] Exchange has been closed indefinitely … The King said emphatically that the only hope for little nations lay in the United States.'[36]

The United States informed neutral governments on 3 April that it would be breaking off diplomatic relations with Germany and invited them to follow suit.[37] But later in April, as we have seen, the United States entered the war. European neutrals were bitterly disappointed that the United States, previously the most vociferous defender of the rights of neutrals, overnight became the most enthusiastic promoter of ever-tighter controls on them.[35] Faced with all these conflicting pressures, the neutrals must have felt as if they had fallen between a bigger hammer and a tougher anvil.

19

Applied Intelligence

The winter of 1916–17 was a critical period of the war. Russia began its collapse into revolution in February and March 1917. The Austro-Hungarian and Ottoman Empires were falling apart. Germany, France and Britain all resolved to intensify efforts to break the stalemate. Talk was of 'total war' – mobilising the whole of society for the war effort. The stalemate gave both sides time to boost production and reorganise their economies to support more intensive fighting.[1]

Power shifted to hardliners committed to fighting for victory. In Britain, France and Italy the politicians established dominance over the military, partly because of the failure of the generals to achieve anything other than mass slaughter.[2] By the end of the year, Asquith had been replaced as prime minister by Dafydd (David) Lloyd George.

Once the radical *bête noire* of British politics, Lloyd George had made his name opposing the Boer War (risking his life to escape a violent pro-war mob in Birmingham) and as a reforming Chancellor of the Exchequer. However, age and several years at the heart of the British Government turned the fiery radical into an equally fiery partisan of Empire. The 'Welsh Wizard' had made his way to power entirely through his exceptional abilities. He had everything against him in his background. His mother tongue was Welsh, not English. In the all-too-typical opinion of one military leader, Lloyd George was 'an underbred swine'.[3] On the other hand, in an intercept decoded by Room 40, Walter Hines Page, the US Ambassador in London, told President Wilson, 'Mr Lloyd George is decidedly not a spent force but the most active and inspiring mind that he knows in England with a most energetic and vivid imagination'.[4] Lloyd George's wartime government has been described as an elected dictatorship, given its wide-ranging powers – one headed by a politician set on victory.

In Germany, a military dictatorship progressively took power, reducing the civil government to an empty symbol. The dictators were Paul von Hindenburg and Eric Ludendorff, victors of the Battle of Tannenberg in August 1914. In August 1916, the Chief of Staff, Eric von Falkenhayn, was demoted to a field command in the Balkans and 'the duo' took control.

Hindenburg was the dictatorship's public face (although never only that). A stickler for status, he once rejected a new portrait of him because his uniform had too few buttons, demanding the painter rework the picture, 'Otherwise posterity will believe that I had run around with missing buttons'.[5]

The hard work of defining policy and seeing it was carried out was the task of Ludendorff, a notably ill-tempered character. He wanted all-out mobilisation of human and material resources in what became known as the Hindenburg Programme. 'The whole German nation must live only in the service of the Fatherland,' said Hindenburg. Germany had to become a 'single munitions factory'.[6] Democratic reform was pushed aside. 'The war does not in any way justify democratisation and parliamentarianism,' said Ludendorff. 'A policy of concessions to the spirit of the age is dangerous.'[7]

During 1916 and 1917 communications intelligence – encompassing interception, direction finding, traffic analysis, codebreaking, intelligence assessment and dissemination – matured into a valuable strategic, operational and tactical tool.[8] The lessons of the early years of the war were reflected in the application of wireless intelligence to a widening range of areas.

★★★

Unrestricted submarine warfare began again on 1 February 1917. Neutral ships stayed in port, waiting to see what would happen. An intercepted message revealed the German Naval Attaché in Madrid informing the *Admiralstab*, 'The arrival of shipwrecked people in Spanish harbours is the best propaganda against proceeding to the blockade area'.[9] In April, the attaché passed on a report from Mallorca: 'On account of shipwrecked persons who have arrived here from the French sailing-vessel, *Andre*, panic has increased amongst the crew of the *SS Agios Georgios*; they refuse to sail.'

Kaiser Wilhelm sent a personal message, which was intercepted by Room 40, to the King of Spain explaining that the British blockade was illegal because it was not close to German shores. Neutrals, he said, had accepted the British rules about where they could sail. So he:

> ... felt sure that in the same way they would not risk facing the new German peril ... [He] expressed himself entirely satisfied with the results of the submarine war, which every day would become more intense, and was confident that it would contribute powerfully towards peace, which had always been the desire of Germany ... [He] laid stress on the great importance in the future of submarines, which he regards as an evolution in the naval art which would reduce the naval power of British domination.[10]

In January, the U-boats had sunk nearly 370,000 tons of shipping. In February the figure rose to 540,000 and continued to rise as spring drew on, reaching a maximum in April when it touched crisis level of just over 880,000 tons. The German advocates of the U-boat war estimated that sinking about 800,000 tons a month would rapidly bring Britain to her knees. Admiral Holtzendorff said, 'We may reckon that in five months, shipping to and from England will be reduced by thirty-nine per cent ... England will not be able to stand that'.

So it looked as if success was close at hand. The collapse of the Russian monarchy in March and subsequent chaos augured well for the Eastern Front. And the German Army was holding its conquered territory on the Western Front. Britain, the hardliners predicted, would soon sacrifice Belgium and northern France for peace.

The effectiveness of the German submarine war was in part thanks to the British Admiralty. One problem was the watertight compartments that separated Room 40 from other sections of the Naval Intelligence Division. A post-war British Intelligence report noted:

> It was not until the summer of 1916 that a little information was allowed to trickle through from the section which dealt with enemy submarine signals to the officer responsible for tracking enemy submarines, and it was not until the autumn of the following year that this officer was allowed access to the records of the cryptographic section ... The activities of several sections ... covered the same ground ... The compartments differed only as to the sources from which each obtained its information ... [and] resulted in very incomplete and patchy knowledge on important matters, which if the information had been properly pooled, would have been [better understood] ... a secret is not worth having at all unless proper use is going to be made of it.[11]

Another problem was that the Admiralty fiercely resisted using convoys. These had proved successful for troop-carrying ships, for cross-Channel colliers and in the Mediterranean (where submarine war had continued unabated).[12] But the Admirals preferred aggressive action, searching out and destroying submarines, not acting as mere escorts for 'shopkeepers'. The scattering of merchant ships, they asserted, provided the best cover for the merchant ships, reducing their chances of coming across a submarine.

In February 1917, the Secretary to the British Cabinet, Maurice Hankey put the case for 'scientifically organised convoys', using information supplied by a junior naval officer who disagreed with his superiors. Lloyd George, already favourable to the idea, was still establishing his power and did not yet feel able to overrule the Admiralty.

Meanwhile, ship losses rose week by week. The dreadful figures for April helped concentrate minds and the Cabinet authorised Lloyd George to review the anti-submarine war – in effect, giving him political backing for overruling the recalcitrant admirals. He announced that on 30 April he would make a personal visit to the Admiralty to discuss the matter – this seemingly insignificant gesture was in fact a quite unprecedented move and a direct challenge to the Admiralty.

Their Lordships were furnished in the Admiralty Boardroom with a dial connected to a wind vane on the roof of the building that showed them at any time the direction from which the wind was coming. This was vital information in the age of sail. However, First Sea Lord John Jellicoe (promoted from his role in charge of the Grand Fleet after the Battle of Jutland) did not need his weathercock to see which way the political wind was blowing.

By the time Lloyd George turned up for the meeting, the Admiralty had already changed position – although reluctantly. Two days before Lloyd George's visit, Jellicoe had received a memo from the naval officer in charge of anti-submarine warfare, Admiral Alexander Duff (until then the leading opponent of convoys), recommending a test of convoys. The navy did not like retreating, and to this day, British naval historians paint this as a voluntary move, not one forced on them by civilians. However, Duff, in a private letter noted, 'The [convoy] system is regarded by the Cabinet as our salvation, and we are being forced into giving it a <u>partial trial</u> [emphasis in the original].'[13]

Despite the slow introduction of the trials, the success of the convoys was remarkable. By October the 'convoy round-trip loss rate was 1.23 per cent, or about one-twentieth of that during April's "Black Fortnight".'[14]

Success did not rest purely on the probabilities of a random encounter between predator and prey in the vast stretches of the ocean, although collecting ships in a convoy was an important factor in making it harder for them to be chanced upon. Wireless intelligence enabled convoys to be routed away from locations where submarines were known to be. This could only happen, of course, once the watertight compartments had been broken through. As Birch concluded, 'Room 40 only became of real value when its material was handed over directly to the Convoy Section ... and was sent out to all commands.'[15]

The officer in charge of tracking U-boats within the Intelligence Division, Fleet Paymaster E. W. Thring, was allowed access to intercept intelligence. The cipher key was changed more frequently, but the new ciphers were usually broken within a few hours of the first intercept landing on the desks of Room 40.

However, there were limits on the accuracy of the intelligence. It was not possible to state exactly where the submarines were at any one time – the direction-finding system giving an accuracy of about 20 miles in home waters and up to 50 miles in distant Atlantic ones. But Room 40 could tell the Admiralty roughly where submarines were lurking, pointing out the likely areas of attack and enemy strength in those areas and diverting convoys. A historian of the submarine war, Robert M. Grant, cites the US Navy Admiral Sims's view:

> More shipping was saved through ... keeping track of submarines and routing ships clear of them than by any other measure ... Toward the end of 1917 the Intelligence Division of the Admiralty compiled the Daily Submarine Return, including all the times, locations, and much of the contents of U-boat signals, as well as notes on the number of days the boats had been in cruise.[16]

'Blinker' Hall ensured that U-boats sunk in accessible waters were searched by divers for code books and other documents. 'Significant material' was recovered from ten U-boat wrecks. The First Sea Lord, writing about the search of the sunken submarine UC-44 in August 1917, said, 'Our principal object is recover all books and documents. We hope to get valuable information. Please send any recovered material direct to me by hand. Utmost secrecy is of course essential.'[17]

The wreck yielded an up-to-date copy of the AFB code book. Active measures were also taken to acquire new code books – when a new one was known to have come into force the Naval Intelligence Division would ask the Operations Division to attack German 'outpost boats off the Ems', for example, on the night of 31 March–1 April 1918.[18]

Having discovered that there were real advantages to be had from sharing and using wireless intelligence to direct merchant shipping away from U-boats, senior naval officers in specialist areas and remote theatres worked with Hall and his Naval Intelligence Department to seek more ways that their work could help. A memo from July 1917 illustrates the new attitude:

> It is proposed that positions of enemy submarines in the southern part of the North Sea, determined by directive wireless telegraphy and plotted in the Admiralty should be passed to the air stations interested, as is already done in the case of Zeppelin positions similarly ascertained.[19]

Special sections were set up to handle air raids, minesweeping, U-boats, direction-finding, the Bight, the Baltic, Austrian naval codes and other specialisms.

An important development was the widening of the number of people who were allowed to see the fruits of Room 40's work through the circulation of 'War Diaries' (daily summaries of intelligence from intercepts)[20] and 'Navintell' telegrams (intelligence by wireless to Dover, Portsmouth and Air Exchanges). The intercepts were no longer passed on in their unedited, unannotated raw form, but were edited and assessed, creating 'reasoned assessments'.[21] Under Ewing's stewardship, Room 40 had no typists or secretaries, something which Hall rectified.

The staff levels were increased. By May 1918 there were seventy-four men and thirty-three women working in Room 40. Also, seven new wireless interception sites were opened up and additional sets put into operation at existing sites.

★★★

The integration of Room 40's output of naval intelligence with convoys was only one of the ways in which British Intelligence and military leaders started to use wireless and cable intelligence to gain an advantage in the war. Captain Round, Marconi's wireless receiver engineer and the developer of the direction-finding networks, had 'reappeared with proposals for intercepting signals in wave-lengths not [previously] taken by any of the stations'.[22] The new and more sensitive receivers meant that signals could be picked from further afield, even from as far as 'Transcaucasia', the region to the east of the Black Sea, where Russia's empire butted up against its Ottoman counterpart.[23]

As more-efficient wireless sets became available, interception signals from many more sources were gathered rather than ignored – 'long range field stations have again been heard … some, at least, appear to be fixed stations at places as far away as Warsaw, Constantinople, Bucharest, Cologne, etc.'[24] So, during 1917 the quantity and variety of intercepted German messages increased significantly. The volume of traffic intercepted reached its maximum towards the end of the year.

Until August 1916, all wireless messages intercepted from the Baltic had been 'put aside and destroyed', as they were not seen as having any relevance to British naval operations. As Birch observed:

> When the reader reflects that Kiel [in the Baltic] was the training base of all new units of the German fleet and that the enemy talked far more garrulously by wireless telegraphy in those waters than in the North Sea he will form some idea of the amount of intelligence which had been wasted for two years of the war.[25]

The German Baltic coast served as the training ground for the entire German Imperial Navy, including submarines, torpedo boats and minesweepers as well as warships. The submarine school at Kiel alone had at any one time 2,000–3,000 officers and ratings, either training or waiting for an assignment. 'In the latter days of the war, the organisation of the [submarine] school assumed huge proportions,' wrote Birch.

The Baltic was also where all new ships and submarines came for trials, so again Room 40 could monitor the ships and submarines soon to be operating in the North Sea and Atlantic. Room 40 could also watch the German Navy developing its tactics. 'Once a year, at dates varying, between January and March, all Battle Squadrons, accompanied by cruisers and destroyers, came to the Baltic simultaneously for battle practice.'[26]

Although Italian and French naval forces were active in the Mediterranean, they had limited resources. Also they did not trust or co-operate with each other, concentrating on their own military interests: France on supplying North Africa and Salonika, where it had troops; Italy almost exclusively on the Adriatic, where it had territorial ambitions in the Balkans. As a result, many of the general naval duties, such as protecting merchant ships, as well as supplying Allied forces in the Middle East, were the responsibility of the Royal Navy.

According to Birch:

> The importance of intelligence concerning the more remote theatres of the war was not realised until late … Mediterranean intelligence was thus

allowed to continue for some time on the simple pre-war system ... The interception of enemy signals, was confined almost entirely to H.M. Ships ... it was subsequently discovered that the French and Italians had been in possession and use of an Austrian codebook – of which a copy had lain untouched for two years at the British Admiralty – until it went out of use, but [the French and Italians] failed to work out its successor, a comparatively simple task afterwards accomplished ... Nor had they any success with the submarine cyphers in use in those waters, a cypher which was a mere variation on the same codebook with periodical changes and easy of elucidation.[27]

Not everyone would agree with Birch's derogatory comments on French codebreaking, which is widely recognised as having been at least as good as British efforts.

In the spring of 1917, Blinker Hall toured the Mediterranean, visiting Rome, Malta and Alexandria to assess how interception and codebreaking operations could be improved. He reported, 'I think the time has come when every effort must be made to assist our joint naval operations in the Mediterranean. The sinkings there are ... a matter of grave concern.'[28] Hall sent one of his best cryptanalysts and most effective administrators, Nigel de Grey, with some seven or eight cryptographers plus several wireless engineers to Italy to set up an interception and cryptanalytic unit. De Grey recalled:

I was given the Austrian Naval cyphers as used in the Adriatic to solve. On the solution of the particular cypher as used by German and Austrian submarines when in the Adriatic I was sent to Malta and Italy to arrange for the establishment of an advanced post for dealing with such messages on the spot. ... I then returned to England having in Paris arranged with the État Major of the ministry of marine to attack the general fleet cypher of the Austrian navy in collaboration – this entailed working out a new book and took about six weeks before messages were readable. ... I was [then] instructed to form two centres in Italy one at Brindisi and another at Rome.[29]

★★★

One of the consequences of the Zimmermann Telegram was that the Germans were denied the use of the reasonably direct US telegraph channel over the Atlantic. However, the Swedish Roundabout remained available. The

German Minister to Argentina, Count Luxburg, sent coded German messages via cable from Buenos Aires to Stockholm for forwarding to Berlin. However, the messages were intercepted en route by the British.

Luxburg's most notorious cables, sent on 19 May 1917, informed the German authorities that two small Argentine merchant steamers were sailing for Bordeaux and asked that they should either 'be spared if possible or else sunk without a trace being left [*spurlos versenkt*]'. Another cable, of 3 July 1917, read:

> I learn from a reliable source that the Acting Minister for Foreign Affairs, who is a notorious ass and anglophile, declared in a secret session of the Senate that Argentina would demand from Berlin a promise not to sink more Argentine ships. If not agreed to relations would be broken off. I recommend refusal.

And on 9 July, Luxburg returned to the 'sink without a trace' theme. 'As regards Argentine steamers, I recommend either compelling them to turn back, sinking them without leaving any trace or letting them through. They are quite small. Luxburg.'

Robert Lansing, the US Secretary of State, agreed that it would be worthwhile making an exception to the customary total secrecy about intercepts. He wrote in his memoirs:

> Although it would disclose to the German Government that the code used and the employment of the Swedish Foreign Office as a channel of communication were known to the Allies, it seemed politic to publish them ... the exposure would have a decided effect on all South American countries ... On September 7 the Argentine Ambassador came to see me and I gave him copies of the three messages. With his strong pro-Ally feelings he was elated at their contents and hastened to telegraph the text to his government. On the eighth the telegrams were published in the American newspapers and caused a tremendous sensation not only in this country but throughout Latin America. The sinister words, spurlos versenkt, formed the text of many editorials, and the wanton inhumanity and cold-blooded cynicism of their author aroused everywhere indignation and abhorrence.[30]

Within days, the Argentine Government had expelled Luxburg, and anti-German riots broke out. However, the government retained its neutrality until the end of the war. The president did not feel justified in taking the country to war because he had been insulted or in response to US pressure. Also, the Argentine Government felt that its one unresolved issue with Europe was British possession of the Falkland/Malvinas Islands.[31] But German influence in South America was severely diminished.

★★★

The First World War saw war take to the air. Battlefield aircraft fought each other, directed artillery fire, bombed and strafed the enemy. Naval aircraft attacked enemy ships and submarines. Aeroplanes also formed an important source of intelligence, being widely used for reconnaissance, both above land and sea (easily spotting minefields, for example). Most shocking, though, was the terror bombing of cities and their populations, however ineffective the raids actually were. As a post-war British Intelligence assessment put it:

> It is difficult to account for the extraordinary widespread interest taken in Count Zeppelin's invention by the German public during the few years preceding the war. More than any other weapon possessed by the Army or Navy, it engaged the enthusiastic attention … of the military and naval authorities who appear to have pinned their faith to the rigid airship rather than the heavier-than-air machine … the Zeppelin had made her debut as a raider, a role she was to play with ever-increasing frequency and which was ultimately to become the chief end of her existence.[32]

During a sustained bombing campaign of British cities, 557 people were killed by Zeppelin raids (they also caused fatalities in Antwerp, Bucharest, Liège, Naples, Paris, Salonika, the Balkans, the Baltic and Russia).[33] The first raid on Britain was on 19 January 1915, with the first on London on 30 May. During that one year, a total of nineteen Zeppelin raids on Britain caused about 180 deaths. The amount of damage was not great, but the raids created considerable panic, especially in London, as well as stoicism and determination to see out the terror.[34]

In response, the War Office organised a system for defending British air space. This air war is now sometimes called the 'First Battle of Britain'. The label is not misplaced. There were several similarities with the battle in Britain's skies in 1940. But there were also differences.

The greatest aid to winning the 1940 battle was radar, which allowed defending fighters to get into the air and meet the raiders. But radar was not available in the First World War. Instead, it was wireless intelligence that gave the defenders notice of air attacks and enabled them to track the Zeppelins in the air. It was impossible to keep defending aircraft aloft all the time in case there might be an attack, so advance knowledge of an incoming flight of raiders was critical.

The solution came in a fine meshing of wireless direction finding, decryption, and sophisticated communications and control systems. A special intelligence section was created within the War Office to handle all the intelligence about air raids (and the navy had a duplicate system). The new section, known as MI1(e), was formed in mid-1916. Initially, it had four cryptographic officers, two collating the Zeppelin messages and two breaking the cipher keys which changed daily.

The German military and naval Zeppelin crews made frequent and systematic use of wireless before and during air raids. Wireless traffic gave an alert that a raid was in the offing, as they were invariably preceded by the transmission of a weather report from Bruges. Once the airships had taken off, they started sending messages, confirming to the British codebreakers as well as their German commanders that they were on their way. The rule was for Zeppelins, immediately after launch, to transmit a standard wireless report, 'Naval Airship [call sign] taking off for distant scouting course [bearing]. Only HVB on board.'[35] The last part of the message was intended to ensure that crews complied with an order that they were only to take the commercially oriented HVB code book aloft.

To the benefit of the British codebreakers, airship crews repeatedly broke this rule and such prizes as the FFB (successor to the SKM) as well as the AFB (which succeeded the HVB) were retrieved from crashed Zeppelins. For example, in September 1916 two Zeppelins were shot down over the east coast. A search of the crash site of L-33 'yielded the key to weather broadcasts, as well as radio log book, with her last signal at 10.58 "from DK to OK, signed KK"'.[36] The other Zeppelin downed that night, over South Green, near Billericay, was L-32. It was caught in the beam of searchlights over London and a Royal Flying Corps pilot shot at the airship from below, at 13,000ft, setting it on fire. Among the first people at the crash site were members of the Naval Intelligence Division, who found a copy of the AFB, 'charred but still readable, in the burned remains of the control gondola'.[37] After another incident, a letter from MI1(e) to the air defences dated March 1917 conveyed thanks for 'what you have done for us in the matter of the books recovered from the Zeppelin … material of immense value'.[38]

A third and most useful indicator of approaching Zeppelins was the system they used for locating themselves over the North Sea (dead reckoning not being practicable for an airship high up in the atmosphere). The Zeppelins would send a wireless signal so that German direction-finding stations could locate them. The German Commander-in-Chief would send a wireless message to the direction-finding stations to 'observe all airships' so they could provide location information.[39] These stations would measure the bearing when the Zeppelins transmitted a request for location information. The result would then be transmitted back to the airship so that its crew could work out an approach route to its target. By listening out for the Zeppelin messages, the British direction-finding stations could also taking bearings on the airships. Indeed, the British stations gave a more accurate triangulation of an airship's position than the Germans could supply to their own airships. This was because the British stations were spread between 49 and 57 degrees of latitude, whereas German stations were limited to a spread between 51 and 55 degrees of latitude.

From April 1915, the Germans had two wireless stations reading bearings, located at Nordholz near Cuxhaven and on the Friesen island of Borkum. These offered a poor level of accuracy, because over northern England they were effectively in line with each other. Towards the end of 1917, two new stations were set up, at Tøndern (now in Denmark) and Cleve, 250km to the south-east near the German–Dutch border. Rather than reading the bearings of messages and replying with location information, these two new stations sent out a transmission every fifteen minutes, which the Zeppelin crew could read and work out their own position, making it somewhat harder for the British to intercept the location data.[40]

Direction finding was one of the areas of wireless intelligence where the British and French co-operated closely so that location information available to MI1(e) was supplemented by the network of French direction-finding stations. Also, the French had several wireless stations which transmitted jamming signals ('*brouilleurs*', or 'foggers') to confuse the Zeppelin navigators.[41] All in all, the British air defenders often had a better idea of the position of the raiders than the raiders themselves.[42]

A raid on the night of 16–17 March 1917 illustrates the point:

> The first indication [of a raid] was obtained at 16.30 when [the German naval wireless station] Nordholz sent out a long weather message of the type usually associated with an aerial raid on this country.

When decrypted, this promised fair weather. However, the German weather forecast was wrong. While at that time conditions over the North Sea were indeed calm, the seas west and north of Britain were already experiencing storms. This meant that the five navy Zeppelins launched into what soon became dense cloud and strong winds. Thus, they were pushed off course and became blinded to where they were. They made repeated requests for location information.

They thought they were above London because the German Navy's direction-finding stations were poorly located for giving precise bearings in the south-east of England. The airships had, in fact, been pushed south by the winds and they were really over the Kent and Sussex coasts, where they let go of their bombs doing just £163 of damage. Indeed, only four of them actually made it to England.

They all had problems on the way home, again through thinking they were further north than they were. As a result, they plotted homeward routes taking them over Allied territory in France, where one was shot down. Due to the bad weather, two crash-landed in German territory. MI1(e) noted in a report that German inter-service rivalry had not helped the aircrews. The German Army's direction-finding stations in occupied France and Belgium could have given better information but made no transmissions that night.[43]

German military engineers responded by building Zeppelins that could go higher, out of reach of heavier-than-air fighters. Yet this just made their

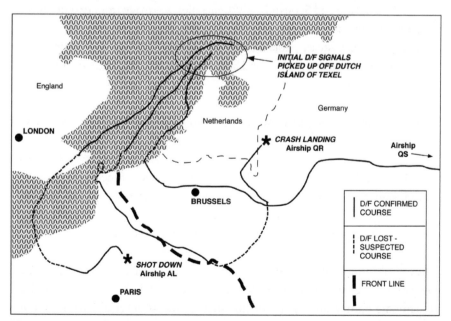

Map 19.1 – Zeppelin raid, 16–17 March 1917

navigation and bomb dropping even more imprecise. Many German officers suspected that the British must have had spies in Germany. Not only could they never find any of these spies, but they could not understand how they could get information to Britain quickly enough for them to intercept the raiders. One suggestion was the possibility of a secret submarine telegraph cable running from near Wilhelmshaven to Denmark where spies' reports could be sent on to Britain.

As one historian has concluded, 'Throughout the first Battle of Britain, wireless sources provided virtually the only operational intelligence available to British air defence. This material was of first rate quality.'[44]

MI1(e) developed into a sophisticated intelligence gathering and disseminating organisation. The individual wireless interception stations were connected:

> ... by direct lines to the War Office telegraph room, and thence by pneumatic tubes to the main plotting centres in Room 417. This was the nerve centre of the organisation and was [the Director of Military Intelligence's] responsibility. As plots of raiding airships came through, warning was passed out via GHQ's Home Forces at Horse Guards, to all Home Commands. Four plotting tables were maintained and bearings were usually received within about 90 seconds of the original transmission. ... The plotting maps covered England and Scotland. ... When a plot was made from two or more [direction finding] bearings, a light was switched on below the map and the appropriate map square could be read out. Different Zeppelins were tracked on the various plotting tables and a master map was maintained to follow the whole raid.[45]

However, for all its sophistication, the system used in the First World War had limitations:

> At best wireless interception might define the number of incoming airships and show that each would enter a given twenty-five mile long section of the coast in a twenty minute period, but it could not define their altitudes and could only approximately estimate speed and direction.[46]

They could not even reach this standard as far as aeroplanes were concerned. Despite the deaths, injuries and heartbreak it caused, the air war on Britain remained a comparatively minor nuisance. It was strategically irrelevant and a waste of resources for the Germans. But, as in codebreaking, it gave the British a precedent that was of inestimable value just over twenty years later.

★★★

On land, thanks to technical improvements, during 1916 and 1917 there was significant growth in the use of wireless communication by both sides – and correspondingly of wireless interception and codebreaking too. British and Indian troops had been engaged since the start of the war in the Middle East, but with mixed results. Military operations took place all across the region, from Persia (Iran), Mesopotamia (Iraq), Syria, Palestine and the Suez Canal, on the borders of British-controlled Egypt. According to one military historian, the Middle East formed:

> … the most complex task of intelligence in the entire First World War …
> This theatre was vast and the needs for intelligence exceptionally precise.
> The Turks had small forces fighting the British but large reserves in Anatolia
> and the unexpected arrival of merely 20,000 Turkish soldiers could over-
> throw the balance of arms in Iraq or Palestine.[47]

British Military Intelligence in the Middle East grew out of small pre-war units but did not do too well in the first couple of years of the First World War, repeatedly overestimating the size of the forces against them and underestimating their enemy's fighting capabilities, and lacking insight into Ottoman military strategy.

In 1915 an Indian Army force was sent to take Baghdad, but the expedition ended in disaster when it had to surrender, having incurred 10,000 casualties, at Kut-el-Amara. An additional 25,000 casualties resulted from fruitless rescue attempts.

The losses at Kut (and at Gallipoli) signalled the end of belief in the invincibility of 'Western' armies. The setback in Mesopotamia prompted fresh thinking. In February 1916, control of forces in the Middle East passed from India to London.

During the winter of 1917, Lloyd George convinced other policymakers of the strategic importance of the Middle East. An indecisive end to the war would leave Germany and its Ottoman ally in control of large parts of the Middle East. The security of the British Empire depended, he argued, on ending German influence in the region. The prize for the British was to link up by land with India. 'As of 1917, Palestine was the key missing link,' wrote historian David Fromkin.[48]

'Although wireless activity on the Western front had entirely died down by the end of 1915, [in the Middle East] it was realised that where his land communications were bad the enemy would still be using his wireless.'[49] Furthermore, sabotage of Ottoman telegraph lines pushed Ottoman forces into making more use of wireless. Initially, interception was handled by army signals units but the intercepted material was cabled back to MI1(b) in London for decryption.

Its attention was drawn to the southern Mediterranean and the Middle East – and specifically to Salonika (in Greece), Egypt, Palestine and Mesopotamia, where interception stations were set up.[50] By August 1916 the Egyptian interception unit was taking in so much material that it started to become impractical to send it all back to London for decoding work. So, 'one of the senior members of the cryptographical section' was despatched to Egypt to set up a local unit there, handling intercepts from Egypt and Salonika. Initially the interception (plus direction finding) and codebreaking staff were managed as one unit, but, as the operation grew, they were separated.[51]

The British intercepted German service messages, German Flying Corps messages, and local purchasing orders as well as 'messages dealing with the activities of German intrigues with Persia ... German intrigues with tribes in Arabia, the Anizah, Shammar, and Dilam and especially Ajaim of the Muntafik'.[52] German and Turkish Army tactical messages were common only during operations or when telegraph wires were interrupted, although there were daily reports to the German Chief of Staff back in Germany.[53]

The most important intercepts were those that helped the British get a view of the Turkish 'order of battle', the names and locations of the army units ranged against them. The interpretation of the intercepts was not as easy as it was on the Western Front. A Turkish 'division' might consist of as many as 10,000 soldiers or as few as 2,000. Or, messages might refer to 'So and So's forces', using the name of a commander. Such a label might be applied to a division when the commander was in charge of a division, but if he was promoted to be in charge of a corps or army, it would still be known by the personal name.

The order of battle had to be built up by extremely careful correlation of intercepts over a long period of time, checking unit names and designations against forces known to be on the ground. Another critical category of intercept contained details of the discussions of strategy and operational planning conducted between senior Turkish and German commanders out at the various fronts (Mesopotamia, Palestine, Syria, the Caucasus) and capital cities. These intercepts allowed British commanders to plan counter operations.

Both the British and the Germans sent new commanders to the Middle East in 1916–17, as they realised the region's strategic importance. The new German commander was Erich von Falkenhayn, Chief of Staff of the German Army until mid-1916. He was first sent to the Romanian front, taking Bucharest in December 1916. From there, he went to the Middle East to command the small German contingent of troops and provide military expertise to the Turkish commanders.

The new British commander, General Edmund Allenby, also came from the Western Front and imported some of the mass-attack techniques used there. A post-war intelligence account notes that Allenby's successes were based, in part at least, on intercepts. 'In the near East wireless was largely employed in operations [by German and Turkish military units] and to the successful interception and solution of wireless signals much of General Allenby's success is said to have been due.'[54]

Another important factor was that Turkey was distracted by the prizes on offer in the disintegrating Russian Empire in the Caucasus. This strategic view was evident in the intercepts that ordered a weakening of the defences of Turkish positions in the Middle East. Early in 1917, British and Indian troops recaptured Kut-el-Amara – 'lost in humiliating circumstances' a year earlier – and then went on to take Baghdad. The force commander, General Frederick Maude, had already planned his operation when intercepts informed him about Turkish debates on whether to reinforce their troops in Baghdad. The intercepts revealed that if the Ottoman high command were to send more troops, it would take a few weeks before they could be got there. This intelligence confirmed Maude in his opinion that it was right to push on immediately towards Baghdad.

Meanwhile, in Palestine, a British attack on Gaza in late March 1917 had been successful, but a foolish error led to the withdrawal of British troops. An intercepted message of 3 April 1917 revealed that Turkish intelligence believed that British 'positions have been withdrawn south of Ghasa [Gaza] to the lines of communication Rasel Markab'.[55] A second battle, between 17–19 April, was a Turkish success.

Allenby arrived in July and spent his time carefully building up his forces, refusing to be hurried by calls for immediate successes. He finally launched an attack on Gaza on 27 October, but it was only a feint. The main attack swung round the defensive forces on the right, attacking Beersheba.[56] Again, it was signals intelligence that confirmed to the British commander that he could strike at an unexpected point. Intercept evidence 'revealed the enemy's reaction to the British breakthrough, its plans for counter-attack – and the weak spot in its line. This was precisely where [Allenby] threw his reserve.'[57]

A key part of the overall British campaign was gaining support from the 'Arab Revolt'. British diplomats promised Arab leaders independence (a promise that was broken). They did not contribute vast numbers of fighters but played an important role in sabotaging (with the involvement of T.E. Lawrence – 'Lawrence of Arabia') telegraph wires and Turkish troop-carrying trains. Intercepts gave the British an oversight of German and Turkish attempts to persuade and cajole rebels and potential rebels into supporting them and not the British.[58]

According to the historian of British Military intelligence in Palestine, 'From mid-1917, wireless intelligence ensured that British forces in Palestine and Mesopotamia would not be taken by surprise operationally by significant enemy forces or a planned hostile initiative on the battlefield.'[59] As the year progressed and into 1918 wireless intelligence became not just a defensive aid but developed into an offensive tool. Three factors were involved in creating this success: first, the rapid expansion of German–Ottoman use of wireless communications; second, 'British proficiency' in integrating interception, direction finding, traffic analysis and codebreaking into a unified system; and third, the competence of British Intelligence in using the intelligence gained. There were limitations and failures but, on the whole, it made 'a significant contribution to the evolution of the campaign in Sinai and Palestine, and as playing an important role in the ultimate victory of the Egyptian Expeditionary Force'.[60]

★★★

With the failure of the submarine campaign to knock Britain out of the war, and with its failure to prevent US troops from starting to arrive in Europe, Germany's great gamble had not paid off. The submarine campaign was neutered but not ended. It limped on, watched over by Room 40, until the end of the war. Like the air war, it remained a death-dealing nuisance to the Allies, but it no longer threatened defeat. Germany's military leaders needed a new military solution.

However, things did not look that bleak for them. In the Balkans and on the Eastern Front there were signs of success for the Germans. In March 1917 the Russian Romanov Empire collapsed under the strain of war and in October 1917 the Bolsheviks took power. The Soviet Foreign Affairs

Commissar, Leon Trotsky, imagined that his historic role would be to publish details of the secret war aims agreed by the Allies, issue a few proclamations calling for worldwide revolution, and then shut up shop.[61] In fact, his first task was to negotiate terms of disengagement with Germany – after all, it was only Russia that had declared an end to the fighting, not Germany.

Trotsky and Lenin (who had been delivered in April 1917 to Russia from neutral Switzerland across Germany in a 'sealed train' precisely to foment revolution) tried to drag out negotiations, fully expecting that German troops would unleash their own socialist revolution. Lenin proclaimed to the Congress of Soviets, that once 'the German proletariat realises that we are ready to consider all offers of peace, revolution will break out in Germany'.[62] But, by January 1918, he began to realise that the world revolution was not imminent, so he sought to prolong the talks even further while the Bolsheviks secured control at home.

By March 1918, Germany's leaders had lost patience and moved forward, occupying large parts of Russia and its empire. As well as occupying the Baltic states and Ukraine, German forces suppressed the Finnish revolution, forced the Russian Navy to withdraw from the Bay of Finland and the coasts of the Black and Azov Seas. The revolutionaries, realising that their bluff had been called, hurriedly agreed the treaty of Brest–Litovsk.

The British Military Attaché in Moscow, during talks leading up to the signing of the treaty, had access to intercepts of telegraph messages sent between Moscow and the Russian representatives at German military headquarters in Brest–Litovsk. The telegrams were copied by political opponents of the Bolsheviks at the telegraph office and passed to British diplomats. The telegraph line had been put in with the agreement of the Germans as it crossed territory controlled by them, so no doubt the German Army negotiators also had access to the Bolshevik communications. One diplomatic historian notes that some of the information used by codebreakers to crack the Russian messages came from a source in the Bolshevik leadership, Trotksy's deputy until January 1918, Zalkind:

> [He] had the reputation in western circles of being a nervous and irascible man, of violent anti–western sentiments. None of the foreigners appear to have been personally drawn to him in any way. In some quarters he was denounced as a likely German agent. On the other hand, a curious unsigned intelligence report … would seem to indicate that Zalkind had been, intentionally or otherwise, the main source of Allied knowledge about Soviet' cryptographic operations.[63]

After Russia and Germany signed the treaty of Brest–Litovsk, Russia's former allies considered giving military aid to opponents of the Bolsheviks in the mistaken belief that a new government could bring Russia back into the war. Up until then, the western governments had ignored the Bolsheviks, expecting their power to collapse. Perhaps for that reason, the British gave little help to the Bolsheviks' opponents.

A letter of 6 April 1918 complained that British telegraph offices were refusing to accept any enciphered messages sent to anti-Bolshevik Russian representatives outside Russia. So, the only people enciphered messages could be sent to were the Bolsheviks. The Russian Ambassador in Tokyo, even though 'loyal to the Allies', was thus denied secure correspondence with Britain.[64]

The treaty gave Germany control of some 1.25 million square miles of Russian territory, 56 million people, one-third of Russia's railways, three-quarters of its iron production and nine-tenths of its coal output. Military leaders and right-wing elements who fantasised about populating a greater Germany were delighted with their gains. War could pay.

But there were downsides, too. What became dubbed the 'peace with violence' shocked the rest of the world and strengthened the conviction of the Allies that they had to win or suffer equally onerous terms. Also, Germany had to keep 1 million soldiers in the occupied territories to control the population and exploit local resources. The great dividend promised by the defeat of Russia – the release of sufficient troops to decisively alter the balance of forces on the Western Front – was sacrificed. In the words of one historian/diplomat, the signing of the Brest–Litovsk treaty:

> … promised at least another year or war, and further casualties on a fearful scale. … The long exertion was now taking its psychic toll. Many people were wretchedly overworked and overwrought. Tempers were frayed, sensibilities chafed and tender.[65]

The only option open to the German Government was yet another big gamble – a final effort to break the Allied line on the Western Front. Hindenburg said, 'In any case, the offensive *had* to be attempted, as the alternative was surrender.'[66]

The troops who were moved to the west brought with them new tactics to burst their way deep into enemy lines.[67] Ludendorff's Spring 1918 Offensive was to be on a gargantuan scale. Millions of men were to be trained in the new tactics. Millions of shells were to be transported to the attack points, as were thousands of guns. All these preparations, even though movement took place at night, could not be hidden from the Allies.[68] When and where they would strike was the daunting military and intelligence question facing Allied intelligence.

★★★

Nearly two years earlier, the Battle of the Somme, launched on 1 June 1916, had revealed the weakness of British intelligence gathering and analysis. According to a historian of BEF Intelligence, 'Working from false assumptions about the state of the German reserves, GHQ Intelligence underestimated consistently the German capacity to reinforce the Somme front.'[69] Behind misplaced optimism lay the persistent belief of the BEF's commander, Douglas Haig, in the idea of creating opportunities for a breakthrough that would allow the cavalry to mop up the German forces from behind. This hope persisted even in November 1917 during the Battle of Cambrai – famous for being the first battle featuring British tanks.

Initially the British assault achieved an astonishing advance of up to 7,000 yards (6,400m). Three days into the battle, on 23 November, Haig wrote in his diary, 'Day was highly successful but I am anxious that everything possible should be done to pass our cavalry through near Bourlon to exploit our success before the Enemy can recover and bring up fresh troops'.[70] This was a false hope and on 30 November a German counterattack drove the British back.

The Ludendorff Offensives, planned to start in March 1918, presented a challenge to the BEF's GHQ Intelligence operation. This was especially so as, apart from Verdun, the Allies had not had to cope with a major German offensive on the Western Front since the onset of trench warfare. Thus, in 1918, according to some historians, the Allies had one of their greatest intelligence failures of the war.[71] However, to others British Intelligence performed pretty well, making use of prisoner interrogations, captured documents, photographic reconnaissance and train-watching espionage groups in enemy territory, as well as placing a growing reliance on wireless intelligence.[72]

The German Army had put a lot of effort into improving their communications since the Battle of the Somme. Then there was limited German wireless activity near the front, but between January and August 1917 the number of German Army wireless sets rose from 125 to some 700.[73] However, as a British Intelligence report noted:

It was plain that the new stations had been rushed up in a hurry, not only from their haphazard method of grouping, but also from the inefficient operation procedure, method of working, and mutual interference with one another. ... In one German Army, during 1916, all the two-letter call [signs] in a group began with the same letter [but from mid-1917] the enemy's wireless system has gradually improved to the present time, when each division on an active front is served by a wireless detachment, consisting of about 12 stations (7 in action, rest in reserve) manned by about 90 operators. ... The need for better communication between artillery units and between infantry and artillery, during severe fighting, is evidently the prime reason for the latest re-organisation of [divisional wireless systems].[74]

By September 1917, the German Army had 110 trench wireless detachments, ninety-six of them on the Western Front.[75] A French report observed that it was 'possible that a complete wireless network is contemplated, which will link up the headquarters of all formations down to divisions'.[76] All the same, some weaknesses were evident. A British report noted, 'There is a very prevalent tendency for German operators to depart from regular procedure. Operating signals and special prefixes are frequently mutilated, and hardly a single [unit] adheres strictly to the rules laid down.'

The BEF responded in mid-1917 by expanding its wireless interception and codebreaking capabilities on the Western Front, setting up a Wireless Observation Group within every British army, each equipped with six interception sets and two direction-finding sets, manned by seventy-five personnel. They mainly gathered intelligence about the placing and movement of different German Army units ('traffic analysis'). This provided information that could reveal forthcoming attacks and troop movements.

One US codebreaker was later to write, 'It is safe to say that in the early days [of US involvement in the war] almost as valuable information was secured from merely an external study of the enemy's wireless traffic as from the actual decipherment and decodement [sic] of his messages.'[77] The British Wireless Observation Groups issued summaries of wireless intelligence (supposedly garnered from 'captured documents' in an attempt to hide the real source in case of capture by the enemy) to senior corps officers.

They also passed on material to the BEF's GHQ Intelligence branch, GHQ I(e), which had been set up under George Church in autumn 1916. It issued its own weekly summaries to all armies, again concealed as ordinary intelligence.[78] 'Messages dealing with plans for [German Army] raids, local attacks or counterattacks, reliefs, etc, were frequently solved in time to be of great value.'[79]

★★★

By March 1918, on the eve of the great German offensive, GHQ Intelligence had detected plans for an offensive and assessed that the German Army still did not have enough troops and reserves on the Western Front to inflict a decisive defeat on the Allies. They correctly identified that the main focus of the German offensive would be directed against the BEF's Third and Fifth Armies, but incorrectly expected it to exclude the southern part of the Third Army's area, next to the French, where the hammer blow did indeed fall.

At first, the German offensive was a great success, capturing many square miles of territory in a few days, so much in contrast to the hard pounding needed under the old tactics to gain a few square yards. Also, while the British had improved communications for when they attacked, they had paid little attention to communications needs in the event of a retreat, making a response more difficult to organise.[80] For the Allies this was a low point. The Kaiser cracked open bottles of champagne to toast the reversal of fortunes. Victory seemed within reach.

In preparation for the great offensives and in an attempt to 'blind' the Allied defensive capabilities, the German Army had undertaken a systematic reorganisation of their codes and ciphers using three new code and cipher systems. Within a 3km 'danger zone' immediately behind the front line, all communication was encoded with three-number code groups from a code book, the *Schlüsselheft* ('Key Book'). For ease of use close to the front line, it was a one-part (alphabetical) code book. But that meant it was also fairly easily subject to being reconstructed by Allied cryptographers. For this reason, encoded messages were also enciphered. Each division had its own cipher using tables known as the '*Geheimklappe*' ('secret flap').[81] The first two numbers in each code group in a message would be substituted by two other numbers using the '*Geheimklappe*' grid (or table). The third number in the code group would remain unchanged – which was a weakness that allowed Allied cryptographers to break the cipher system even when the grid was changed as often as daily.

To use the '*Geheimklappe*' to encipher a code group, say '453', the operator would locate '4' in the left-hand column and '5' in the topmost row in the '*Verschlüssingstafel*' (enciphering table). The cipher result, '15', would then be read where the column and row intersected (see Diagram 19.1), giving '153' as the enciphered result.

Deciphering the message used a separate accompanying '*Entschlüsselungstafel*' (deciphering table) in similar manner, looking up '1' in the left-hand column and '5' in the uppermost row and to read '45' in the grid at the intersection point to reveal the unenciphered code group of '453'. The pair of enciphering and deciphering '*Geheimklappe*' grids currently in use would be inserted into a flap at the back of the *Schlüsselheft* code book, with the flap folded out so that the tables could be seen when in use and folded in when not in use. When the pair of grids was changed the old pair was slid out of the foldout flap and a new pair slid into it.

The *Schlüsselheft* was introduced on 10–11 March 1918, just before the great offensive, timed to sow confusion among the Allied cryptographers. However, early on the morning of 11 March, a message of thirteen code groups in the

Geheimklappe
Verschlüsselungstafel (Encipherment table)
Source: ADM137/4399

	0	1	2	3	4	*5*	6	7	8	9
0	11	45	77	30	14	64	51	98	23	87
1	29	92	27	65	46	38	10	61	40	94
2	56	12	99	52	06	31	86	71	78	24
3	37	89	43	13	79	44	76	22	68	41
4	28	07	57	00	01	*15*	95	54	39	88
5	70	82	36	66	47	32	21	62	97	26
6	58	20	69	02	85	60	80	16	72	90
7	83	08	59	74	09	63	35	05	55	42
8	18	19	48	93	75	49	73	81	17	91
9	25	50	67	33	53	96	04	34	84	03

Diagram 19.1 – *Geheimklappe* enciphering grid

new code was intercepted by a US wireless operator and passed on to the US cryptographic unit. This intercept was followed a few minutes later by a much shorter message from the German receiving operator. This reply was in the old code and contained the code group for '*ohne Sinn*' (unreadable) and two other code groups. One of them had been reconstructed and meant '*alt*' (old); the other was unknown to Allied codebreakers. It was assumed to be a request for the original message to be re-sent in the old code.

Half an hour later a message in the old code, of the same length as the original message in the new code, was indeed intercepted. When decoded it consisted mainly of spelling code groups detailing a planned German operation on the British sector. The US cryptographer noted the urgency of the information:

> These solutions were telegraphed immediately to the French Code Office. We had not as yet adopted a method of secret communication by telegraph with the British Code Office ... [so] these solutions were despatched to the British by special aeroplane. The first break was sufficient. The new code was attacked at once, ... [and the] principle classes of groups soon manifested themselves.[82]

The French captured a copy of the code book on 25 March which confirmed the Allied work on the code.[83]

★★★

Behind the 3km 'danger zone', communications between regiments, divisions and artillery groups had to use a code book with three-letter code words, *Satzbuch* ('sentence book'). Orders specified that copies of the *Satzbuch* were not to be taken closer than 3km from the front line to minimise chances of capture.

Initially, it had 2,208 entries but this was increased to 3,380 by expanding it to use five-letter code words and then increased again to 4,205 by introducing the extra letters, Ä, Ö and Ü. As it was a 'two-part' (randomly organised) code book it was considered harder for the Allies to reconstruct, so messages were not enciphered. Each German Army on the Western Front had its own version of the *Satzbuch* so that at any one time there were about ten in use.[84] The code book was broken by the techniques described in Chapter 14, and provided further useful intelligence.

Further back still from the front line, for communications between divisions, corps and army headquarters, a special cipher system was introduced (without a code book). Initially known to the Allies as ADFGX, it used two cipher stages, with an initial substitution stage followed by a transposition stage. It was considered by the German cipher authorities to be unbreakable.

For the first stage, it used a grid providing twenty-five possible cipher substitutions (one for each letter in the alphabet, except J). Messages consisted only of the letters ADFGX – thus, the name given to it by Allied cryptographers. These letters were chosen because their Morse code versions are very different from one another, so it was hoped mistakes in transmission would be minimised. It was then expanded to add a sixth letter to the grid, so becoming known as the ADFGVX cipher, allowing for thirty-six possible cipher substitutions (twenty-six letters of the alphabet and the digits 0 to 9).

In the enciphered messages each plain-language letter would be substituted by two letters, so plain letter H would become GV (see Diagram 19.2), X would become AF, W would become FD, etc. (thus, the enciphered messages were twice as long as the plain-language versions). After the substitution stage, the second stage shuffled the enciphered characters around using the transposition technique described in Chapter 7, with a pretty long key (such as 6, 16, 7, 5, 17, 2, 14, 10, 15, 9, 13, 1, 21, 12, 4, 8, 19, 3, 11, 20, 18). The transposition had the effect of splitting up the two letters determined by the grid to represent the plain-language letter. Thus, the combined two-stage cipher system presented the Allied codebreakers with a very difficult task.

It took a lot of effort by the brilliant French codebreaker Georges Painvin to break the system in June 1918.[85] He first worked out how to break it using two messages either beginning or ending with the same sequence of jumbled characters in intercepted messages.[86] This allowed him to start unravelling the transposition columns and then the substitution grid. Initially it took Painvin several sleepless days to make a break, but he eventually honed down his methods to take just twenty-four hours. However, he did not manage to develop a general technique to unravel any message and remained dependent on messages with the same beginning or ending (indeed, it was only after the war was over that a general solution was worked out).

This restriction did not prevent Painvin deciphering one crucial message that was intercepted on 1 June. Twenty-six hours later he was able to inform the Deuxième Bureau that one of the messages read, 'Hasten supplies of munitions. Stop. Send by day if [it can be done] unseen [*Munitionierung beschleunigen. Punkt. Soweit nicht eingesehen auch bei Tag*]'.

ADFGVX cipher
Source: J Rives Childs: German Military Ciphers

Example - *H* is enciphered as *GV*

	A	D	F	G	V	X
A	C	O	8	X	F	4
D	M	K	3	A	Z	9
F	N	W	L	0	J	5
G	5	S	1	Y	H	U
V	P	I	Y	B	6	R
X	E	Q	7	T	2	G

Diagram 19.2 – ADFGVX cipher grid

British direction-finding records showed that the munitions were to be sent to a location near the front in the French sector. As it was most unusual to risk transferring supplies by day it was guessed that the munitions were needed urgently for an imminent attack. This assumption was backed up by air reconnaissance and information from captured German soldiers. This intelligence allowed the French to prepare for the onslaught that was launched on 9 June and thus blunt it, preventing a breakthrough of the so-called Gneisenau Offensive.

By 14 June, the attack had ground to a halt. 'The German army was never so dangerous again, and from now on even its tactical effectiveness diminished, while the Allies perfected methods that checkmated its assault procedures.'[87]

The German Army message decrypted by Painvin went down in French historiography of the war as the '*télégramme de la victoire*' (the telegram of victory).[88] In reality, French, US and British cryptographers had all jointly contributed vital intelligence to aid the Allied defeat of Germany's last great gamble.

★★★

Although the Ludendorff Offensive consisted of a series of major attacks, each of which initially made big gains, in turn, they petered out as supply lines became stretched and the Allies organised resistance. Ludendorff lost sight of his objectives. He started switching the focus of attacks, thus blunting them. And, crucially, German soldiers stopped fighting to gorge themselves on captured supplies of food and wine. After years of minimal rations, they preferred the opportunity to indulge themselves to more fighting. The soldiers also realised that the propaganda they had been fed about the poor conditions on the Allied side were lies. This was the first major sign of the collapse of morale in the German Army.[89] Many German troops allowed themselves to be captured to avoid more fighting.

When the last German offensive failed in July, the German Army had suffered some 250,000 casualties – killed, wounded or captured. The British suffered some 236,000 and the French 75,000. But Germany could no longer replace its losses while US troops were arriving at a rate of 125,000 a month and, in May, near the end of the offensive, there were already some 670,000 fresh US troops in northern France.

Ludendorff hid the full extent of the German losses from the Kaiser, the Chancellor, German troops and the German public. Propaganda lauded great German gains, but the news of the failure could not be entirely suppressed. The submarine assault had not ended the war and the blockade was biting. Rations were again reduced. 'The entire army had anticipated an overwhelming victory from the March offensive, and when this did not occur morale sunk.'[90]

Ludendorff, however, blamed inadequate efforts by his subordinate commanders, his troops and civilians on the home front. 'In some places,' he said, 'wages are so high that there is no longer any incentive to work. On the contrary, disinclination to work, love of pleasure and high living are on the increase. Workmen often lounge about all day.'[91]

War, Revolution and Peace

In mid-1918 it was Germany that appeared to be on the brink of a communist revolution. Ludendorff thought repression of the German population was justified because he imagined that its will to fight was being undermined by agitators and militants. In reality, it was his own domestic policies that pushed German workers – and soldiers and sailors – into the radical camp, opening their minds to socialist arguments, and weakening morale among society at large and within the armed forces. 'Whatever the problem, [Ludendorff] insisted on giving priority to narrow military considerations,' wrote one historian.[1]

Germany's allies, too, were faltering under the pressure of war. As early as February 1918, the new Austrian Emperor Karl (86-year-old Franz-Joseph having died in November 1916),had sent a wireless message to the Austrian Ambassador in Madrid asking the Spanish King to approach the United States about peace talks. The message was intercepted by Room 40, decoded and passed on to Lloyd George. He therefore knew the full details of the proposal before it was presented to Wilson. Room 40 also intercepted a message from Berlin to Madrid informing Prince Ratibor, the German Ambassador, that Germany opposed Austria's move and hoped it would fail.

The initial success of the German offensive of March 1918 had put an end to any continuation of these peace feelers. After the failure of the offensive, German military morale started to collapse. Yet, so traumatised by the apparent closeness of defeat, Allied governments and the military:

… continued to anticipate a final victory [only] in 1919 or even 1920 …
Only when the Allied armies suddenly delivered a series of spectacular

successes on all fronts did it become conceivable that the war might end that autumn … The tide turned first [on the Western Front], where from mid-July to September the Allies regained the territory lost since March. They then broke through the strongest German positions. In later September the Allied armies in the Balkans knocked out Bulgaria and those in Palestine annihilated the Turkish forces opposite them. A month later the Italians broke the main Austro-Hungarian army, while the Allies in the west herded their enemy towards the German border.[2]

When the French counter-attacked on 18 July, followed by the British, Canadian and Australian troops (along with 600 tanks) on 8 August, it was the start of the end for the German occupation of Belgium and northern France. Up until then the German Army had successfully used 'traffic analysis' of wireless communications to work out the Allied 'order of battle' and 'had easily traced British dispositions and deployments'. But, 'British signals security was radically improving, and thus also the ability to conceal British operations. Without knowing it the Germans had lost their enemy.'[3]

The careful use of wireless and the creation of 'dummy' wireless traffic was employed to deceive the German Intelligence Service about where Allied forces were located and thus where they were intending to attack. As happened in Mesopotamia and Palestine, this use of wireless deception helped the Allied offensives succeed.

The British Army (with Dominion troops), the French Army and the US Army attacked repeatedly, each time taking more territory from the German troops. A British report noted:

> The enemy has generally made great use of his wireless during the last two months, very high activity having been noticed following our attacks. As a result of our offensive of 8 August there was a considerable disorganisation of his wireless system: several messages were sent in clear and there were repeated requests for repetitions of messages etc. Activity ceased altogether at 11.00 evidently owing to the compulsory withdrawal of his stations.[4]

On 4 October, the German Government sent a 'peace note' to President Wilson and the next day announced it was seeking an armistice. It took until early November to agree terms, but the war was clearly ending.

Military historians identify the cause of the German defeat as the adoption by Allied commanders of winning tactics. They had adopted a concept of war fighting and had the weapons systems they needed. The concept was 'bite and hold' – taking small chunks and holding on to them, rather than always expecting a major breakthrough and the 'rolling up' of the enemy lines. The weapons systems were 'combined arms', using infantry, tanks, artillery, aircraft and command-and-control systems to overwhelm the enemy defences. But while these factors were no doubt of great importance, they are insufficient to account in mid-1918 for the collapse of the morale of the German Army, affecting the lower ranks through to the highest commanders.

The Allied offensives were also successful because the German troops were increasingly unwilling to fight on and surrendered in droves. The German soldiers' awareness of the arrival of large numbers of US troops contributed to the decline in morale. The United States started to join battle in mid-1918. German soldiers, tired after four years of war and lacking in reinforcements, were faced with fresh troops in increasing numbers.

Ludendorff later wrote:

> I was told of deeds of glorious valour, but also of behaviour which, I openly confess, I should not have thought possible in the German army; whole bodies of our men had surrendered to single troopers or isolated squadrons. Retiring troops, meeting a fresh division going bravely into action, had shouted out things like 'Blackleg' and 'You're prolonging the war', expressions that were to be heard again later. The officers in many places had lost their influence and allowed themselves to be swept along with the rest.[5]

Given his role as commander and his persistent refusal over the years to listen to any suggestion of peace, Ludendorff had little choice but to remain a believer in ultimate victory. If he failed to demonstrate to his subordinates, and through them to the troops, his complete commitment to victory, then the morale essential to maintain an army in fighting mode would dissipate.

The British attack on 8 August threatened to send him over the edge. He needed a consultation with a psychiatrist following the crisis on that day. Shortly afterwards, he told Hindenburg, Kaiser Wilhelm, the Chancellor, the Crown Prince and the Austrian Emperor that the war could not be won.

On 26 September, the US Army commander unleashed an attack by 550,000 US and 110,000 French and French colonial troops. Two days later, Ludendorff cracked. He demanded an immediate peace. The politicians to whom he turned pointed out that it would take some time. They began to make contact with President Wilson, who, it was assumed, would demand a less onerous peace than the bitter French and avaricious British. Meanwhile, the Allied offensive continued pushing the German Army back towards the German border.

★★★

At sea, the submarine war also carried on. On 4 October a U-boat sank a passenger vessel with the loss of 292 lives. On 10 October, another ship was sunk with the loss of 176 out of 720 passengers on board. Wilson demanded an immediate stop to the sinking of passenger ships. Ludendorff, who now started to insist that he had never asked for peace, opposed giving in to Wilson's demands, as did the new navy chief, Scheer. But on 20 October, the Kaiser finally found the will to overrule Ludendorff and called off the submarine attacks on passenger vessels. An angry Scheer recalled all submarines to base. The submarine ports at Ostend and Zeebrugge were closed as Allied armies pushed their advance towards Germany. The submarine war was over.

Scheer, however, was hatching another idea. In the words of one German historian, 'Among the naval commanders the idea still held force that the navy had to demonstrate and justify its future existence. This could now only be done through a last decisive battle with the British.'[6] Scheer did not inform the *Admiralstab*, the Kaiser or the Chancellor about his plans. On 22 October, he began planning a final naval sortie with as many German ships as were available, including the entire fleet of U-boats, for 30 October. An intercepted letter from a naval officer on a torpedo boat describes what happened:

> At the end of October, just as we were getting ready for the second part of our exercises, every single available boat was ordered to Wilhelmshaven … We knew at once that some sort of enterprise was underway although it was officially stated that the fleet was going to carry out manoeuvres … Had the raid taken place a naval engagement would have been fought, besides which the Battle of Jutland would have been mere child's play. Our entire fleet would have been thrown into the scale and this would have led to the long-expected decisive battle ending in the total destruction of our forces and of the greater part of the British fleet … Had the losses been in our favour, the war might have taken a different turn, at any rate there would have been no armistice, or else a different one.[7]

But news of the 'suicide mission' spread around the German ships' crews, despite attempts to keep them in the dark. A couple of days before the operation was due, the first sign of trouble was when stokers from some ships in Cuxhaven hid themselves when their ship was ordered to get up steam. The insubordination turned into mutiny and spread to other warships at Cuxhaven, with mutineers taking control of the warships (only larger ships were affected, not minesweepers, submarines and the like).

A threat to fire on rebel ships led to the arrest of some 200 'ringleaders'. Scheer decided to disperse the affected ships, sending them to other ports such as Kiel and Wilhelmshaven. This backfired as it spread the revolt. There, too, ships' crews took control of their vessels, snatched down the imperial flag and raised the red flag.

In Kiel, thousands of armed sailors marched in the streets and formed a Soldiers' Council ('*Soldaten Rat*') in imitation of the Russian Soviets. The fever spread to other naval and then commercial ports, such as Hamburg and Bremen, and to inner Germany, Cologne, Hanover, Frankfurt, Dresden, Munich and eventually to Berlin itself. Mutiny threatened to turn into revolution.

From intercepted messages, Room 40 was able to pick up some hints of the plan for a final battle and, with delays, of its mutinous consequences. Room 40 had refined its operations so that in 1918 it could intercept German wireless messages, decode them and then get the intelligence out to ships at sea in less than thirty minutes once the cipher key had been broken.[8] The German Imperial Navy had reorganised its wireless call-sign system in September but this had not stopped Room 40 from continuing to harvest the fruits of German naval wireless traffic.

However, not all orders were sent by wireless. Scheer travelled from Berlin to Wilhelmshaven to personally deliver his orders to Hipper to organise the grand sortie. The intelligence analysts had to infer what was going on from orders sent to vessels at sea.

On 22 October, intercepted messages showed that all German submarines were ordered to concentrate in the middle of the North Sea, but no one in the Naval Intelligence Division was sure what this implied. Then, overnight on 23–24 October there was an unusually high number of messages – and they were sent in an unknown cipher.

It seems that Room 40 was unable to break this cipher, so the content remained a mystery, but the unusual flurry of messages put it on alert. And it was still watching those submarines, although noting that otherwise there was little naval activity. On 28 October, some messages were decoded showing that five submarines had been ordered to start patrolling in the North Sea and also that a squadron of warships had been ordered to take on coal. These were sure signs of a sortie in the offing.

An assessment sent to Beatty, then Commander-in-Chief of the Grand Fleet, stated, 'Dispositions of enemy submarines combined with position of their large minefield recently laid and now clear constitutes fairly decisive evidence of his desire to draw the Grand Fleet out.' However, it was thought 'unlikely that the enemy will risk fleet action until Armistice negotiations are settled one way or another'.[9]

In fact, at this time, the German fleet had been gathering in Schillig Roads, ready to launch the sortie. Senior British naval commanders already suspected (and, in not a few cases, hoped) that Scheer would launch a final attack. This intelligence allowed them to confirm by 28 October that such a sortie was likely. All the same, they still underestimated the extent of the German plans to draw the British Grand Fleet into a massive battle.

On 29 October, wireless messages revealed that the *Hochseeflotte* was beginning to assemble in Schillig Roads. Early the next day, the Naval Intelligence Division expected the sortie to begin that day. But just after 8.30 a.m. Room 40 learned that the fleet was to remain at anchor for the time being. Early in the afternoon more messages showed that the sortie had been postponed until the next day.

Room 40's first guess was that this was probably due to poor weather in the German Bight. But then messages to submarines were intercepted informing them that all operations up to 5 November had been cancelled. On 31 October, more decodes showed that minesweeping and other operations had also been cancelled and one squadron of warships had been sent to the Baltic. For a few days nothing out of the ordinary appeared in the airwaves, although an expected change in the cipher key did not take place.

On 1 November, Room 40 intercepted several messages referring to courts martial and deserters. Over the next few days, messages could be at best only partially decoded. However, on 5 November a message was decoded instructing all ships that cipher documents were to be locked up immediately and messages were only to be decoded by officers. Shortly later, a message sent to U-139 informed them that there had been a 'revolution' at Kiel and a Soldiers' Council had been set up.

Early in the morning of 6 November, a message instructed all submarines to fire without warning on any ships displaying a red flag. Blinker Hall is alleged to have arranged for the distribution in Germany of postcards showing red flags hoisted on British ships, hoping to spread the revolt of German sailors. But this final piece of skulduggery by the Naval Intelligence Chief, if true, was superfluous. The German Imperial Navy, like the army, had lost its desire to continue the fight. Officers may have wanted a conflagration and a glorious death, but not the men. They knew the war was over and had no intention of prolonging it. The German revolution was an outcry against the failed war and the sacrifices it had demanded among the armed forces and their families at home.

On 11 November, the Armistice came into force, but German naval wireless stations remained as garrulous as ever. A selection of intercepted messages from that day illustrates how the war ended in confusion and revolt for the German Imperial Navy. At 1.40 p.m. U-boat U-70 reported that it was off Emden, but 'says she will not proceed into Emden unless an assurance is given she will not be put under the red flag'. The Soldiers' Council gave the submarine permission to come in using the naval ensign.

Meanwhile, the *Admiralstab* sent out a message announcing, 'Armistice concluded. Therefore all acts of war are to cease and all warships are to [head for port] at full speed according to directions.' A short while later, another message was sent in the name of the Soldiers' Council announcing the formation of a new government. The next day, a message related that the previous 'order dealing with treating the Red Flag as an enemy flag is cancelled. Make sure this is transmitted to all submarines in the neighbourhood. Secondly, proceed to your base.' Later that day, another message from the Soldiers' Council at Augsburg was intercepted:

> With reference to wireless of this morning and a telephone order ... we request that the Soldiers' Council at Cuxhaven to have the 1,000 sailors armed and in good order ready at the station at 1 o'clock. The courier of the Imperial government will arrive there about 1 p.m. with sufficient train accommodation to fetch the crews. We are hastening the execution (of this order) as the Imperial government of the Socialists in Berlin is in a perilous position.[10]

The 'German Revolution', and similar ructions in Austria and Hungary, sputtered on but never really threatened to take Germany and central Europe down the road to Bolshevism. In Germany, the army general staff, police and national bureaucracy survived the upheavals. Fear of Bolshevism and chaos restrained the radical government, its failure leading to the rise of the right-wing *Freikorps* and other counter-revolutionary paramilitary organisations embittered by the war and drawn to continuing violence.[11]

The war to end all wars was over, although a new war was brewing in Russia where the Bolsheviks, now lacking widespread support, resorted to terror to prolong their rule, taking the exhausted nation into a civil war that cost the Russians more lives than the Great War they had revolted against. Vicious fighting also continued for a few years in the east as the German, Habsburg and Ottoman empires imploded (and on the western periphery of Europe in Ireland, and Belgium even made territorial demands on the Netherlands).[12]

★★★

After the Armistice, Room 40's work dwindled, but MI1(b)'s expanded for a few months. The peace talks at Versailles presented MI1(b) with stiff new challenges. It had to increase the number of staff working on diplomatic codebreaking from seventy at the end of the war to 100. According to one original document, Room 40 handled some 37,000 intercepted naval messages during the war, and sent out about 54,000 messages to the navy's Operations Division between October 1914 and June 1918.[13] Another document claims 'some 200,000 signals' were dealt with.[14]

It seems most likely that all these figures account only for German naval messages and exclude 'political/diplomatic' messages. The diplomatic section alone handled another 30,000 intercepted messages of which 90 per cent were decoded.[15] There are no comparable statistics for MI1(b)'s and MI1(e)'s throughput. For MI1(b), the number of diplomatic messages handled was probably not much lower than Room 40's diplomatic tally, and army field units must have decoded many thousands of field messages. We do know:

> At the time of the Armistice the total number of diplomatic [code] books solved [by MI1(b)] was fifty-two … Trench codes had been solved to a number of forty-eight; while of German and Turkish field ciphers a total of over 700 different keys, etc., had been dealt with.[16]

The tally of codes and ciphers broken by the Allies was anything but an amateur effort that just chanced to succeed. Furthermore, the experiences of the First World War laid the ground for the even more professional achievements at Bletchley Park some twenty years later. The staff at lower levels may well have been 'amateurs', rather than professional intelligence operatives, but as one historian points out:

> They operated within a rigid framework designed and controlled by a cadre of professionals, many of whom had long experience in intelligence work. The colourful characters that joined the system in the early years may have left compelling and entertaining memoirs, but there is a danger of their folklore becoming an immoveable orthodoxy.[17]

Notes

Prologue

1 Neiberg, *Dance of the Furies*, pp.9–14.
2 Bostridge, *The Fateful Year: England 1914*, p.xxvii.
3 Lloyd George, *War Memoirs*, Vol. 1, pp.32–33.
4 Neiberg, *Dance of the Furies*, p.12.
5 Hastings, *Catastrophe 1914*, p.66.
6 Albertini, *Origins of the War*, Vol. 3, p.495.
7 Nickles, *Under the Wire*, p.132.
8 Lloyd George, *War Memoirs*, Vol. 1, pp.45–46.
9 Albertini, *Origins of the War*, pp.500–02, adds an extra layer to the account: The British Government prepared a 'note' of reply in advance of a response to its ultimatum. At 9.40 p.m. a Foreign Office Private Secretary 'dashed in to say that Germany declared war … [so the prepared note] was hurriedly re-drafted and typed … "The German Empire having declared war upon Great Britain …".' This note, along with the ambassador's passports, was delivered to the German Ambassador at 10.15 p.m. but it was learnt that the Private Secretary's information (acquired from the Admiralty) was wrong. 'It was ascertained that this information was based on an intercepted wireless message by which German shipping were warned that war with England was imminent.' The delivered note had to be retrieved from the German Ambassador who, it is claimed, had not opened it.
10 John Ferris, 'Before Room 40: The British Empire and Signals Intelligence 1898–1914', *Journal of Strategic Studies*, Vol. 12, No. 4.
11 ADM137/4065 at the National Archives (TNA) contains a logbook of handwritten translations of intercepts between 18 March 1914 and 27 January 1915. All the messages cited in the remainder of this chapter come from this document. A note at the start of the logbook states, 'Early telegrams, chiefly relating to the beginning

of the war – Partly Admiralty Staff and partly Colonial – Began to be read in November 1914'.

12 Hew Strachan, *First World War*, (3 vols) p.38.

13 ADM137/4065.

Chapter 1: Munitions of War

1   ADM137/2804.

2   Lawford and Nicholson, *The Telcon Story*, p.9.

3   Dr R. Prakash et al, 'Gutta-percha – an untold story'.

4   Lawford and Nicholson, *The Telcon Story*, p.13; Kunert, *Telegraphen-Landkabel...*, pp.5, 10.

5   Kunert, *Telegraphen-Landkabel...*, p.14.

6   Beauchamp, *History of Telegraphy*, pp.135–37.

7   Offer, *The First World War*, p.81.

8   Cain and Hopkins, *British Imperialism 1688–2015*, p.39; Joll and Martel, *The Origins of the First World War*, p.204.

9   Beauchamp, *History of Telegraphy*, p.138.

10 Beauchamp, *History of Telegraphy*, p.155.

11 Evans, *The Pursuit of Power*, pp.284–85.

12 Evans, *The Pursuit of Power*, pp.295–96.

13 Evans, *The Pursuit of Power*, p.300.

14 Steiner and Neilson, *Britain and the Origins of the First World War*, pp.65–66.

15 Lambert, *Planning Armageddon*, p.21.

16 Evans, *The Pursuit of Power*, p.306.

17 Evans, *The Pursuit of Power*, pp.641–43.

18 Röhl, John, *Kaiser Wilhelm II*, Vol. 3, p.24 (Cambridge University Press, 2017).

19 MacMillan, *The War that Ended Peace*, pp.89–91.

20 Wolz, Nicolas, *From Imperial Splendour to Internment*, p.5 (Seaforth, 2015).

21 Kennedy, *The Rise of the Anglo-German Antagonism*, p.416.

22 Röhl, *Kaiser Wilhelm II*, Vol. 3, pp.208–10, 475–92.

23 Röhl, *Kaiser Wilhelm II*, Vol. 3, pp.632–33.

24 Joll and Martel, *Origins of the First World War*, pp.207–08.

25 Clark, *Kaiser Wilhelm II*, pp.181–83.

26 Headrick, *Invisible Weapon*, p.80.

27 Clark, *Kaiser Wilhelm II*, pp.182–83; Clark's view is not shared by Röhl, *Kaiser Wilhelm II*, pp.75–76.

28 Headrick, *Invisible Weapon*, pp.81–82.

29 Röhl, *Kaiser Wilhelm II*, p.44.

30 Headrick, *Invisible Weapon*, p.88.

31 Röhl, *Kaiser Wilhelm II*, Vol. 3, pp.21–22.

32 Röhl, *Kaiser Wilhelm II*, Vol. 3, p.214.

33 McMeekin, *The Berlin–Baghdad Express*, p.46.

34 Röhl, *Kaiser Wilhelm II*, Vol. 3, pp.88–90.

35 Röhl, *Kaiser Wilhelm II*, Vol. 3, pp.89–94.

36 CAB17/75; POST83/56; Headrick, *The Invisible Weapon*, p.108.

37 Smit, *Nederland in de Eerste Wereldoorlog*, Vol. 2, pp.219–21.

Chapter 2: Breakout

1   Raboy, *Marconi*, pp.328–32.

2   Jolly, *Marconi*, 176–77; Raboy, *Marconi*, pp.331–32.

3   Raboy, *Marconi*, pp.333–34.

4   Raboy, *Marconi*, p.31.

5   Raboy, *Marconi*, pp.572, 507.

6   Raboy, *Marconi*, p.19.

7   ADM116/523, 16/9/1896.

8   ADM116/569; ADM116/570.

9   ADM116/595, 13/8/1900.

10 Bonatz, *Die Deutsche Marine-Funkaufklärung 1914–1945*; Hezlet, *The Electron and Sea Power*, p.38; Pocock, *The Early British Radio Industry*, p.170.

11 Jolly, *Marconi*, p.133.

12 Raboy, *Marconi*, pp.99–102.

13 ADM116/523.

14 ADM116/523.

15 Raboy, *Marconi*, p.102.

16 Röhl, *Kaiser Wilhelm II*, pp.60–61; Clark, *Kaiser Wilhelm II*, p.81.

17 Friedewald, *Telefunken und der deutsche Schiffsfunk 1903–1914*.

18 Friedewald, *Telefunken und der deutsche Schiffsfunk 1903–1914*.

19 Raboy, *Marconi*, 340–41.

20 Raboy, *Marconi*, p.341.

21 ADM137/986; Donaldson, *The Marconi Scandal*.

22 CAB16/32, 17/6/1914; F. Ullrich, *Die Station Rabaul (Südsee) bei Kreigsausbruch, in Telefunken Zeitung Nr 18, Austellungsnummer 3, Jahrgang Oktober 1919.*

23 Thiele, *Telefunken Nach 100 Jahren*, p.19.

24 Baker, *A History of the Marconi Company*, p.158.

25 Mombauer, *The Origins of the First World War: Controversies…*, p.17; Clark, *The Sleepwalkers*; Mombauer, *The Origins of the First World War: Documents*; Albertini, *Origins of the War*; Geiss, *July 1914: The Outbreak of the First World War*; Otte, *The July Crisis*; McMeekin, *July 1914*; Joll and Martel, *The First World War*; Macmillan, *The War That Ended Peace*.

26 Watson, *Ring of Steel*, pp.8, 28.

27 Otte, *July Crisis*, pp.84–85.

28 Albertini, *Origins of the War*, Vol 2, p.185.

29 Otte, *July Crisis*, p.521.

Chapter 3: The Longest Link

1 Headrick, *The Invisible Weapon*, p.142; Winkler, *Nexus*, pp.28–33.
2 Grant, *U-Boat Hunters*, pp.16–17.
3 Headrick, *The Invisible Weapon*, p.142; Barty-King, *Girdle Round the Earth*, p.166.
4 Kennedy, 'Imperial Cable Communications and Strategy, 1870–1914' in Kennedy, *The War Plans of the Great Powers 1880–1914*, pp.80, 90.
5 ADM137/4; R Bruce Scott, *Gentlemen on Imperial Service*, pp.35-39.
6 Helmuth von Mücke: *The "Ayesha"* (modern reprint with no page numbers).
7 Barty-King, *Girdle Round the Earth*, p.167.
8 ADM137/3893.
9 von Mücke, *The 'Aeysha'*.
10 ADM137/4699; Grant, *U-Boat Hunters*.

Chapter 4: Urgent Imperial Service

1 CAB16/189.
2 Kennedy, 'Imperial Cable Communications and Strategy, 1870–1914' in Kennedy, *The War Plans of the Great Powers 1880–1914*, p.82.
3 CAB18/16; see also E. Bruton, *The Cable Wars: Military and State Surveillance of the British Telegraph Cable Network during World War One*.
4 Kennedy, 'Imperial Cable Communications and Strategy, 1870–1914' in Kennedy, *The War Plans of the Great Powers 1880–1914*, p.77.
5 CAB16/14.
6 CAB16/14.
7 POST56/55.
8 POST56/55.
9 POST56/55.
10 Headrick, *The Invisible Weapon*, p.141.
11 Olusoga, *The World's War*, p.101.
12 Michael Friedewald, *Funkentelegrafie und deutsche Kolonien: Technik als Mittel imperialistischer Politik, Fraunhofer Institute for Systems and Innovation Research*, January 2009.
13 CAB45/110.
14 WO32/5788.
15 Strachan, *First World War*, Vol. 1, p.507.
16 CAB45/110.
17 Klein-Arendt, *Kamina ruft Nauen!*, p.265.
18 CAB45/111.
19 Dr A. Esau, 'Die Grossstation Kamina und der Beginn des Weltkrieges', in *Telefunken Zeitung*, No. 16, Zweitekriegsnummer, 3 Jahrgang, Juli 1919.
20 Klein-Arendt, *Kamina ruft Nauen!*, p.273.
21 Esau, *Die Grossstation Kamina und der Beginn des Weltkrieges*.
22 Esau, *Die Grossstation Kamina und der Beginn des Weltkrieges*.
23 Olusoga, *The World's War*, p.106.

24 CAB45/110.

25 CAB45/110.

26 ADM137/18.

27 ADM137/3893.

28 ADM137/27.

29 ADM137/3893.

30 ADM137/27.

31 ADM137/3893.

32 Olusoga and Erichsen, *The Kaiser's Holocaust*.

33 Olusoga and Erichsen, *The Kaiser's Holocaust*, pp.124–25, 130–33.

34 Olusoga and Erichsen, *The Kaiser's Holocaust*, pp.235, 351–52; Röhl, *Kaiser Wilhelm II*, Vol. 3, p.505; the Kaiser dissolved the Reichstag and called an election. This was the so-called 'Hottentot election', where nationalist and racist themes were played up, resulting in a shift to the right in the new Reichstag.

35 L'Ange, *Urgent Imperial Service*, pp.7–9; Strachan, *First World War*, Vol. 1, p.565.

36 ADM137/986.

37 Hancock, *Smuts*, pp.379, 380–81.

38 ADM137/4177.

39 ADM137/4177.

40 ADM137/4177.

41 L'Ange, *Urgent Imperial Service*, pp.258–60.

42 L'Ange, *Urgent Imperial Service*, pp.281, 333.

43 Paice, *Tip and Run*; Klein-Arendt, *Kamina ruft Nauen!*, pp.292–326.

44 R. Hirsch, 'Funkentelegraphische Skizzen aus der Kriegszeit in der Südsee (Samoa)', *Telefunken Zeitung* No. 18, Austellungsnummer 3, Jahrgang Oktober 1919. Other sources give the date of the shelling of the wireless station on Yap as 12 August.

45 F. Ullrich, 'Die Station Rabaul (Südsee) bei Kreigsausbruch'. *Telefunken Zeitung* No. 18, Austellungsnummer 3, Jahrgang Oktober 1919.

46 F. Ullrich, 'Die Station Rabaul (Südsee) bei Kreigsausbruch'.

47 https//en.wikipedia.org/wiki/History_of_wireless_telegraphy_and_broadcasting_in_Nauru.

48 ADM137/4; CO881/14/9.

49 R. Hirsch, 'Funkentelegraphische Skizzen aus der Kriegszeit in der Südsee (Samoa)'.

50 R. Hirsch, 'Funkentelegraphische Skizzen aus der Kriegszeit in der Südsee (Samoa)'.

51 ADM137/4.

52 Stephenson, *The Siege of Tsingtao*; Dixon, *Clash of Empires, 1914*.

53 Yates, *Graf Spee's Raiders*, pp.83–84, 127–28.

54 ADM137/4.

55 ADM186/591.

56 ADM137/4802; Keegan, *Intelligence in War*, p.161.

57 HW3/7.

58 Bernstorff, *My Three Years in America*, p.21.

59 Kennedy, 'Imperial Cable Communications and Strategy, 1870–1914' in Kennedy, *War Plans*, p.94.

Chapter 5: Birth of a Legend

1   Beesly, *Room 40*, p.9.
2   Hezlet, *The Electron and Sea Power*, p.89.
3   Hoy, *40 O.B.*, p.23.
4   Headrick, *Invisible Weapon*, p.158.
5   Cited in Beach, *Haig's Intelligence*, p.326.
6   Headrick, *The Invisible Weapon*, pp.159–60, 170–71, citing Alberto Santoni, *Il Primo Secret: L'influenza delle decrittazioni Brittaniche sulle operazioni navali della Guerra 1914–1918* (Milan, 1985).
7   Headrick, *The Invisible Weapon*, says Santoni cites intercepted messages in ADM137/4065 (TNA), saying Santoni gives as a title for this document, 'Log of intercepted German signals in Verkehrsbuch (VB) code from various sources. March 1914–January 1915'. However, this is actually the file reference name in the National Archives catalogue – the catalogue names can be imprecise (for example, in this case the document includes SKM and HVB encoded messages as well as VB). The first entry in the document itself says, 'Early telegrams, chiefly relating to the beginning of the war – Partly Admiralty Staff and Partly Colonial – Began to be read in Nov. 1914'.
8   Ferris, 'The Road to Bletchley Park'.
9   Freeman, *Origins*, p.224.
10 Ferris, 'Before Room 40', p.438.
11 Ferris, 'Before Room 40', pp.441–42.
12 Ferris, 'Before Room 40', p.432.
13 Sheffy, *British Military Intelligence in the Palestine Campaign*, p.4; Fergusson, *British Military Intelligence, 1870–1914*.
14 Fergusson, *British Military Intelligence*, p.160.
15 Fergusson, *British Military Intelligence*, 1870–1914, p.220.
    Fergusson, *British Military Intelligence, 1870–1914*, pp.219–20.
16 Lambert, *Planning Armageddon*, p.34.
17 Seligman, *Naval Intelligence from Germany.*
18 Ferris, 'Before Room 40', pp.442–45.
19 ADM137/4065.
20 Strachan, *The First World War*, Vol. 1, p.381.
21 Ramsay, *'Blinker' Hall: Spymaster*, p.29, citing 'Recollections of Admiral of the Fleet, Sir Henry Oliver'.
22 Ewing, *The Man of Room 40*, p.198.
23 Ewing, The Man of Room 40, p 79
24 Ewing, *The Man of Room 40*, pp.79–127.
25 Ewing, The Man of Room 40, p144
26 Ewing, *The Man of Room 40*, p.144.
27 William F. Clarke papers.
28 Beesly, *Room 40*; Denniston, *Thirty Secret Years*.
29 HW3/3; Hall papers; Denniston papers.

30 HW3/3; HW3/35.

31 Denniston papers.

32 ADM223/767. This file is an important source of information about MO5(e), later known as MI1(b), between July 1914 and March 1915. It is a handwritten copy of various documents (including captured German military cipher instructions) and a log of important events.

33 WO32/10776, cited in Freeman, *Origins*, p.208.

34 Freeman, *Origins*, pp.206–07. August 1914 to April 1915, under Director of Military Operations, as MO5(d); April 1915 to January 1916, part the Directorate of Special Intelligence, as MO5; from January 1916, within the Directorate of Military Intelligence, as MI1(b).

35 ADM223/767.

36 Freeman, *Origins*, p.210.

37 Denniston papers.

38 HW3/6.

39 Denniston papers – the typescripted document states 'Norddeich' on one page, with a pencil crossing out and a marginal entry in handwriting, 'Nauen?' and just 'Nauen' on a later page. ADM137/4065 gives both stations as sources of messages in August and September.

40 Spears, *Liaison 1914*, pp.58–59.

41 Spears, *Liaison 1914*, p.63.

42 HW3/183.

43 Denniston papers.

44 ADM223/767.

45 ADM223/767.

46 Denniston papers.

47 Degoulange, *Les Écoutes de la Victoire*, pp.25, 29, and Chapters 2 and 3 generally.

48 Degoulange, *Les Écoutes de la Victoire*, pp.31–33.

49 Blond, *The Marne*, p.93, describes the Germans' resorting to plain language on the Western Front as '*Schlamperei*' (sloppiness).

50 Degoulange, *Les Écoutes de la Victoire*, p.80; Heydorn, *Nachrichtenaufklärung*....

51 Occleshaw, *Armour Against Fate*, p.111.

52 Degoulange, *Les Écoutes de la Victoire*, p.31; for the role of intercepts by the German Army of plain-language Russian messages during the Battle of Tannenberg in August 1914, see Showalter, *Tannenberg*, pp.95, 99, 169, 229 and 328; for the role of intercepts of Russian messages by the Austro-Hungarian Army in the opening battles on the Galician Front, see Max Ronge, *Zwölf Jahre Kundschaftsdienst Kriegs- und Industrie Spionage*; Albert Pethö, *Agenten für den Doppeladler: Österreich-Ungarns Geheimer Dienst im Weltkrieg*; for the Italian Front, see Kahn, *The Codebreakers*, pp.316–20.

53 Ferris, *The British Army and Signals Intelligence*, p.5.

54 Dooley, *Codes, Ciphers and Spies*, p.62; Kahn, *The Codebreakers*, pp.301–04.

55 ADM223/767; Degoulange, *Les Écoutes de la Victoire*, pp.94–96.

56 ADM223/767.

57 HW7/3.
58 ADM223/767.
59 ADM223/767.
60 ADM223/767.
61 ADM223/767.
62 ADM137/767
63 ADM223/767.
64 Baker, *A History of the Marconi Company*, pp.163–66.
65 Beesly, *Room 40*, p.70.
66 Baker, *A History of the Marconi Company*, pp.281–82; Degoulange, *Les Écoutes de la Victoire*, pp.117–26, 171–76.
67 Kahn, *The Codebreakers*, p.313.
68 Heydorn, *Nachrichtenaufklärung*, pp.30–34.

Chapter 6: Code Capture

1   Several different dates are cited by various sources for the *Magdeburg* grounding, ranging from 20 August to 26 August.
2   Churchill, *The World Crisis, 1911–1918*, pp.255–56.
3   HW3/1 (p.14 of the section on 'Codes and Ciphers').
4   Denniston papers.
5   Denniston papers.
6   Denniston papers.
7   Denniston papers.
8   ADM137/4065; ADM223/767.
9   ADM223/767.
10 Denniston papers.

Chapter 7: Codes and Ciphers

1   HW3/1.
2   ADM137/4156 '*Signalbuch der Kaiserlichen Marine*', 'Magdeburg Copy', p.151; ADM137/4331.
3   HW3/1; HW7/3; ADM137/4156; ADM137/4331.
4   See note 1.
5   HW3/1; HW7/3; ADM137/4329; ADM137/4388.
6   HW3/1; HW7/3; ADM137/4374; ADM137/4671.
7   HW3/1.
8   HW3/1.
9   HW3/1.
10 HW137/4320.
11 Mendelsohn, *Studies in German Diplomatic Codes*....
12 HW137/4314.

13 HW3/1; HW7/3.

14 Souchon, *Break Through*.

15 Van der Vat, *The Ship that Changed the World*, p.46.

16 Many of these messages are recorded in the National Archives file, ADM137/4065 (see prologue).

17 Van der Vat, *The Ship that Changed the World*, p.139.

18 Lasry, Niebel and Andersson, *Deciphering German Diplomatic and Naval Attaché Coded Messages from 1900–1915*. I am grateful to George Lasry for providing me with details of his and his colleagues' work in unravelling the coding and enciphering process used for the *Goeben* messages and sharing documents on German codes and ciphers.

19 BAMA RM 92/2545; BAMA RM 92/2523; BAMA RM 92/2544.

20 Some other encoded or enciphered messages can be found in the archives at Kew, but these tend to be partially worked out encoded messages or training material.

21 Mendelsohn, *Studies in German Diplomatic Codes Employed During the World War*, 1927.

22 ADM 137/4703.

23 ADM 137/4703.

Chapter 8: Early Days

1 Denniston papers.

2 ADM137/986.

3 POST56/55.

4 POST56/55.

5 ADM137/4065.

6 Denniston papers.

7 Baker, *A History of the Marconi Company*, p.159.

8 HW3/5.

9 HW3/5.

10 A.J. Alan, 'My Adventure at Chislehurst', in Foss (ed), *The Best of A.J. Alan*, pp.105–17.

11 HW3/35.

12 It is commonly suggested that Lambert was involved in cryptography, but his contribution was to wireless interception procedures and techniques.

13 Denniston papers.

14 Denniston papers.

15 Ewing, *The Man of Room 40*, p.160.

16 The original is in the Clarke papers at Churchill Archives, Cambridge; a copy is in held in the National Archives, HW3/4.

17 Beesly, *Room 40*, p.18.

18 Denniston papers.

19 Gannon, *Colossus*.

20 HW3/3; Beesly, *Room 40*, p.125, says that Montgomery came to Room 40 from the Censorship Department.

21 HW3/3.

22 HW3/3; Denniston papers.

23 HW3/3.

24 HW3/3.

25 ADM137/4169; ADM137/4686.

26 ADM137/4065.

27 HW3/3; Denniston papers.

28 Bird and Hines, *In the shadow of Ultra*, pp.110–11.

29 Bird and Hines, *In the shadow of Ultra*, pp.112–13.

30 Bird and Hines, *In the shadow of Ultra*, pp.114–16.

31 Grant, *U-Boat Hunters*, p.53.

32 Grant, *U-Boat Hunters*, pp.11–12.

33 Cited in Massie, *Castles of Steel*, p.20.

34 HW7/1.

35 Strachan, *The First World War*, Vol. 1 'To Arms', pp.406–07.

36 Halpern, A *Naval History of World War I*, p.22.

37 HW7/1.

38 HW7/1.

39 Corbett, *Naval Operations*, Vol. 2, p.22.

40 Cited in Massie, *Castles of Steel*, p. 312.

41 Watson, *Ring of Steel*, p.238.

42 ADM137/4067.

43 ADM137/3893; ADM186/610.

44 Corbett, *Naval Operations*, Vol. 2, p.28.

45 Cited in Massie, *Castles of Steel*, p.353.

46 Gordon, *The Rules of the Game*, p.25.

47 Cited in Massie, *Castles of Steel*, p.358.

48 ADM186/610.

49 ADM137/4067.

50 ADM137/4067.

51 ADM137/4067.

Chapter 9: Blockade

1 Lambert, *Planning Armageddon*, pp.4–5.

2 Lambert, *Planning Armageddon*, p.21.

3 Quoted in Lambert, *Planning Armageddon*, p.40.

4 Ferguson, *Pity of War*, p.191.

5 Lambert, *Planning Armageddon*, pp.185-191.

6 Lambert, *Planning Armageddon*, pp.185-191.

7 Lambert, *Planning Armageddon*, p.5.

8 Lambert, *Planning Armageddon*, pp.98-99.

9 Moeyes, *Buiten Schot*, p.179.

10 Derry, *A History of Scandinavia*, p.303.

11 Albertini, *Origins of the War*, p.662.

12 Derry, *A History of Scandinavia*, pp.303–05.

13 Albertini, *Origins of the War*, pp.665, 670.

14 Moeyes, *Buiten Schot*, p.8.

15 ADM137/1640.

16 Marc Frey, 'Bullying the Neutrals: The Case of the Netherlands', in Chickering & Foerster, *Great War, Total War*.

17 Mecking, *Neutraal Nederland in Oorlogstijd*, pp.103–18.

18 ADM137/2805; E.H. Kossman, *The Low Countries*, pp.545–46.

19 ADM137/2805; ADM137/2837.

20 Moeyes, *Buiten Schot*, pp.217, 220.

21 Moeyes, *Buiten Schot*, p.219; Smit, *Nederland in de Eerste Wereldoorlog*, Vol. 2, pp.74, 77–78.

22 Moeyes, *Buiten Schot*, p.212.

23 ADM137/2805.

24 ADM137/2805.

25 Moeyes, *Buiten Schot*, p.223.

26 Osborne, *Britain's Economic Blockade of Germany*, pp.2–4.

27 Kennedy, 'The War at Sea', in Winter et al (eds), *The Cambridge History of the First World War*, Vol. 1, p.345.

28 Lambert, *Planning Armageddon*, p.501.

29 Watson, *Ring of Steel*, p.232.

30 Devlin, *Too Proud to Fight*, p.157.

31 Watson, *Ring of Steel*, pp.232–35, p.346.

32 Chatterton, *The Big Blockade*; Hampshire, *The Blockaders*.

33 Lambert, *Planning Armageddon*, pp.211–12.

34 Lambert, *Planning Armageddon*, p.241.

35 Lambert, *Planning Armageddon*, p.500.

36 ADM223/738.

37 ADM223/738; ADM137/2988.

38 ADM137/2988.

39 ADM137/2085.

40 Devlin, *Too Proud to Fight*, p.140.

41 Devlin, *Too Proud to Fight*, p.174.

42 Striner, *Woodrow Wilson and World War I*, p.36.

43 Lambert, *Planning Armageddon*, pp.260, 246.

44 Devlin, *Too Proud to Fight*, pp.214–15.

Chapter 10: Counter-Blockade

1   HW7/1.
2   Wolz, *Imperial Splendour*, p.36.
3   ADM137/3958.
4   Wolz, *Imperial Splendour*, p.60.
5   Watson, *Ring of Steel*, p.239.
6   HW7/1.
7   Bernstorff, *My Three Years in America*, p.42.
8   Gerard, *My Four Years in Germany*, Chapter 12.
9   Gerard, *My Four Years in Germany*, Chapter 12.
10 Massie, *Castles of Steel*, p.514
11 Devlin, *Too Proud to Fight*, 188.
12 Cited in Devlin, *Too Proud to Fight*, 200.
13 ADM137/3958.
14 ADM137/3958.
15 Grant, *U-Boat Intelligence 1914–1918*.
16 ADM137/3958; ADM137/4177.
17 ADM137/3958.
18 ADM137/4066.
19 Beesly, *Room 40*, p.92.
20 ADM137/3960.
21 ADM137/4128.
22 Simpson, *The Lusitania*; Ramsay, *The Lusitania Saga and Myth*; Larson, *Dead Wake*.
23 Devlin, *Too Proud to Fight*, p.216.
24 Bernstorff, *My Three Years in America*, p.78.
25 Cooper, *Woodrow Wilson*, p.287.
26 Blum, *Dark Invasion*.
27 HW7/1.
28 Gerard, *My Four Years in Germany*, Chapter 12.
29 Devlin, *Too Proud to Fight*, pp.286–87.
30 HW7/1.
31 HW7/1.
32 Gordon, *The Rules of the Game*, p.397.
33 Massie, *Castles of Steel*, p.639.
34 ADM223/737.
35 Massie, *Castles of Steel*, p.659.

Chapter 11: 'For You the War is Over'

1   Malcolm Hay ('Exchange Officer'), *Valiant for Truth*, pp.69-70.
2   Harris, *Haig*, p.91.
3   Denniston papers.
4   HW3/183.

5   Hall, *Communications and British Operations on the Western Front, 1914–1915*, p.58.

6   Spears, *Liaison 1914*, p.142.

7   Beach, *Haig's Intelligence*, p.115.

8   Morgan, *The Secrets of Rue St Roch*; Mecking, *Neutraal Nederland in Oorlogstijd*, p.55; Ruis, *Spynest*, pp.93–98.

9   Degoulange, *Les Écoutes de la Victoire*, pp.135–46.

10 N. Barr, 'Command in the Transition from Mobile to Static Warfare', in Sheffield and Todman, *Command and Control*, pp.20–21.

11 HW3/183; Hall, *Communications and British Operations*, p.94.

12 HW3/183.

13 Sheffy, *British Military Intelligence in the Palestine Campaign*, p.90.

14 ADM223/767.

15 ADM223/767.

16 WO106/6398.

17 ADM223/767.

18 Freeman, *Origins*, p.210.

19 Hay, *Valiant for Truth: Malcolm Hay of Seaton*, p.58.

Chapter 12: 'The Pillars of Hercules have Fallen'

1   Hay, *The Jesuits and the Popish Plot*, p.124.

2   Hay, *The Jesuits and the Popish Plot*, pp.203–07.

3   Hay, *Valiant for Truth: Malcolm Hay of Seaton*, pp.76–77.

4   HW7/35.

5   ADM223/767.

6   ADM223/767; Lambert, *Planning Armageddon*, pp.263–64.

7   Freeman, MI1(b), gives the January 1916 as the date of the first surviving US decode.

8   Hay, *Valiant for Truth: Malcolm Hay of Seaton*, p.59.

9   Hay, *Valiant for Truth: Malcolm Hay of Seaton*, p.77.

10 HW7/35.

11 HW7/35.

12 HW3/185.

13 HW3/1.

14 Lüdke, *Jihad Made in Germany*.

15 Hopkirk, *On Secret Service East of Constantinople*, p.105.

16 Hall papers.

17 Cited in Beesly, *Room 40*, p.131.

18 Cited in Beesly, *Room 40*, p.132.

19 HW3/1.

20 Denniston papers.

21 For a detailed discussion, see Freeman, *Zimmermann Telegram*, pp.138–41.

22 McMeekin, *The Berlin–Baghdad Express*, p.221.

23 Beesly, *Room 40*, p.123.

24 ADM223/768.

25 ADM223/773.

26 Cited in Beesly, *Room 40*, p.134.

27 Beesly, *Room 40*, p.173.

28 HW3/1; HW7/3.

29 ADM223/773.

30 Denniston papers.

31 ADM137/4357.

32 HW7/4.

33 HW7/1 HW3/1; HW7/3; HW7/4.

34 HW3/1; HW7/3.

35 James, *The Eyes of the Navy*, p.132.

36 Hall papers.

37 Hall papers.

38 Hall papers.

39 ADM223/784.

40 Hall papers.

41 Bernstorff, *My Three Years in America*, p.78.

42 Doerries, *Prelude to the Easter Rising*, p.161.

43 Freeman, *MI1(b)*, p.213; Bernstorff, *My Three Years in America*, p.86.

44 HW3/184.

45 HW7/17.

46 HW7/1.

47 Hall papers.

48 HW3/177.

49 Hall papers.

50 HW3/184.

51 HW3/184.

52 HW3/184.

53 HW3/184.

54 HW3/186.

Chapter 13: Inside Room 40

1   William James, *The Eyes of the Navy*, pp.xviii, xxiii–xxiv.

2   HW3/8.

3   Clarke papers.

4   Fitzgerald, *The Knox Brothers*, p.99.

5   Fitzgerald, *The Knox Brothers*, pp.59, 127–28.

6   Batey, *Dilly: The Man Who Broke Enigmas*, pp.11–12.

7   Fitzgerald, *The Knox Brothers*, p.99.

8   Fitzgerald, *The Knox Brothers*, p.55.

9   Fitzgerald, *The Knox Brothers*, p.56.

10 Batey, *Dilly: The Man Who Broke Enigmas*, p.49.

11 Batey, *Dilly: The Man Who Broke Enigmas*, p.x; interview on Radio 4, November 2008. The file in question is HW43/7, catalogued as 'GC&CS Secret Service Sigint Volume II: Cryptographic Systems and their Solution. I Machine Cyphers', and apparently entitled, 'A History of the Solution of Unsteckered Enigmas and Abwehr Machine Ciphers 1941–1945'.

12 All quotes from Clarke in this section from HW3/3; copy in Clarke papers.

13 Denniston papers.

14 Clarke papers.

15 Thompson, *The White War*, pp.40–47.

16 HW3/35.

17 HW3/8.

18 HW7/35.

19 HW7/35.

20 Rinke, 'Luxburg Affair', Online International Encyclopedia of the First World War.

21 HW3/35; HW3/6.

22 HW3/35.

23 HW3/35; Clarke papers.

24 HW3/35; Clarke Papers.

25 HW3/35.

Chapter 14: Codebreakers

1 ADM137/4077.

2 HW3/183.

3 HW3/183.

4 This chapter has been drawn together using, in particular, ADM223/773 (history of Room 40 political branch), ADM137/4652 ('Solution of codes') and ADM137/4659 ('Solution of field codes, Enemy codes and their solution'), Friedman, *Solving German Codes in World War I*, (1919) and Mendelsohn, *Studies in German Diplomatic Codes Employed During the World War*, (1936).

5 In the German language, the thirty most common 'wordforms' (*die, der, und, in, zu, den, das, nicht, von, sie, ist, des, sich, mit, dem, dass, er, es, ein, ich, auf, so, eine, auch, als, an, nach, wie, im, für*) account for 32 per cent of an average German language text (based on a count performed in 1911 of just under 11 million words of text from a variety of sources). The next seventy most common wordforms (including *man, aber, aus, durch ... ohne, eines, können, sei*) account for 15 per cent and the next 207 words for another 7 per cent. In all, these wordforms account for just about 50 per cent of all words in a text (Werner König, *DTV-Atlas zur deutschen Sprache*, pp.114–15 (1994). In English, the fifteen most frequently occurring words account for 25 per cent of an average text, the first 100 words for 60 per cent, the first 1,000 for 85 per cent and the first 4,000 for 97.5 per cent (David Crystal, *The Cambridge Encyclopedia of Language*, 2010).

6 ADM137/4652.

7 ADM137/4659.

8   Cited in Ferris, *The British Army and Signals Intelligence*, pp.9–10.
9   Ferris, *The British Army and Signals Intelligence*, p.10.
10 Cited in Ferris, *The British Army and Signals Intelligence*, pp.10–11.
11 ADM137/4701.
12 Ferris, *The British Army and Signals Intelligence*, p.327.
13 ADM137/4701.
14 Mendelsohn, *Studies in German Diplomatic Codes*....
15 ADM137/4659.
16 ADM137/4701.
17 ADM137/4659.
18 ADM137/4659.
19 ADM137/4701.
20 Mendelsohn, *Studies in German Diplomatic Codes*..., p.99.
21 ADM137/4659.
22 ADM137/4659.
23 ADM137/4659.
24 Ferris, *The British Army and Signals Intelligence*, p.9.
25 ADM137/4701.
26 ADM137/4659.
27 ADM223/773.
28 HW7/4.
29 Gannon, *Colossus: Bletchley Park's Greatest Secret*.
30 ADM223/773.
31 ADM223/773.
32 See Jon Agar, *The Government Machine: A Revolutionary History of the Computer* (2003) for a discussion of the 'machine' as metaphor for 'administration' and its reflection in the development of computerised administration.
33 Beach, *Haig's Intelligence*, pp.176–77.
34 ADM223/738; ADM223/773.
35 ADM223/773.
36 HW3/16.
37 Ewing, *The Man of Room 40*, p.269.

Chapter 15: The Spanish Interception

1   Ramsay, *'Blinker' Hall: Spymaster*; James, *Eyes of the Navy*; Beesly, *Room 40*.
2   See the Hall papers at the Churchill Archives, Cambridge.
3   Hall papers.
4   Hall papers.
5   Daniel Larsen, 'British Signals Intelligence and the 1916 Easter Rising in Ireland'.
6   ADM137/1187; ADM137/4152.
7   Schmuhl, *Ireland's Exiled Children: America and the Easter Rising* (2016) pp.27–28.
8   Doerries, *Prelude to the Easter Rising*, p.4.
9   Doerries, *Prelude to the Easter Rising*, p.20.

10 HW7/1; Beesly, *Room 40*, p.187.

11 ADM137/1187.

12 Doerries, *Prelude to the Easter Rising*, pp.214–15.

13 ADM137/4152.

14 ADM137/1187.

15 Doerries, *Prelude to the Easter Rising*.

16 James, *Eyes of the Navy*, pp.110–15.

17 Raymond Carr (ed.), *Spain 1808–1975: A History* (Oxford University Press, 1982).

18 Carden, *German Policy Toward Neutral Spain*, pp.11–19.

19 Salvado, *Spain 1914–1918*, p.67.

20 ADM223/736.

21 ADM223/737; ADM223/738.

22 ADM223/737.

23 ADM223/739.

24 ADM223/737.

25 ADM223/738.

26 ADM223/738.

27 ADM223/738.

28 ADM223/739.

29 ADM223/739.

30 ADM223/737.

31 ADM223/739.

32 ADM223/737.

33 ADM223/739.

34 Carden, *German Policy Toward Neutral Spain*, p.43.

35 ADM223/738.

36 ADM223/736.

37 ADM223/738.

38 Hall papers.

39 ADM223/738.

40 HW7/27.

41 ADM223/739.

42 ADM223/736.

43 ADM223/739.

44 ADM223/739.

45 ADM223/736.

46 ADM223/739.

47 ADM223/739.

48 ADM223/736.

49 ADM223/736.

50 ADM223/736.

51 ADM223/737.

52 The French did indeed intercept German Berlin–Madrid diplomatic wireless traffic from early on in the war at the Bureau de Chiffre in the French Foreign Office (the Deuxième Bureau cryptographic unit being part of the French Army).

53 ADM223/737.

54 ADM223/737.

55 ADM223/740; ADM223/738; ADM223/739.

56 ADM223/738.

57 ADM223/737.

58 ADM223/740.

59 ADM223/739.

Chapter 16: 'Most Secret: Decipher Yourself'

1   Tooze, *The Deluge*, p.45.

2   Striner, *Woodrow Wilson and World War One*, p.81.

3   Tooze, *The Deluge*, pp.12–13.

4   Stevenson, *1917*, pp.46–49.

5   Gregory, *Walter Hines Page*, p.188.

6   Cited in Freeman, *Zimmermann Telegram*, p.101.

7   Gregory, *Walter Hines Page*, pp.48–89.

8   HW7/17.

9   HW7/17.

10 Kennan, *Soviet–American Relations*, Vol. 1, p.28.

11 Gerard, *My Four Years in Germany*.

12 HW7/17.

13 HW7/34.

14 HW7/17.

15 HW7/19.

16 Bernstorff, *My Three Years in America*; Doerries, *Imperial Challenge*.

17 HW7/17.

18 HW7/17.

19 Tuchman, *The Zimmermann Telegram*, p.107.

20 Stevenson, *1917*, p.14.

21 Tuchman, *The Zimmermann Telegram*, p.134.

22 Cited in Tuchman, *The Zimmermann Telegram*, p.138.

23 Joachim von zur Gathen, 'The Zimmermann Telegram: The Original Draft', *Cryptologia*, 31 (2007) pp.2–37.

24 Doerries, *Imperial Challenge*; Katz, *The Secret War in Mexico*.

25 Rinke, *Latin America and the First World War*, p.55.

26 Thomas Boghardt, *The Zimmermann Telegram: Intelligence, Diplomacy, and America's Entry into World War I*.

27 Gathen, *Zimmermann Telegram*, pp.18–19.

28 Clarke papers.

29 ADM223/788.

30 Freeman, *The Zimmermann Telegram*, p.115.

31 Freeman, *The Zimmermann Telegram*, pp.116–17.

Chapter 17: 97556 = Zimmermann

1 Freeman, *The Zimmermann Telegram*, p.119.

2 HW3/35.

3 Hall papers.

4 HW3/35.

5 HW3/187.

6 Hall papers.

7 Hall papers.

8 HW3/177.

9 Hall papers.

10 Hall papers.

11 Hall papers.

12 ADM223/738; sources differ on how many numbers made up a code word in 7500, but this working document written at the end of the war puts 7500 in a category with six other 'four-figure [hatted] ciphers'; the five-figure code words, as noted, use the additional figure for grammatical information.

13 HW3/177.

14 Freeman, *The Zimmermann Telegram*, pp.26–27.

15 ADM223/773.

16 Freeman, *The Zimmermann Telegram*, p.122.

17 HW3/178.

18 Mendelsohn, *Studies in German Diplomatic Codes....*

19 ADM223/738; for more details on other diplomatic codes see ADM223/773.

20 HW3/35.

21 HW3/177.

22 HW3/182.

Chapter 18: On Timing and Treachery

1 HW7/19.

2 HW7/19.

3 HW7/20; HW7/17; HW7/16.

4 HW7/19.

5 Freeman, *Zimmermann Telegram*, p.123.

6 HW7/8.

7 Freeman, *Zimmermann Telegram*, p.125.

8 Cited in Ramsay, *'Blinker' Hall*, p.205.

9 HW3/179.

10 HW3/178.

11 Beach, *Haig's Intelligence*, pp.329–30.

12 HW3/178.

13 Lansing, *War Memoirs*, pp.227–28.

14 Tuchman, *The Zimmermann Telegram*, p.172.

15 HW3/180.

16 HW7/20.

17 HW3/180.

18 Tuchman, *The Zimmermann Telegram*, p.184.

19 Lansing, *War Memoirs*, pp.230–32.

20 HW3/180.

21 Stevenson, *1917*, p.61.

22 Cited in Neiberg, *The Path to War*, p.221.

23 Neiberg, *The Path to War*, pp.221–23.

24 HW3/180.

25 HW3/180.

26 HW7/8.

27 HW7/8.

28 HW7/8.

29 Beesly, *Room 40*, p.234.

30 Katz, *The Secret War in Mexico*, pp.417–21; a sending station was also opened in July 1918 but Nauen was unable to receive its transmissions.

31 Hall papers.

31 HW3/181.

32 HW7/8.

33 HW7/8.

34 HW3/181.

35 HW7/20.

36 HW7/19; ADM223/742.

37 Holger Herwig, 'Total Rhetoric, Limited War: Germany's U-Boat Campaign 1917–1918', in Chickering and Förster, *Great War, Total War*, pp.202–03.

Chapter 19: Applied Intelligence

1 Martin van Creveld, 'World War I and the Revolution in Logistics', in Chickering et al, *Great War, Total War*, pp.66–68.

2 Pearton, *The Knowledgeable State*, p.155.

3 Grigg, *Lloyd George: War Leader, 1916–1918*, p.225.

4 HW7/20.

5 Asprey, *German High Command*, pp.295–96.

6 Ferguson, *The Pity of War*, p.290.

7 Asprey, *German High Command*, p.358.

8 Agathe Couderc, 'Transmettre, chiffrer, écouter et intercepter sur le front française 1914–1918', in Forcade and Vaïsse (eds), *Espionnage et renseignement pendant la Première Guerre mondiale*, pp.107–19.

9 ADM223/741.

10 HW7/21.

11 HW7/1.

12 Halpern, *A Naval History of World War I*, pp.387–88.

13 Stevenson, *1917*, p.81.

14 Stevenson, *1917*, p.83.

15 HW7/1.

16 Grant, *The U-Boat Hunters* ..., p.41.

17 Grant, *The U-Boat Hunters* ..., pp.32, 56.

18 Grant, *The U-Boat Hunters* ..., pp.50, 37.

19 HW7/24.

20 HW3/1.

21 James, *Eyes of the Navy*, pp.172–73.

22 James, *Eyes of the Navy*, p.129.

23 Not all wireless signals were best intercepted closer to source. 'The great strides in wireless reception enabled the German communications in the Caucasus and South Russia to be intercepted with great accuracy in England itself, with greater accuracy and precision indeed than at Salonika or Egypt', HW7/35.

24 HW3/183.

25 HW3/8.

26 HW3/8.

27 HW7/1.

28 ADM137/4699.

29 HW3/35.

30 Lansing, *War Memoirs*, pp.326–28.

31 Rinke, *Latin America and the First World War*, pp.147–52.

32 HW7/1; ADM137/4124.

33 Powis, *The Defeat of the Zeppelins*, p.x.

34 White, *Zeppelin Nights*, p.126.

35 John Ferris, 'Airbandit: C3I and Strategic Air Defence During the First Battle of Britain', in Dockrill and French (eds), *Strategy and Intelligence*, p.38.

36 Grant, *The U-Boat Hunters* ..., p.50.

37 Powis, *The Defeat of the Zeppelins*, pp.159–60.

38 ADM137/4305.

39 ADM137/4177.

40 Grant, *The U-Boat Hunters*, pp.30–31.

41 Degoulange, *Les Écoutes de la Victoire*, pp.123, 124.

42 HW3/88; ADM137/4124.

43 ADM137/4305.

44 Ferris, 'Airbandit: C3I and Strategic Air Defence During the First Battle of Britain', in Dockrill and French (eds), *Strategy and Intelligence*, pp.44–45.

45 Ferris, 'Airbandit: C3I and Strategic Air Defence During the First Battle of Britain', in Dockrill and French (eds), *Strategy and Intelligence*, p.40.

46 Ferris, 'Airbandit: C3I and Strategic Air Defence During the First Battle of Britain', in Dockrill and French (eds), *Strategy and Intelligence* , pp.44–49.

47 Ferris, *The British Army and Signals Intelligence*, p.297.

48 Fromkin, *A Peace to End All Peace*, pp.276–81; ADM223/767.

49 HW7/1.

50 ADM223/782; HW7/32.

51 Sheffy, *British Military Intelligence in the Palestine Campaign*; ADM223/787.

52 Sheffy, *British Military Intelligence in the Palestine Campaign*.

53 HW7/3.

54 HW7/3.

55 ADM223/782.

56 Sheffy, *British Military Intelligence in the Palestine Campaign*; Stevenson, *1914–1918*, pp.339–40; Barr, *Setting the Desert on Fire*, pp.156, 176; Strachan, *The First World War*, pp.275–78; HW3/88.

57 Ferris, *The British Army and Signals Intelligence*, pp.299, 341–42.

58 HW7/32.

59 Sheffy, *British Military Intelligence in the Palestine Campaign*, p.256.

60 Sheffy, *British Military Intelligence in the Palestine Campaign*, pp.326, 330.

61 Figes, *A People's Tragedy: The Russian Revolution*, p.537; Deutscher, *The Prophet Armed*, p.271.

62 Wheeler-Bennett, *Brest–Litovsk*, p.69.

63 Kennan, *Soviet–American Relations*, vol. 1, pp.401–02, 454–55.

64 HW3/185.

65 Kennan, *Soviet–American Relations*, Vol. 2, pp.3–4.

66 Stevenson, *With Our Backs to the Wall*, p.35.

67 Dowling, *The Brusilov Offensive*.

68 Stevenson, *With Our Backs to the Wall*, p.42.

69 Beach, *Haig's Intelligence*, pp.206–07, 211–12.

70 Sheffield and Bourne (eds), *Douglas Haig: War Diaries and Letters*, p.350.

71 French, *Failures of Intelligence*, p.95.

72 Beach, *Haig's Intelligence*, pp.301–02.

73 Beach, *Haig's Intelligence*, p.159, WO157/160.

74 HW3/183, WO157/20.

75 HW3/183.

76 HW3/183.

77 Friedman, *Solving German Codes*, p.88.

78 Beach, *Haig's Intelligence*, pp.160–62, WO158/898.

79 Friedman, *Solving German Codes*, p.57.

80 Hall, *Communications and Operations*, p.241; 246–49.

81 ADM137/4399.

82 Friedman, *Solving German Codes in World War I*, pp 112–15

83 Friedman, *Solving German Codes in World War I*, pp.112–15.

84 ADM137/4661.

85 Degoulange, *Les Écoutes de la Victoire*, pp.194–205.

86 Lasry, *A Methodology for the Cryptanalysis of Classical Ciphers with Search Metaheuristics*.

87 Stevenson, *With Our Backs to the Wall*, p.88.

88 Degoulange, *Les Écoutes de la Victoire*, p.204.
89 Martin Kitchen, *The German Offensives of 1918*, p.256.
90 Asprey, *The German High Command at War* ..., p.398.
91 Asprey, *The German High Command at War* ..., p.403.

Chapter 20: War, Revolution and Peace

1   William Carr, *A History of Germany 1815–1985* (London: 1987), p.225.
2   Stevenson, *With Our Backs to the Wall*, pp.112–13.
3   Ferris, *The British Army and Signals Intelligence*, pp.16–21.
4   ADM223/789.
5   Asprey, *The German High Command at War*, p.448.
6   Jost Duelffer, 'Deutschland als Kaiserreich 1871–1918', in Martin Vogt, *Deutsche Geschichte*, p.565.
7   ADM137/4186.
8   ADM137/4185.
9   Cited in Beesly, *Room 40*, pp.294–95.
10 ADM137/4184.
11 Carsten, *Revolution in Central Europe 1918–1919*, p.11.
12 Gerwarth, *The Vanquished: Why the First World War Failed to End*; Smit, *Nederland in de Eerste Wereldoorlog*, Vol. 3, pp.137–40.
13 HW3/3.
14 HW7/1.
15 ADM223/773.
16 HW7/35.
17 Beach, *Haig's Intelligence*, pp.326–27.

Select Bibliography

A bibliography with full titles, and other books and papers that have been consulted is available on www.paulgannonbooks.co.uk.

Abbenhuis, *The Art of Staying Neutral* (2006).
Albertini, L. *Origins of the War of 1914,* Vol. 3.
Andrew, *Secret Service: The Making of the British Intelligence Community* (1985).
Baker, *A History of the Marconi Company* (1970).
Barr, *Setting the Desert on Fire* (2007).
Barty-King, *Girdle Round the Earth* (1979).
Batey, *Dilly: The Man Who Broke Enigmas* (2009).
Beach, *Haig's Intelligence* (2013).
Beauchamp, *History of Telegraphy* (2001).
Beesly, *Room 40* (1982).
Bell, *A History of the Blockade of Germany* (1937).
Bernstorff, *My Three Years in America* (1920).
Blum, *Dark Invasion* (2014).
Bonatz, *Die Deutsche Marine-Funkaufklärung 1914–1945* (1970).
Bostridge, *The Fateful Year: England 1914* (2014).
Bourachot, *Marshal Joffre* (2014).
Brownrigg, *Indiscretions of the Naval Censor* (1920).
Cain and Hopkins, *British Imperialism 1688–2015* (2016).
Carden, *German Policy Toward Neutral Spain, 1914–1918* (1987).
Carr, *Spain: A History 1808–1975* (1982).
Chatterton, *The Big Blockade* (undated).
Chickering, et al. (eds), *Great War, Total War* (2000).
Childers, *The Riddle of the Sands* (1903).
Childs, *German Military Ciphers* (undated).

Churchill, *The World Crisis 1911–1918* (1943).

Clark, *Kaiser Wilhelm II* (2009).

Clark, *The Sleepwalkers* (2013).

Cooper Jnr, *Woodrow Wilson* (2009).

Corbett, *Naval Operations, Official History of the Great War*, Vols 1–5 (1921).

Degoulange, *Les Écoutes de la Victoire* (2019).

Denniston, *Thirty Secret Years* (2007).

Deutscher, *The Prophet Armed* (2003).

Devlin, *Too Proud to Fight* (1974).

Dixon, *Clash of Empires, 1914* (2008).

Dockrill and French (eds), *Strategy and Intelligence* (1996).

Doerries, *Imperial Challenge* (1989).

Doerries, *Prelude to the Easter Rising* (2000).

Donaldson, *The Marconi Scandal* (1962).

Dooley, *Codes, Ciphers and Spies* (2016).

Duffy, *Through German Eyes* (2007).

Evans, *The Pursuit of Power* (2017).

Ewing, *The Man of Room 40* (1939).

Ferguson, *The Pity of War* (1999).

Fergusson, *British Military Intelligence, 1870–1914* (1984).

Ferris, *The British Army and Signals Intelligence* (1992).

Fitzgerald, *The Knox Brothers* (2000).

Forcade and Vaïsse (eds), *Espionnage et reseignement pendant la Première Guerre mondiale* (2017).

Foss (ed.), *The Best of A.J. Alan* (1954).

Friedewald, 'Telefunken und der deutsche Schiffsfunk 1903–1914' (2001).

Friedman, *Solving German Codes in World War I* (1977)

Fromkin, *A Peace to End All Peace* (2000).

Geiss, *July 1914: The Outbreak of the First World War* (1967).

Gerard, *My Four Years in Germany* (1917).

Gerwarth & Manela (eds), *Empires at War: 1911–1923* (2014).

Gill, *War, Wireless and Wangles* (1934).

Gordon, *The Rules of the Game* (2005).

Grainger (ed.), *The British Maritime Blockade of Germany in the Great War* (2003).

Grant, *U-Boat Intelligence 1914–1918* (1969).

Grant, *The U-Boat Hunters: Code Breakers, Divers and the Defeat of the U-Boats* (2003).

Gregory, *Walter Hines Page* (1970).

Grigg, *Lloyd George: From Peace to War 1912–1916* (1997).

Grigg, *Lloyd George: War Leader 1916–1918* (2003).

Gudgin, *Military Intelligence* (1999).

Hall, *Communications and British Operations on the Western Front, 1914–1915* (2017).

Halpern, *A Naval History of World War I* (1994).

Hampshire, *The Blockaders* (1980).

Hancock, *Wireless at Sea* (1950).

Hancock, *Smuts* (1962).

Hastings, *Catastrophe 1914* (2013).

Hay ('Exchange Officer'), *Wounded and a Prisoner of War* (1917).

Hay, *The Jesuits and the Popish Plot* (1934).

Hay, *Valiant for Truth: Malcolm Hay of Seaton* (1971).

Headrick, *The Invisible Weapon* (1991).

Hertog and Kruisinga (eds), *Caught in the Middle: Neutrals, Neutrality and the First World War* (2011).

Herwig, *The First World War* (1997).

Herwig, *The Marne* (2011).

Heydorn, *Nachrichtenaufklärung (Ost) und sowjetrussisches Heeresfunkwesen bis 1945* (1985).

Hezlet, *The Electron and Sea Power* (1975).

Hopkirk, *On Secret Service East of Constantinople* (2001).

Hoy, *40 O.B.* (1935).

Jeffery, *1916: A Global History* (2016).

Jellicoe, *Jutland* (2016).

Joll and Martel, *The Origins of the First World War* (3rd edition, 2007).

Jolly, *Marconi* (1972).

Kahn, *The Codebreakers* (2nd edition, 1996).

Katz, *The Secret War in Mexico* (1983).

Keegan, *Intelligence in War* (2003).

Kennedy, *The Rise of the Anglo-German Antagonism 1860–1914* (1980).

Kennedy, *The Rise and Fall of British Naval Mastery* (2001).

Klein-Arendt, *'Kamina ruft Nauen!'* (1996).

Kitchen, *The German Offensives of 1918* (2005).

Kunert, *Telegraphen-Landkabel einschließlich der Flußkabel* (1940).

Lambert, *Planning Armageddon* (2012).

Landau, *The Spy Net* (1938).

Landau, *The Enemy Within* (1937).

L'Ange, *Urgent Imperial Service* (1991).

Langford, *Somme Intelligence* (2013).

Lansing, *War Memoirs* (1935).

Larson, *Dead Wake* (2015).

Lawford and Nicholson, *The Telcon story 1850–1950* (1950).

Le Queux, *The Invasion of 1910* (1906).

Lloyd George, *War Memoirs*, Vol. 1 (2-volume 'new' edition, 1938).

Lüdke, *Jihad Made in Germany* (2005).

MacMillan, *The War that Ended Peace* (2014).

McMeekin, *The Berlin–Baghdad Express* (2011).

McMeekin, *July 1914* (2013).

McMeekin, *The Ottoman Endgame* (2015).

Massie, *Castles of Steel* (2005).

Mecking, *Neutraal Nederland in Oorlogstijd* (2014).

Mendelsohn, *Studies in German Diplomatic Codes Employed During the World War* (1937).

Moeyes, *Buiten Schot* (2005).

Mombauer, *The Origins of the First World War: Diplomatic and Military Documents* (2013).

Mombauer, *The Origins of the First World War: Controversies and Consensus* (2013).

Morgan, *The Secrets of Rue St Roch* (2005).

Neiberg, *Dance of the Furies* (2011).

Neiberg, *The Path to War* (2016).

Nickles, *Under the Wire* (2003).

Nicolai, *The German Secret Service* (2015).

Occleshaw, *Armour Against Fate* (1989).

Offer, *The First World War* (1991).

Olusoga & Erichsen, *The Kaiser's Holocaust* (2011).

Olusoga, *The World's War* (2014).

Osborne, *Britain's Economic Blockade of Germany, 1914–1919* (2013).

Otte, *July Crisis* (2014).

Paice, *Tip and Run* (2007).

Pearton, *The Knowledgeable State* (1982).

Pethö, *Agenten für den Doppeladler* (1988).

Pocock, *The Early British Radio Industry* (1988).

Powis, *The Defeat of the Zeppelins* (2018).

Prior and Wilson, *Command on the Western Front* (2004).

Raboy, *Marconi* (2016).

Ramsay, *'Blinker' Hall, Spymaster* (2008).

Ramsay, *The Lusitania Saga and Myth: 100 Years On* (2015).

Rinke, *Latin America and the First World War* (2017).

Roberts, *Battlecruisers* (1997).

Rogan, *The Fall of the Ottomans* (2015).

Röhl, *Kaiser Wilhelm II*, Vol. 3 (2017).

Ronge, *Kriegs- und Industrie-Spionage: zwölf Jahre Kundschaftsdienst* (1930).

Scott, *Gentlemen on Imperial Service* (1994).

Seligmann, *Naval Intelligence from Germany* (2007).

Seligmann, *Spies in Uniform* (2006).

Seligmann, *The Royal Navy and the German Threat* (2012).

Sheffield and Bourne (eds), *Douglas Haig: War Diaries and Letters 1914–18* (2006).

Sheffield and Todman (eds), *Command and Control on the Western Front* (2007).

Sheffy, *British Military Intelligence in the Palestine Campaign, 1914–1918* (1998).

Showalter, *Tannenberg* (2004).

Smit, *Nederland in de Eerste Wereldoorlog*, 3 Vols (1971).

Spears, *Liaison 1914* (2014).

Stafford, *Churchill and Secret Service* (Woodstock, 1998).

Steiner and Neilson, *Britain and the Origins of the First World War* (2nd edition, 2003).

Stephenson, *The Siege of Tsingtao* (2017).

Stevenson, *1914–1918* (2005).

Stevenson, *With Our Backs to the Wall* (2012).

Stevenson, D., *1917* (2017).

Strachan, *The First World War*, Vols 1–3.

Striner, *Woodrow Wilson and World War I* (2014).

Tarrant, *Jutland* (1995).

Thiele, *Telefunken Nach 100 Jahren* (2003).

Thompson, *The White War* (2008).

Tuchman, *The Zimmerman Telegram* (2001).

van der Bijl, *To Complete the Jigsaw* (2015).

van der Vat, *The Ship that Changed the World* (1985).

von Kluck, *The March on Paris* (2012).

von Mücke, *The 'Ayesha'* (1917).

von Rintelen, *The Dark Invader* (1933).

Wade, *Spies in the Empire* (2007).

Watson, *Ring of Steel* (2015).

Wawro, *A Mad Catastrophe* (2015).

Weightman, *Signor Marconi's Magic Box* (2004).

White, *Zeppelin Nights* (2015).

Winkler, *Nexus* (2013).

Winter, *Haig's Command: A Reassessment* (2001).

Winter, et al. (eds), *The Cambridge History of the First World War, Volume 1: The Global War* (2014).

Yates, *Graf Spee's Raiders* (1995).

Young, *With the Battle Cruisers* (1921).

Index

Italicised page references indicate illustrations and bold page references indicate tables.